BUFFY IN THE CLASSROOM

BUFFY IN THE CLASSROOM

Essays on Teaching with the Vampire Slayer

Edited by Jodie A. Kreider *and*
Meghan K. Winchell

McFarland & Company, Inc., Publishers
Jefferson, North Carolina, and London

LIBRARY OF CONGRESS CATALOGUING-IN-PUBLICATION DATA

Buffy in the classroom : essays on teaching with
the vampire slayer / edited by Jodie A. Kreider
and Meghan K. Winchell.
p.   cm.
Includes bibliographical references and index.

ISBN 978-0-7864-5964-3
softcover : 50# alkaline paper ∞

1. Television in education.   2. Buffy, the vampire slayer
(Television program)   I. Kreider, Jodie A., 1969–
II. Winchell, Meghan K.
LB1044.7.B785   2010   371.33'58 — dc22   2010030109

British Library cataloguing data are available

Cover images ©2010 Shutterstock

Manufactured in the United States of America

*McFarland & Company, Inc., Publishers
Box 611, Jefferson, North Carolina 28640
www.mcfarlandpub.com*

To Mackenzie and Kelsey.
M.K.W.

In memory of Nancy.
J.A.K.

Table of Contents

Acknowledgments

This project came out of our participation in the Slayage Conference on the Whedonverses at Henderson State University in Arkadelphia, Arkansas where we met a vibrant group of scholars, including several of our contributors. We fondly remember talking about our *Buffy* classes while about seven of us were crammed inside Jodie's car on the way to dinner after a pedagogy panel. Since then that community of scholars and teachers has expanded and shared their ideas via email, the U.S. Postal Service, on the highways between Lincoln, Denver and Minneapolis, over dinner tables, in the collaborative spaces provided by the Slayage conferences, and in classrooms from Australia, Canada, Britain, and the U.S. Our contributors have been patient, cooperative and generous in sharing their innovative teaching methods. Their ideas inspire us and we look forward to trying them out in our own courses. We thank them for their participation and enthusiasm.

We also thank our home institutions for financial support of this project. Nebraska Wesleyan University provided funding to attend conferences and help move the book through the final publication process. We thank John Montag of the Cochrane-Woods Library for regularly adding the latest *Buffy* books to NWU's collection. Both the NWU History Department and the Liberal Arts Seminar program fostered a creative space where this project could develop. The Center for Teaching and Learning at the University of Denver graciously supported travel to several Slayage conferences, while the Marsico Visiting Scholar Program allowed both editors the chance to interact with *Buffy* Seminar students in Denver.

We owe great thanks to all of our First Year Seminar and Liberal Arts Seminar students on both campuses over the years, whose sophisticated comments and lively participation inspired us to tell others about our experiences teaching with *Buffy*. Their feedback was invaluable as we revised our classes each year. We thank one of those former students, NWU's Alex Bednar for aiding in the final production of the manuscript.

Several members of the *Buffy* Studies community helped us from the beginning including Kevin Durand who graciously supplied a list of teachers who incorporate *Buffy* into their classrooms. Rhonda Wilcox helped us publicize our call for submissions and encouraged us along the way.

Amongst our colleagues and friends Elizabeth Escobedo, Laura Shelton, and Shannon Brence read early versions of the manuscript and provided valuable feedback. Tanya Cochran acted as cheerleader, publishing sage, and enthusiastic supporter throughout the entire process. She even read a full draft of the collection, while on a trip to Japan no less! We gratefully thank her for all of her help and insights.

Finally we must thank our family and friends. Guy, Mackenzie and Kelsey Davenport tolerated lots of academic *Buffy* speak from Lincoln to Denver and back again. We both appreciate their good humor and patience. Thank you to Laura Tabili, Alison Futrell, Christy Rowe, Ingrid Tague, Rahul Nair and Scot, Chandra, and Marlin Kreider for support and in some cases, dog sitting services. And thanks to all of those friends, family, and colleagues who knew nothing about *Buffy*, thought this was an odd project for historians, but backed us anyway!

Introduction:
"Let's Have a Lesson Then"

Jodie A. Kreider and Meghan K. Winchell

Like students today, the titular heroine of *Buffy the Vampire Slayer* frequently finds herself sitting in a classroom contemplating metaphorical demons such as her social life, troubles at home, her friends' antics, the agonies of impending adulthood, and only peripherally, the actual process of learning something from her instructors or the academic experience. Unlike our students, vampire-fighting teenager Buffy Summers slays real demons throughout high school, college and young adulthood. While our own classrooms are not situated atop a Hellmouth like Buffy's, real teachers often see their students struggle with the same distractions that plague Sunnydale teens. Perhaps this is part of the reason that academics took such a keen interest in Joss Whedon's critical hit. This interest led to the now well-established field of *Buffy* (Whedon) Studies. Long after *Buffy* ended as a first run series, living on in DVD, comic book form, and syndication, scholars continue to analyze the series, its interpretations, and its reflections of larger historical, artistic, literary, and cultural contexts (Edwards et al.; Durand; South; Dial-Driver). These scholars demonstrate that *Buffy* is a canonical text worthy of study across many disciplinary divides and international borders (Wilcox; Wilcox & Lavery; Jowett; Adams).[1] These efforts coalesced into *Slayage: The Whedon Studies Association Journal*.[2] Over the past decade scholars also brought *Buffy* into their classrooms to enliven and illustrate multiple concepts within disciplines such as English, history, communications, sociology, psychology, and media production. This collection of essays aims to bridge the gap between scholarly criticism of *Buffy* and its application in the classroom. The contributors include international teacher-scholars from both secondary and university institutions who teach single lessons, entire units, or full courses on *Buffy*. For teachers both familiar and unfamiliar with *Buffy* as a television series and text, these essays present tested and honed ideas about themes to address, texts to compare, sources to reference, assignments to give, field trips to take, and questions to ask students. Ironically, bringing the Hellmouth into the classroom can prevent students from feeling the educational ennui and negativity experienced by Buffy and her fellow classmates.

Sharing experiences about lessons from the Hellmouth in numerous panels on pedagogy at Slayage Conferences on the Whedonverses inspired this project. These sessions on teaching sparked intense discussion between scholars who teach, or hope to teach with

Buffy. We then explored the extant literature and use of *Buffy* in the classroom and learned that more than 200 teachers at all levels of secondary and post-secondary education across the globe currently employ *Buffy* to teach multiple subjects in diverse styles in disciplines such as religious studies, gender studies, English literature, composition, film studies, first-year seminars, philosophy, linguistics, history, American studies, and communications. Some people are fortunate to teach entire courses on *Buffy.* Based on these factors it was evident that a book on teaching with *Buffy* would centralize these exciting contributions to the fields of *Buffy* Studies and education into one volume accessible to secondary school teachers and college professors.

While many teachers at all levels bring popular culture into the classroom as a way to connect with millennial students whose childhoods included easy access to the Internet and mass media, this book argues that *Buffy* remains a stellar and long-lived example of an ideal classroom text. Much like Jane Austen's and Charles Dickens' works were popular in their day, *Buffy* garnered significant public attention, but its popularity is not what makes it a unique and effective teaching tool. Like teaching with other popular texts now considered classic, the instructor's job is to introduce students to new, rich texts that contain depth, rather than to appeal to them via texts they already know. While some scholars argue that millennial students[3] are no longer familiar with the show from its initial broadcast, we challenge the interpretation that popular culture can only be defined as that which is broadcast in the immediate present.

Quality matters more than timeliness. Even Shakespeare appears dated until scholars demonstrate why he is still an important playwright and teach his works to the next generation. Currently, teachers are discovering that, like great works of literature or classic films, *Buffy* remains a useful text to teach complex ideas to students because of its quality, depth, and wide appeal, even though its creators, like Austen or Dickens, are no longer producing new televised episodes. *Buffy* and other quality texts must be taught and disseminated to a wider audience and a new generation to keep them alive and relevant. As in the show itself, the classroom and the school campus are the battlegrounds where *Buffy* Studies will live or die.

This collection combines the academic and the practical aspects of teaching by exploring the ways in which *Buffy* is taught in international classrooms through both interdisciplinary and discipline-based approaches. It focuses on methodology and practice in order to encourage and guide others interested in adding *Buffy* to their pedagogy. The contributors share pragmatic lesson plans and assignments from their own teaching experience and offer recommendations about how to apply *Buffy* as a tool to explain a variety of concepts such as morality, good, evil, self-actualization, feminism, gender, heroism, mythology, allegory, narrative, and intentional action. For example, for the historian, the essay on archetypes or teaching narrative structures will help them broaden their lessons on *Buffy* as a text to include new concepts that they rarely discuss but are routinely taught in English classrooms. Likewise, essays written by historians discuss ways to integrate field visits to cemeteries, as well as public history, witchcraft, romanticism, and women's history into interdisciplinary or straight history courses. The English teacher can use the chapters on the depiction of morality and violence in *Buffy* to broaden their classroom lessons on narrative and character development. For those readers not familiar with *Buffy,* each chapter provides episode numbers, synopses, and references to supporting literature that facilitate relatively easy adoption.[4]

The nature of *Buffy* as a series of breadth and depth allows the individual instructor to use the show in myriad ways. Teachers from multiple disciplines should heed Joss Whedon's advice and "bring [their] own subtext" to class lessons (Koontz 8). For example, readers may be surprised to learn that the two historians in this collection do not often choose to use the Native-American genocide-themed Thanksgiving episode "Pangs" (4.8) in their courses. Instead, due to their own training and interests, they focus on the supernatural theme of witchcraft from different perspectives and contexts. Moreover, for historians, integrating *Buffy* into classes on American or British history is not easy to do. Students, however, find that integrating *Buffy* and its reflection of a historical context and historical references into an interdisciplinary seminar exciting and accessible. Ideas about using *Buffy* to teach Shakespeare might never occur to an historian, but to an English teacher, this connection seems obvious. The episode "Hush" (4.10) is so unique that it makes an appearance in classrooms throughout the disciplines ranging from psychology, first-year seminars, and media production. Perhaps it most obviously deserves placement in a communications course. This volume provides a taste of *Buffy*'s value and application in today's classroom.

The collection begins with a discussion of the pedagogical and logistical issues involved with teaching a text like *Buffy* that involves 144 episodes/103 hours of television, a spin-off series, and an additional season in comic-book form. David Kociemba explores the question "to spoil, or not to spoil." He argues that teaching quality television forces the instructor to make decisions about this issue. Drawing upon five years of experience teaching a full-length *Buffy* course, Kociemba notes the drawbacks and benefits of spoiler-heavy versus spoiler-free television viewing and crafts a new question, "Does teaching canonical television like *Buffy* require a new pedagogy?" Teachers who choose *Buffy* episodes to illustrate any number of topics or themes to their students must also confront their own fandom in order to teach successfully. Jason Lawton Winslade argues that all instructors must wrestle with this "awkward dance between experiential viewing pleasures and thoughtful analysis." He prompts teacher-fans to recognize their love for the show and offers insights into how to negotiate their own status as fans, as well as dealing with student-fans in the classroom. The authors in this collection adjust the amount of information they give to their students about the show based upon their own answers to these questions.

Buffy emerges as an effective text to teach myth and archetypes in a number of college classrooms. Tanya R. Cochran describes her experience teaching Joseph Campbell's monomyth to first-year students through an exploration of how *Buffy* both embraces and challenges aspects of the hero's journey. She helps them make connections between their favorite stories and the significance of story to the way they see the world. Barry Morris outlines the major archetypes of the Western canon and shows students how to identify them in multiple episodes of *Buffy*. Morris' "usable suspects" include "The Chosen One," the "Regular Guy" and the "Girl Next Door." K. Dale Koontz creates units constructed around "Prophecy Girl" (1.12), "Bad Girls" (3.14), "Who Are You?" (4.16), and "The Body" (5.16) to teach "morality and contemporary views of heroism." These episodes address personal sacrifice, boundaries, redemption, questions of identity and reactions to loss. *Buffy* brings these philosophical concepts to life for students through a medium that they are comfortable with.

Buffy has found a home in a number of first-year college seminars in part because its characters, like real life college students, make the transition both from high school to college, and adolescence to young adulthood. Meghan K. Winchell argues that Whedon's *Buffy* renders feminism understandable as well as embraceable to otherwise skeptical students. She screens Whedon's 2006 Equality Now speech with her students alongside multiple episodes of *Buffy* to help them shape an active definition of gender equity and its historical development. Similarly, Rod Romesburg teaches seminars in which episodes of *Buffy* spur discussions of "stages of life, femininity/feminism, and masculinity." He argues that "Out of Mind, Out of Sight" (1.11), "The Replacement" (5.3), and "I Was Made to Love You" (5.15) offer the best starting points for discussing identity development in early adulthood, explaining that traditionally college students are at a point in their lives where they are searching for their identity. Keith Fudge teaches a unit on ethics with *Buffy* at its center in his first-year composition course. He discusses the challenges of time apportionment, episode selection, and student reactions to episodes that address the moral choices behind Willow's abuse of magic, Dawn's kleptomania, and Buffy's decision to sacrifice herself to save the world. Melissa C. Johnson prompts students in her first-year seminar course to talk about the awkwardness of the transition from high school to college through a discussion of "The Freshman" (4.1). She asks students to explore their own reasons for seeking a college degree and compares them to the reasons depicted in popular culture of various sorts, including *Buffy*.

Media Studies and Communications scholars have put *Buffy* at the center of lessons designed to highlight the visual aspects of the text and its effects. Brian Cogan draws on "Hush" (4.10) to teach a number of concepts, including "haptics, territoriality, kinesics, and expressions of gender-related non-verbal communication" to students. His students are better able to understand complicated concepts when they are acted out on screen by characters they enjoy and relate to. Jane Martin shows scene selections or full episodes including "Welcome to the Hellmouth" (1.1), "Storyteller" (7.16), "The Body" (5.16), and "Once More with Feeling" (6.7) to teach film production students how to identify the elements of setting and content, the significance of "sets, props and costumes for character development," and the importance of sound and editing to the development of theme. Rosie White pairs "Earshot" (3.18) with Michael Moore's *Bowling for Columbine* to open valuable discussions among students about the representation of violence on television, the degree to which it influences the viewer, and how quality television complicates the often simplistic view that all violence depicted on television is problematic. She outlines a unit which focuses solely on *Buffy*, but places it within the larger context of an entire course on violence and television.

Buffy is a flexible teaching text, which works well as a teaching tool when paired with other reading, creative assignments, and societal debates, thereby setting up a context in which students can draw their own conclusions about *Buffy's* multiple meanings. Australian secondary school teacher Leith Daniel includes *Buffy* in his classroom because the episodes are "technically advanced," "accessible to students, but academically challenging."

He introduces high school composition students to stereotypes, intertextuality and allegory through "Beauty and the Beasts" (3.4), and shows "Gingerbread" (3.11) to lead students through an engaging role-play about the dangers of censorship. Jodie A. Kreider shares several different types of assignments for investigating historical themes in a seminar on *Buffy*. These include taking students on field excursions to historical cemeteries and reading both *Buffy* literature and historical scholarship, including a monograph on witchcraft cases in 17th century England. Her students then plan their own thematic units for the course using a wide range of texts, which reveal how they see *Buffy* fitting into the larger scope of their educations and experiences. Kristopher Karl Woofter includes "Buffy vs. Dracula" (5.1) in a complete and balanced pedagogical unit around fairy tales as a genre of literature. Rather than making the more obvious comparisons to *Dracula* and other vampire myths, this unit makes creative connections between an episode that is sometimes overlooked by teachers due to its campy and satiric tone, and "Little Red Riding Hood." Woofter's unit illustrates the polysemic nature of Whedon's texts. Patrick R. Grzanka demonstrates how *Buffy* facilitates the teaching of the complex concept of intersectionality, namely the idea that "all people have a race, gender, sexual identity, and social class status." The characters in *Buffy* demonstrate that every person has multiple identities and chooses to privilege one or more of those identities at a certain time. *Buffy*'s complexity as a text encourages students to break down simplistic categorizations of people, race, identities, and characterizations in both real life, and the series. In the collection's final essay, Julia L. Grant compares "Out of Mind, Out of Sight" (1.11) and "Earshot" (3.18) to two of Shakespeare's plays, *The Merchant of Venice* and *Othello*, arguing that they provide a counterpoint to each other. This unit teaches secondary school students to identify and explore themes like stereotyping, bigotry, bullying, exclusion and inclusion in *Buffy* and Shakespeare.

Buffy, Willow, Xander and the rest of the Scooby Gang spend a lot of their classroom time doodling, chatting, staring out of windows; mostly wishing they were someplace else. Our students, no matter their level or discipline, are not much different. As instructors we are always looking for new ways to enliven the classroom, engage students in difficult conversations about complicated topics, and spur them to think critically about the text in front of them and the world outside. By exposing our students to *Buffy the Vampire Slayer*, we accomplish all of these goals. Our students, in turn, show us how they interpret *Buffy*, why the show is relevant to their lives and how they apply its lessons to their own worlds. And now, it is time to take Spike's advice — "Let's have a lesson, then" ("Becoming" 2.21).

NOTES

1. See the larger listing at the Academic Buffy Studies and Whedonverse Bibliography *http://www. alysa316.com/Buffyology/* and Don McNaughtan's *Bibliography of* Buffy the Vampire Slayer *and* Angel. (McFarland, forthcoming).

2. Go to *http://slayageonline.com/* for information on the Whedon Studies Association, previous and future Slayage conferences, and access to the online journal, hereafter referred to as *Slayage*.

3. For a discussion of millennial students, also called Generation Next or Generation Y, see Pletka 27, and Diana Oblinger.

4. For further episode detail, including writer and director credits, we recommend the episode guide included in Roz Kaveney, *Reading the Vampire Slayer.*

WORKS CITED

Adams, Michael. *Slayer Slang. A* Buffy the Vampire Slayer *Lexicon.* New York: Oxford University Press, 2003. Print.

Dial-Diver, Emily, Sally Emmons-Featherston, Jim Ford and Carolyn Anne Taylor, eds. *The Truth of Buffy: Essays on Fiction Illuminating Reality.* Jefferson, NC: McFarland, 2008. Print.

Durand, Kevin, ed. *Buffy Meets the Academy: Essays on the Episodes and Scripts as Texts.* Jefferson, North Carolina: McFarland, 2009. Print.

Edwards, Lynn, Elizabeth Rambo, and James South, eds. *Buffy Goes Dark: Essays on the Final Two Seasons of* Buffy the Vampire Slayer *on Television.* Jefferson, NC: McFarland, 2007. Print.

Jowett, Lorna. *Sex and the Slayer: A Gender Studies Primer for the* Buffy *Fan.* Middletown, CT: Wesleyan University Press, 2005. Print.

Kaveney, Roz, ed. *Reading the Vampire Slayer: An Unofficial Critical Companion to* Buffy *and* Angel. 2nd edition. New York: IB Tauris, 2004. Print.

Koontz, K. Dale. *Faith and Choice in the Works of Joss Whedon.* Jefferson, NC: McFarland, 2008. Print.

Oblinger, Diana. "Boomers, Gen-Xers, and Millenials: Understanding the New Students." *EDUCAUSE* (July/August 2003): 37–47. Print.

Pletka, Bob. *Educating the Net Generation: How to Engage Students in the 21st Century.* Santa Monica, CA: Santa Monica Press, 2007. Print.

South, James B., ed. Buffy the Vampire Slayer *and Philosophy: Fear and Trembling in Sunnydale.* Chicago: Open Court Press, 2003. Print.

Wilcox, Rhonda. *Why Buffy Matters: The Art of* Buffy the Vampire Slayer. New York: IB Tauris, 2005. Print.

Wilcox, Rhonda, and David Lavery, eds. *Fighting the Forces: What's at Stake in* Buffy the Vampire Slayer. Lanham, MD: Rowman Littlefield, 2002. Print.

To Spoil or Not to Spoil: Teaching Television's Narrative Complexity

David Kociemba

I suppose I was nervous. It was a few weeks before the start of my first seminar devoted to *Buffy the Vampire Slayer*, and even at a communications school like Emerson College it felt as though I was taking a risk. I wanted my first batch of seniors to have the best capstone experience I could offer, lest it be the last seminar on *Buffy* I got to teach. But I discovered a problem when I re-read my syllabus a week or so before the semester began. In the first month, my reading assignments would spoil how Angel lost his soul, Tara's surprise death at the end of Season Six and all of the best jokes from Season Three. These assignments went beyond simply revealing the ending to *The Crying Game*. I would be fundamentally changing how some of my students first experienced the entire series. Did I want to do that?

Lengthy television series present a set of practical problems in the classroom as well as in syllabus construction. Students without knowledge of the series often feel at a competitive disadvantage to those students who are fans. After all, how are they to write a midterm paper on *Buffy* when they do not know how the series ends? Even in courses not devoted to a single series, teachers often feel they must sacrifice narrative complexity and artistic excellence in favor of simplicity for students new to the series.[1] Both teachers and students face a difficult choice not encountered in film studies courses. In a film class, teachers can avoid spoilers by showing the work in its entirety in one class and assigning readings to foster discussion for the next one. A teacher cannot do that with *Buffy*, because it is 103 hours long and it is only that short if one excludes the crossover episodes in *Angel* and the comics. While some film studies professors show clips of lengthy works like *Birth of a Nation*, an entire course based on that principle can produce an unsatisfying game of "Guess what the teacher is thinking?" Students are led by the nose rather than given the tools to come to their own informed conclusions about the work. Nor can one teach a television series as if it were a novel by assigning suitable chunks of the text as homework until the students finish. Over a 13-week semester, I would have to assign 11 *Buffy* episodes each week, or roughly eight hours of viewing alone. These "spoiler virgins" face a choice between two unpalatable options: do 100 hours of work to "catch up" to fan-students (and protect the purity of their first time watching the series) or risk a fundamentally altered experience of an important text that is the center of the educational experience in that classroom.

The sheer size of *Buffy* combined with their finite time in the classroom forces teachers to make a choice when assigning readings. Teachers want to assign the kind of rigorous textual analysis that makes for nuanced observations and persuasive argumentation because such scholarship provides a model for students to emulate. Yet the use of spoiler-heavy scholarship when teaching serial narratives (or lengthy novels) can encourage bad reading habits. Rather than discover the text as they go, students end up reading to confirm or refute the opinions of authorities. Students become more critical viewers due to the spoilers functioning as a distancing device. But teachers risk students becoming less critical readers of the scholarship, as they must take the author's word for it without having fully experienced the artwork themselves. How can students learn to read an artwork that they cannot reasonably be expected to "read" in its entirety before the course starts and which there is not enough class time to fully "read" during the semester? Which is better: a virginal first experience or the distanced reading position produced by spoilers? Does teaching a canonical series like *Buffy* require a new pedagogy?

Television studies as an academic field has been around for quite some time. Perhaps these issues have already been solved. After all, spoilers have existed since the earliest days of the internet allowed East Coast posters to reveal narrative details to Usenet users on the West Coast, where the networks had not yet aired the episodes. Television scholar Jason Mittell offers two reasons why the discipline is only just now grappling with narrative complexity. First, most television scholars have not particularly cared about the artistry of a television series. Second, television now airs more challenging narratives worthy of close reading due to changes in the industry, media technologies and audience behavior. Mittell argues that television scholars have been reluctant to focus their analysis on narrative form because the discipline emerged from cultural studies (e.g., Stuart Hall) and mass communications (e.g., Denis McQuail). Both approaches tend to foreground social impacts over close reading approaches. Mittell observes that there is a surprisingly limited supply of analyses of the narrative form.[2]

The television industry produces more complex narratives more frequently, so spoilers bedevil more than those who are teaching with *Buffy*. This model of storytelling is neither entirely episodic nor serial, but it is also not a complete merger of both forms. Mittell argues that this new approach rejects "the need for plot closure within every episode" while "individual episodes have a distinctive identity as more than just one step in a long narrative journey," "foregrounds ongoing stories across a range of genres," may downplay or reject the melodrama style and relationship-centered structure, "rebel against episodic conventionality," and ultimately it "invites us to care about the storyworld while simultaneously appreciating its construction" (32–35). Such series make narrative evolution, convolution and involution central. Mittell traces the approach's evolution from its roots in the late 1970s and early 1980s (with *Dallas, Soap, Hill Street Blues,* and *Cheers,* among others) to late 1980s programs like *Moonlighting, thirtysomething,* and *Star Trek: The Next Generation* to *Twin Peaks* and *The X-Files* in the early 1990s, to *The Wire, Lost, Buffy, West Wing, Veronica Mars,* and *Battlestar: Galactica* today (Mittell, 32–33). Teachers never had to worry about spoilers when teaching *I Love Lucy.*

The new factors that helped this creative strategy flourish ensure that teachers in television studies will have to face these issues for many years. There has been an influx of talent from creators seeking more control as producers in television than they could reliably retain in film. Long-form series present an artistic challenge impossible in film's constrained time span. Shrinking audiences have re-shaped networks' expectations and forced them to consider the viability of cult shows with so-called boutique audiences. Narrative complexity provides brand separation from reality television's exclusive focus on relationships. New revenue streams push the industry away from least objectionable programming towards most repeatable programming. *Battlestar: Galactica* was a smash hit for the Sci-Fi cable network with just 2.3 million viewers, due to new revenue streams like DVD rentals and sales, digital downloads, and expanded merchandizing opportunities. The financial incentives for repeatable programming became so powerful by 2008 that ABC devoted an hour of primetime to the television version of the *CliffsNotes* for *Lost* by airing prime time reruns of the prior week's episode, complete with pop-up information clarifying plot and character arcs. Under the old broadcast model, the network insisted on repetitive explanatory dialogue, marring each episode and alienating its most devoted fans. Finally, new technological shifts connected audiences and allowed for greater scrutiny of television narratives (Mittell 30–32). Dedicated viewers no longer have to wait a decade for a film journal to publish frame-by-frame analysis of the shower sequence of *Psycho*. They can do it themselves with their remote control, then tell the world online. Henry Jenkins quotes one online fan, "Can you imagine *Twin Peaks* coming out before VCRs or without the net? It would have been Hell!" (54). Instructors who grapple with the issue of spoilers in teaching *Buffy* prepare the way for the difficulties to be posed by *Lost*. Mittell and others argue that this new breed of television requires a new television scholarship to be written. I agree. But my experience teaching *Buffy* suggests that we also need adaptable methods to teach the new television aesthetic and the new scholarship. These pedagogical issues are here to stay.

One potential model is the spoiler-free class, which I tried in my *Buffy* seminar back in 2004. I rewrote the syllabus so that I screened crucial episodes earlier in the semester and assigned readings that spoiled crucial narrative events, character arcs and formal strategies in assignments towards the end. During the first class meeting, I asked my 17 students how many of them were fans of *Buffy*. Three students raised their hands. Only a few others had seen more than a handful of episodes. (Little did I know that four students were closeted fans.) I paused. I thought a bit. Then I promised to run a spoiler-free class.

I wanted a classroom where students who were not fans[3] felt safe to try out new ideas without fear of being refuted based on evidence from parts of the series they had not yet seen. When the question of whether the series was feminist came up in the first two weeks, I made my case for its gender politics based only on the first season. When Kendra the Vampire Slayer came on the scene in the second season, we talked about how the series made us participate in Buffy's racism and whether doing so presented an opportunity for viewers to consider the role of whiteness in the series. Only when the class reached the third season did we compare all three slayers, this time adding class, sibling rivalry, and education theories to the mix.[4]

The spoiler-free classroom presented quite a rhetorical challenge. After seeing the first season, the majority of my class remained skeptical that this series was worth a seminar. I think a few of them suspected me of having unclean thoughts about Sarah Michelle Gellar. I ached to tell them about innovative episodes like "Restless" (4.22) and "The Body" (5.16). Their skepticism eased with the screening of the second season's "Surprise" and "Innocence" (2.13–14), episodes in which Buffy loses her virginity. Angelus came on the screen, having had sex with Buffy the previous night. He utterly humiliates Buffy, calling her "a pro" while hinting that her inexperience made the sex commonplace. And then he promised to call. He walked out, leaving Buffy emotionally devastated. That's when one male student said, loudly, "DAMN!"

Everything changed. I caught several students wiping tears away during the final credits of "Becoming" (2.21–22) as Buffy flees Sunnydale, having damned her true love to a hell dimension. They analyzed "The Zeppo" (3.13) as a satire on how they had been reading the series during the first weeks of the semester. The closeted fans came out and talked about why they had been in the *Buffy* closet in the first place. Students started reconsidering all of their opinions about the series to that point. They were reading and re-reading the series at the same time. I had never seen that happen with such intensity in a film studies classroom. Several students' written work — previously held back by unfounded assumptions about the intellect, gender, age and desires of the audience and thus the intentions of the series' creator — used more details to support their points and became more thoughtful about the text's implications.[5]

Television studies courses should not be taught like film, theater or literature courses. Television studies needs a pedagogy that is informed by the experiences of our peers in those disciplines but responsive to the unique possibilities and problems of teaching serial television's texts. Discovering how to use spoilers is a crucial element of this new approach. I taught courses where the first experience of the series was not held sacrosanct. I ran seminars where I told students that I would not spoil anything until after we had watched Season Three, but that after that point, all bets were off due to time constraints. In 2008, I ran the seminar as an all-spoiler course. My positive experiences there make me ambivalent, conflicted, on what role spoilers should play in the classroom. There may be no one best approach.

Television studies professors might simply borrow a technique from their peers in English departments. Some literature professors expect students to enter the class having read the novels and poems to be assigned that semester. They can suggest that students should enter the class having seen the series if they wish; an unsullied first read. In my last seminar, one senior watched the series for the first time over the summer to prepare for my course. On our course website blog she shared with me what she gained from that experience:

> I really appreciate that you emailed us at the beginning of the summer, asking who was familiar with the series etc. Seeing how I signed up for the class with no knowledge of the series, the fact that everyone else was so familiar [with it] was a little bit intimidating. And I am so glad that in the last month before class started that I watched it. Maybe it is just this specific group of students but there have been spoilers even in discussions. I think it is effective to examine the text as a whole, referencing different parts at different times. It is also important to experience the series as it was originally broadcast, thus I appreciate how in class we watch episodes sequentially.

The knowledge disparity between fan-students and others can be intimidating and watching the entire series before class starts is one way to defuse that fear. Several students in the past read Roz Kaveney's detailed summary of *Buffy* and *Angel* in *Reading the Vampire Slayer* at the start of the semester instead. Typically, they do not find even her 82 pages recounting plot and theme to be an effective means of catching up. I try to bridge the gap between a summary article and 103 hours of viewing by highlighting essential episodes in the syllabus as "suggested viewing." Unfortunately, this tactic does not seem to have a great impact on fan-students or those new to the series. Only students with a middling knowledge of the series have told me that they found it helpful as a way to refresh their memory.

There are costs to having students see the series on their own time. Teachers who assume that students will do significant amounts of course work on their own give a clear advantage to those students who have no family or work commitments that might interfere. Completing *Buffy* by watching three hours a day would take more than a month, a period that might be longer than winter break. Should departments only schedule television studies classes during the fall semester to give students the summer to see every episode? That seems to be a solution most department heads are unlikely to endorse due to the obvious scheduling difficulties it entails. Students who do not finish catching up often continue the process during the semester. Every semester that I have taught *Buffy*, some students try to catch up by watching the series as quickly as possible during the semester, averaging over seven hours a week in extra work. Such a viewing commitment makes completing the assigned reading and writing assignments more difficult, let alone how it must affect their work for other professors. Finally, every class would run better if students put in 100 hours of preparatory work prior to the start of class. Why should this expectation apply only to literature and television courses?

A student who once watched the series does not escape the problems of knowledge-disparities in the classroom. Many saw it in initial broadcast when they were young. Some do not remember the series particularly well, or did not see it sequentially, or it meant something very different at the age of 12 than at 20. They remember the big plot points, usually. But the rest has an aura of familiarity, where the details are forgotten but the exposure is remembered. More students encounter this series in that manner. As Laura Carroll puts it, "When gossip about a text circulates and infiltrates and sediments to the point where it coalesces into the common shared culture, and if a text endures long enough then that inevitably happens, foreknowledge becomes a normal element of reception, not some kind of aberration."

The fact that Angel is a vampire with a soul was a spoiler in 1997. It is not one now. Similarly, the success of the "Once More, with Feeling" (6.7) screenings that encourage audiences to sing along to the musical ensures that some students enter the class knowing about the series' extreme genre hybridity.[6] Buffy's deaths or Willow's relationship with Tara were culturally prominent enough to be increasingly part of the evolving common knowledge about the series. That is why some students watch the series again, either before the course starts or as the class progresses through each season. They do not wish to depend on their memory or on common knowledge.

Some texts depend on audiences having that common knowledge to achieve certain effects. When teaching ancient texts, one teacher on *The Chronicle of Higher Education*'s discussion boards tries to replicate the initial audience's knowledge entering the story:

> If my students are reading a work for which the original audience was generally expected to know the ending and most of the details, then I give the students some of those same details. For example, I give them a summary of the events of the Trojan War before we read the Iliad. I think that the students need to know that Hektor will never see his wife or son again when they have their parting scene, and I even note the ultimate fate of that son according to some traditions. In cases like this one, knowing how things turn out is what gives emotional weight to the scene [mended_drum].

I have found this to be a useful approach with "Once More, with Feeling" (6.7). The promotional ads for that episode featured the actors singing in the studio, which shaped the reception of the musical (cf. Halfyard, Albright).[7] Halfyard observes that in those ads, "their voices sound quite small and very 'natural,' lacking the timbral sophistication and vibrato of trained singers, which itself may very well be a crafted illusion" (para 42) that connotes their sincerity (which itself is a genre convention). Their voices remind viewers of the actors carefully hidden in the roles. The suspense of whether this cast will be able to rise to the challenge of singing and dancing doubles that of whether the characters will survive the musical demon. Reminding the audience that the characters are performed identities establishes the central theme of the season, as Buffy hides her depression behind a mask of acceptable behavior, the Trio seek to become the arch-villains of the fictions that inspire them and Willow's long-term mask of the "good girl" is ripped off.[8] Yet, the diversity of information available to modern viewers online and through broadcast promotions — as well as the global market for *Buffy*— makes figuring out who knew what, when, a hugely complex task with rapidly diminishing returns in all but exceptional cases. Did viewers in Turkey get the same effect from the series if they did not see the promos broadcast in the United States?

While exposure to spoilers varies by locale, reactions to spoilers are historically variable. Television scholars Jonathan Gray and Jason Mittell observe that "the long history of storytelling suggests that unspoiled narratives are far less common than spoiled ones — traditional drama and literature often retells well-known source material like myths and history, and many published works were preceded by summaries of each chapter or the entire narrative, ensuring that readers knew what to expect before encountering it." Of course, those literary spoilers often were written by the author, rather than imposed on the text by others. They were partially a response to cultural fears about the immersive pleasures of the novel when compared to more refined forms like poetry or scriptures. A certain critical distance from them was "healthy" because novels were bad for you; one might lose oneself in a story rather than find oneself. In short, our present obsession with spoilers may be generational and technological, but history suggests that the ambivalence to textual immersion demonstrated by readers of spoilers might be a common response.

In addition, not all spoilers have the same impact. *Buffy* scholar Rebecca Williams provides the following list of types:

> The different types of spoiler that have been identified through my research are episode titles, information on writers and directors, basic plot outlines, information on guest stars (and possible returning characters), information on character deaths, information on roman-

tic developments, information on locations used, extracts from shooting scripts and wild-feeds (special transmissions of a show that networks use to transmit to local television stations).... These spoiler types ... vary ... in their "intensity." For instance, a fan knowing the title of an upcoming episode is less "intense" a spoiler than having read the wildfeed and knowing exactly what, and how, something will happen before the episode airs [para 13].

So the disruption of a spoiler varies. Some episodes are thoroughly spoiled in the scholarship through in-depth analysis of form and narrative, such as ones on the series' opening credit sequences (Kociemba) and "Hush" (4.10) (Wilcox), or Matthew Pateman's book, much of which reads the entire series through the fourth season finale, "Restless." But many other articles have spoilers that reveal little more than what happens and not how it happens. These articles may be more concerned with understanding how the series works culturally than artistically, for example. Students who have not had even one full viewing of the series will have to take the scholar's article at face value. Teachers end up exchanging a student lacking the tools and distance necessary to provide a critical reading of the series, for a student lacking the experience with the text to come to their own decisions about the worth of the scholar's arguments.

Many critics who decry spoiler paranoia argue that this concern over-emphasizes the importance of plot. Williams' definition, like many others, does not list artistic techniques as a type of spoiler. Film critic Jonathan Rosenbaum, writing in defense of spoilers, observes that it is not considered a spoiler to state that *Touch of Evil* begins with a long tracking shot. Laura Carroll writes, "the underlying assumption doesn't imply much respect for anything that a fiction might offer you except abrupt and sensational narrative developments, or much confidence in the long-term durability of a story (i.e., its ability to withstand and reward repeated engagements)." Carroll and Rosenbaum have a point that spoilers are focused on plot. The definition of spoilers, however, should include revealing important artistic techniques. The details of how voice-over narration is used in "Passion" (2.17), how the absence of score in "The Body" (5.16) functions, the use of pantomime in "Hush," and which musical sub-genres are used in "Once More, with Feeling" are just as much spoilers as the fact that Angel loses his soul during the afterglow of having sex with Buffy, or that Tara gets killed by a stray bullet.

Some spoilers might be necessary. The syllabus for my "spoiler-free" course listed episode titles and information on writers and directors. The fact my students would see an "Espensode" is a spoiler as the identity of the writer hints at the nature of the episode (Kociemba).[9] The identity of various creators is vital knowledge for students to have if they are to learn how communal television production really is. The strategic use of spoilers can save class time by eliminating the need to use long tedious re-caps to get the class up-to-date. For example, if a teacher does not wish to show much of the seventh season, Elizabeth Rambo's fine close reading of its first episode, "Lessons" (7.1), provides so much detail that I use it to keep students up-to-date on that season's plot and theme. With minimal loss to plot comprehension, teachers can focus more on episodes in other seasons or on ambitious seventh season episodes like "The Killer in Me" (7.14), "Storyteller" (7.17), or the series finale, "Chosen" (7.22).

In addition, some researchers into spoiler fandom argue that reading spoilers produces more active, and frankly better, viewers. Williams, Gray and Mittell, and Jenkins all describe spoiler fans as viewers who seek out spoilers before watching an episode because they treat episodes as codes to be cracked through textual and extra-textual information.[10] Gray and Mittell's research on spoiler fans of *Lost* shows that they "see the revelatory aspect of the plotline and pleasures of suspense as relatively unimportant, obscuring more enjoyable textual qualities that they seek out such as narrative mechanics, relationship dramas, and production values." It is a different pleasure for them, not the loss of pleasure. They care more about understanding how a text works, which is an important skill for television studies professors to teach students. A class designed primarily to accomplish this goal might treat *Buffy* as a codex, a multiple-entry point text.

These authors all found that spoiler fans argued that spoilers allowed them to avoid being distracted by the task of plot comprehension or the emotional turmoil of suspense. Gray and Mittell refer to spoilers as permitting a shortcut to the more considered approach of a second viewing. If true, that efficiency is exactly what television studies needs. Unfortunately, one spoiler avoider accidentally exposed to a spoiler actually found the opposite to be true: "I spent too much time waiting for 'the big moment' and not enough time enjoying the show" (Gray and Mittell). Perhaps viewing through the lens of spoilers requires practice and skill.

Embracing spoilers may not be necessary to teach how a text works. Jes Battis noted that "Buffy 'double-codes' many of its scenes, using a combination of foreshadowing and subtextual references that the more discerning reader can access" (para 17). Even if one teaches without spoilers, students can talk about how such narrative techniques work. Students can learn to re-read the series' past in light of present developments while simultaneously earmarking elements as possible foreshadowing. These suppositions can then be re-evaluated in class discussions later in the semester as the narrative unfolds. The heaviest burden of that interpretative work occurs, however, during the final weeks of the semester. As students write their final papers, not only must they talk about the weighty issues brought up by the end of Season Six,[11] but they also revisit all the moments that might have foreshadowed them. It is easier to discuss these techniques fully when they come up.

Some people avoid all spoilers in pursuit of an unsullied first experience. Yet, avoiding only some spoilers may help viewers experience the series in the way that the authors of complex serial narratives do as they create it. Spoilers tend to imply that the authors of complex television narratives intend their every effect. In the case of *Buffy*, Whedon did not know that his series would return after its first season. While the creators planned season arcs far in advance—Buffy's Season Five death is foreshadowed in "Graduation Day Part II" (3.22)—generally episodes separated by such a time span do not intentionally foreshadow, as in the case of Willow's discovery of her homosexuality in Season Four. Rhonda Wilcox examines how foreshadowing gets produced in complex media narratives:

> Certain tropes are established which parallel and symbolically foreshadow later events. Since Whedon and Co. knew the overall arc of a season, it is possible that the early versions of a pattern are purposeful foreshadowing; it is also possible that they are preliminary explorations or first inklings of an idea which writers will choose to develop more fully later. Retroactive continuity allows for the effect of foreshadowing. Roz Kaveney has queried Jane Espenson about "inadvertent foreshadowing"; Espenson noted that Joss Whedon had

on occasion asked, "'Were we planning this back then?' And even he didn't know for sure" (Espenson, 107–108). She also comments, "Some of it is conscious and some of it is not conscious, but it is clearly there anyway" (107). The method is not unlike that of Charles Dickens, who wrote his novels in serialized form, knowing the overall arc but creating week by week, following where the characters led [115].

Students as readers may mirror the creator's own writing position by discussing "Nightmares" (1.10) without spoiling the dreams shown in "Restless," Willow's "kinda gay" vampire double in "Doppelgangland" (3.17) without spoiling the Willow-Tara relationship the next season, or Buffy's unusually vehement protests at the prospect of being hospitalized for the flu in "Killed by Death" (2.18) in light of the discovery in "Normal Again" (6.18) that she had been involuntarily committed by her parents when she first discovered she was a vampire slayer. Students need to learn that creators intend future narrative developments and formal approaches. Spoilers highlight that technique. Spoilers that do not include the production history details that inform those events give students the mistaken impression that all developments are planned far in advance, eliding how creators react to unexpected developments in their own work.

There are certain practical advantages to using spoilers in the classroom. In researching *Lost*'s spoiler fans, Gray and Mittell found that some use spoilers to reassure themselves that their time investment will be worthwhile, that the show will not "fall from grace." Gray and Mittell noted that:

> some cautious fans remain worried, hiding a touch of fear behind their pleasures, a tinge of apprehension that their show might start to decline or take an undesirable narrative turn to break their fannish hearts. For such cautious fans, spoilers work as a form of narrative insulation, revealing potential miscues in [a] less emotionally charged medium....

Indeed, during my first "spoiler-free" course, I felt that there might be an advantage in using spoilers to signal to skeptical students that this seminar would be worthwhile because the series will be worthwhile.

Premature information may prepare rather than spoil. *Buffy* packs an emotional wallop at times. I had one student who had just lost a parent leave the classroom during "The Body." A number of events in the series might hit students close to home: the attempted rape of Buffy in "Seeing Red" (6.19), Willow and Angel's grappling with addiction, or Dawn's self-cutting in "Blood Ties" (5.13). (Indeed, some cutters find that the depiction of such events — however positively or negatively represented — cues the past problematic thought patterns that led them to cut themselves.) Difficult as it may be, it is best that my students hear from those affected by media content, as many of them seek to make media products professionally. Joss Whedon revealed how "I knew we were doing the show right" when he read one girl's online post after Angel lost his soul as a result of sleeping with Buffy in "Innocence," which read, "This is unbelievable. This exact same thing happened to me" (quoted in "Wit and Wisdom of Joss Whedon," 7). In teaching a series that aims for emotional authenticity, teachers should do what they can to help students who have personal experience with these issues talk about them in the classroom. With spoilers providing the time to consider the issues, these students may be more able to make persuasive cases for how their experiences inform their views on the subjects covered by the series.

Along with such benefits, there are costs to using spoilers in the classroom. Williams's research finds that spoilers split *Buffy* fan communities into an information hierarchy of haves and have-nots:

> ...these fans will be in possession of the greatest levels of fan "discursive power," as they are able to control the flow of spoilers to fans and to set the agenda of fan discussion through the revelation or concealment of specific spoilers.... "[T]he unspoiled ones [...] are a bit 'late' then and a lot of discussion has already taken place" [Frances para 21].

She is not alone in noting the power disparities within fan communities. John Fiske detailed how fan knowledge "serves to distinguish within the fan community. The experts — those who have accumulated the most knowledge — gain prestige within the group and act as opinion leaders. Knowledge, like money, is always a source of power" (43). Henry Jenkins noted the importance of "a certain common ground, a set of shared assumptions, interpretations and rhetorical strategies, inferential moves, semantic fields and metaphors [...] as preconditions for meaningful debate over specific interpretations" ("Textual Poachers" 89). Such executive fans become a little like professors, responsible for enforcing and controlling appropriate fan interpretations, what Jenkins (1992) refers to as "the right way" of reading a text.

Teachers and students can abuse that power. Many times early in the semester non-fan students have asked whether they will face a competitive disadvantage with fan-students for the grades that determine eligibility for scholarships and academic prizes and honors.[12] Some students without pre-existing knowledge of the series do feel late to the class discussion. Some students use their greater "discursive power" to control the classroom. Two spoiler fans in Gray and Mittell's *Lost* fandom study noted the appeal of intellectual superiority. One woman wrote that she liked spoilers "honestly so I can sit back and laugh at people making stupid posts and stupid theories." That statement articulates the worst fears of non-fan students sharing a classroom with fan-students. Will they be mocked publicly or privately for their ignorance? Even professors can get sucked into this power dynamic when they "correct" students based on unseen narrative developments. Spoilers may silence even as they open up new ways of looking at the text. I have seen students grow tentative when they are corrected even a few times in this manner by their peers. Requiring all students to enter the course having seen the series may be the only way to even the playing field between experienced and inexperienced *Buffy* readers in the classroom. But that solution, as noted previously, can be impractical and discriminatory.

Using spoilers to cushion the emotional impact of the text comes with hidden costs. First, breaking the students' fannish hearts may be the best way to teach Spike's attempted rape of Buffy, the fan outrage resulting from the violent end to network television's longest running lesbian relationship and the mistakes the creators made in responding to these two crises (Wilts; Ryan). Students who approach this case study only with critical distance may miss the crucial role that emotions like anger, guilt, shame, and pride played in the actual reception of the text and its lingering cultural impact. Second, failure can be educational, as is deciding what failure really means. Joss Whedon described how he learned from some of the failures in *The X-Files'* plotting. I teach at a media arts school where the vast majority of my students are preparing to go into media production. They need to study the second season of *Twin Peaks* without being told whether it was a success or a failure. They need to come to their own conclusions about whether the final episode of *The Prisoner* works. And they need to see that seasons in *Lost* or in *Buffy* can have the reputation of being artistic failures to some people while being triumphs to others, all without ruining the series in question. Stating whether a series or a season succeeds or fails is itself a spoiler that teachers must mull over whether to share. Third, spoilers allow students to avoid being implicated as viewers. Joss Whedon finds the loss of narrative surprises troubling:

> Surprise is a holy emotion.... [It is] a reminder of the limits of our frame of reference.... [It] makes you humble. It makes you small in the world and takes you out of your own perspective. It shows you that you're wrong, the world is bigger and more complicated than you'd imagined. The more we dilute that with insider knowledge, with previews that show too much, with spoilers, with making-of specials, the more we're robbing ourselves of something we essentially need [Nussbaum 1].

One point of a liberal arts education is to see yourself in a new light through the catalyst of art. When *Buffy* is spoiled, you never have to face the possibility that you might react viscerally and uncomfortably to Willow coming out of the closet. The student will never risk reacting like Buffy did or like a number of fans online did. Without surprises, viewers have the time to orchestrate their reactions, to prepare them. The student will get only the reflective experience, instead of both the reflective and the responsive experience. To argue for spoilers is to argue that the only valuable mode of response is a reflective one. To argue against spoilers is to argue that both the reflective and responsive modes have their value.

Worse yet, students exposed to too many spoilers do not engage in the process of re-reading a work in light of later supplements to it. They crack the code and discover how the series works and they are done. But a work one cares about is not something one has read but rather something one reads. Knowledge becomes a goal rather than a process of continual engagement, a mode of alertness, sensitivity and openness. Knowing becomes a passive event, a set of facts (about culture, history, medium, and artistic techniques) to be discovered and recognized rather than actively made. Knowledge is not an interaction with the world but something realized and appreciated for that which it already unalterably is and was. It is disposable knowledge for a consumer culture. That is not true to my responsive or my considered experiences of the series. Independent media scholars Philip Mikosz and Dana C. Och observe that episodes like "Superstar" (4.17) model a different way to view the series:

> To write about *Buffy* is to write about a relationship, a certain investment across a serialized duration, as well as the cognitive relations that are elaborated at all levels of the series, from the season right down to a single shot.... Season by season, and even episode by episode, the series accumulates a multiple past, elements of oftentimes incongruous combinations" [para 2–3].

Knowledge about *Buffy* is actively made and remade as the series evolves. Rather than lending itself to be read once, it asks to be read multiple times. Such a reading position is necessarily speculative and imaginative. Spoilers undo an unusual feature of the storytelling of the *Buffy*verse, which always acknowledges the possibility of alteration:

"The Wish" (3.9) speculates on how single decisions can radically alter history, Jonathan rewrites the narrative in "Superstar" to make himself its star, the insertion of Dawn as Buffy's sister in "Real Me" (5.2) or the revelations of Buffy's involuntary committal in "Normal Again" rewrite the background of its central family. The crossover episode "I Will Remember You" (1.8) in *Angel* makes the unilateral decision to rewrite a relationship central to its profound emotional impact when Angel rewrites history to continue to fight the good fight rather than live as an ordinary man as Buffy's lover. Spoilers risk transforming stories into a story, without us ever experiencing the possibilities of stories. David Lavery asserts that because the series offers no closure at the level of questions "the text of *Buffy* invokes the imagination of the reader ... to finish the story in their own fashions, ... to write, and live, our own stories" (42). With spoilers, students never have to live in the question of what might happen and thus never get any practice completing stories in their own fashion. From this perspective, spoilers make reading more of a passive act of reception than an act of imagination.

Given the technological and economic changes in the television industry over the past twenty years, more series will be made that are, like *Buffy*, worthy of sustained classroom inquiry. Thus, more teachers will have to decide how to handle the power disparity implicit in a class in which some students enter with a body of narrative knowledge that others do not have. The traditional solution offers students the option of either putting in dozens of hours of extra work or face a competitive disadvantage in writing assignments and the possibility of being silenced in class discussions. Those teachers without such implicit course requirements must choose whether and how much to use spoilers. Using spoilers in reading assignments and discussions promotes several outcomes. Scholarship with many spoilers tends to model the kind of nuanced, detailed analysis students should emulate in their own writing. As spoilers foster plot comprehension and undermine suspense, class discussions will be less about whether the series works and more about how it works. Texts become codes to be cracked to foster an analysis of its underlying cultural and artistic structures. These classrooms value the more reflective posture typical of a more experienced reader. The teacher who avoids spoilers finds value in the responsiveness, investment and emotional commitment of a student's first reading experience. This approach encourages students to learn a doubled reading style in which they experience the narrative's momentum while reflecting on the text's construction. Such teachers risk stifling fan-students' enthusiasm in course discussions and craft vastly more complex lesson plans because they desire to be true to narratives that invite viewers to both invest in and critique the experience at the same time. As experienced readers, spoiler-averse teachers may even feel a responsibility to ensure that a student's first time with a text is a rewarding one, as it is a unique experience. There may be no best way to teach television's narrative complexity in the classroom, but then, no pedagogy has ever enjoyed a monopoly in classrooms for long. There is no answer. There are only choices.

NOTES

1. Tamara Wilson describes choosing to use "Never Kill a Boy on a First Date" (1.5) "precisely for its early date because I doubted any students in the class followed the series with academic intent. Most

had not followed the series at all" (212). After recounting the disappointing discussion that followed, she speculates about other episodes she could have chosen for what she was trying to accomplish, such as the (to my mind) superior episodes "Halloween" (2.6), "The Initiative (4.7) and the paired episodes "Surprise" and "Innocence" (2.13–14).

2. He notes that the bulk of this approach can be found in classics by Horace Newcomb, Robert Allen, Sarah Kozloff, John Ellis, Jane Feuer, Thomas Schatz, and Marc Dolan (Mittell 30).

3. While I recognize that "fan" is a loaded word to some readers, I use the term for two important reasons. First, some students in my seminars on this series describe themselves with that term. To describe them otherwise is to believe that "fan" is or should be a pejorative term, as if being a committed and enthusiastic reader is something they should be ashamed of or somehow is inferior to a pose of objectivity. Second, the term "fan" connotes someone with a body of knowledge superior to a student who has watched the series in part or idly in broadcast. Later in the essay, this distinction becomes important. Spoilers affect students differently based on whether they have never seen the series, saw the series once, or are active fans of the series.

4. Kendra became a vampire slayer after Buffy's heart temporarily stopped at the end of Season One, entering the series in "What's My Line, Part I" (2.9). The character used a bad Jamaican patois and Buffy's animosity to this rival consequently demands reading along racial lines. Faith, described by Eliza Dushku on the Season Three DVDs as a "working class Slayer," was activated by Kendra's death to end the second season. For two excellent articles of the many on them, I recommend Lynne Edwards' chapter, "Slaying in Black and White: Kendra as Tragic Mulatta in *Buffy*," in *Fighting the Forces* and Sue Tjardes' chapter, "'If you're not enjoying it, you're doing something wrong': Textual and Viewer Constructions of Faith, the Vampire Slayer," in *Athena's Daughters*.

5. For a more in-depth analysis on how a viewer's perception of the author and intended audience can shape that viewer's understanding of the text, as well as reported demographics and ratings, see my article, "'Over-identify much?': Passion, "Passion," and the Author-Audience Feedback Loop in *Buffy the Vampire Slayer*" in *Slayage*. 19. As that article notes, even professional scholars can fall victim to this dynamic. For the record, Joss Whedon said, "They charted it in our second year, and the median viewer age is 26. There are young kids watching it, but I consider it a college show." (Longworth 215).

6. See Holly G. Barbaccia on the slasher genre in "Helpless," Steve Wilson on the series' word play, my own writing on its use of black comedy, Scott Westerfield on its use of the alternate world fantasy sub-genre, Rhonda Wilcox on the Quality Television movement and "The Body," Elizabeth Krimmer and Shilpa Raval on how the Liebstod marks the Buffy-Angel relationship, Cynthea Masson and Marni Stanley on camp and Spike, and Wilcox, Janet K. Halfyard and Richard S. Albright on "Once More, with Feeling," the musical episode.

7. These promos continue to influence viewers. "*Buffy the Vampire Slayer*— Making of the Musical" on YouTube got nearly 200,000 views at the time of publication, with other similar versions having more than 80,000 views. Broadcast-quality versions of the aired 30-second, one-minute and two-minute length promos can be found at the series' sixth season page of Howard Russell's Buffy world.com.

8. See Christie Golden on Wicca and Willow's witchcraft, Jes Battis on Willow's growth into a heroic figure and Caroline Ruddell on Willow's split identity.

9. Jane Espenson is a writer recognized by fans, television critics and scholars for having a distinctive style somewhat independent of the series she writes for and may function as an auteur despite not serving as the executive producer, or even a director. For more, turn to my chapter, "Understanding the Espensode," in *Buffy Goes Dark*.

10. Indeed, Henry Jenkins has an amusing anecdote about the time spoiler fans of *Survivor* got free use of a satellite to spy on the set of the series, as the producer had negotiated a no-fly zone in the air space overhead. Some spoiler fans are simply fans of a series who seek out spoilers, while other spoiler fans are both fans of the series and spoilers in their own right. See his chapter, "Spoiling *Survivor*" in his book, *Convergence Culture*.

11. See Alissa Wilts and Brandy Ryan's paired articles about the end of the Willow-Tara relationship, Peg Aloi's evocative response to Tara's murder and Dawn Heinecken's documentation on fan readings of sex and violence at the end of the sixth season.

12. In my experience, fan-students either do very poorly or very well. Some simply cannot step outside what the series means to them to think critically about how it works. Others take advantage of the knowledge base with which they enter the class.

WORKS CITED

Albright, Richard S. "'Breakaway pop hit or ... book number?': "Once More with Feeling" and Genre." *Slayage: The Whedon Studies Association Journal* 5.1 (June 2005): n.pag. Web. 16 March 2010.

Aloi, Peg. "Skin Pale as Apple Blossom." *Seven Seasons of* Buffy. Ed. Glen Yeffeth. Dallas: BenBella Books, 2003. 41–47. Print.

Barbaccia, Holly G. "Buffy in the 'Terrible House.'" *Slayage* 1.4 (December 2001): n.pag. Web. 16 March 2010.

Battis, Jes. "'She's Not All Grown Yet': Willow as Hybrid/Hero in *Buffy the Vampire Slayer.*" *Slayage* 2.4 (March 2003): n.pag. Web. 24 March 2009.

Buffy the Vampire Slayer: The Chosen Collection. Twentieth Century–Fox Home Entertainment, 2005. DVD.

Carroll, Laura. "Cruel Spoiler, the Embosom'd Foe." *The Valve: A Literary Organ* (9 October 2005): n. pag. Web. 24 March 2009.

Edwards, Lynne. "Slaying in Black and White: Kendra as Tragic Mulatta in *Buffy.*" *Fighting the Forces: What's at Stake in* Buffy the Vampire Slayer. Eds. Rhonda Wilcox and David Lavery. New York: Rowman & Littlefield, 2002. 85–97. Print.

Fiske, John. "The Cultural Economy of Fandom." *The Adoring Audience: Fan Culture and Popular Media.* Ed. Lisa A. Lewis. London: Routledge, 1992. Print.

Golden, Christie. "Where's the Religion in Willow's Wicca?" *Seven Seasons of Buffy.* Ed. Glen Yeffeth. Dallas: BenBella Books, 2003. 159–166. Print.

Gray, Jonathan, and Jason Mittell. "Speculation on Spoilers: *Lost* Fandom, Narrative Consumption and Rethinking Textuality." *Participations* 4.1 (May 2007): 47 pars. 24. Web. March 2009.

Halfyard, Janet K. "Singing Their Hearts Out: The Problem of Performance in *Buffy the Vampire Slayer* and *Angel.*" *Slayage* 5.1 (June 2005): n.pag. Web. 16 March 2010.

Heinecken, Dawn. "Fan Readings of Sex and Violence on *Buffy the Vampire Slayer.*" *Slayage* 3.3–4 (April 2004): n.pag. Web. 16 March 2010.

Jenkins, Henry. *Convergence Culture: Where Old and New Media Collide.* New York: New York University Press, 2006. Print.

_____. "'Do You Enjoy Making the Rest of Us Feel Stupid?' Alt.Tv.Twinpeaks, the Trickster Author, and Viewer Mastery." *Full of Secrets: Critical Approaches to Twin Peaks.* Ed. David Lavery. Detroit: Wayne State University Press, 1995. 51–69. Print.

_____. *Textual Poachers: Television Fans and Participatory Culture.* New York: Routledge, 1992. Print.

Kaveney, Roz. "'She Saved the World. A Lot.' An Introduction to the Themes and Structures of *Buffy* and *Angel.*" *Reading the Vampire Slayer.* Ed. Roz Kaveney. New York: Tauris Parke Paperbacks, 2004. 1–82. Print.

Kociemba, David. "'Actually, It Explains a *Lot*': Reading the Opening Title Sequences of *Buffy the Vampire Slayer.*" *Slayage* 6.2 (Winter 2006): n.pag. Web. 24 March 2009.

_____. "'Over-identify Much?': Passion, "Passion," and the Author-Audience Feedback Loop in *Buffy the Vampire Slayer,*" *Slayage* 5.3 (February 2006): n.pag. Web. 24 March 2009.

_____. "Understanding the Espensode," *Buffy Goes Dark.* Eds. Lynne Edwards, Elizabeth L. Rambo, and James B. South. Jefferson, NC: McFarland, 2009. 23–39. Print.

_____. "'Where's the Fun?': The Comic Apocalypse in 'The Wish,'" *Slayage* 6.3 (Spring 2007): n.pag. Web. 24 March 2009.

Krimmer, Elizabeth, and Shilpa Raval. "'Digging the Undead': Death and Desire in *Buffy.*" *Fighting the Forces: What's at Stake in* Buffy the Vampire Slayer. Eds. Rhonda Wilcox and David Lavery. New York: Rowman & Littlefield, 2002. 153–164. Print.

Lavery, David. "Apocalyptic Apocalypses: The Narrative Eschatology of *Buffy the Vampire Slayer.*" *Slayage* 3.1 (August 2003): n.pag. Web. 24 March 2009.

Longworth, James L., Jr. "Joss Whedon: Feminist." *TV Creators: Conversations with America's Top Producers of Television Drama.* 2. Syracuse, NY: Syracuse University Press, 2002: 197–220. Print.

Masson, Cynthea, and Marni Stanley. "Queer Eye of That Vampire Guy: Spike and the Aesthetics of Camp." *Slayage* 6.2 (Winter 2006): n.pag. Web. 16 March 2010.

mended_drum. "Re: Spoilers in Your Reading Assignments." *Chronicle of Higher Education.* (30 May 2008). Web. 19 March 2010.

Mikosz, Philip, and Dana C. Och. "Previously on *Buffy the Vampire Slayer*...." *Slayage* 2.1 (May 2002): n.pag. Web. 24 March 2009.

Mittell, Jason. "Narrative Complexity in Contemporary American Television." *The Velvet Light Trap*. 58 (Fall 2006): 29–40. Print.

Nussbaum, Emily. "The End of the Surprise Ending." *New York Times* 9 May 2004: Section 2, Pg. 1. Print.

Pateman, Matthew. *The Aesthetics of Culture in* Buffy the Vampire Slayer. London: McFarland, 2006. Print.

Rambo, Elizabeth. "'Lessons' for Season Seven of *Buffy the Vampire Slayer*." *Slayage* 3.3-.4 (April 2004): n.pag. Web. 24 March 2009.

Rosebaum, Jonathan. "In Defense of Spoilers." *Chicago Reader* (14 November 2006). n.pag. Web. 24 March 2009.

Ruddell, Caroline. "'I am the law' I am the magicks': Speech, Power and the Split Identity of Willow in *Buffy the Vampire Slayer*." *Slayage* 5.4 (May 2006): n.pag. Web. 16 March 2010.

Russell, Howard. "*Buffy the Vampire Slayer* Season Six (2001-2002)." *BuffyWorld.com*. BuffyWorld. n.d. Web. 19 March 2010.

Ryan, Brandy. "'It's complicated ... because of Tara': History, Identity Politics, and the Straight White Male Author." *Buffy Goes Dark*. Eds. Lynne Edwards, Elizabeth L. Rambo, and James B. South. Jefferson, NC: McFarland, 2009. 57–74. Print.

Tabron, Judith L. "Girl on Girl Politics: Willow/Tara and New Approaches to Media Fandom." *Slayage* 4.1–2 (October 2004): n.pag. Web. 16 March 2010.

Tjardes, Sue. "'If you're not enjoying it, you're doing something wrong': Textual and Viewer Constructions of Faith, the Vampire Slayer." *Athena's Daughters: Television's New Women Warriors*. Eds. Frances Early and Kathleen Kennedy. Syracuse, NY: Syracuse University Press, 2003. 66–77. Print.

Westerfield, Scott. "A Slayer Comes to Town." *Seven Seasons of Buffy*. Ed. Glen Yeffeth. Dallas: BenBella Books, 2003. 30–40. Print.

Wilcox, Rhonda. *Why Buffy Matters*. New York: I. B. Tauris, 2005. Print.

Wilson, Steve. "Laugh, Spawn of Hell, Laugh." *Reading the Vampire Slayer*. Ed. Roz Kaveney. New York: Tauris Parke Paperbacks, 2002. 78–97. Print.

Wilts, Alissa. "Evil, Skanky and Kinda Gay: Lesbian Images and Issues." *Buffy Goes Dark*. Eds. Lynne Edwards, Elizabeth L. Rambo, and James B. South. Jefferson, NC: McFarland, 2009. 41–56. Print.

"The Wit and Wisdom of Joss Whedon." *Slayage*: n.pag. Web. 24 March 2009.

Williams, Rebecca. "'It's About Power': Spoilers and Fan Hierarchy in On-Line *Buffy* Fandom." *Slayage* 3.3-.4 (April 2004): n.pag. Web. 24 March 2009.

Wilson, Tamara. "Keeping *Buffy* in the Classroom." *Buffy Meets the Academy*. Ed. Kevin Durand. Jefferson, NC: McFarland, 2009. 211–218. Print.

"Have You Tried Not Being a Slayer?" Performing *Buffy* Fandom in the Classroom

Jason Lawton Winslade

Whenever my first-year writing students write about popular culture, I generally work hard to suppress the inevitable cringe. Usually, their assessment of popular culture amounts to a moralistic condemnation of a media entity typically characterized as monolithic, faceless, and potentially dangerous. And understandably so, as students are undoubtedly parroting the simplistic, dichotomous rhetoric of their high school literature courses or of endless news stories that have blamed teen violence on Marilyn Manson, *Grand Theft Auto*, or any cultural phenomenon that challenges mainstream values. In the tradition of Frederic Wertham's postwar classic of cultural paranoia, *Seduction of the Innocent*, which decried the scourge of comic books as the source for the societal ills perpetrated by wayward juveniles, this type of media coverage inevitably dominates the first stage of research that students embark upon. And many students willfully reproduce this rhetoric, even when they do not seem to believe a word of it themselves, and even when they seem to value their entertainment more highly than mere escapism.

In the conclusion to his groundbreaking study, *Convergence Culture: Where Old and New Media Collide*, media scholar Henry Jenkins regrets that universities often encourage this limited point of view, lamenting that "more focus is placed on the dangers of manipulation rather than the possibilities of participation, on restricting access — turning off the television, saying no to Nintendo — rather than in expanding skills at deploying media for one's own ends, rewriting the core stories our culture has given us" (259). Jenkins advocates introducing students to participatory culture as a way to both validate their experiences with popular culture and offer them a stake in co-creating that culture. He further advocates "rethink[ing] the goals of media education so that young people can come to think of themselves as cultural producers and participants and not simply as consumers, critical or otherwise" (259). As I teach a first year undergraduate seminar course on *Buffy the Vampire Slayer* for the fifth time, Jenkins' proposal haunts me. I often wonder if, through the class, I am simply creating a more critical consumer and not doing enough to encourage students to become cultural producers. These issues inevitably revolve around the notion of fandom, and what role fandom plays in scholarship of popular media.[1] Jenkins characterizes fandom as "born of a balance between fascination and frustration:

if media content didn't fascinate us, there would be no desire to engage with it; but if it didn't frustrate us on some level, there would be no drive to rewrite or remake it" (247). It is this frustration that urges me to question my own fandom and how students navigate fandom in their critical study of *Buffy*.

An essential part of introducing students to *Buffy* discourse is my own insider scholarship, consisting of a personal approach to scholarly writing on the subject and the integration of a television program that I personally treasure into a university course. Teaching *Buffy* itself requires an awkward dance between experiential viewing pleasures and thoughtful analysis, one that reflects many issues in my training as a Performance Studies ethnographer. Despite its inherent challenges, fandom can be put to good use in teaching a course on *Buffy the Vampire Slayer*. By addressing the issues of fandom head on, teachers can examine how students choose to navigate these tensions and internalize their experience of the show and its characters. One method available for students to articulate their experience is incorporating analysis of their own and others' attempts at engaging the show through fan creations, as well as the program's own acknowledgment of these processes. By constantly acknowledging the pleasures and pitfalls of fandom in the classroom, educators can engage students on a personal level that allows for fruitful critical discussions. In my case, that fandom was often shared between students and myself.

In a strange coincidence, *Buffy the Vampire Slayer* appeared on television in the Spring of 1997, at the same time I was finishing my PhD coursework in Performance Studies at Northwestern University. I was immediately drawn into the show and identified strongly with the character of Xander. That fall, fresh out of coursework, I began my first adjunct teaching job at DePaul University, and over the seven years of the show's run, my life changed, as I married and gained a family. By the end of the show, I had been a composition and rhetoric professor for seven years, and at that point, while I still felt connected to the Xander character, I found myself relating to the character of Giles even more, as a mentor, teacher and parent.

This kind of identification with the characters is certainly what Joss Whedon had in mind when he created a show and characters that he knew would be "an emotional experience [...] loved in a way that other shows can't be loved" (Thompson et al., 375). David Lavery, one of the founders of an academic subculture known as "*Buffy* Studies," professes this very love in his essay, "'I wrote my thesis on you!' *Buffy* Studies as an Academic Cult." Answering to charges that *Buffy* scholars are "repressing, projecting and 'acting out' their own fantasies in relation to the program" (Levine and Schneider 299), Lavery defends this emotional identification, claiming that the love of *Buffy* scholars for the show is more "agape" than "eros": "Loving *Buffy* need not be a swoon. It may be the means to really know the show, know it as only love can know" (par. 38).[2] With this clarification of the nature of *Buffy* love, he also answers to criticism from the other end of the spectrum, those who accuse Lavery and Rhonda Wilcox, the co-founders and editors of *Slayage*, of "sucking the life" out of the series by overanalyzing what is ostensibly throw-away entertainment.[3] Though the purpose of this essay is not to defend the value of *Buffy* scholarship, these questions are fundamental when approaching scholarship in both a conference and a classroom setting dedicated to studying the series.

I struggled with these questions of fandom early on with my own foray into *Buffy*

Studies. One of my earliest publications was an article in the premiere issue of *Slayage*, dealing with *Buffy*'s participation in the contemporary commodification of witchcraft.[4] That brief article has remained the most cited and referenced of my published works, both in other essays, books, and class syllabi, while leading to several interviews that cite me as an authority on occultism and pop culture.[5] These various interpellations of my *Buffy* knowledge and my class gave me status as an "insider," either as an academic, a *Buffy* fan, or in some cases, my role as a member of the practitioner communities studied as part of my dissertative work on magick and occultism.

This participant/observer confusion, while initially troublesome, was ultimately supported by my field: performance studies. As a discipline, performance studies highlights the "constructed nature of most human activity" and examines the "performances" that individuals and communities produce, either consciously framed as such, or unintentional (Carlson 191). In order to examine performance, however, the researcher must go beyond reductive textual readings and actually engage with those who are performing, while still acknowledging his or her own performances as an ethnographer. In her essay on performance pedagogy, Elyse Pineau succinctly describes the task of the performance ethnographer, which is to "replace distanced observation with active participation in the host community, arguing that sensuous engagement and kinesthetic empathy between researchers and subjects can best illuminate the experiential complexities of human interaction, the texture of a living moment" (47). Thus, performance studies ethnographers, or researchers who wish to engage their subjects through a methodology of embodiment, must pay close attention to their "active participation" and the effect such interactions have on their scholarship. Thus, performed roles in the ethnographic encounter, particularly within the realm of alternative subcultural activities, are always contingent, always changing, resisting stratification into easy participant/observer poles as questions of sincerity and authenticity inevitably come to the fore, and the term "performance" takes on many contested meanings.

This is no less true in the realm of *Buffy* Studies, as noted by ethnographer Asim Ali, in his study of the online *Bronze* community, the posting board for *Buffy* fans named after the teen hangout depicted in the television program. Describing the process by which he was "de-lurked" — called out by a Bronzer he had met and interviewed in person — Ali acknowledges his initial discomfort with becoming a poster himself: "I suddenly found myself not the observer but the observed, the newbie trying to learn the community rules to fit in. The ethnographer's gaze had been reflected back, and the (artificial) distinction between observer and observed irrevocably confused" (110). Ultimately, Ali accepts this slippage as a result of a false binary that many anthropologists and performance studies scholars have acknowledged which, in turn, have opened the door to insider scholarship conducted by those who are members of the community they are studying.[6] When teaching a class on a popular television program from the perspective of a scholar *and* a fan, I consciously foreground the slippage between observer and observed, no less than my own students would, considering that a significant number might sign up for the course because they are fans of the show.

I saw my fandom as a potential problem in teaching *Buffy* to first year college students, wondering how much of our discussions would be based on personal opinion of the show and its characters. I was certainly not alone in these concerns. In an essay investigating the first *Slayage* conference, Vivien Burr notes that almost everyone who responded to her email request for reactions to the conference "wrote of the tension between their academic and fan identities" (2). Many of these respondents seemed uncomfortable with their dual identities, while some framed their fandom as analogous to their general work as scholars who are "fans" of literature or other scholars' work. During my own attendance at the conference, I was certainly troubled by how fandom could prevent critical discourse, as post-panel discussions would often devolve into academics gushing about a particular episode or character. In the article, Burr quotes my response at length:

> I feel that fandom can certainly inform a scholar's work and adds to the playfulness that can make scholarly papers interesting. But a scholar needs to balance that with a more measured approach. I refrain from using the term "objectivity," since that notion is as mythical as vampires are. But an academic writing on these topics needs to learn to coax his or her fandom into the service of scholarly inquiry[7] [Burr 3].

I carried this cautious attitude about fandom into the creation of my *Buffy* course as I determined my own position in this fray.

As a performance studies scholar, my approach to analyzing *Buffy* tended to focus on how the program constantly highlighted performance, from its construction of Buffy's vampire-slaying as a conscious performance complete with punning, martial arts, and gymnastics, to the notion of identity creation as a performance, especially on the part of Spike, who willfully changes his demeanor, his clothes, and even his accent, from upper-class dandy to working-class bad boy. Willow was also a character primarily defined by how she claimed identity based on her performance of magical acts, not to mention her conscious performances of gender and sexual orientation. In addition, the show featured traditionally framed performances as well as "meta" acknowledgements of the show's action within a performance frame (as in the popular musical episode, "Once More, With Feeling" (6.7)).[8] In approaching the creation and implementation of my own course on *Buffy*, I was convinced that these performance elements, along with explorations of fandom, would be the way to reach first-year students.

Inspired by the scene in "The Freshman" (4.1), in which Buffy expresses incredulity at the idea that college students can get credit for taking courses on popular culture and television, I proposed a course to the First Year Program at DePaul University. Unlike classes at other universities that incorporated *Buffy* into teaching various subjects, I worked the other way around. My job was actually to teach the show itself within a course, working with various discourses and fields that the show engages, most prominently feminism and gender studies, ethics and philosophy, cultural and media studies, and performance studies. The course was proposed as a Focal Point Seminar, one of a wide selection of such seminars that first year DePaul students choose from in the Winter and Spring terms. Every student must take one Focal Point as a requirement for the First Year Program.[9] These courses are meant to be interdisciplinary in nature, in which a single topic (a person, place, text, idea, or event) is explored at length through "multiple methodological or disciplinary perspectives," offering students the opportunity to experience the "active learning" and critical analysis of a seminar setting. The course description also mentions that the various topics "are framed from the faculty member's experience and intellectual perspective," therefore I felt somewhat justified in my personal approach to the topic.[10]

Before the term began, I contacted students, recommending they spend some time familiarizing themselves with the show, while reassuring them that lack of prior knowledge of the show would not necessarily put them at a disadvantage in the class. In the first half of the course, taught in a ten-week quarter, I approached each season as a distinct unit, a chapter in a broader literary text, in order to discuss the story developments and themes for that particular season. Sometimes the "season summary" features on the DVD sets aided with this, though I encouraged students to question and critique statements made by writers, directors and actors in these interviews. Students were responsible for viewing at least one episode from each season, in addition to whatever episodes or clips I screened in class in a given week, and to write a two to three page response paper for their chosen episode. For this assignment, I required students to contextualize the episode within the season or entire series, emphasizing character, thematic, and technical analysis, while discouraging plot summary for its own sake, or tone and diction that too closely approached a review (avoiding language such as "I liked that..." or "x was well done"). For their midterm paper, students were required to extend this analysis of an episode to a five-page paper, sometimes expanding a response paper or choosing a new episode to analyze. Here, I encouraged students to incorporate scholarly work that particularly addressed their chosen episode, and offered them the opportunity to present their thesis in a brief class presentation, which sometimes utilized clips from the episode. I let students know that viewing these episodes outside of class was their responsibility, through renting or buying DVDs. I also relied upon the vast amount of online documentation to fill in the blanks, providing links to several websites that provide episode summaries and transcripts, encouraging students to review these summaries in order to get a sense of the narrative flow for any given season. As this supplementary material was not required reading, students determined for themselves what level of knowledge was necessary for completing the assignments. The only assessment of this knowledge was in the form a midterm exam that asked them to address broad themes of the show and its characters, rather than any factual knowledge of plots or trivia. For most students, this worked out fine. A few enterprising students eagerly bought the seven season boxed set, while most rented DVDs, and some even shared episodes with each other.

In the first half of the course, we analyzed episodes in context with the season arcs until we had more or less covered the narrative of the entire series. In the second half of the course we focused more on scholarly work on the show itself, dealing with broader issues like ethics, violence, gender, and power. Every reading in the course is specific to *Buffy* itself, but I do emphasize *Buffy* scholarship that builds on the work of authors like Goffman, Barthes, and Jenkins, in accordance with my emphasis on performance theory. Along these lines, I pointed out instances within the show itself where the writers insert metatextual references, such as the episode "Storyteller" (7.16), which features the character of Andrew, the ultimate "fan" within the *Buffy*verse, or when characters demonstrate or acknowledge their performative natures, as in the previously mentioned case of Spike. Therefore, we also discussed actor performances in this light, applying these discussions to performance in everyday life, in which we all, consciously or not, portray characters.

The final paper for the course consisted of several options, including an extended character or thematic analysis, incorporating scholarly work on the show, a critical comparison between *Buffy* and another show or text, an analysis of other ancillary texts, either "official" or fan-based. The few students who chose this option attempted, some more successfully than others, to compare how these objects tended to either support or undermine the ethos of the show. For instance, one student wrote on fan fiction accounts that rejected the show's tendency to keep its romantic couples in turmoil and offer more traditional, "romantic" happy endings. Students also had the option to write about how the show might influence their personal approaches to ethics, religion, and current events (for instance, one student wrote a paper on how Buffy might solve the situation in Iraq), while others took a creative option to come up with a continuation of the show's events after it ended. In these cases, students wrote full story arcs and attempted to address the themes of the show given the new circumstances they would create. Students also created, with varying degrees of success, their own scripts, fan music videos (or "vids"), or fan fiction, accompanied by a short paper that critically justifies the work. This option particularly encourages students to be actively engaged producers rather than just consumers watching a TV show.

Throughout the course, I try to prepare students for this kind of active producer role by discussing fandom in general and the impact of the audience on the initial broadcast of the show as well as fan readings of the series, its surrounding "universe" and the consumer franchise itself.[11] For instance, we look at fan-created texts that comment on the show or display an individual's reading of the show, whether or not that reading coincided with the program creators' intent. Some examples of this are "wallpapers," online artwork that feature an image or many images from the program with text from the show or even text from classic poetry or a popular song that might provide a perspective on the visuals. In other cases, "vids" provide similar examples of scenes selected and edited by the fan, put to music and lyrics that foreground a particular element of the show, or bring forward subtextual elements, sometimes introducing a "slash fiction" element, depicting same sex characters as lovers simply by selective editing.[12] This form of fan "poaching," Henry Jenkins' term borrowed from Michel de Certeau, becomes the basis for a discussion of Roland Barthes' "readerly text" where readers have the ability to change the text to reflect their own desires and needs, even when those desires may undermine the program's feminist message. To explore these topics, I provide students with links to a few examples of wallpapers, fan fiction, and music videos, modeling analysis of these new media products in class, and requiring that students find their own examples of *Buffy* new media and analyze them in a response paper.

Student reactions to the series and the class have been noticeably varied. David Kociemba, writing about his experiences teaching *Buffy*, relates students' reluctance and even hostility towards critically discussing television programs they personally find entertaining, while studying more highbrow viewing is acceptable (par. 3). The risk for students is that analyzing something they actually enjoy may pose a risk of crossing too many boundaries between personal life and academic life. In my class, although I initially encountered some resistance to the notion that *Buffy* was worthy of study, many students unfamiliar with the show eventually discussed their surprise that a series called *Buffy the*

Vampire Slayer could be intelligent and interesting. The first four times I taught the course, roughly one third said that they were already fans prior to taking the course (in a class of approximately 20 students), another third were vaguely familiar with the show (either had seen an episode or two or had heard of it), with another third having no knowledge of it whatsoever. This distribution may be due to the service nature of the course, with students taking it because it fits their schedule or it "sounded cool." Some were even confused in that they thought the course was going be about vampire folklore and not a television show.

Students with greater familiarity with the show had more material to draw from in discussions and papers, but since I provided links to websites with extensive information, the opportunity for familiarity was available to everyone. According to one set of course evaluations, some students felt that their unfamiliarity with the show put them at a disadvantage and they would have done better if they had more prior knowledge of the show. However, I often found this not to be the case. In some instances, a few students who had never even heard of the show before taking the course performed excellently and consistently received some of the highest grades on their papers. In one case, this high performance was due to the student's prior training in literary criticism (and she was a devout *Harry Potter* fan, which prepared her for analyzing fantasy). These students may have had an advantage because they could approach the series from a fresh, critical perspective. As one of these students put it in a survey, "my lack of fandom made it easier for me to analyze the show critically and explore negative views." Indeed, one young woman who admitted to being a fan often had a hard time seeing past her fandom in order to achieve critical depth. Her response papers tended to focus more on her personal attachments to characters rather than on thematic analysis.

As more time passed from *Buffy's* final airing in 2003, I assumed that students' awareness of the program would lessen. However, in the fifth iteration of the course, I was pleasantly surprised to learn that, of the eighteen students who signed up for the course, the majority considered themselves fans of the show, and those students who were not as familiar with the show considered themselves to be fans of genre fiction, television, and comics. Unlike previous classes, I did not have to spend any time proving that *Buffy* was worthy of study and our discussions were immediately fruitful because of a shared familiarity with the conventions of genre fiction and film, as well as an awareness of fan culture. Usually, students like these are the exception in a course, but in this case, they were the rule. While this interaction was initially exciting and energizing, especially since I did not have to be embarrassed about my own fan identity, I quickly became concerned that our discussions would lack critical depth. Thankfully, a group discussion after a viewing of the popular episode "Hush" (4.10), in which we addressed issues of communication and community, allayed those fears. The students translated their enjoyment of the show into a detailed discussion about the symbolism of the episode. The key here was bringing together a screening with a critical text. In this case, it was "Hush" with an article by Patrick Shade, entitled "Screaming to Be Heard: Community and Communication in 'Hush.'" Shade's article set the stage for a discussion of the episode that allowed them to apply the themes of speaking, communication, and community to their keen observations of the episode.

In my experience, although teaching the course to fans may at times be more personally enjoyable, the challenges of keeping discussions and student papers critical and scholarly are significant. Generally, reading scholarly work about *Buffy* helps students to contextualize popular culture within academic discourse. Conversely, these readings helped convince non-fans that the program was worthy of study and could be a part of discursive fields like literature, philosophy, gender, and politics. Steering class discussions toward a critical edge was also crucial. In some cases, I let "fan discussions" occur just so we could blow off steam as a class and simply enjoy an episode or aspect of the show. But I always looked for ways to take a "fan discussion" and make it work for the purposes of the course. For instance, at one point female students engaged in a debate over which vampire was more attractive: Angel or Spike. We were able to turn this potentially mind-numbing discussion over who is "cutest" into a discourse on the characters themselves, what makes them attractive, what relationship pitfalls each represents, and ultimately, how both symbolize different gendered power conflicts that challenge young women in modern society.

Overall, this course has been extremely successful. It has consistently been a popular course among the first year students, often filling up immediately after registration, and its student evaluation marks are usually higher than the department mean, making it one of the more highly student-ranked classes in the First Year Program. In a short, informal survey that I distributed to my second class, many students acknowledged that the course had taught them to view popular culture with a more critical eye and to assess television through the lens of discourses like feminism and performance studies. In addition, several commented about how the course helped them to fully integrate other ideas that they have encountered in their other university classes. For instance, Allison spoke to me about how her familiarity with fan fiction and the notion of role-playing and identity construction aided her subsequent pursuits in her college major in social work.

Madeline, one of the students with little prior knowledge of the show, articulately outlined how studying *Buffy* is an example of "the struggle to understand the human condition through multiple frames of human experience." She also related how class discussions of *Buffy* balanced out gender studies courses she had taken that tended to present reductive views of gender:

> I really think that one of Buffy's saving graces is that she embraces the mainstream — she doesn't want to kill the prom queen, she wants to be the prom queen. She functions within her culture as [a] self-realized woman ... often times in my other [gender studies] course I felt shamed for being "too feminine," but Buffy doesn't necessarily say that in order to be a strong woman you have to be A, B, and C ... rather [the show] encourages self-respect.[13]

While not every first year student who takes this course may be able to process its content at such a high level and integrate it with broader disciplinary issues, Madeline stands as a model for how students might interpret the show and its characters as examples of processual, contingent identities, and in turn incorporate that interpretation into academic work that itself contributes to the *Buffy* Studies discourse. Madeline eventually entered her final paper in DePaul's First Year Program Writing Showcase. She won the top prize with her essay entitled "The Dead Poets Society," comparing the relationship between Spike and Buffy with that of the main characters of Nabakov's *Lolita*, and eventually published the essay in the peer-reviewed online journal, *Watcher Jr.*, the Undergraduate Journal of *Buffy* Studies.[14] Therefore, Madeline, who became a fan of the program through the class, parlayed her emotional and political identification with the character of Buffy into an opportunity to become an active academic producer. Madeline also articulates a fairly common identification with Buffy among students in the current post-feminist academic environment, particularly with regards to her identity struggles between "normal girl" and "Slayer."

In an essay on performativity and *Buffy*, Rob Cover argues that in more recent serialized television, particularly in the genres of fantasy and science fiction, "subjecthood is shown to be torn between an enlightenment era notion of wholeness and a postmodern fragmentation, selective diversity and internalized variances" (par. 5). Thus, while Buffy yearns for the normalcy of traditional feminine roles within family, dating, school, and work — even within her proscribed role as the Slayer — she acknowledges the impossibility of maintaining such an identity. She rejects the hegemony of the Watcher's Council and, ultimately, the program's established mythos, upturning her own "Chosen One" status in order to empower the other potential Slayers in the series finale. This torn subjecthood not only speaks to the confused identities of the aforementioned fan scholar, but of students themselves. University students, especially first-year students newly adjusting to the demands of college life (just as Buffy did at opening of the fourth season), struggle to negotiate their student identities with their various roles as family members, employees, athletes, musicians, friends, boyfriends or girlfriends.

Audrey, a student in the fourth iteration of my *Buffy* class, initially displayed this reluctance, entering the class unfamiliar with the series, outside of some negative impressions of *Buffy* fans at her high school ("overweight Goth girls," she claimed). Although she admits that she became a fan after the class, she maintains that her non-fan status helped her approach the show critically:

> Since I had no personal biases against it, nor did I particularly like it, I was able to go into watching the episodes with an open mind. Watching the show in the classroom context helped me learn, because I am not one to delve deep into something I don't find to be outwardly emotional or critical. Having a *Buffy* expert for a professor as well as my classmates helped me to examine the show and see many of the underlying meanings I would never have caught. I notice that when I look at media now I am much better at spotting what is truly the meaning.[15]

Not only was Audrey able to "spot the meaning," her final paper successfully addressed the series' issues in relation to her personal life, describing her feelings of alienation based on a "punk" identity that set her apart. Describing her discomfort with the "punk" label bestowed upon her by her peers, Audrey compares herself with Buffy's "Slayer" identity, asserting, "I was constantly undermined by an image I could not control." She introduces her paper with a cogent assessment of Buffy's journey of selfhood:

> Throughout the many years I have spent striving to reach societal standards, I have realized that "normal" girls are a figment of the media's imagination. Once I was able to confront this idea, I, like Buffy, was able to form my own identity. Buffy's identity construction throughout the series has mirrored my own and demonstrated my own steps toward entering the next phase of my life.

Audrey's self-assessment mirrors Buffy's conclusions at the end of the show that she is "cookie dough."[16] Ultimately, Cover argues,

> for Buffy, contentment with selfhood is not about a resolution of the struggle between a "chosen" slayer identity and her attempts to participate in everyday life ... nor is it about finding a stability in the context of modernist notions of identity fixity. Rather the process of identity transformation is represented as existence itself— only by embracing the process of transformative selfhood as existence does she find that contentment [par. 21].

Thus, through her various struggles to fit into a "normal" feminine role, Audrey, like Buffy is able to acknowledge the processual nature of identity and prepare herself for the coming changes that college life will bring. Students like Madeline and Audrey certainly offer evidence that students are able to grasp some of the course's more complex notions of gender, identity, and performance theory.

But what of students who claimed to be fans prior to the class? Jenny, one student who admitted to not only being a fan but an avid reader and writer of *Buffy* fan fiction, even incorporated some of that fan fiction into her final paper. In correspondence after the course, Jenny spoke of how her fandom enhanced her class experience:

> Knowing all the characters' relationships, history, struggles, and quirks, I felt I had an advantage. I was able to see more of the possibilities that a character might potentially choose — with regards to discussions about his/her moral choices, etc. Class discussions revolving around themes like morality/good vs. evil, or female empowerment often involved doing close readings of a character's personality to see why this worked for the plot, how it was supported in the *Buffy*verse. Here this type of critical and hypothetical dialogue was easier as a fan.
>
> My familiarity with fan fiction definitely aided me in these "hypothetical" situations about what characters may or may not do. Through reading fan fiction, I knew these writers were already asking these "what if?" questions that take characters in different directions.[17]

Jenny's work is representative of many students' projects that engage the show on creative levels. Before "Season Eight" of the *Buffy* comics was released, several students attempted to continue the story after the series finale. Some of these assignments were clever variations and even critiques of the show's plot and themes, such as one student who imagined the fallout of too many active Slayers and how an increase in violence around the world would result, a plot point quite prophetic of the current comic series, in which the Slayers are deemed a threat by the U.S. military. However, many student projects displayed little beyond the student's avid fandom itself. My continued struggle is to find ways to direct students' fandom towards critical ends. I am pleased that the class has created fans of the show, but that cannot be my only goal.

Part of the problem here is the way that the show itself is marketed and structured. By encouraging students to either purchase or rent DVDs, or purchase reference books such as *The Watcher's Guide*, I am ostensibly turning students into pop culture consumers. Unlike the typical purchase of college books, these items are actual merchandising for a vibrant franchise. Amelie Hastie argues that ancillary texts like *The Watcher's Guide* and various novelizations "create a self-enclosed world of *Buffy* (and *Buffy*'s fans) based on the interdependence of knowledge and consumerism.... [T]hey regulate a desire for and a production of knowledge" (82–83). Further, Hastie notes that, similar to genre shows like *Twin Peaks* and *The X-Files*, the show's plots are based on the seeking of knowledge and research, and that academic inquiry into these programs mirrors this "epistemological economy" (83). In her essay, Hastie questions how academic texts on *Buffy* (and I would add, classes) can avoid becoming just another example of fan merchandising. This seems to be an inescapable trap. In her recent study of online *Buffy* fandom, sociologist Mary Kirby-Diaz divides fans into "story-oriented" (productive) and "series-oriented" (consumptive), subsequently including academic conferences in this latter category (67). So are we just producing *Buffy* consumers by furthering academic discourse and pedagogy about the show? In some cases this might be literally true, since my initial email in November to pre-registered students usually includes a link to the complete series box set on Amazon, and some students have told me that they put it on their Christmas list before class starts. However, the question of whether or not academic discourse is reproducing pop culture consumption is dependent on the content of that discourse. If an academic text is a balanced approach that is not merely celebratory of the program, then surely that text counts as criticism, not merchandising, especially when 20th Century–Fox does not receive any profit from it (and indeed, in many cases, neither do the actual publishers). Ultimately, "academic merchandising" associated with a television program bears little difference to films, DVDs, and books about Shakespeare, Dickens, or Austen, besides having the stigma of mass culture rather than "high art."

A further solution to these issues returns us to Henry Jenkins' celebration of convergence culture, which advocates a "politics of participation" and extols the resistant potential of fan fiction that "rejects[s] the idea of a definitive version, produced, authorized, and regulated by some media conglomerate. Instead, fans envision a world where all of us can participate in the creation and circulation of central cultural myths" (256). Papers like Audrey's that examine the show's themes of identity transformation and compare them to the student's own experiences may be the first step. Fan fiction, or other creative ventures, that do more than just establish odd romantic relationships, that offer critique and analysis of the program, and of popular culture in general, could be another. Ultimately, it is up to professors to engage with participatory culture themselves, to educate themselves about best new media practices and find ways that students can enter into this world, perhaps through understanding performance theory and discussing the ways in which students form their own identities through their own "slaying" performances, similar to Audrey's approach to the program. The question, then, is not "Have you tried not being a Slayer" or fan, but "how can your slaying be more effective and integrative?"

NOTES

1. I would also include comic books in this, a subject matter I also teach in a first year seminar.

2. Here, Lavery invokes a distinction made in Greek philosophy and Christian theology between the purer "divine" love (agape) and the messier, more passionate erotic love that reflects the desires of the individual (eros).

3. Six years after the show's demise, the journal has expanded its scope to "Whedon Studies." encompassing all of Joss Whedon's material, usually including *Buffy*, *Angel*, *Firefly*, *Dollhouse*, *Dr. Horrible's Sing-Along Blog* and the Whedon-penned comics. The journal is also home to the "Whedon Studies Association," a nascent academic organization that will be a presence behind the journal, website, and various conferences.

4. This was borne out in a subsequent study on teen witchcraft by Helen Berger and Doug Ezzy. In their many interviews with teenage witches, Berger and Ezzy mention the influence of *Buffy* and other programs on these practitioners' approaches to magic and witchcraft.

5. The article, by Nathan Ronchetti, published 8/23/2007, may be found online at www.daily herald.com/story/?id=21880. In addition, a Chicago suburban newspaper featured my *Buffy* class as one of several pop culture-oriented university classes in the Chicago area. The original article included a picture of series star Sarah Michele Gellar with the headline, "Buffy 101: Local Colleges Offer Many Ways to Put the B.S. in Your Degree." Since the article described all the courses positively as fresh ways to approach college education, I would like to think that the B.S. in the title stood for "*Buffy* Studies."

6. See especially Rosaldo and Conquergood for theories on auto-ethnography and Bado-Fralick as an example of a community member studying her own community and its processes.

7. Though Burr cautiously uses the pseudonym "Alan" for my comments in her article, I have no problem claiming responsibility for my assertions.

8. See especially Halfyard (2005). Of course, I am not the only scholar to apply performance theory to *Buffy*. Engaging with topics of fandom and new media, Rebecca Bley has utilized Erving Goffman's classic *Presentation of Self in Everyday Life*, a standard text in performance studies, to investigate the creation of fan personas and role-playing on LiveJournal.

9. Both full time and adjunct faculty from various departments may propose their own Focal Point courses, and the courses go through a vetting process between the First Year Program and the faculty member's respective department before they are scheduled.

10. Taken from the Focal Point course description: (http://condor.depaul.edu/~firstyr/focal/index. html).

11. Fan posting boards like the Bronze were valuable in assessing fan reactions while the show was on, while DVD commentaries and numerous interviews with Whedon and the show's writers often referenced fan reactions, especially to extreme situations like the death of Tara in Season Six. For more on this phenomenon, see Tabron (2004).

12. Another salient example of a fan vid that students found themselves and analyzed is a recent "mash-up" vid of dialogue and scenes from *Buffy* and the popular vampire film *Twilight*. In a critique of the film craze and its regressive views of gender relations, the vid characterizes *Twilight's* main heartthrob vampire, Edward, as a creepy stalker and continually shows Buffy rejecting his advances and eventually staking him. See "Buffy vs. Edward" at http://www.youtube.com/user/rebelliouspixels or www.rebelliouspixels.com.

13. Email correspondence, 5/24/06.

14. Since Madeline has actually published her essay, I am using her name. All other student names are pseudonyms.

15. Email correspondence, 6/2/09.

16. In this scene in "Chosen" (7.22), the final episode of the series, Buffy confesses to her longtime love Angel that even after seven years of being the Slayer, she is still in process. In other words, she is like "cookie dough," unfinished and still not baked into cookies.

17. Email correspondence, 6/3/09.

WORKS CITED

Ali, Asim. "Community, Language, and Postmodernism at the Mouth of Hell." *Buffy and Angel Conquer the Internet: Essays on Online Fandom*. Ed. Mary Kirby-Diaz. Jefferson, NC: McFarland, 2009. 107–125. Print.

Bado-Fralick, Nikki. *Coming to the Edge of the Circle: A Wiccan Initiation Ritual*. New York: Oxford University Press, 2005. Print.

Barthes, Roland. "From Work to Text." *Image/Music/Text*. Trans. by Stephen Heath. New York: Farrar, Straus, and Giroux. 155–164. Print.

Berger, Helen A., and Douglas Ezzy. *Teenage Witches: Magical Youth and the Search for the Self*. New Brunswick: Rutgers University Press, 2007. Print.

Bley, Rebecca. "RL on LJ: Fandom and the Presentation of Self in Online Life." *Buffy and Angel Conquer the Internet: Essays on Online Fandom*. Ed. Mary Kirby-Diaz. Jefferson, NC: McFarland, 2009. 43–61. Print.

"Buffy vs. Edward" Remix. <www.rebelliouspixels.com>.

Burr, Vivien. "Scholar/'shippers and Spikeaholics: Academic and Fan Identities at S*CBtVS*." *European Journal of Cultural Studies* 8.3 (2005): 375–383. Print.

Carlson, Marvin. *Performance: A Critical Introduction.* New York: Routledge, 1996. Print.

Conquergood, Dwight. "Performance Studies: Interventions and Radical Research." *Performance Studies Reader.* Ed. Henry Bial. New York: Routledge, 2003. 311–322. Print.

Cover, Rob. "From Butler to *Buffy*: Notes Toward a Strategy for Identity Analysis in Contemporary Television Narrative." *Reconstruction* 4.2 (2004): n.pag. Web. 13 May 2009.

de Certeau, Michel. *The Practice of Everyday Life.* 1974. Trans. Steven Randall. Berkeley: University of California Press, 1984. Print.

Halfyard, Janet K. "Singing Their Hearts Out: The Problem of Performance in *Buffy the Vampire Slayer* and *Angel*." *Slayage: The Whedon Studies Association Journal* 17 (2005): n.pag. Web. 9 June 2009.

Hastie, Amelie. "The Epistemological Stakes of *Buffy the Vampire Slayer*: Television Criticism and Marketing Demands." *Undead TV: Essays on* Buffy the Vampire Slayer. Ed. Elana Levine and Lisa Parks. Durham: Duke University Press, 2007. 74–95. Print.

Jenkins, Henry. *Convergence Culture: Where Old and New Media Collide.* New York: New York University Press, 2006. Print.

Jowett, Lorna. *Sex and the Slayer: A Gender Studies Primer for the Buffy Fan.* Middletown, CT: Wesleyan University Press, 2005. Print.

Kirby-Diaz, Mary. "So, What's the Story? Story-Oriented and Series-Oriented Fans: A Complex of Behaviors." *Buffy and Angel Conquer the Internet: Essays on Online Fandom.* Ed. Mary Kirby-Diaz. Jefferson, NC: McFarland, 2009. 62–86. Print.

Kociemba, David. "'Over-identify much?': Passion, 'Passion,' and the Author-Audience Feedback Loop in *Buffy the Vampire Slayer*." *Slayage* 19 (2006): n.pag. Web. 9 June 2009.

Lavery, David. "'I Wrote My Thesis on You': *Buffy* Studies as an Academic Cult." *Slayage* 13/14 (2004): n.pag. Web. 9 June 2009.

Levine, Michael P., and Steven Jay Schneider. "Feeling for Buffy: The Girl Next Door." Buffy the Vampire Slayer *and Philosophy: Fear and Trembling in Sunnydale.* Ed. James B. South. Chicago: Open Court Publications, 2003. 294–308. Print.

Morehead, John. "Jason Winslade Interview: Esotericism and Witchcraft in Entertainment and Commodification." *Theofantastique: A Meeting Place for Myth, Imagination and Mystery in Pop Culture.* n.p. 2 Aug. 2007. Web. 9 June 2009.

Pineau, Elyse Lamm. "Critical Performance Pedagogy: Fleshing Out the Politics of Liberatory Education." *Teaching Performance Studies.* Ed. Nathan Stucky and Cynthia Wimmer. Carbondale: Southern Illinois University Press, 2002. 41–54. Print.

Ronchetti, Nathan. "Buffy 101: Local colleges offer many ways to put the B.S. into your degree." *The Daily Herald* 23 Aug. 2007. Web. 9 June 2009.

Rosaldo, Renato. *Culture & Truth: The Remaking of Social Analysis.* Boston: Beacon Press, 1993. Print.

Shade, Patrick. "Screaming to be Heard: Community and Communication in 'Hush.'" *Slayage* 21 (2006): n.pag. Web. 4 Feb 2010.

Tabron, Judith L. "Girl on Girl Politics: Willow/Tara and New Approaches to Media Fandom" *Slayage* 13/14 (2004): n.pag. Web. 11 Mar 2010.

Thompson, Steven. "Joss Whedon." *The Tenacity of the Cockroach: Conversations with Entertainment's Most Enduring Outsiders.* Ed. Thompson et al. New York: Three Rivers Press, 2002. 369–378. Print.

Wilcox, Rhonda. *Why Buffy Matters: The Art of* Buffy the Vampire Slayer. New York: I.B. Tauris, 2005. Print.

Winslade, J. Lawton. "Teen Witches, Wiccans and 'Wanna-Blessed-Bes': Pop-Culture Magic in *Buffy the Vampire Slayer*." *Slayage* 1 (2001): n.pag. Web. 9 June 2009.

And the Myth Becomes Flesh

Tanya R. Cochran

In the beginning was the *mythos*, from the Greek, meaning speech and thought and story. According to comparative mythologist Joseph Campbell, myth is the very essence of being human, an epic story — not the summary of one's day but the narrative of one's lifetime — replete with villains and heroes, hinderers and helpers, loss and love, monsters and angels, life and death and rebirth. In fact, though minute details distinguish the grand stories we tell, Campbell realized that around the world and across time humans continue to tell one story over and over and over again. He called that story the monomyth, the hero's journey.[1] Though some scholars have disparaged his work, Campbell's extensive inventory of myths remains culturally significant and deserves a place in the curriculum. I teach the monomyth because it teaches students about language, about power, and about what it means to be human. I teach the monomyth through Joss Whedon's *Buffy the Vampire Slayer* because *Buffy* (mis)behaves. For the most part, Buffy Summers follows the path Campbell draws for the typical hero, but when she occasionally chooses the uncut route, Buffy's choices hold deep meaning for the audience, and for students. If students understand *Buffy*, they understand that myth explains where we come from, determines how we act in and upon the world, and shapes who we will become. If they understand *Buffy*, they understand that power resides in language, in the very words we use to create our realities. If they understand *Buffy*, they understand that *we* — like Buffy herself — are always already story embodied. We are our own myths become flesh.

Several years ago, I began guest-speaking on the monomyth for a first-year university seminar that focuses on *Buffy*. The goals of the lesson include the following: (1) define myth and discuss its potential outcomes or consequences, (2) introduce Joseph Campbell and his scholarship on mythology — particularly the stages of the hero's journey, (3) demonstrate the ways in which *Buffy* compares to and contrasts with the monomyth, and (4) draw significance for students' everyday experience out of those similarities and differences.[2] Because I have only one class period and less than fifty minutes with students, I move quickly to accomplish these goals.[3] Certainly, my presentation would not be effective if it had no context. But when I arrive close to Halloween each year, I am greeted by students who already have familiarity with *Buffy*. Though not a requirement for the course, a few of them have watched the entire series before beginning the semester. Because I encourage group discussion, I find that the more versed students are in *Buffy*, the better the lesson unfolds.

35

My presentation, simply titled "*Buffy the Vampire Slayer* and Myth," follows this topical outline:

   I. Introductions — Getting to Know Each Other — *5 minutes*
  II. Background — Write, Share, Discuss — *10 minutes*
       A. Favorite Book, Film, or Television Series
       B. Favorite Character
       C. Major Events in Favorite Character's Life
 III. Myth — Its Purposes and Power — *15 minutes*
       A. Joseph Campbell
          1. Biography
          2. Scholarship
             a. The Hero's Journey
             b. The Monomyth
       B. Write, Share, Discuss
          1. Purposes of Myth
          2. Local, State, and National Myths
          3. Power and Consequences of Myth
  IV. *Buffy* and Myth — From the Hero's to Her Journey — *15 minutes*
       A. The Rites and Stages of the Hero's Journey
          1. Rites of Passage
             a. Separation
             b. Initiation
             c. Return
          2. Stages of the Journey
          a. Birth
          b. Call to Adventure
          c. Helpers/Amulet
          d. Crossing the Threshold
          e. Tests
          f. Helpers
          g. Climax/Final Battle
          h. flight
          i. Return
       B. Discussion
          1. Comparing *Buffy* to the Hero's Journey
          2. Contrasting *Buffy* with the Hero's Journey
   V. Significance — Answering the "So What" Question — *5 minutes*

This outline also reflects the worksheet I give to students, one that asks questions and provides space for handwritten answers which become the springboard for our group conversation.

After I briefly introduce myself, describe my Whedon scholarship, and share my interest in the study of fan communities, I begin the lesson with what should be most familiar and interesting to students: their own passion for stories. I distribute my prepared handout and ask everyone to immediately do some writing. First question: *What is your favorite book, film, or television series?*[4] After a minute, I invite class members to share their responses. Occasionally, I get unique answers, including *The Notebook* by Nicholas Sparks, *A Little Princess* by Frances Hodgson Burnett, the film *Little Giants*, or the television series *Grey's Anatomy*. But most answers are predictable, likely because they represent big budget, mass-distributed texts: *Star Wars, Star Trek, The Matrix, Lord of the Rings, Harry Potter,* and most recently *The Twilight Saga.*

My verbal follow-up question prompts students to articulate as best they can why that story is their favorite: *What is it about this story that draws you in and keeps you coming back for more?* Often, they cannot immediately articulate answers. In fact, some students seem frustrated by the question, as if they want me to be satisfied with a "just because." The importance of pushing students to contemplate this question, though, lies in the self-reflexivity necessary to answer. Having to voice why a particular story has power hints at the personal meaning all of us make out of the texts we let enter and reenter our thoughts, let play and replay on our emotions. These same thoughts and emotions may even result in our actions. Without being didactic, I intend the question to lead students into a deeper understanding of a story's power. As Todd Ramlow argues, the popular narratives we tell, write, film — whether ancient or contemporary — do "real cultural work." In his commentary on *Buffy*'s sixth season and the relationship between Willow Rosenburg and Tara Maclay, Ramlow passionately insists that that work entails

> [reflecting] and [helping] to reproduce contemporary zeitgeists; this is how pop culture functions as an apparatus of dominant ideology. The refusal to consider any social or political import to popular culture demonstrates how ideology functions through media to promote certain social and cultural values as "natural," and to make particular political investments and disseminations transparent.

Though I do not let this relevant but tangential point derail the conversation, I do want students to begin sensing the social and even political weight of story.

To sharpen students' understanding of the power of grand narratives, I ask them to respond to the next question on the handout: *Who is your favorite character from that book, film, or series?* Out loud, I follow that question with another: *Why do you identify with that particular character?* Among others, responses include Izzie Stevens (*Grey's Anatomy*), Lois Lane (*Smallville*), Angel (*Angel*), Harry (*Harry Potter*), and Edward Cullen (*The Twilight Saga*). The last time I guest-lectured, one student explained that she identifies with Izzie Stevens because Izzie experiences many hardships but grows stronger through her trials. Another student noted that she feels drawn to the character Lois Lane because Lois, though independent and tough, knows that she sometimes needs the help of her friends. Another student cited Angel's search for redemption as a reason for affiliating with the soulful vampire. These and other responses illuminate for students how significant character-audience identification can be. A story is not a story without actors, agents, heroes with whom audience members connect. Being conscious of why we emotionally or psychically bond with certain characters further establishes for students the influence of myth, especially the myths conveyed through popular, cultural artifacts. By identifying with a character, I explain, we symbolically take that character's journey, seeing the world through those eyes.[5] In essence, the audience "uses" the text in personal — hopefully productive — ways.[6]

Next on the handout, I ask students to name pivotal moments: *Can you identify the major events in the character's life?* I remind the class of a story's structure, a pattern most of them learned in high school or even middle school. I draw a bell shape on the board and see if they can remember the five parts: exposition, rising action, climax, falling action, and dénouement. Then I ask the follow-up questions: *What are some of those major events? What shape do the events seem to take? Could you depict the events in a graph, chart, or timeline?* I encourage them to sketch and label. Students note that, mapped out, some character's lives look like erratic EKG readings — all melodrama; as soon as one conflict resolves, another begins. Among others, the characters and storylines of *Grey's Anatomy* are perfect examples. As one student last fall noted, Izzie Stevens already lives a crazy life as first an intern and then a resident at Seattle Grace. Added to the daily hospital drama are matters of the heart — metaphorically and literally. Izzie falls in love with her cardiac patient Denny Duquette who eventually proposes. Izzie accepts and Denny receives the heart transplant he desperately needs only to suffer a stroke and die soon after the surgery. For a long time, Izzie mourns his loss but finally falls in love with "frenemy" Alex Karev. Just when life seems good again, Izzie learns she has terminal cancer. Miraculously, she beats the cancer just before sabotaging her marriage with Alex and falling victim to job cuts during a hospital merger. Up and down, up and down — I draw the pattern on the classroom white board. Other students comment that occasionally a story moves in a circle or remains level from beginning to end. The more examples they cite, though, the more students see that most stories have a similar shape. Still, this point remains: the differences — however small — that distinguish one story from another can be extremely important. Realizing that they can discover profound meaning in those small distinctions will be essential later when we talk about how *Buffy* compares to and contrasts with the typical hero's journey. First, though, I define that quest.

I came to the scholarship of Joseph Campbell late — in graduate school, so I should not be surprised when first-year college students respond with blank stares when I ask them, "Are you familiar with Joseph Campbell? Do you know what the monomyth is? Have you heard of the hero's journey?" Now that I am familiar with it, the research Campbell completed strikes me as common knowledge for the culturally literate. Also, the hero's quest seems to so infuse our humanity that I always assume — every single time — that a few students, even just one student, will say "yes" to one of my questions. I have yet to find right away the affirmation I seek, and since I believe students must know the man behind the monomyth, I share with them a biographical sketch:

> Campbell spent most of his teaching years at Sarah Lawrence College in New York, where he was a professor of mythology. Among the general public he may be best known for his PBS shows with Bill Moyers, a television series called *The Power of Myth* which first aired in 1988 — before most if not all of you were born. Scholars and other myth enthusiasts are likely to refer to Campbell's book *The Hero with a Thousand Faces*, published first in 1949, than any other of his works. In *Hero*, Campbell outlines the hero's journey or quest and demonstrates that the pattern emerges across cultures and time periods; it is the very fabric of human existence. And so he called this meta-story the monomyth.

After I have briefly introduced students to the teacher and scholar and the terms *hero's journey* and *monomyth*, I offer an example. Their blank stares fade and sparks of recognition brighten their eyes when I make for them the Joseph Campbell-George Lucas-*Star Wars* connection, noting that Lucas intentionally created his characters and their stories in the image of the "one story to rule them all," my paraphrase for the monomyth. "Oooohhh," they exclaim.

But even more important than students' familiarity with Campbell or his scholarship is their understanding of how powerful and culturally significant myth or story has been, is, and always will be.[7] Stories allow us to form and nurture meaningful relationships between and among friends, families, local communities, states, and nations. At the same time, the stories we tell ourselves about who we are — as individuals, as intimate partners, as neighbors, as national or global citizens — can convince us to sever, undermine, and cripple relationships. Narratives cleave us, bind *and* tear us apart.

Just telling students that myth has great power, of course, does not educate them; they need to discover that truth for themselves. At this point, then, I ask for more writing. Students take a few minutes to answer the next three questions on the handout: (1) *What purposes do you think myths might serve among friends and family, among local communities, and in a nation?* (2) *Can you identify a myth we share here in Lincoln, in Nebraska, in the United States? How powerful are these myths?* (3) *What could be some of a myth's outcomes or consequences?* These questions stimulate eager discussion and are good ones for the pair-share strategy: after a minute or so of writing, students pair with a classmate, share their answers, and then report each other's responses to the class at large.[8]

Responses to the first question — the purpose of myth — sometimes need a little prompting from me, but students catch on quickly. I explain that the stories extended families tell provide relatives a sense of identity.[9] The stories towns and cities tell instill in residents a sense of community. The stories nations tell offer citizens a sense of purpose in the world. As examples, students cite tales of Mayflower ancestors, pistol-toting grandmothers, and Mafia-connected great, great uncles. They mention Husker football and Nebraskan's frugality. As they call out what they see as national myths, I write on the board: "World War II was 'the good war,'" "Abraham Lincoln freed the slaves," "the United States is a 'free' country," "the South will rise again," "America is a beacon of good will to the rest of the world," "the foundation of our country is the Christian Bible." I emphasize that we should not think of myths as inherently good or bad, moral or immoral. Rather, we should pay attention to how myths work. Among other functions, I summarize, myths frame how we understand our experience as well as afford us a way to discover common ground with other people (Cochran and Edwards 155). In other words, the stories we tell form and even constitute our world(s), act as "social glue" (Nimmo and Combs 13), and help us define "we."[10] On the other hand, myths can do the very opposite: give us ways to establish uncommon ground and to define "them."

Once students have even a loose grasp on the purpose of mythic storytelling and identify a few substantive examples, they find it easy to name possible outcomes or consequences of myths. For instance, the mythic account of Nebraskans' financial prudence continues to influence how state representatives — regardless of party leanings — vote. Nebraskans' devotion to their sports teams unifies residents, gives them a sense of belonging. The American belief that the United States has been divinely elected, some students note, may explain the country's self-confidence and its sense of obligation to promote democracy or "police" other countries. Usually, by the time class members complete this portion of the lesson, they recognize myth as fundamental to and considerably influential on our daily lives — the ways we think, feel, believe, speak, and act. With this concept settling in their minds, we turn to the rites and stages of the monomythic quest and the story of *Buffy.*

According to Joseph Campbell, a hero embarks on a journey marked by three rites of passage, rites that form the core of the monomyth: departure, initiation, and return. Among these three rites are various stages, seventeen in all. Scholars at the University of California-Berkeley have synthesized those seventeen into a more manageable eleven. I include and cite these stages on the handout I give to students:

- **Birth**— Fabulous circumstances surrounding conception, birth, and childhood establish the hero's pedigree, and often constitute their own monomyth cycle.

- **Call to Adventure**— The hero is called to adventure by some external event or messenger. The hero may accept the call willingly or reluctantly.

- **Helpers/Amulet**— During the early stages of the journey, the hero will often receive aid from a protective figure. This supernatural helper can take a wide variety of forms, such as a wizard, an old man, a dwarf, a crone, or a fairy godmother. The helper commonly gives the hero a protective amulet or weapon for the journey.

- **Crossing the Threshold**— Upon reaching the threshold of adventure, the hero must undergo some sort of ordeal in order to pass from the everyday world into the world of adventure. This trial may be as painless as entering a dark cave or as violent as being swallowed up by a whale. The important feature is the contrast between the familiar world of light and the dark, unknown world of adventure.

- **Tests**— The hero travels through the dream-like world of adventure where he [or she] must undergo a series of tests. These trials are often violent encounters with monsters, sorcerers, warriors, or forces of nature. Each successful test further proves the hero's ability and advances the journey toward its climax.

- **Helpers**— The hero is often accompanied on the journey by a helper who assists in the series of tests and generally serves as a loyal companion. Alternately, the hero may encounter a supernatural helper in the world of adventure who fulfills this function.

- **Climax/The Final Battle**— This is the critical moment in the hero's journey in which there is often a final battle with a monster, wizard, or warrior which facilitates the particular resolution of the adventure.

- **Fight**— After accomplishing the mission, the hero must return to the threshold of adventure and prepare for a return to the everyday world. If the hero has angered the opposing forces by stealing the elixir or killing a powerful monster, the return may take the form of a hasty flight. If the hero has been given the elixir freely, the flight may be a benign stage of the journey.

- **Return**— The hero again crosses the threshold of adventure and returns to the everyday world of daylight. The return usually takes the form of an awakening, rebirth, resurrection, or a simple emergence from a cave or forest. Sometimes the hero is pulled out of the adventure by a force from the daylight world.

- **Elixir**— The object, knowledge, or blessing that the hero acquired during the adventure is now put to use in the everyday world. Often it has a restorative or healing function, but it also serves to define the hero's role in the society.

- **Home**—"...the hero comes back from this mysterious adventure with the power to bestow boons on his [or her community," writes Campbell]. (Office of Resources)

As we consider each stage of the quest, the students recall bits of their preferred stories. For example, as a baby Harry Potter survives Voldemort's attack on his family but receives a literal mark on his forehead that symbolizes his being "the chosen one" as well as the quest that will later be handed him. A mysterious letter marks the call to adventure, an acceptance to Hogwarts School of Witchcraft and Wizardry. At Hogwarts, the wise mentor Dumbledore teaches and protects Harry over the next few years. Among other items, Harry's amulets include his wand and a cloak of invisibility that allow him to move about the school undetected, for the most part. Once students begin to connect their favorite tales with the stages of the journey, we fold in examples from Whedon's series. On the handout, I pose two questions: (1) *What scenes do you recall from* Buffy *that match the stages of the hero's journey?* (2) *Are there ways in which* Buffy *or* Buffy *does not fit?* The first requires class members to compare *Buffy* to the monomyth, to identify how Whedon's text mirrors the Campbellian quest. The second involves a more critical eye; it requires students to contrast, to pinpoint how Whedon's text undoes the monomyth.

Together, the students and I note comparisons that I write on the board. Buffy has been selected from birth because she is born a "potential" slayer, a young woman in a mystical line of chosen ones who could be triggered at any moment by the death of the current Slayer. According to the myth, one woman at a time bears the responsibility and possesses the supernatural power to carry out her calling. As a result, the teenage Buffy becomes conscious of her pedigree quite abruptly, her call to adventure arriving in the person of an overly serious, wool-suited British man named Merrick who approaches her on a hot, sunny day at a California high school. Buffy sits on the cement steps, lollipop clicking her teeth as she waits to be picked up after classes. Suddenly, Merrick appears in front of her ("Becoming, Part I" 5.21):

MERRICK: Buffy Summers?... I need to speak to you.... There isn't much time. You must come with me. Your destiny awaits.

BUFFY: I don't have a destiny. I'm destiny-free, really.

MERRICK: Yes, you have. You are the Chosen One. You alone can stop them.

BUFFY: Who?

MERRICK: The vampires.

BUFFY: Huh?

According to the description of this early stage, the hero does not always accept the call immediately or happily. Such is the case for Buffy. In fact, soon she and her newly divorced mother find themselves moving to an entirely new location to escape sour relationships — at home and at school.

In Sunnydale, Buffy meets her new Watcher, Giles. Taking Merrick's place, Giles attempts to train and mentor the still-reluctant young hero. He stands for the wise, usually senior helper (arguably, Angel also fits this role). And the comparisons continue; students — sometimes with my help, sometimes on their own — note the following:

- Buffy wears or carries **amulets**— a cross necklace from Angel, holy water, cross bows, rocket launchers, and her favorite stake Mr. Pointy.

- Buffy crosses many **thresholds**—her first night in the cemetery with Merrick, her descent into the Master's lair, her death at the hands of the Master, her self-sacrificial death to save her sister Dawn and seal the tear between human and demon dimensions. In fact, Buffy crosses an ordinary threshold everyday: when the sun goes down, she literally enters the dark on her nightly patrols.

- Buffy endures many **tests**—a "Big Bad" every season in addition to a giant praying mantis, a pack of possessed hyenas, a couple of super-sized reptiles, a step-dad-ish robot, a cyber demon, and plenty of run-of-the-mill vampires. When she turns eighteen, her test comes from the human realm, specifically the Watcher's Council. Locked in an abandoned house with a vicious vampire, Buffy must defeat her foe despite being temporarily stripped of her powers ("Helpless" 3.12).

- Buffy surrounds herself with **helpers**—first Willow Rosenberg, Xander Harris, and Angel; later Oz, Cordelia Chase, Wesley Wyndam-Pryce, Anya, Dawn, Riley Finn, Tara Maclay, Spike, Faith, and Robin Wood.

- Buffy **fights** *several* **final battles**[11]—with the Master and his minions, Angelus, Mayor Richard Wilkins, Adam and the Initiative, Glorificus (Glory), the Trio (Warren Mears, Jonathan Levinson, and Andrew Wells), and The First; there never seems to be a resolution to Buffy's adventure.

- Buffy **returns**—from the Master's lair, from the Hellmouth, from the grave.

- Buffy bears **home** many **elixirs**—objects, knowledge, blessings.

Together, the students and I cite scenes and discover the obvious similarities between *Buffy* and the monomyth. The importance of doing this work of comparison rests in students' understanding that *Buffy* is one more tale in an historical cycle of retold tales that make up the meta-story. Next we discuss the importance of *Buffy* taking its audience a few steps outside of that traditional circle of storytelling.

With a little more effort and guidance, the students and I mark contrasts. A number of scholars have analyzed *Buffy* and the hero's journey (Cochran and Edwards 148; see especially Bowman; Buttsworth; Early; and Wilcox). While some of them explore likenesses, others mention differences. Laurel Bowman understands Buffy herself, the hero, as the most prominent yet distinct monomythic marker because most journeyers fit the violent-loner-male profile. While clearly a hero figure, Buffy defies that profile: she is a woman who relies heavily on her friends and dispatches her enemies as swiftly (and tidily) as possible — vampire meets expertly placed stake which results in conveniently self-vaporizing, vampiric particles. Even more so, posits Bowman, Buffy could be read as stereotypically feminine — thin, pretty, clothes-conscious, obsessed with dating. Buffy herself often queries aloud why she cannot be more normal. What Buffy touts as "normal" for a teenage girl contradicts most notions of a "normal" hero.[12] After I explain this argument to the class, students suggest other ways *Buffy* revises the monomyth, evidence that the lesson achieves its purposes:

- Giles cannot always be trusted or relied upon to give the wisest counsel — as any human, he is vulnerable to spells, he sometimes defers to the Watcher's Council rather than standing up for Buffy, and he has his own complex past to confront.

- The tests that Buffy faces are not always external but also internal, other-imposed *and* self-imposed — she chooses the world over her love for Angel, she sacrifices herself to save her sister and the planet, and to live to fight another day she leaves Spike at the mouth of hell.

- The elixirs do not always solve every problem or heal every relationship — she knows that she must kill Angel, her own lover, to save the world; witchcraft cannot return the mother she so longs for from a natural death.

- Final battles do not always mean resolution — after Buffy defeats the Master, her feelings of vulnerability do not fade; surviving high school does not fend off college; and finally knowing that she really does love Riley does not stop his helicopter from taking off and carrying him away from her.

- When Buffy wins her battles, obtains the elixir, and returns home, the community at large — the very world she has been chosen to defend — neither welcomes her back nor embraces or praises her heroic efforts.[13] In fact, most of the time they remain completely (and intentionally) oblivious to Buffy's deeds.

- Possibly most important of all, even if she wavers about her and her companions' roles, Buffy and her chosen family of friends — especially Willow and Xander — see the journey through together, together until the very end (Cochran and Edwards 152–166).

With a (mis)behaved hero at its heart, *Buffy* demonstrates that though the differences from the monomyth may be few and may be slight, those differences are noteworthy and they matter.

Ideally, students take from the lesson a beginning understanding of the monomyth, its purposes and power, and an appreciation of how *Buffy* and Buffy mirror yet shatter the archetypal pattern. Students should be able to answer for themselves the question, "So what?" Why does understanding the hero's journey and its use in popular fiction, film, television, video games, and other texts matter? I can think of at least one good answer. Understanding the monomyth helps all of us pay attention to what the stories we read, listen to, watch, and role play teach us about who we are and who we are not, how we should and should not think and believe and hate and love. Whether bad or good, whether debilitating or inspiring, whether we like it or not, our grand narratives become reality; story is power. So it matters that women play heroes and that heroes collaborate with others rather than isolate themselves from their communities and that "ordinary" people, people without a remarkable birth and with no special powers — like Xander and Dawn — get to be heroes too. The significance of understanding myth lies in our ability to be the champions of our own fabulously and heroically mundane experience, to recognize in our mirrors the stories we tell — in the flesh.

NOTES

1. In a footnote to *The Hero with a Thousand Faces*, Campbell cites *Finnegans Wake* by James Joyce as the original source of the term *monomyth* (30).

2. This lesson grew out of an anthologized essay I coauthored with Jason A. Edwards titled "*Buffy the Vampire Slayer* and the Quest Story: Revising the Hero, Reshaping the Myth."

3. The four objectives could be expanded into a much longer unit for various subject areas. History, psychology, sociology, literature, and media studies courses are particularly suited for a discussion of the monomyth and its significance.

4. The next time I teach this lesson, I will add video, role-playing, and multi-player online games to the list, especially considering that many games have fully-developed plots, story arcs, and characters. In other words, they are mythic in nature.

5. For an in-depth treatment of symbolic journeying through popular texts, see Roger C. Aden, *Popular Stories and Promised Lands*.

6. Catharsis is one of those productive ways in which identification proves useful, an argument often employed in defense of violent video games, films, or television series such as Showtime's *Dexter*.

7. For a longer, more in-depth unit, these authors — alongside Joseph Campbell — and their texts may be particularly useful: Karen Armstrong, *A Short History of Myth*; Roland Barthes, *Mythologies*; Laurence Coupe, *Myth*; William Doty, *Myth: A Handbook*; Mircea Eliade, *Myth and Reality* and *Myth, Dreams and Mysteries*; Robert Jewett and John Shelton Lawrence, The *American Monomyth* and *The Myth of the American Superhero*; Carl Jung, *Jung on Mythology*; Carol Pearson and Katherine Pope, *The Female Hero in American and British Literature*; Robert Segal, *Myth: A Very Short Introduction*; and Andrew Von Hendy, *The Modern Construction of Myth*.

8. The pair-share strategy works well to get everyone — even the quiet or disengaged students — talking and requires partners to truly listen to each other so they can paraphrase their partner's answer for the class.

9. For extended discussions of myth and identification, see Dorsey; Fuller; Kluver; and Nimmo and Combs, among others.

10. See Edwards; Kluver; and Starr for more about how humans come to define "we."

11. In "A New Man" (4.12), Riley declares, "Buffy. When I saw you stop the world from, you know, ending, I just assumed that was a big week for you. It turns out I suddenly find myself needing to know the plural of apocalypse."

12. As Cochran and Edwards note, "In their analysis of the Buffy video game released in 2002 for X-Box, Labre and Duke ... found that 'the type of heroism portrayed in the Buffy video game is characterized by the Warrior archetype, the male shadow, and an ethic of justice rather than care' [(152)]. This characterization complicates a more progressive and positive depiction of [what Early calls] the female just warrior ... and is in stark contrast to the series' portrayal of heroism" (168). See Labre and Duke; Early; and Owen for more on this discussion.

13. The notable exception comes in "The Prom" (3.20) when Buffy's schoolmates award her with an umbrella that symbolizes her role as "Class Protector."

WORKS CITED

Aden, Roger C. *Popular Stories and Promised Lands: Fan Cultures and Symbolic Pilgrimages*. Tuscaloosa: University of Alabama Press, 1999. Print.

"Becoming, Part I." *Buffy the Vampire Slayer*. WB 12 May 1998. Television.

Bowman, Laurel. "*Buffy the Vampire Slayer*: The Greek Hero Revisited." University of Victoria, 2002. Web. 12 May 2006.

Buttsworth, Sara. "'Bite me': *Buffy* and the Penetration of the Gendered Warrior Hero." *Continuum: Journal of Media & Cultural Studies*, 16.2 (2002): 185–199. Print.

Campbell, Joseph. *The Hero with a Thousand Faces*. New York: MFJ Books, 1949. Print.

Cochran, Tanya R., and Jason A. Edwards. "*Buffy the Vampire Slayer* and the Quest Story: Revising the Hero, Reshaping the Myth." *Sith, Slayers, Stargates + Cyborgs: Modern Mythology in the New Millennium*. New York: Peter Lang, 2008. 134–69. Print.

Dorsey, Leroy G. "The Frontier Myth in Presidential Rhetoric: Theodore Roosevelt's Campaign for Conservation." *Western Journal of Communication* 59.1 (1995): 1–19. Print.

Early, Frances H. "Staking Her Claim: Buffy the Vampire Slayer as Transgressive Woman Warrior." *Journal of Popular Culture* 35.3 (2001): 11–27. Print.

Edwards, Jason A. "The Demonic Redeemer Figure in Political Myth: A Case Study of Vladimir Zhirinovsky." *Journal of the Wisconsin Communication Association* 31 (2000): 17–32. Print.

Fulmer, Hal W. "Mythic Imagery and Irish Nationalism: Henry Grattan Against Union, 1800." *Western Journal of Speech Communication* 50 (1986): 144–157. Print.

"Helpless." *Buffy the Vampire Slayer*. WB. 19 Jan. 1999. Television.

Kluver, Alan R. "Political Identity and National Myth: Toward an Understanding of Political Legitimacy." *Politics, Communication, and Culture*. Eds. Alberto Gonzalez and Delores V. Tanno. Thousand Oaks, CA: Sage, 1997. 48–75. Print.

Labre, Magdala P., and Lisa Duke. "'Nothing like a brisk walk and a spot of demon slaughter to make a girl's night': The Construction of the Female Hero in the *Buffy* Video Game." *Journal of Communication Inquiry*, 28.2 (2004): 138–156. Print.

"A New Man." *Buffy the Vampire Slayer*. WB. 25 Jan. 2000. Television.

Nimmo, Dan, and James E. Combs. *Subliminal Politics: Myths and Mythmakers in America*. Englewood Cliffs, NJ: Prentice-Hall, 1980. Print.

Office of Resources for International and Area Studies (ORIAS). University of California–Berkeley. N.d., n.p. Web. 10 February 2010.

Owen, Susan. "*Buffy the Vampire Slayer*: Vampires, Postmodernity, and Postfeminism." *Journal of Popular Film and Television*, 27.2 (1999): 24–31. Print.

Ramlow, Todd R. "Ceci n'est ce pas une lesbianne." *PopMatters* 18 June 2002. Web. 1 Feb. 2010.

Starr, John B. *Ideology and Culture*. New York: Harper & Row, 1973. Print.

Wilcox, Rhonda. *Why Buffy Matters: The Art of* Buffy the Vampire Slayer. New York: I. B. Tauris, 2005. Print.

Round Up the Usable Suspects: Archetypal Characters in the Study of Popular Culture

Barry Morris

The term "popular culture" is a magnet when attached to a class. It connotes the scholarly legitimacy of "what I like" and favors the young and fresh over the "dead and dull." Having a course in popular culture is an effective way to engage students in the methods of critical inquiry and the discipline to produce rigorous aesthetic criteria. On the down side teachers and students often treat popular media as though the content *is* the culture — as though the world and its depiction are the same. The myth is that to analyze the product comprehensively is to analyze the culture completely.

Popular art is not popular culture. Popular culture is a complex chemistry of informal relationships intended to imbue in the institutions of law and economics the community out of which they evolved and exist to serve.[1] We should perceive the institutions of popular media not as a storehouse of culture but as a massive Global Positioning System using each song, show and sketch as a reference point for triangulating our position on the terrain. This GPS locates individuals in time as well as place. Where we are cannot be comprehended without reference to where we have been and are likely to end up. Deriving the context of its production from a text creates a trajectory for the trip instead of a mere list of stops along the way. The task for the students is to recover artifacts and divine the needs and desires that shaped them. The most reliable artifacts in popular texts are characters who embody and describe the needs and desires of their times. The navigator can study characters to tell where the travelers have come from and where they will venture next.

Buffy the Vampire Slayer is the best text for digging into the relationship between a text and its times — an outstanding body of work for learning to navigate American popular culture.[2] It is densely populated and intimate. It is rich in mythology, but since virtually all the mechanics of that mythology (e.g., types of monsters, sources, and powers) were invented by its creators it requires little outside annotation or experience. The high-school-as-hell metaphor is apparent — the teacher who eats her male students alive literally eats her male students alive ("Teacher's Pet" 1.4) — yet poignantly developed within the vernacular of its time. The "monsters cannot be defanged and declawed by being called metaphors, symbols, nightmares or childish misunderstandings of the adult world. They are real" (Skwire 204).

Buffy's strongest feature is that over seven years creator Joss Whedon developed a cohesive and consistent universe. The characters mature as products of the social forces the text-as-artifact illuminates.[3] Just as people create and embody the meaning of their times, so do the characters in our fictional performances record and store those meanings. Whedon claims that "the mythic structures we base all our stories on ... most of the stories and the myths we're creating, we carry with us already" (*Master at Play*). This chapter will discuss how to link characters to those mythic structures and archetypal histories in the classroom. In so doing instructors help students see that even the most transitory artistic expression bares its cultural history. Every text does this. *Buffy* makes it fun. The characters represent classic archetypes — categories that exist back to the beginning of storytelling. Students learn how these archetypal characters endure from generation to generation and how each generation adds its unique contribution to the history of the archetype. In so doing, students come to appreciate how each culture is both connected to the past and unique.

Even with a complex text like *Buffy* a teacher needs a strategic framework for using the rich content. The framework introduced here focuses on characters. The structure of Western storytelling from *Gilgamesh* to *Gilligan* has consisted of placing volitional characters in circumstances where their beliefs and values are tested by equally volitional opponents.[4] Over a few thousand years of human storytelling, a population of fluid and adaptable character types in a stable set of recurring categories emerged to embody those values. I have distilled a representative cast that I call the Usable Suspects — a collection of commonly used and almost universally embraced archetypes. The list of usable suspects identifies this stable set of archetypes and organizes them into a sort of meta-narrative — a western saga within which our personal narratives unfold.

What are "archetypal" characters? In any era, decade or marketplace, people identify enough similarity among individual characters to categorize them. Those categories are called stereotypes. In any social era, people tend toward the conceit that everything they create is original, but as generations of literature and history teachers have taught us everything "new" is really rooted the past. The characters of Greek theater, Ajax, Oedipus, Clytemnestra and Antigone fought over the same issues as the heroes and villains of our time. We re-imagine *Romeo and Juliet* in every generation and across cultures, because its themes of love, loyalty and irrational generational hatred are universal.[5] Buffy Summers is a product of that tradition: the vampire-slayer in love with the avatar of evil. Not just a vampire — Angelus! The worst of the worst ("Innocence" 2.14). So everything old becomes new again.

Binding the illicit love of Buffy, Juliet, Electra and others is a more substantial category than stereotype, one that exists at a level of abstraction up from that of characters and stories of the era that displays those similarities. That is the level of Archetype. A cultural stereotype is enriched by the capacity of the historical archetype to root the conditions of the moment — conventions, politics, values and technologies of the specific periods in which they are employed — to the generations of cultures out of which those "conditions of the moment" evolved. Characters are closely moored to the specific social currents that shape them at the level of stereotype but more fully fleshed out in the archetype.

One of the advantages of employing *Buffy* as a text is that "the vampire" is a perfect example of how character, stereotype and archetype combine to encapsulate meanings. Every new version of the vampire story can be traced from its current incarnation backward through history.[6] Each of the iterations employs and reinvents elements of the vampire tradition — how they became vampires, their powers and weaknesses — to comment on the myth's contemporary social conditions. Sometimes the point is to provoke society into confronting its excesses, sometimes its repressions. Each characterization is more stereotype than archetype. Each is inextricably tied to its cultural time and place. When Buffy Summers recognizes a vampire in the crowd at The Bronze in "Welcome to the Hellmouth" (1.1) because his outfit is "carbon-dated," she is the arbiter of cool, commenting on her subculture's opinion of his "monstrous" fashion sense.[7] Of course the vampire is no more "monstrous" according to that criterion than was Cordelia who had earlier victimized Buffy's new friend Willow for having found "the softer side of Sears." The Anne Rice slurs in *Buffy* are more recent and hence more relatable but emblematic of the same effect.[8] Stereotypes are archetypes distilled through the filter of now.

Using archetypes entails deciding how deeply and into which philosophical minefield one dares to skulk. The term is applied along a confusing array of intersecting continua, some so completely abstract that they cannot even be applied in the "real" world, some rooted in the human subconscious, and some distilled from history. Archetypes are formally defined as "recurrent patterns of actions, character types, or identifiable images whose expression is an unconscious mental record of such experiences, the collective unconscious" (O'Donnell 83). The simplest way to think of them is as fundamental tools for meaningfully comparing the alien to the familiar. Remembering that our purpose is to use recurring character types as a tool for exploring culture, each instructor has a choice: Do you do it the hard way or simply define archetype operationally as the evolving and sustained version of familiar stereotypes?[9] In most cases simple works best. Simply conceive of archetypes as the starting points that allow us to make sense of the obscure by comparing it to the familiar. On the first day of class, with little introduction, the instructor should screen the two-part pilot, "Welcome to the Hellmouth" (1.1) and "The Harvest" (1.2). The students will be introduced to a universe in which a typical high school girl is fated to save the world from the forces of darkness. The student will meet several typical characters. When we say a character is "typical" we are saying that he or she conforms to a type. Every student has met a stranger and thought "I know your type!" Stereotypes are categorical generalizations of those types. The compelling thing about archetypes is that they relate to something comprehensive about all of human experience. The recurrence of basic archetypal images, forms and characters suggests the existence of universal structures all humans use to connect to the world. They allow us to refer to "memories" of experiences that we as individuals have never had. They also give us the ability to "invent" what has always existed by experiencing a sincere, authentic moment of discovery. Issues relating to the origins and constitution of the collective unconscious persist, but they do not enjoin us from using archetypes as a means of finding the *everything* in the *every thing* of popular culture.

Archetypal characters are not just ways to categorize the people who appear in fictional texts. Simply deciding that a character represents a category tells us little about the text or the conditions under which it was created and distributed. Rather we should ask: What do I learn about the character as a representative of this archetype as opposed to how he or she might operate as a member of a different one? "The slayer" serves as the archetypal Chosen One. The implications of that perspective are best illuminated by also considering Buffy from another "correct" perspective — that of the Girl Next Door. Does Buffy embody a newly empowered version of the traditionally cast female victim, or can she still "justifiably be accused of subscribing to ... commercial and patriarchal standards of feminine beauty" (Pender 36)? The instructor should remind students that simply categorizing a character is the beginning not the end of the investigation.

Here is a partial list of the archetypal characters I have employed.[10] Drawing on the seven-year run of *Buffy,* an instructor can introduce almost all of them and engage in comprehensive study of the roots and traditions of American Popular Culture.

| The Chosen One | The Regular Guy | The Girl Next Door | The Working Stiff |
| The Rogue | The Mystic/Savant | The Mentor | The Innocent |

The *Buffy*verse is sufficiently vast, well developed and internally consistent to teach the course and several of the most integral Usable Suspects. The instructor has at his or her disposal 144 episodes featuring hundreds of compelling characters, spanning seven years of American popular culture history. Joss Whedon is an articulate student of the history and theory of western drama. He was educated at Wesleyan University not as a writer or director but as a student of "film genre, mythos, and mis-en-scene" (*The Master at Play*). His plots and characters embody popular stereotypes, then negotiate, exaggerate and eviscerate them. Of course, an analysis of the archetypal characters in *Buffy* has to begin with the archetype around which the others congregate.

The Chosen One

The Chosen One archetype performs in a setting of dialectical tension. In the fact of being exceptional, she draws attention to the frailties and inadequacies of the community she considers worth saving. Characters go into situations with intentions — outcomes they hope to achieve — but circumstances inevitably intervene. Buffy Summers is a high school student who like all high school students wants to find some way to be special (Brown and Gilligan). Then she discovers that she is not only unique she is literally one-of-a-kind — the "one girl in all the world with the strength and skill to hunt the vampire." Good news, super powers; bad news, the slayer is fated to fight alone. Buffy cheats fate to become the longest-lasting and most accomplished slayer by enlisting her friends and family in the fight (Wilcox 4–6). Fate however gets the last laugh. Throughout the series circumstances remind her, often tragically, that the Chosen One is the chosen *one.* As the series progresses, Buffy becomes more and more powerful." In "The Harvest" she tells her friends that she cannot break down the solid steel door of The Bronze (1.2). Five years later in "Once More, With Feeling" (6.7) she blows through that door barely breaking stride. The more Buffy saves the world, though, the less adept she becomes at living in it. The tension between living in the world and defending it exists throughout the series.[11]

In "The Prom" (3.20) Buffy's classmates honor her as "Class Protector." The proclamation reads:

> We're not good friends. Most of us never found the time to get to know you, but that doesn't mean we haven't noticed you ... but whenever there was a problem or something creepy happened, you seemed to show up and stop it. Most of the people here have been saved by you, or helped by you at one time or another. We're proud to say that the Class of '99 has the lowest mortality rate of any graduating class in Sunnydale history, and we know at least part of that is because of you. So the senior class, offers its thanks, and gives you, uh, this [3.20].

The tribute is moving, because it is delivered to a girl who in any normal American high school would have been popular, but who by virtue of having been "chosen" remained a stranger.

At the end of Season Five, Buffy defeated a god. By the middle of Season Six she was a barely functional server at the Double Meat Palace. Even at the end, in the final battle between good and evil, The First evil taunts Buffy: "There's that word again. What you are. How you'll die. Alone." ("End of Days" 7.21). In *Buffy* education is compelled by thoughtful questions not by easy answers. Whedon believes the same is true of television. He says that movies are "about answers" while television has to have more. "Movies are about a girl coming to power" he says, "but on television you can't do that. You have to have a question" (*The Master at Play*).

What kind of world is worth saving at such a sacrifice? The inspiration of *Buffy* is that the Chosen One is the ideal archetype against which to compare and contrast the kinds of middle American daily life that one could choose. Why? Because being "chosen" implies the influence of major ontological forces:

- Chosen by whom?
- Chosen through what process?
- Chosen for what?

To choose is a deliberate act. The capacity to choose indicates authority, control over resources and status. In a nutshell, the mythology of the Chosen One in *Buffy* is that the demon world existed prior to the world of humans. When humanity developed and the two worlds interacted, the vampire — a hybrid of demon and human — was created and preyed on humankind. An authority not hinted at until the end of Season Four ("Restless" 4.22) and not directly discussed until near the end of the series ("Get It Done" 7.15) used its mystical powers to imbue into a young woman the skills necessary to make it a fair fight. A vampire slayer is "chosen" when the previous slayer dies. Having witnessed the outcome of the selection process (in this case the nomination of the new slayer), the community has the opportunity to investigate and evaluate the dynamics of the process.

The Regular Guy and the Girl Next Door

American popular culture is "American" and "popular" because one does not have to be royalty to be worthy of artistic consideration. The great tradition of American art has been the elevation of the Willy Lomans and the Huckleberry Finns to the dramatic heights of the Henrys, the Richards, the Antigones and Ophelias. The population from which American culture is drawn is the "traditional" family unit. Orbiting that family unit are character types whose abilities, viewpoints and circumstances inform and challenge the familial stasis, and in so doing provide the conflict necessary to any good story.

After being introduced to a Chosen One whose destiny it is to keep the world safe for the traditional family by denying herself its security and pleasures, the class should explore the archetypes that comprise that family, such as the Regular Guy, so they have a fuller understanding of who she is fighting for and why. The predominance of the American "everyone" is most obvious in Arthur Miller's *Death of a Salesman*, where the gods squash the ambitions and ruin the family of a man whose only ambition was to be somebody on the job and mean something when he was gone. No one was going to confuse Willy Loman with Ajax or Hamlet, but the theatergoer saw the folly in his unwillingness to see the dignity a person could obtain just getting through life. The honor of common guts and wisdom was parodied in *Huckleberry Finn*, made fantastical in George Bailey of *It's a Wonderful Life*, propagandized in the character of Forrest Gump, and sloganeered in the person of Hope Steadman who encouraged her husband Michael in the pilot episode of *thirtysomething* by declaring that "it's such a brave thing you do going to work everyday!" (1.1).

The Regular Guy (and his blue collar corollary the Working Stiff) is the linchpin of the entire American popular culture artifice.[12] Because America has undergone a transformation since the Industrial Revolution from a production economy to an information economy, a distinction needs to be made between The Regular Guy, who aspires to be a mid-level professional and The Working Stiff, who embodies those values in the blue collar social class. The tragic and comedic friction of these archetypes generally derives from the difference between the stated ambitions of the supposedly ambitious regular guy and actual decisions that lead more to cooperation and compliance. He plays the rogue yet depends on the security of the system. He is trapped in a perpetual state of becoming, always striving for the next promotion or the "big deal." He is perpetually subordinate to other forces.[13]

Xander Harris provides this perspective in *Buffy*. Xander dedicates his high school life to surviving the onslaught of the dark forces of existence, believing that being a good person will result in a justly rewarded life. He wants what the pecking order says he should not have, and however consistently he is punished for reaching too high, he continues to reach. We first see Xander racing through a school-day crowd on his skateboard, only to be upended by the distraction of the new girl in school — Buffy Summers ("Welcome to the Hellmouth" 1.1). He gravitated to Willow as most small children do through proximity. They were neighbors growing up. He was attracted to Willow's simplicity and her ability to help him with his homework. She was attracted to his sense of humor and sincerity. Throughout the first couple of years of the series, Willow harbored a crush on Xander. Of course Xander, for whom Willow would have been an ideal mate, was fixated on the unattainable.

From the beginning, Xander is gung ho about confronting forces far above his ability. When his best friend Jesse is captured by vampires, Xander does not think twice about wading into battle. Buffy rebuffs him. He shows up in the sewers anyway, both motivated to help and aware of his mortality. When Buffy asks why he did not bring a flashlight, he replies "The part of me that would have told me to do that is still telling me not to come" (1.1). Xander lived his life subject to the same kind of internal narration as the young Michael Doonesbury.[14] As he walked down the hall or hung out at the Bronze, he was constantly in story mode, but when push came to shove, as in the case of the kidnapping of his best friend, he reacted with an admirable sense of purpose. Even when confronted by vampire–Jesse in the final battle of the pilot ("The Harvest" 1.2), he could not help trying to reach the inner spirit that was no longer there. He only survived the encounter through a slapstick accident.

Whedon cements Xander's low status as a member of the team in "The Zeppo" (3.13). While the gang is researching Sunnydale's latest apocalypse, Xander becomes virtually useless. He goes out on his own, encounters, befriends and eventually defeats a gang of zombie hoodlums intent on blowing up Sunnydale High. At the end of the episode his friends tell him about all of the excitement he had missed. Xander reacts with quiet confident humility grounded in the realization that while he has no "powers" he can rise to the occasion when needed. In order to defeat the primary villain of Season Four, Buffy has to subsume the essences of her friends into herself. Buffy supplies the strength. Willow supplies the intellect. Xander's contribution is "heart"—again defining him as the weak but plucky sidekick to those with actual power, and once again, heart being necessary to the equation, good triumphs over evil ("Primeval" 4.21).

The comrade of the Regular Guy is the Girl Next Door—who popular myth called upon since *The Wizard of Oz* to teach children that no matter how ambitious one might be, the important things in life were there all along. The Girl Next Door possesses "hidden beauty." The flash and trash of the overtly beautiful "dream girl" is exposed as so much iron pyrite. Love is purest when it is alloyed with friendship, but friendship is a difficult current to navigate. Early in the series Cordelia, the unattainable, terrorizes Willow. To make matters worse, Willow who has a crush on Xander is forced to watch him lust after Buffy, Cordelia, and even a reanimated Incan mummy ("Inca Mummy Girl" 2.4). The one guy in Season One who does show an interest in Willow turns out to be a demon whose goal is to seduce her into releasing him from his imprisonment in cyberspace ("I Robot, You Jane" 1.8).

Throughout the first two seasons, Buffy is torn between her loyalty to Girl Next Door Willow and the allure of Cordelia's world. In Season One, Buffy tries out for the cheerleading squad ("The Witch" 1.3). In Season Two, she follows Cordelia in search of "older men" ("Reptile Boy" 2.5), and in Season Three Buffy and Cordelia battle for the ultimate mantle of supremacy—Homecoming Queen ("Homecoming" 3.5). All the while, Cordelia is drawn farther into the circle of the Scooby Gang and her status declines. At one point, her social stock falls so low that she makes a deal with a demon creating an alternate universe in which she is still popular, Buffy has never come to Sunnydale, and both Willow and Xander are the ultimate social outcasts—vampires ("The Wish" 3.9).[15]

As Willow grows she reinforces the point that applying archetypal labels is the beginning not the end of the process. As Willow evolves through seven seasons of *Buffy*, the social currency of the Girl Next Door inflates. Willow goes from wallflower to intentional character while in high school. When she gets to college, she gains self-confidence and a status nearly equal to Buffy's. By the end of Season Six, she surpasses Buffy in power and nearly loses herself to that power. By the beginning of the final episode of the series — standing in the Summers' living room before the apocryphal battle — her status as the most powerful person in the room is touchingly packaged within the self-effacing non-verbal posture of the high school sophomore who offered to help the new girl catch up with her assignments. The nature of an archetypal character at any given time is less important overall than how and under what influences that character grows and changes. Students should be prodded not just to categorize a particular character but to chart that character's evolution through the series.

This chapter began with the invocation that students need to be able to expand their perspectives beyond the narrow confines of the social moment — to see the connection between mass media in the "here and now" and the broad social and historical forces that influence them. The best way to use archetypes is a three-step process. First locate a character as a particular usable suspect such as Buffy as the Chosen One, Xander as the Regular Guy, and Willow as the Girl Next Door. The series contains hundreds of characters many of which serve as worthy exemplars of the cast of Usable Suspects. It can be argued that one of my favorite characters, Jonathan, represents at one time or another nearly half of the archetypes on the list.[16]

The second step is to demonstrate that a character who might appear new to students actually has a history. Having established for the class that Buffy is the Chosen One, the instructor can illuminate the archetype by comparing her to other prominent characters within the same category — first those with whom the student is familiar, then those from older and broader cultural perspectives. I have included at the end of the chapter *Archetype Data Sheets* for each of the categories. The data sheet for the Regular Guy includes brief statements of theme, utility, values and foundations in culture. It also includes exemplars — other "regular guys." The data sheets guide discussion of how some exemplars are similar to and distinct from others. Another fruitful discussion is how specific social, political and economic circumstances influence the creators of texts to define, develop and even deviate from the standard. Did Whedon conceive of Willow as an unaware lesbian when he defined her, or was lesbianism the best avenue of development when he found a need to evolve the character in Season Four? Would he have been able to get that choice past the network in the 1970s or 1980s?

It is difficult to find exemplars of people like the Regular Guy and the Girl Next Door in ancient literature, because the elevation of the common man and woman to the status of tragedy is a relatively recent phenomenon,[17] but my students have had no trouble finding prominent characters from antiquity who wrestled with the same issues as the characters in *Buffy*. Was Buffy any less challenging a student to Giles than Arthur was to Merlin? The boy who would become King David had issues with authority and problems with the ladies that rival any of those in modern texts.[18] Cordelia Chase was so direct of thought and unequivocating of voice, that when Buffy was able to read minds (3.18) Cordelia's internal thoughts differed not at all from what she said aloud. In that way she is like her namesake whose unwillingness to flatter or appease led her father, King Lear, to banish her. Theseus, led by Ariadne, went into the cavern and slew the Minotaur.

Polyphemus lured victims to his cave. Buffy fought her first villain in a cavern after having been led there by a child. She fought her last battle when lured into the bowels of the earth below the Hellmouth.[19]

The third step is for students to challenge the efficacy of archetypes as they are represented in the present. This is the occasion for students to apply alternative and contested interpretations of the legitimacy of certain categories and to put the categories into conflict with one another.[20] Did Xander's designation as the "the heart" of the Scooby Gang constitute another example of the gender-swap at the center of the *Buffy* myth? Was Mayor Wilkins the antithesis of the Regular Guy in his relationship with Faith, the fallen slayer of Season Three, or was he a deliberately distorted reinforcement of it?[21] Some of the issues that arise can be used to spur conversation. Others can be turned into useful assignments combining *Buffy* with other social and historical texts. Following are a few assignments that have worked well for me.

- Which Usable Suspect are you? Put yourself into the category that best fits you. Discuss your life using the data sheet for that archetype. Is this the category you would prefer to be in? If you could choose another what would it be, and what is keeping you from becoming that?

- Prophecy almost always figures heavily in texts that revolve around a Chosen One. What recent stories have revolved around prophecy? Why do outlets like the Discovery Channel and the History Channel win loyal audiences when they discuss the subject? Examine a specific prophecy. Discuss its source, its possible interpretations and whether or not it has or might come true.

- What are the social and political implications of being a potential slayer? While the mechanism of how the slayer is chosen was an afterthought of the idea to have a high school cheerleader be the savior of the world, its conditions and ramifications are worthy of investigation.[22] The slayer is chosen shortly after reaching puberty. Is this coincidental or is there a natural dualism between giving life and slaying demons?

- What are the social, racial and/or historical assumption and biases in a contemporary example of the vampire?

The immediacy of popular art is both its greatest draw and its biggest challenge. A person who wants to appreciate the text completely has to be able to appreciate the culture that created it. Popular culture is a living, thriving and evolving organism. It must be considered in its historical context to be considered at all. The most compelling way to do that is to link the immediate to the past by connecting our most vibrant characters to those who came before. Employing the archetypal characters called The Usable Suspects is a heuristically sound and consumer friendly means of doing so. Turn the students into cultural archeologists. Have them mine the current culture for stereotypes that might not yet be on the radar. Have them discover archetypes that are not on the list. Spike's love for Buffy as it develops in Season Six has a profound effect on the narrative. Students will be able to identify popular culture texts with which they are already familiar that discuss the same themes and, with the classics Oedipus and David as starting points, be able to research the cultural antecedents. The Usable Suspects will engage the class in fun and enhanced learning. Luckily the instructor has in *Buffy* a deep and complex mythology to mine. The characters live and grow. The stereotypes morph and evolve. The products of culture illuminate that culture, and the culture illuminates our places in it.[23] That is a worthy ambition for any course.

Archetype Data Sheets

The Chosen One

Theme:	The world is in trouble, but a savior is on the way.
Utility:	To reinforce the notion that we are not alone, that a higher power is looking out for us.
Relevant values:	Spirituality, Optimism, Virtue, Charity
Foundations:	Individualism. Judeo-Christian Dogma, Lure of the Supernatural.
Limitations:	The price of service to the masses, the trap of fate
Exemplars:	Buffy Summers	*Buffy the Vampire Slayer*
	Neo	*The Matrix*
	Harry Potter	*Harry Potter and the Sorcerer's Stone*
	Aang	*The Avatar*
	Hal Jordan	*The Green Lantern*

The Regular Guy

Theme:	There is value and even nobility in simply maintaining an average middle class or lower middle class existence.
Utility:	To reinforce the notion that being part of the whole is sufficient cause to exist. To confirm that "average" is not a pejorative term.
Relevant values:	Loyalty, Moderation, Reliability.
Foundations:	The corruption of power. The centrality of family. Judeo-Christian/Protestant Capitalism.
Limitations:	Cannot have a glamorous job. Should either know or come to know domestic bliss. Can neither be too rich nor too poor.
Exemplars:	Bud Baxter	*The Apartment*
	Homer Simpson	*The Simpsons*
	Willy Loman	*Death of a Salesman*
	Michael Steadman	*thirtysomething*
	Mike Brady	*The Brady Bunch*

The Girl Next Door

Theme:	Your Soul Mate is Your Best Friend.
Utility:	Provides "safe harbor" for the adventurous acquisitive male.
Relevant values:	Virtue. Authenticity. Familiarity. Self-Reflective Value.
Foundations:	Social Science (proximity). Redemption. Domesticity. Moderation.
Limitations:	Counter-Ambitious. "Class-based." Anti-Feminist.
Exemplars:	Mary Jane Watson	*Spiderman*
	Lizzie McGuire	*Lizzie McGuire*
	Winnie Cooper	*The Wonder Years*

Willow Rosenberg	*Buffy the Vampire Slayer*
Melanie Smooter	*Sweet Home Alabama*

The Working Stiff

Theme:	You get what you earn through your own sweat.
Utility:	Values the creation of quality through modes of action available to anyone.
Relevant values:	Virtue. Authenticity. Self-reliance. Concentration. The Value of Skill.
Foundations:	Domesticity. Moderation. Extended Family. Craft.
Limitations:	Counter-Ambitious. "Class-based." Socially Limiting. Potentially Anachronistic.
Exemplars:	Xander Harris *Buffy the Vampire Slayer*
	Ralph Kramden *The Honeymooners*
	Sookie St. James *Gilmore Girls*
	Doug Heffernen *The King of Queens*
	Dan Conner *Roseanne*

The Rogue

Theme:	Society establishes rules of decorum; rules are for suckers.
Utility:	To allow the consumer to play out the need for social rebellion in a harmless environment.
Relevant values:	Individuality, Romance, Democracy.
Foundations:	Individualism. Class Consciousness. Tradition of Satire.
Limitations:	Deciding for one's self when to ignore the guidelines of social decorum can quickly deteriorate into dangerous hedonism.
Exemplars:	Spike *Buffy the Vampire Slayer*
	Eric "Otter" Stratton *Animal House*
	Barney Stinson *How I Met Your Mother*
	Pepe Le Pew *Merrie Melodies*
	Danny Ocean *Ocean's Eleven*

The Mystic/Savant

Theme:	There are people among us who fulfill more of our human potential.
Utility:	Provides a glimpse at the "higher-level" capabilities of humanity
Relevant values:	Spirituality, Optimism, Sense of Mystery.
Foundations:	Lure of the Supernatural, Fear of those who are different.
Limitations:	There is an inevitable cost associated with gifts.
Exemplars:	Winifred "Fred" Burkle *Angel*
	George Malley *Phenomenon*
	River Tam *Firefly/Serenity*
	Harrison Bergeron *Harrison Bergeron*
	Will Hunting *Good Will Hunting*

The Mentor

Theme:	Truth and Wisdom can be handed down if the student is ready and worthy.
Utility:	Provides social foundations for generational perspectives and respect for tradition.

Relevant values:	Wisdom, Patience, Education.
Foundations:	Patriarchal Society, Propositional Ethics (as opposed to situational).
Limitations:	Is open to overuse, Moderate challenge to innovation (discover rather than create).

Exemplars:		
	Rupert Giles	*Buffy the Vampire Slayer*
	Mr. Miyagi	*The Karate Kid*
	Wilson Wilson, Jr.	*Home Improvement*
	Mickey Goldmill	*Rocky*
	Master Po	*Kung Fu*

The Innocent

Theme:	Virtue is power, and the greatest virtue is the utter lack of corruption. The seed of corruption is ambition.
Utility:	To reward cooperation and passivity. To reinforce the "burden of proof" which supports defending the status quo, unless there exists sufficient evidence to alter it. To extol the virtue of passivity. To argue against the value of curiosity and extremism.
Relevant virtues:	Virtue, Chastity, Virginity. Passivity.
Foundations:	A more Protestant version of Christianity lacking the notion of original sin.
Limitations:	The innocent must often threaten his/her innocence. He or she may often be unaware of his or her innocence and portray himself/herself as anything but, and in so doing triumph despite himself/herself. Innocence is almost invariably lost.

Exemplars:		
	Forest Gump	*Forest Gump*
	Wilton Parmenter	*F Troop*
	Laurie Strode	*Halloween*
	Spongebob Squarepants	*Spongebob Squarepants*
	Navin Johnson	*The Jerk*

NOTES

1. Two camps present conflicting views. Raymond Williams argues that the term culture has in part evolved to include "the idea of a general process of intellectual, spiritual and aesthetic development ... applied and effectively transferred to the works and practices which represent and sustain it. He relates that to one notion of the term "popular" that specifies work deliberately setting out to win favor." Another camp more vested in postmodern theory locates popular culture as the ground on which common people contest centers of power for control of their meanings (Storey). In the words of Edward Hirsch, "we make our meaning within a text, we wrestle with what we see and talk back to it, and we become more fully ourselves in the process" (O'Donnell 137).

2. "Theorists from Eric Erickson to Milton Rokeach to Claude Lévi-Strauss and Joseph Campbell argue that we share these experiences, struggles, goals, values, and stories ... the human experience is, for all intents and purposes, universal. And *Buffy* personifies this sentiment on so very many levels...." (Lynne Edwards, *Furthering Buffy Studies.*)

3. The story extends in comic book form in *Buffy the Vampire Slayer*, Season Eight. Dark Horse Comics.

4. Volition in this case refers to the ability of an actor to define then accomplish goals.

5. See *The Archetypes and the Collective Unconscious* by Jung, *Archetypal Patterns in Fairy Tales* by van Franz, and *Jung and Education: Elements of an Archetypal Pedagogy* by Mayes.

6. Among other examples are *The Twilight Saga*, the *True Blood* television show, *Forever Knight* (1992), *The Night Stalker* (1972), the Anne Rice book *Interview with the Vampire* (1976) and the subsequent film (1994).

7. "Buffy doesn't choose to be the Slayer, but she chooses how to be the Slayer. She chooses to have friends and to share her mission with them. She chooses to wear cool clothes" (Postrel 73).

8. Gothic author Anne Rice's *Interview with the Vampire* books are often credited with jump-starting the contemporary fascination with vampires. Spike refers directly to Rice's influence ("School Hard" 2.3). Angel does so more obliquely ("Reptile Boy" 2.5).

9. Carl Jung used the term archetype to describe the influence of the shared human spirit on the conscious individual. His motivation was to find a rationally satisfying way to explore what is not directly observable in people. According to Jung, "only the psyche can observe the psyche" (75). We cannot observe it directly. He conceived of the human spirit — be it deific, biologically or socially supplied — as existing deeper in us than our consciousness could reach and as having an "original autonomy" which makes it "quite capable of staging its own manifestations spontaneously" (83). The spirit or unconscious does this primarily by swiping the content of our conscious frames of reference and subverting that content to give us dreams in which it can manifest its influence. He studied thousands of dreams of people from many backgrounds and found an amazing recurrence of content. Without worrying about whether the chicken or the egg first dreamed up the other, he labeled these recurring structures archetypes.

10. The archetypal characters employed here should not be considered pure archetypes like those discussed by Jung. Those archetypes are much more abstract and amorphous. I use these recurring archetypal characters because I see them recur over time and across genres. Instructors and students should be encouraged to identify their own and to take exception if they so choose to the ones that I suggest.

11. In middle-class America, and especially in televised middle-class America, aggression and anger are contrary to the skill set generally expected of a young woman in transition from school to the professional world. The more she defines herself by her skills of aggression, the farther she drifts from the ability to assimilate into a normal, middle-class life. When the subject of a career comes up in "What's My Line?, part 1" (2.9) she tells Willow, "Do the words 'sealed in fate' ring any bells for you?" (Helford 22–26). Zaslow writes that "we are not free to create any identity that we select but rather one that reflects the reality of our material conditions and the ideologies in which we come to know the self" (36). Buffy's "self" as determined by her calling then will sadly be constantly in conflict with her socializing conditions.

12. The American intention to divorce its culture from Europe's by glorifying the common man reaches at least back to Abraham Lincoln, about whom was said, "He was not of course the first eminent American politician who could claim humble origins, nor the first to exploit them ... none has maintained so completely while scaling the heights the aspect of extreme simplicity" (119). John Hay referred to Lincoln as "the greatest character since Christ" (Hofstadter 118) another person of humble origins who rose to prominence. The Christian ethic was written into the American working pattern early on by Calvinism's relation of hard work to good works as they relate to predestination. Gothein "rightly calls the Calvinistic diaspora the seed-bed of capitalist economy" (Weber 43).

13. See Camron; Hollis.

14. In the early days of Gary Trudeau's comic strip, Michael Doonesbury described his inner thoughts with a pseudo-sportscaster's running color commentary of his life. The frame, for instance, would have him bumping into a co-ed, while the caption read "And the kid goes for broke!" Xander and Jesse employ the same kind of self-referential conversational ploys in the first couple of episodes of *Buffy*.

15. See McAvin and Kessenich.

16. Jonathan — who awarded Buffy the Class Protector Award — was first credited as a character under the name "Hostage Kid" in the episode "School Hard" (2.3). He was more prominently featured as an outcast in "Earshot" (3.18), a rogue and/or superman in "Superstar" (4.17), and a mystic/savant as a member of the "brotherhood of the dim" in most of Season Six.

17. Northrop Frye writes that "if superior neither to other men nor to his environment, the hero is one of us; we respond to a sense of his common humanity and demand from the poet the same canons of probability that we find in our own experience." (34). He refers to this theme as the low mimetic mode and identifies it in history as having developed around the end of the 19th century. Also, the emergence of Freudian psychology made it more acceptable to dramatize the plight of the common man because the battle between the id and the ego could be portrayed as titanic (Schafer).

18. See for example, Hodge's "Dead or Banished": A Comparative Reading of the Stories of King Oedipus and King David." It speaks to the issue of King David's tragedy and reinforces the theme that such stories recur over time.

19. *King Lear*, William Shakespeare. For the story of Ariadne and Theseus see Ruck et al. For the story of Polyphemus, the Cyclops see Homer's *The Odyssey*.

20. One of the sources employed in the writing of this chapter, *Fighting the Forces*, is an anthology of such investigations. I recommended the book for upper-level college students, while the instructor can frame the basic issues in simpler terms for younger ones.

21. In the Season Three finale, after explaining to the vampires how they would come up through the sewers and attack the high school commencement ceremony, giving him time to morph into a monster-snake and take over the world, he admonished them to watch their language while in public ("Graduation Day, Part 2" 3.22).

22. Whedon's commentary from *Buffy the Vampire Slayer: The Complete First Season*. 20th Century–Fox. DVD.

23. As Richard W. Bailey says: "*BTVS* is a twenty-first-century incarnation of other serials involving groups of young people in combat with malefactors, but none of these older sagas inspired scholars to drop everything and hasten to do philology, philosophy, and anthropology to explicate the agon" (93).

WORKS CITED

Bailey, Richard W. "Neologize Much?" *American Speech* 79.1 Spring 2004. 92–97. Print.

Brown, Lyn Mikel, and Carol Gilligan. *Meeting at the Crossroads*. Cambridge, MA: Harvard University Press, 1992. Print.

Buffy the Vampire Slayer: The Complete Series. 20th Century–Fox. 1997–2006. DVD.

Burke, Kenneth. *A Grammar of Motives*. Berkeley: University of California Press, 1962. Print.

Camron, Marc. "The Importance of Being the Zeppo: Xander, Gender Identity and Hybridity in *Buffy the Vampire Slayer.*" *Slayage: The Whedon Studies Association Journal* 6.3: n.pag. Web.

Edwards, Lynne. "Furthering *Buffy* Studies." *Diverse: Issues in Higher Education*, Vol. 25, Issue 10:5. (June 26, 2008): 5. Print.

Frye, Northhrope. *Anatomy of Criticism: Four Essays*. Princeton, NJ: Princeton University Press, 1957. Print.

Helford, Elyce R. "'My Emotions Give Me Power:' The Containment of Girls' Anger in *Buffy*." Eds. Rhonda V. Wilcox and David Lavery. *Fighting the Forces: What's at Stake in Buffy, the Vampire Slayer*. Lanham, MD: Roman Littlefield, 2002. 18–34. Print.

Hodge, Joel. "'Dead or Banished': A Comparative Reading of the Stories of King Oedipus and King David." *Scandinavian Journal of the Old Testament*. Vol. 20 Issue 2 (Nov. 2006): 189–215. Print.

Hofstadter, Richard. *The American Political Tradition*. New York: Vintage, 1974. Print.

Hollis, Erin. "Gorgonzola Sandwiches and Yellow Crayons: James Joyce, *Buffy the Vampire Slayer*, and the Aesthetics of Minutiae." *Slayage* 6.2: n.pag. Web.

Joss Whedon: The Master at Play. Creative Screenwriting Publications. 2005. DVD.

Jung, C.C. *The Archetypes and The Collective Unconscious, Collected Works*. 2nd ed. Princeton, NJ: Bollingen,1981. Print.

_____. *Psyche and Symbol*. Ed. Violet S. DeLaszlo. Princeton, NJ: Princeton University Press, 1991. Print.

Kessenich, Laura. "'Wait Till You Have an Evil Twin': Jane Espenson's Contributions to *Buffy the Vampire Slayer.*" *Watcher Junior* Issue 3 (July 2006): n.pag. Web.

Mayes, Clifford. *Jung and Education: Elements of an Archetypal Pedagogy*. Lanham, MD: Rowman and Littlefield, 2005. Print.

McAvin, Em. "'I Think I'm Kinda Gay': Willow Rosenberg and the Absent/Present Bisexual in *Buffy the Vampire Slayer.*" *Slayage* 6.4: n.pag. Web.

Miller, Arthur. *Death of a Salesman*. New York: Penguin, 1998. Print.

O'Donnell, Victoria. *Television Criticism*. Thousand Oaks, CA: Sage, 2007. Print.

Osborn, Michael. "Archetypal Metaphor in Rhetoric: The Light-Dark Family." *Quarterly Journal of Speech* 53 (1967): 115–126. Print.

_____. "The Evolution of the Archetypal Sea in Rhetoric and Poetic." *Quarterly Journal of Speech* 63 (1977): 347–363. Print.

Pender, Patricia. "'I'm Buffy and You're ... History': The Postmodern Politics of Buffy." Eds. Rhonda V. Wilcox and David Lavery. *Fighting the Forces: What's at Stake in Buffy, the Vampire Slayer*. Lanham, MD: Roman Littlefield, 2002. 35–44. Print.

Postrel, Virginia. "Why Buffy Kicked Ass." *Reason* Vol. 35 Issue 4 (Aug/Sep 2003): 72–73. Print.

Ruck, Carl A. P., and Danny Staples. *The World of Classical Myth*. Durham: Carolina Academic Press, 1994. Print.

Schafer, Roy. "Narration in the Psychoanalytic Dialogue." *On Narrative*. Ed. W.J.T. Mitchell. Chicago: University of Chicago Press, 1980: 25–50. Print.

Skwire, Sarah E. "Whose Side Are You On Anyway? Children, Adults and the Use of Fairy Tales in *Buffy*." Eds. Rhonda V. Wilcox and David Lavery. *Fighting the Forces: What's at Stake in Buffy, the Vampire Slayer*. Lanham, MD: Roman Littlefield, 2002. 195–204. Print.

Storey, John. *Cultural Theory and Popular Culture*. Athens: University of Georgia Press, 2006. Print.

thirtysomething: The Complete First Season. Shout! Factory. 2009. DVD.

Weber, Max. *The Protestant Ethic and the Spirit of Capitalism*. New York: Scribner's, 1958. Print.

Wilcox, R.V. "Who Died and Made Her the Boss? Patterns of Mortality in *Buffy*." Eds. Rhonda V. Wilcox and David Lavery. *Fighting the Forces: What's at Stake in Buffy, the Vampire Slayer*. Lanham, MD: Roman Littlefield, 2002. 3–17. Print.

Williams, Raymond. *Keywords*. Rev. Ed. New York: Oxford University Press, 1983. 87–93. Print.

Zaslow, Emilie. *Feminism, Inc.: Coming of Age in Girl Power Media Culture*. New York: Palgrave MacMillan, 2009. Press.

Heroism on the Hellmouth:
Teaching Morality Through *Buffy*

K. Dale Koontz

A common lament among college faculty is that students arrive ill-prepared to tackle the literature and lessons of the "Western canon." While there may be heated discussion about which authors, artists, and philosophers have earned a place on this lofty list, discussants rarely consider television shows for inclusion. This is a pity, since many educators have found Joss Whedon's *Buffy the Vampire Slayer* to be a high quality text that adapts easily to the classroom. *Buffy* is particularly useful in introducing students to literary criticism and philosophical positions. Moreover, I have successfully used guided viewing and discussion of *Buffy* as a text to introduce concepts of both morality and contemporary heroism to students.

My experience has shown me that *Buffy* is quite at home in the college classroom. The use of television shows in the classroom makes logical sense — while few students come to the classroom already conversant with classical philosophers, they all have watched television. Without the commercials, an hour long television episode of *Buffy* is roughly 44 minutes; a length that easily fits most classroom sessions. Further, unlike the experience of solitary reading, the shared viewing experience removes much of the apprehension students often have toward open discussion of loaded concepts such as morality. By watching the same episode together, students experience the same plot at the same time and this shared experience creates common ground for guided discussions.

While *Buffy* can easily be utilized within a vast array of disciplines,[1] this chapter focuses on its portrayal of morality and contemporary views of heroism through four specific episodes, among many that could have been chosen, that provide a unified arc of contemporary heroic behavior. This arc of heroism is discussed in more detail for each episode within the chapter. Each episode serves to illustrate particular aspects of the modern hero as well as to demonstrate how the character of Buffy Summers is a continuation of the rich tradition of heroes in myth and literature. Since the course centers on contemporary depictions of heroism, each episode chosen illustrates a particular theme as one of the focal points of the course.[2] My discussion also provides examples from the classical canon to incorporate with each episode. While each episode is discussed separately, the primary course themes are as follows: "Prophecy Girl" (1.12) explores personal sacrifice, "Bad Girls" (3.14) explores boundaries, "Who Are You?" (4.16) explores redemption and identity, and "The Body" (5.16) explores reactions to loss. Prior to beginning the discussion of each episode, I provide a basic overview in preparing the class to watch television critically. Then, within each section, I discuss how to prepare the class, present the particular episode for that session, and guide the discussion. The viewing and discussion of each episode as detailed below takes approximately two hours. Each section can either be conducted as one unified class session or divided into two sections with the first session consisting of background information and viewing the episode with the guided discussion comprising a second class session. Additional relevant "Whedon readings" such as journal articles or published essays are noted in the notes for each episode.

There is no one right way to present these lessons to a particular class. As with other canonical works such as those of Shakespeare, Austen, or Dickens, some students may well be avid fans; others may not be even fleetingly aware of the text. I prepare students for each lesson by introducing the characters and parameters of the show first. When instructors use traditional dramatic literature such as Shakespeare's *King Lear*, a student can simply flip back to the cast of characters at the beginning of the play to sort out confusion about whether Edmund or Edgar is the bastard; an option television does not provide. If time allows, instructors may wish to begin with a plot synopsis for each episode to provide context.[3]

Creating a simple PowerPoint presentation containing a visual representation of the characters the class will encounter in that particular episode, along with a brief description of essential personality traits and relationships, is useful in preparing students. Printing out the slides in handout form has the added benefit of giving students a portable "cheat sheet." A "spoke and wheel" diagram for the first episode with Buffy at the center and arrows to indicate her relationships with other major characters establishes the links between characters. While covering the cast and relationships of the central characters takes some time during the first class, taking this time is effective and it is also quite simple to add new characters for subsequent episodes. The object is to give the class enough background to easily follow the plot ("Who's that?" is *not* a question the instructor wants students whispering when a major character appears!) without spoiling the viewing experience. Within the discussion of the four episodes, key characters and relationships are identified. I introduce these to students prior to the viewing of each episode.

Once students are clear on "who's who," I use additional PowerPoint slides or handouts to emphasize particular questions and themes regarding heroism that the students should focus on as they watch the episode. The following discussion of each episode includes suggestions in bullet point form for both before and after viewing. If desired, these can easily be incorporated into each episode's PowerPoints.[4] These questions are the heart of the guided discussion for each episode and serve as the springboard to assess students' increasing understanding of central concepts of heroism.

"Prophecy Girl"

The Season One finale "Prophecy Girl" examines the concept of personal sacrifice in the hero character. This episode provides an excellent starting point, since the ongoing tension between Buffy's recognition of her duty and her reluctance to fulfill that duty is in full swing. Heroes ranging from Jesus Christ of the Gospels to Sydney Carton of *A Tale of Two Cities* have faced their desire to simply walk away and live a "normal" life; Buffy is a continuation of that noble line of heroes who do the right thing, but think twice about it.

I make a point of introducing the characters of Buffy, her mother Joyce, her Watcher Giles, a computer teacher at the local high school named Jenny, Buffy's friends Willow, Xander, Cordelia, and Buffy's love interest Angel. As discussed above, each slide also contains a brief description to help students understand how each character fits into the mosaic of the episode.

Once characters and relationships have been clarified, I introduce the central theme toward the end of the PowerPoint. I explain to the class that each episode will concentrate on a particular theme that is a common aspect of both the classical and the modern hero. For "Prophecy Girl," the class explores a common element of hero epics — the willingness of the hero to undertake hardship for others. It is important to brief the class on the recurring metaphor of "high school as Hell" and the basic rules of Slayers, which echo many classical heroes who are "chosen" for their destiny, ranging from the Biblical Jonah to Tolkien's Frodo. In the world of *Buffy*, these rules are (a) the Slayer is *chosen*; she does not *choose* this life and (b) there is only one Slayer at a given time and when that girl falls, the next is called. "Prophecy Girl" centers on what happens when Buffy must confront the harsh reality of her calling as a Slayer by discovering a prophecy that foretells more that she wants to know.[5] The final slide asks the class to watch for three things:

- Rebellion/denial
- The turning point for Buffy; that is, the instant at which she makes a conscious choice to risk her life
- Why her non-superpowered friends choose to put themselves at risk

For me, next comes the hard part. That is, showing the episode, but resisting the temptation to call out, "See that? That's what you need to notice!" Allowing students to first view the episode without interjection permits them to locate their own understanding of the episode. Following that viewing, I give the students a short span of time to discuss what they have just seen in an unstructured manner. Ten minutes spent in informal discussion aids in creating a spirited guided discussion.

Next, I reconvene the class and collect general thoughts and observations. Quite often, the details the students noticed surprise me. I gradually steer the conversation to the idea of sacrifice, beginning with Buffy's reluctance to accept the prophecy that she will not survive her coming battle. The following questions guide the discussion and encourage students to make notes:

- What is a general definition of the term "sacrifice?"
- What is Buffy's "sacrifice" in this instance?
- What is the difference between "courage" and "sacrifice?"
- Buffy tries to balance her duties as the Slayer with her desire to be a "normal" girl.

In this episode, she rebels against her duties. At some time, you have probably rebelled against an obligation — how did you resolve the conflict?

- Everyone has to make choices in life. What is the difference between "prioritizing" and "sacrifice"?

- It is common in many religious traditions to deny yourself something you enjoy as part of a religious ceremony or ritual (giving up chocolate during the season of Lent, for example). To what extent is sacrifice linked to atonement?

- Buffy comments that she feels "stronger" after Xander revives her. How does sacrifice make a person stronger?

I point out the repetition of the line "I like your dress" referring to Buffy's white, bride-like gown which she topped with a black leather jacket. I then ask if this blending of the vulnerable and the tough is an accident. *Buffy* is justly famed for twisting traditional tropes such as the vulnerable blonde victim.[6] I want to encourage students to identify stereotypes of hero stories and ask how "Prophecy Girl" challenges or reinforces those tropes. I further remind students to listen carefully to both dialogue and background music, as lyrics are often used to comment on or foreshadow the events of the episodes. For the first week, I simply ask students to be aware that music and clothing can play a part in the action. In later weeks, we explore in more depth the episodes' attention to elements such as costuming and sound.

In "Prophecy Girl," despite her triumph over the Master and her flaunting of prophecy, Buffy is called upon to make the ultimate heroic sacrifice — she dies. While her death may have been temporary, it was sufficient to activate another Slayer, a young woman named Kendra. When Kendra is murdered by a vampire in Season Two, yet another Slayer is called. This Slayer — named Faith — has her own way of looking at the rules that have been set down, both for Slayers and for ordinary humans. The contrast between these two Slayers is the focus for Week Two.

"Bad Girls"

Heroes are distinguished from ordinary humans by possessing extraordinary abilities. A traditional marker of the hero is the willingness to use these powers only for good and not for selfish personal gain or glory. Therefore, the next concept of the hero that the class will discuss is limitations and boundaries. The character Faith was first introduced earlier in Season Three of *Buffy*; however, this lesson focuses on a later episode entitled "Bad Girls." I begin by asking the class to consider the following:

- Just as vampires straddle the line between the living and the dead, Slayers Buffy and Faith straddle the line between human and superhuman. What rules apply to such beings?

- Who has the authority to make those rules?

- How are such rules enforced?

"Bad Girls" is an action-packed episode that permits students to explore these questions and also opens the door to discussion of the responsibility of the powerful and privileged towards the rest of humanity. Nietzsche's "übermensch" and Dostoyevsky's *Crime and Punishment* both raise questions about the responsibilities of the powerful toward the powerless. Another potential link is Arthur Miller's *The Crucible*, which includes both power-mad girls and a righteous man who refuses to allow his name to be dragged through the mud.[7] Regardless of which works the instructor may choose to illustrate the central concepts under discussion in *Buffy*, be sure to prepare a brief handout to remind students of what they are seeking to connect to in viewing this episode.[8]

I introduce new characters in this session's PowerPoint overview, including Faith, Oz, the Mayor, Mr. Trick, and Wesley Wyndam-Pryce. Once students have been briefed on both the new residents of Sunnydale and changes in relationships — for example, it is important to note that Joyce is now aware of her daughter's role as the Slayer — I ask the class to answer one question: Should rules be different for people based on their abilities? To answer this question, I tell the class to watch for three items:

- The personality contrasts between Buffy and Faith, including their different approaches to slaying
- The attitude of the new Watcher, Wesley, toward the slayers
- Costuming choices — pay careful attention to who wears what in this episode

By now, students usually understand what is expected of them in terms of focused viewing and watch this and subsequent episodes with increased attentiveness.

After watching "Bad Girls," I allow students to simply talk about what they noticed about the episode with little interference. Then gradually I lead the discussion around to the theme of boundaries, which can be used to discuss consequences. *Buffy* often deals head-on with some thorny issues, including concepts of free will and the results of abusing it. These are themes that are clearly evident in "Bad Girls."[9] Faith assumes her powers give her the right to scorn her obligations. I ask the following questions to guide the discussion:

- What boundaries did the characters cross in this episode?
- Who and what does Buffy feel a sense of obligation toward in determining her behavior?
- What about Faith — to whom and what does she feel she owes an obligation?
- Buffy distinguishes herself as a "Slayer" rather than a "killer." What is the difference?
- Buffy seems both attracted to and repelled by the very violence she engages in every night, yet Faith does not have the same problem. Both are Slayers, yet the two are very different. Why?
- What colors are the Slayers wearing when first seen? How do these colors change as the episode progresses?
- What problems arise from people trying to avoid the consequences of their actions?
- To what degree are boundaries necessary in a free society? Why?

"Bad Girls" serves as an excellent gateway into a discussion of the Nietzschean ideal, which is defined as "a powerful physicality, a flourishing, abundant, even overflowing health, together with that which serves to preserve it: war, adventure, hunting, dancing, war games, and in general all that involves vigorous, free, joyful activity" (Nietzsche 469). I ask the class how this definition applies to Faith and what seems to be missing from the definition, then I explain that this concept of the rules being different for people based on their own abilities and attributes is a common thread running through both literature (Dostoyevsky's *Crime & Punishment* is one example) and life ("Only the little people pay taxes," as wealthy hotelier Leona Helmsley famously stated). Stan Lee's *Spider-Man* puts it succinctly: "With great power comes great responsibility." (Sanderson 78). I ask students if they agree with this position or if they believe that unusual power grants unusual privilege. As the students discuss these positions, I prod them to supply additional examples and support for their opinions on this disparity. By doing so, the students begin to engage in comparative criticism.

Despite her actions in killing an innocent man, Faith is not beyond the possibility of redemption. Instead, the troubling question is whether Faith *wants* to be redeemed; a question to which the answer appears terribly murky at the end of "Bad Girls." This question of redemption will be the focus of Week Three.

"Who Are You?"

A common characteristic of many contemporary hero characters is the degree of darkness in their pasts that informs their present course. The third episode taught in this course focuses on the concept of redemption; in this particular case, Faith's redemption. The class views the episode "Who Are You?" to explore this theme. Aspects of redemption — the possibility, desirability, and the mechanics of it — are an overarching theme in Whedon's work.[10] All of these facets can be seen in this episode, along with ideas about personal identity and self-awareness.

The PowerPoint for this episode introduces six new characters: Tara, Anya, the monster Adam, Spike, Riley, and Forrest. I make a point to note that at the very end of the previous episode (which is not shown in this course) Faith confronted Buffy and used a device to swap bodies with her. It is crucial for the class to understand that throughout this episode, "Buffy" is Faith and "Faith" is Buffy.[11] I find that this is an appropriate time to mention the literary device of the foil with classic examples ranging from Hector and Achilles in Homer's *Iliad* to King Lear and the Fool in Shakespeare's *King Lear*. More modern examples include Batman and the Joker, as well as the "subplot foil" of "Tales of the Black Freighter" contained in Alan Moore's *Watchmen* which informs and comments on the main plot of that graphic novel.[12]

Once the class is comfortably up to speed on the new developments, I give them their assignment for this episode. Specifically, they need to watch carefully for the following:

- External identity (how others see us) vs. a more internal (how we see ourselves) view of identity

- The role of action in redemption
- The use of Christian symbols throughout the episode

Next I show the class "Who Are You?" By now, the class is familiar with the routine and settles in eagerly to critically watch the episode. As with previous episodes, I must resist the temptation to point out anything in the episode and, once the episode concludes, I permit the class to spontaneously discuss what they have just seen before beginning the guided discussion. I gradually lead the discussion around to the theme of redemption. *Buffy* often deals with the concepts of redemption and identity and this episode brings those subjects into sharp focus.[13] Among the questions I pose to the class are the following:

- Is there a link between forgiveness and redemption?
- Where does Faith's journey of redemption begin?
- What is the catalyst for Faith's desire to change?
- What insights do Buffy and Faith gain from their time in the other's skin?
- What is the most unsettling part of the action in the church?
- Whedon, the creator of *Buffy*, is an avowed atheist. Why is there so much Christian imagery in this episode? What point is being made here?
- Is Faith redeemed at the end of the episode? If not, what remains for her to do?

In addition to examining redemption, "Who Are You?" also stimulates a discussion of identity. I ask some additional questions to bring this to the students' attention:

- How much of Faith's desire to act heroically in this episode stems from the way other people treat her?
- How do Faith and Buffy compare to examples such as King Lear and his Fool?
- Are Buffy and Faith the inverse of the other, such as Batman and the Joker?

As Buffy, Faith is treated with respect, shown love and tenderness, and is the recipient of gratitude. As Faith, Buffy is scorned, reviled, and even spat upon by representatives of the Watcher's Council. Faith-as-Buffy alludes to this treatment when she says, "I guess you never really know someone until you've been inside their skin." This sentiment is echoed in Harper Lee's classic novel *To Kill a Mockingbird* when Atticus Finch advises his son Jem that he will "never really understand a person until you consider things from his point of view ... until you climb into his skin and walk around in it." (Lee 33). Having had the opportunity to see life through the eyes of the other, both Slayers are changed. I ask the class to consider two questions at this point — How is this change shown to the viewers? Moreover, what will happen to both Slayers now that they each have knowledge of the other's point of view?

This is also an appropriate time to discuss the power of personal creeds to guide the actions of a hero. In contrast to the Musketeers' famous creed of "All for one and one for all" ("*un pour tous, tous pour un*"), Faith's creed is self-centered: "Want. Take. Have." However, people can change and throughout this episode, Faith adopts what she believes is Buffy's creed. Buffy fights evil "because it's wrong." I want to lead the class discussion toward examination of these personal codes. Using the bedroom scene with Riley, I point out how Faith's internal conflict is shown externally through techniques such as off-balance camera angles and sharp editing cuts. Helping students focus their attention on such details allows them to recognize the high degree of craft and skill that goes into creating quality television.

"The Body"

From Antigone to Buffy, heroes are not immune from loss and the class explores that concept by watching "The Body." This Season Five episode is often listed as one of the most emotionally wrenching of the series and provides students with a gateway to discussing different approaches to the subject of loss. Throughout the series, Whedon emphasizes that while Buffy is "the Chosen One" and is gifted with abilities far beyond those of ordinary people, she is far from invulnerable. One of Buffy's greatest sources of strength is her ability to form meaningful relationships with other people; however, those same relationships leave her open to the possibility of emotional heartbreak. In "The Body" viewers see the full extent of that vulnerability and its aftermath. In the final episode of this course, students learn the harsh truth that there are some things not even a Slayer or a hero can defeat.[14]

I use the PowerPoint for this episode to introduce Dawn and Glory. While the web of backstory is considerably more complicated, I let students know that Dawn is Buffy's younger sister and Glory is the chief villain of Season Five. Further, I inform students that Buffy's mother Joyce has been suffering from a brain tumor — not due to any magic spell or demon curse, but just because human beings sometimes get sick. The previous episodes all feature Joyce as a compassionate mother. That is a deliberate choice I made to help the class form a connection with Joyce, which makes the character's sudden death resonate with students. Cruel perhaps, but this tactic has proven to be effective in eliciting engaged reactions from the class who are often visibly affected by Joyce's death.[15] Rather than have the entire class look for certain themes in the episode, I divide the class into small groups, with three or four students per group and have the groups sit together to watch the episode. Each group is given a particular topic to watch for in the episode. Among the topics that I have assigned are:

- Family
- Use of light and dark
- Body language
- Sound (excluding voice)
- Vocal expression
- Color — the instructor may want to get more specific and assign particular colors such as yellow or blue to different groups
- Thresholds/boundaries

Once the groups understand their assignments, we begin viewing the episode. At the conclusion of the show, I permit the groups informally to discuss what they have seen and ask each group to appoint a "spokesmodel" to address the rest of the class and explain their group's observations and findings.

"The Body" deals honestly and unflinchingly with the absolute bewilderment that comes with the death of a loved one.[16] While the focus is on Buffy, the effect of Joyce's death on secondary characters is an important part of the episode, since all the characters must deal with the loss. In fact, Buffy's Slayer strength is presented as a *negative* trait here—I have pointed out the sharp cracking sound as Buffy inadvertently breaks her mother's sternum while attempting to revive her with CPR. The group with the assignment of focusing on sound will probably mention this, as well as another significant absence in the episode—there is no background music in "The Body." I remind the class that the absence of background music is particularly significant since most television shows, including *Buffy*, use background music to indicate mood. Viewers are so accustomed to music in television programs that students frequently comment on its absence here.[17]

Once the students have concluded their group discussions within the class, I ask them for their reactions to the following:

- The episode contains a series of "flashbacks" as Buffy tries to re-order events to have a different outcome. Why is this sort of "if only" a common reaction to bad news?
- Why is only the lower half of the paramedic's face shown when he is delivering the news of Joyce's death to Buffy?
- What is the significance of the title?
- What is the significance of the art lesson about "negative space"?
- How do the different characters—Xander, Willow, Giles, Anya—react to Joyce's death?
- What is the significance of Buffy's battle with the vampire in the morgue?

"The Body" is an episode which leaves viewers with a number of questions. Perhaps that fact makes this a good place to stop the formal inquiry into the show and leave students free to continue their own quests for meaning within *Buffy* as a text. In the short span of four weeks, students begin to use basic critical thinking skills to delve beneath the surface of a quality television show, explore deeper themes and learn to pay closer attention to what is contained within the frame. Once students understand that everything is in the frame (or, in a written text, on the page) for a reason, they often have a desire to ascertain what the reason is for the inclusion. Far from taking the joy out of experiencing the story, my students noted that such close attention deepened their pleasure in watching a well-crafted show—or reading well-crafted literature.

The key to success in using televisual texts in the classroom lies in selecting a quality show which contains well-rounded characters, memorable dialogue, and compelling narrative arcs and then providing a context for viewing the show within the classroom. All too often, visual texts such as film and television are used carelessly in the classroom and students walk away with the mistaken idea that films such as *The Alamo* are documentaries rather than creatively dramatized depictions of events. By providing specific guidelines to tailor the initial viewing and guiding the subsequent discussion along the lines of a particular theme, I help students discover a framework by which to explore their own ideas and those of their classmates. The resulting give-and-take of discussion is crucial for students to learn both how to articulate their own ideas and how to listen and critique those of other viewers. These same skills easily translate into more traditional text-based discussions. After all, Buffy Summers in "The Body" has certain commonalities with Shakespeare's Hamlet, including indecision about how to proceed in life after a parent's death. While there are many ways to effectively evaluate what students have learned about thinking critically about heroism throughout these lessons, one suggestion is to have students write essays comparing and contrasting themes discussed in these episodes with those from written literary forms. Topics include comparing Faith with Abigail Williams from *The Crucible* to explore the consequences of misusing power, or comparing Buffy with Antigone to explore reactions to loss and duty. Another option is to have students write essays tracing the heroic character throughout literature and then argue how Buffy Summers fits that lineage. The methods of evaluating student progress are limitless and can be tailored to the subject matter, student population and individual instructor style.

Viewing television shows such as *Buffy* is a worthy supplement to reading and discussing traditional texts in the classroom.[18] While I have described using *Buffy* here to teach concepts of morality and heroism, the show can also be used effectively in many disciplines ranging from philosophy to the performing arts, for the need to tell stories as a way to find meaning in the events in our lives is an ongoing one. Technology simply provides new methods to accomplish the same goals. Instructors have long embraced technology in the classroom to reach students. We now use online resources to communicate with students via e-mail, blog posts, and instant messaging. In fact, I created a blog to supplement this class. The blog was a means of posting relevant links to online articles such as those contained in *Slayage*. I also posted links to transcripts of the episodes and to lists of relevant articles that students might be interested in locating. Further, the blog provided students with a place to discuss the episodes beyond the time limitations of the class permitted. The blog was such a successful part of the class that I maintained it even after the class concluded.[19]

Regardless of the form used, the essential lessons to be taught remain. Instructors must apply the same degree of care to the selection of television episodes as is used in the selection of traditional texts. Based on my experiences in using *Buffy* within the confines of an academic setting, I find that my students are thoroughly engaged in the narrative. Moreover, they quickly begin to use the tools of critical thinking to move beyond a mere "Wow! Did you see that?" to a deeper analysis of story, characterization, and theme, as well as applying what they see in the episodes to the larger discussion of heroism and morality outside of the show. Therefore, I am confident that quality television, including Whedon's *Buffy*, has earned a place within the academic canon.

NOTES

1. The fields of religion, sociology, communication, and psychology all leap to mind, although the themes of *Buffy* are so wide-ranging that the show can be successfully incorporated into just about any

discipline. I have seen effective presentations using *Buffy* in the fields of business, education, and criminal justice, for example.

2. In its original form, this was a course taught through the continuing education department of my college, so I had the luxury of tremendous freedom in structuring the course and assessing the progress of the participants, some of whom were great fans of *Buffy* prior to taking the course and others who had never heard of the show. Throughout the chapter, I noted suggestions for evaluating the progress of students, but I invite instructors to use their own initiative in adapting my experiences to their own particular situation.

3. Howard Russell's site, which can be accessed at http://www.buffyworld.com/, is especially useful for plot synopses. This site is full of information, including episode transcripts, summaries, and trailers.

4. I also suggest including a handout of further readings for the end of class. I chose particular essays and articles from *Slayage* and other related Whedon works, but this could easily be adapted to include material specific to the individual class.

5. I found it useful to provide students with a list of relevant readings for each episode. For "Prophecy Girl," I would suggest Anderson's "Prophecy Girl and the Powers That Be: The Philosophy of Religion in the *Buffyverse*" in South, Erickson's "'Sometimes You Need a Story': American Christianity, Vampires, and Buffy" in Wilcox and Lavery, and McClelland's "By Whose Authority? The Magical Tradition, Violence, and the Legitimation of the Vampire Slayer" in the first issue of *Slayage*. Longer texts include Battis; Reiss.

6. The introduction to Roz Kaveney's *Reading the Vampire Slayer* (titled "She Saved the World. A Lot.") is an excellent place to begin the study of the themes and structure of *Buffy*.

7. Alan Moore's graphic novel *V for Vendetta* could also be used to provide a basis for comparison.

8. Relevant Whedon readings for "Bad Girls" include Forster's "Faith and Plato: 'You're Nothing! Disgusting, Murderous Bitch!,'" Kawal's "Should We Do What Buffy Would Do?," Marinucci's "Feminism and the Ethics of Violence," Miller's "'The I in Team': *Buffy* and Feminist Ethics," and Stroud's "A Kantian Analysis of Moral Judgment in *Buffy the Vampire Slayer*." All of these essays are found in South.

9. Schudt's "Also Sprach Faith: The Problem of the Happy Rogue Vampire Slayer" *is* quite useful on this point. This essay can be found in South (2003).

10. Relevant material for "Who Are You?" includes Keller's "Spirit Guides and Shadow Selves: From the Dream Life of Buffy (and Faith)" in *Fighting the Forces* and Sakal's "No Big Win: Themes of Sacrifice, Salvation, and Redemption" in South. Longer texts include Koontz (2008) and Riess.

11. Since the discussion of this episode will also touch on issues of identity, you may want to suggest that the class take note of how the actresses convey this — especially through the mannerisms and speech patterns of Faith as she tries to remember that she is in Buffy's body.

12. Moore's *Watchmen* is an excellent modern reference and is the only graphic novel included on *Time* magazine's list of All-Time Best 100 English language novels as compiled by critics Lev Grossman and Richard Lacayo. Should the instructor wish to include the subplot foil of *Watchmen* in the discussion of literary foils, note that the subplot is contained only in the novel itself, not the 2009 film version of *Watchmen*.

13. Battis discusses these concepts at length in *Blood Relations*, as does Wilcox in *Why Buffy Matters*.

14. Much has been written about "The Body," but of particular usefulness are Riess' "Death Is Our Gift" in *What Would Buffy Do?* and Wilcox's "Who Died and Made Her Boss? Patterns of Mortality in Buffy" in *Fighting the Forces*.

15. From Shakespeare's *Hamlet*, Act 3, Scene 4, line 199: "I must be cruel, only to be kind." Hamlet knows a thing or two about the loss of a parent. Whedon is known for snatching away beloved characters, often in nasty, seemingly undeserved ways. Joyce's death would not matter as much if the audience did not care about her welfare. Further, just as I am indebted to Diane Wilson's work on the Website *The Unitarian Slayer* for providing much of the initial framework for the earlier three sections, I wish to acknowledge Rhonda Wilcox's workshop on "The Body" for pioneering many of the ideas in this section.

16. It should be noted that Whedon routinely cites his late mother, Lee Stearns, as one of his greatest influences (Havens 6).

17. In addition to previously mentioned works regarding "The Body," see Dechert's "'My Boyfriend's

in the Band!' *Buffy* and the Rhetoric of Music" in *Fighting the Forces* for a discussion of *Buffy*'s use of music.

18. The ever-growing shelves of scholarly and academic texts attest to this fact! The methodical study of *Buffy* as a text continues to expand. One notable addition to this field is Kevin Durand's edited collection *Buffy Meets the Academy*, which focuses on the episodes and the scripts as texts. Tamara Wilson's essay in that collection, "Keeping *Buffy* in the Classroom," is particularly illuminating.

19. In fact, I continue to maintain the blog as a place to connect with other Whedon scholars. I should re-emphasize that while I did not use the blog posts as part of the students' grade in this course, that could certainly be a viable option, should the individual instructor wish to do so.

WORKS CITED

Battis, Jes. *Blood Relations: Chosen Families in* Buffy the Vampire Slayer *and* Angel. Jefferson, NC: McFarland, 2005. Print.

Buffy the Vampire Slayer: The Chosen Collection. Twentieth Century–Fox Home Entertainment, 2005. DVD.

Carnes, Mark C. *Past Imperfect History According to the Movies* (Henry Holt Reference Book). New York: Owl Books, 1996. Print.

Dickens, Charles. *A Tale of Two Cities.* Oxford: Oxford University Press, 1991. Print.

Dostoyevsky, Fyodor. *Crime and Punishment.* Trans. David McDuff. London: Penguin, 2003. Print.

Dumas, Alexandre. *The Three Musketeers.* Trans. Lord Sudley. New York: Penguin, 1982. Print.

Durand, Kevin K., ed. *Buffy Meets the Academy.* Jefferson, NC: McFarland, 2009. Print.

Grossman, Lev, and Richard Lacayo. "All-Time 100 Novels." *Time.* Time Mag., 2005. n.pag. Web. 11 Nov. 2009.

Havens, Candace. *Joss Whedon: The Genius Behind Buffy.* London: Titan, 2003. Print.

Homer. *The Iliad.* Cambridge: Cambridge University Press, 2004. Print.

Kaveney, Roz. *Reading the Vampire Slayer.* London: I.B. Tauris, 2004. Print.

Koontz, K. Dale. *Faith and Choice in the Works of Joss Whedon.* Jefferson, NC: McFarland, 2008. Print.

_____. Weblog. *Unfettered Brilliance.* 2007–2009: n.pag. Web. 11 July 2009. <www.unfetteredbrilliance. blogspot.com>.

Lee, Harper. *To Kill a Mockingbird.* 35th Anniversary Edition. New York: HarperCollins, 1995. Print.

The Living Bible. Wheaton, IL: Tyndale, 1973. Print.

McClelland, Bruce. "By Whose Authority? The Magical Tradition, Violence, and the Legitimation of the Vampire Slayer." *Slayage: The Whedon Studies Association Journal* 1 (2001): n.pag. Web. 11 Nov. 2009.

Miller, Arthur. *Arthur Miller's Collected Plays: With an Introduction.* New York: Viking, 1981. Print.

Moore, Alan. *V for Vendetta.* New York: DC Comics, 2009. Print.

_____. *Watchmen.* New York: DC Comics, 1995. Print.

Nietzsche, Friedrich. *Basic Writings of Nietzsche.* Trans. Walter Kaufmann. New York: Random House, 2000. Print.

Reiss, Jana. *What Would Buffy Do? The Vampire Slayer as Spiritual Guide.* San Francisco: JosseyBass, 2004. Print.

Sanderson, Peter. *Marvel Universe.* New York: Harry N. Abrams, 1996. Print.

Shakespeare, William. *The Tragedy of King Lear.* Ed. Barbara A. Mowat and Paul Werstine. New York: Washington Square, 2005. Print.

Sophocles. *Antigone.* Trans. Richard Braun. New York: Oxford University Press, 1989. Print.

South, James B., ed. Buffy the Vampire Slayer *and Philosophy Fear and Trembling in Sunnydale.* Chicago: Open Court, 2003. Print.

Tolkien, J.R.R. *The Fellowship of the Ring: Being the First Part of The Lord of the Rings.* Boston: Houghton Mifflin, 1994. Print.

Wilcox, Rhonda. *Why Buffy Matters: The Art of* Buffy the Vampire Slayer. I.B. Tauris: London, 2005. Print.

_____. "Workshop on 'The Body.'" Popular & American Culture Associations in the South Conference. Marriott Savannah Riverfront, Savannah, GA. Oct 2006. Workshop.

_____, and David Lavery, eds. *Fighting the Forces: What's at Stake in* Buffy the Vampire Slayer. New York: Rowman and Littlefield, 2002. Print.

Wilson, Diane. *The Unitarian Slayer.* Unitarian Universalist Fellowship of Raleigh, 2003–2005. Web. 11 July 2009. <http://dianewilson.us/buffy/>.

Whedon Takes "the Scary"
Out of Feminism

Meghan K. Winchell

"Scary." "Extreme radicals." "Hillary Clinton." These are some of the descriptors first-year seminar students offered in answer to my question, "What is feminism?" They characterized feminists as "loud, obnoxious" women who are "female dominant and demeaning to men;" they are "unattractive" women who "hate men" and are "not normal." Therefore, it did not come as a surprise to me that when I asked the next question, "Are you a feminist?" not a single student raised a hand, even though some had offered a more positive view of feminism as "girl power" and "independence" in response to the original question. Negative views of feminists and feminism far outweigh the positive for millennial students. Some students believe that "women already have rights so feminism is no longer needed." Most, however, have fallen for the negative stereotypes that the media perpetuate about feminism. Media Studies scholar Susan Douglas has shown that the media has distorted feminism, creating the enduring and false notion that feminists just don't have any fun (7). Buffy Summers belies this image. She not only has fun at work, slaying vampires and foiling apocalypses, she does so with a razor sharp vocabulary and near perfect hair, thereby making Joss Whedon's *Buffy the Vampire Slayer* the ideal text to introduce young skeptics to feminism.

Critics and scholars have debated *Buffy's* identification as a feminist text since the show's first season, never quite coming to full agreement. Some scholars embrace the series as a feminist mantra for the ages. A young blond girl defies stereotypes to take on the forces of evil (and patriarchy) all the while enveloped in the supportive cocoon of community (Levine, Hibbs, Miller, Marinucci). Others contend that Buffy Summers' hyper-femininity, brought to life in halter-topped glam by Sarah Michelle Gellar perpetuates negative stereotypes of women held hostage by the male gaze (Vint, Fudge). Patricia Pender opts for a middle ground in which Whedon's heroine and the show itself display all of the contradictions inherent in young women's lives. *Buffy* is "a site of intense cultural negotiation" rather than simply feminist or not (Pender 43). It has been my experience in the classroom that eighteen and nineteen-year-old college students warm to Buffy and her friends exactly because she faces the kinds of problems that they deal with. Buffy wants to be a partner in a stable relationship and has a difficult time balancing her multiple commitments to friends, family, school and work. She wants to be a "normal girl" but cannot live up to the image suggested by that category. Students in my *Buffy* course ask similar questions about their own competing responsibilities, as well as their feminine and masculine identities. The show's "emotional realism" speaks to young women and men whose feet continue to move over the shifting terrain of power and gender relations (Wilcox 8).

To a great extent, feminism is the philosophy responsible for shifting that terrain and creating a wider set of opportunities for women and men. Female workers currently make up half the paid labor force, 40 percent of whom hold management positions, and most American women have wide access to safe legal birth control and abortion, however tenuous that guarantee might be (*The Shriver Report*). Men and women of all ages benefit from the successes of feminism, but many are unwilling to associate themselves with that movement.[1] The label "feminism" scares students far more than the idea that men and women ought to have equal access to power in society. Over the past four years, for example, my first-year seminar classes have included male and female students in equal numbers, with female students outnumbering men in the most recent class. The fact that today women earn 60 percent of college degrees reflects modern patterns in education and reinforces the notion that feminism is no longer necessary because it has achieved its central goal — equal access to opportunity (*The Shriver Report*). When prompted, students in my classes generally agree that changes such as these in the United States are positive, but they worry that feminists are interested in creating a system in which women dominate men. To many of them, this domination is what feminism means.

We know that the feminist movement has had many successes, but a fundamental redistribution of power between men and women remains in the works. One needs to look no further than the membership of the Supreme Court, the U.S. Senate or poverty statistics to see that full parity in American life has not been achieved. At present, women earn seventy-six cents on the male dollar and women are "40 percent more likely [than men] to be poor" (Valenti 111). Couples continue to battle over the "second shift," struggling to assign childcare, housecleaning and cooking responsibilities equally between them. Men continue to do less housecleaning than women even if both partners work outside the home, and many families find it difficult to afford childcare in a nation that does not subsidize it for all citizens (Valenti 123). These inequities reveal little about the sexist stereotypes that wander freely through Hollywood blockbusters and television shows where women do not enjoy equal representation behind the cameras, in boardrooms or in the writers' room (Casey et al., 96).

Hollywood filmmakers and network television executives have long depended upon the exploits of male heroes to engage audiences. It is "their action that is central to the narrative" and their perspective through which the story is told (Heinecken 8–9). Blockbusters typically place male characters in dangerous situations where they prevail based upon their intellect, strength and masculine prowess. When women appear in such films, often, they are depicted as corollary to men: perhaps as wives, girlfriends, or victims. Television shows began to shift their representation of women near the time that second-wave feminism emerged. As they switched the dial in the sixties, seventies and eighties, women caught glimpses of smarts and ability in Samantha Stevens, Jill Munroe and Diana Prince (Douglas). Networks continued to glamorize and sexualize these women, especially the likes of *Charlie's Angels*, reminding the audience that women should not abandon physical beauty in their quest to free the nation of criminals (Douglas 212–216; Levine 169). In the 1980s when television shows expanded fictional women's career options further, as in *thirtysomething*, they also questioned their decision to leave home and family for the workplace (Douglas 274; Faludi 160–167). Fully-formed complex female characters were still hard to find on television in the early 1990s when Whedon stepped in to fill this void. His stories are peopled by "girls who can fight, who can stand up for themselves, who have opinions and fears and cute outfits" (Whedon qtd. in Stuller 74). Whedon's writing does not separate physical appearance from female empowerment. At the same time, *Buffy* is "critical of traditional femininity" (Heinecken 110). Like Buffy, Willow and Xander, college students routinely attempt to balance the value of physical appearance with their own self-concept and desire for personal relationships.

My course, "Decoding *Buffy the Vampire Slayer*," exposes first-year students to these issues and creates an environment for them to critique and assess gender relations through the medium of popular culture. This course is one of Nebraska Wesleyan University's Liberal Arts Seminars (LAS) designed to teach first-semester college students how to think critically, conduct research, synthesize information from multiple sources, and to write and present their analytical findings clearly ("Preparing for Global Citizenship" 44). Students select the topic for their LAS from a list of courses. Not every student records my course as their top choice and occasionally one or two find themselves in the class not having listed it as a preference at all. As a result, I teach a mix of fans and first-time viewers. Nebraska Wesleyan University encourages instructors to choose a topic that will pique student interest and supply texts worthy of analysis and research. *Buffy* is such a topic and text and I am an historian of women's history, a feminist and a Whedon fan. Creating a full course around *Buffy* has made it possible for me to bring together all of these identities. By semester's end, students have learned to approach popular culture with a critical eye and to make connections between what they see on screen and the world around them. Feminism forms the subtext of the course, but it is not the central focus. It is one of the themes that a concentrated study of *Buffy* lends itself to, alongside those of identity, race, and sexuality.

I have taught this course four times and varied my pedagogical approach to feminism each academic year. I never begin the semester by teaching about feminism per se, though the theme is embedded in the course syllabus, assigned readings and in *Buffy*. Instead, I take a back-door approach in which I wait for the students to appreciate and critique *Buffy* first, then break the news to them about five weeks into the semester that a show they respect and enjoy is indeed feminist in origin. I take this subtle line because it is less threatening to students who initially have a negative view of feminism. Perhaps I am catering to their distorted perception of the subject, fearful of challenging them as soon as they walk through the classroom door. I prefer to think that this course design cultivates open minds that would otherwise snap shut without ever contemplating *Buffy* as a serious text, let alone consider feminism as a worthwhile philosophy. I have had more success teaching feminism to first-semester college students without labeling it as such right away than I would have had otherwise.

Most students enter the class having only fleeting memories of *Buffy*, while a few recall watching it as children with their parents. Their limited knowledge about the series is not a problem and can sometimes be an asset.[2] I introduce the core Scooby Gang members Buffy, Giles, Willow and Xander over the first two class periods. During the second and third weeks of the semester, students quickly get up to speed about life in Sunnydale by researching a specific character and presenting information about that character, including a two minute episode clip, to the class. With 15–18 students in the class these presentations cover a great deal of territory and serve as a tutorial overview for all seven seasons. I do not teach a spoiler-free course, so students become scholars first, and many become scholar-fans by the end of the semester. Rhonda Wilcox's *Why Buffy Matters* serves as the course reader and shows students by example how to make connections between *Buffy* and other texts. The students watch and analyze the episodes highlighted in her book, discussing "The Zeppo" (3.13), "Surprise" (2.13), "Innocence" (2.14) and "Hush" (4.10) during the first half of the course, and "Restless" (4.22), "The Body" (5.16) and "Once More, with Feeling" (6.7) at the end. They answer a set of questions that I provide them with before they watch each episode. We spend a full class period discussing the episodes, some of which they view outside of class. Students soon discover that Wilcox is correct. *Buffy* is a significant piece of art, part of the television canon that offers a rich variety of episodes to unravel, critique and compare to other significant works produced across time and place.

Students put Wilcox's thesis into practice throughout the semester when they read, discuss, and write about historical documents and novels paired with pertinent *Buffy* episodes. For example, they evaluate documents from the 1691–1692 Salem Witch Trials including excerpts from the court cases against accused witches Sarah Good and Martha Corey. I contextualize these documents with information about women's place and value within Puritan society, as well as some characteristics about Puritan New England in general. Puritans for example, abided by a special covenant with God in which they were his "chosen" people. They privileged hierarchy, order, and patriarchy to fulfill the covenant and avoid God's wrath. Puritan neighbors policed one another in a practice called "holy watching" (Winthrop 26). After an in-class viewing of "Gingerbread" (3.11), students answer questions from the handout that ask them to compare the actions of Sunnydale residents with those of seventeenth-century New Englanders. They quickly observe that Sunnydale's adult residents engage in their own version of "holy watching" as they pry into their children's lives, checking lockers and invading student spaces. They also discuss the misgivings Joyce and Sheila have about their teenage daughters, Buffy and Willow. They make comparisons between Buffy's competing identities (daughter, slayer, girlfriend, student) and the multiple identities they embody as students, friends, children, and siblings. J.P. Williams' article "Choosing Your Own Mother" provides additional material for the class discussion. "Gingerbread" is an effective text to spur critical thinking because it encourages students to draw comparisons across time and space about women's fraught relationships with one another and their communities.

The course material then moves from Puritan New England to European Romanticism, followed by Victorianism. Students read Mary Shelley's *Frankenstein*, after which we view clips from "Goodbye Iowa" (4.14) and then we discuss the similarities and differences between Shelley's Creature and Whedon's Adam. They also read Anita Rose's article "*Buffy* Does Frankenstein." This combination of texts leads to provocative in-class discussions during which students draw comparisons between Whedon's discomfort with attempts to perfect humanity through technology, Shelley's fear of "man playing God" and their own concerns about cloning and stem cell research. Just as *Frankenstein* maintains its relevance to today's society, so too does *Buffy*. Bram Stoker's *Dracula* makes up the final significant piece of reading that the students do in the course. I situate *Dracula* in the Victorian era and help students connect Lucy's hypersexuality, and Mina's chaste embodiment of womanhood with Victorian notions of female deviance and respectability. They read a number of articles which yield fruitful discussion about the persistence of the vampire myth in literature, television, and films (Cox; Erickson; DeKelb-Ritten-house). Students eagerly compare the seductive Count Dracula with Whedon's depictions of Angelus and Spike. We spend a full class period comparing the qualities and skills of Stoker's Dracula with those of Whedon's vampires. Inevitably, a number of students also draw comparisons to Stephanie Meyer's Edward Cullen from the *Twilight* novels. When students compare *Buffy* alongside other texts, they express a greater appreciation for modern television's place in the larger sphere of popular culture.

I reveal *Buffy's* feminist origins to the class after students have completed character presentations, studied the Salem Witch Trials, and critiqued several episodes. The two-class-period lesson begins when I ask students the question that introduces this essay, "What is feminism?" After listing their frequently negative responses on the board, I ask another question, "Do you like *Buffy the Vampire Slayer*?" Every semester, nearly every student in the room has said yes. With some glee in my heart, I then say, "Guess what? Whedon created *Buffy* as a feminist show." They usually respond with looks of surprise and mild discomfort at this news. I continue the lesson by delivering a "race through women's history" lecture. This lecture is fast-paced, relies heavily on images, and its purpose is to move students through U.S. women's history from the seventeenth century to the present. I touch on the American Revolution and Republican Motherhood, chattel slavery, the Cult of True Womanhood, separate spheres ideology, industrialization, poverty and immigration, married women's property laws, the Seneca Falls Convention, Victorian sexual ideology, the Comstock Act, passage of the 19th Amendment, flappers, the Great Depression, Rosie the Riveter, the baby boom and "return to domesticity," the Student Non-Violent Coordinating Committee (SNCC), Students for a Democratic Society (SDS), and the Women's Liberation Movement (Evans; Rosen). Then, with the help of Susan Douglas's *Where the Girls Are*, I trace the ways in which popular culture has chosen to deal with women's empowerment or invisibility on television from *I Love Lucy* to *Bewitched* and *I Dream of Jeannie*, then to *Wonder Woman* and *Charlie's Angels*, and on to *Cagney & Lacey*, *Full House*, and finally ending with *Buffy*. The purpose of the lecture is not to do a thorough study of women's history, but to reinforce the notion that the actions of men and women over time have created a much more equitable society in which contemporary students now live. This society emerged despite the persistence of the very "blond girl in the alley gets killed first" representation that Whedon attempted to remediate through *Buffy*. I end this lecture with Whedon's own words, "this show is designed to be a feminist show, not a polemic, but a very straight-on feminist show" ("Innocence," 2.14). Students respond thoughtfully and tentatively to the women's history lecture and news that *Buffy* can be seen as a feminist text. For example, they do not immediately jump up and cry, "I have seen the light! I am now a feminist!" Instead, they process this information throughout the rest of the semester and beyond.

While Whedon has asserted *Buffy's* feminist nature and mission, the primary characters within the series never identify themselves as such. Much of the time, they simply behave as independent women and supportive men who work in concert to save the world from monsters and apocalypses. This is not to say character relationships are free of conflict. In fact, Buffy, Xander, Willow, Giles, and everyone else in Sunnydale are at times selfish, arrogant and thoughtless. Yet in the *Buffy*verse these behaviors have consequences that ultimately remind the characters that sharing power with friends and family, as well as in intimate sexual relationships is healthier than amassing power and privileging oneself above others. In essence, feminist communities are stronger and more nourishing than ones rooted in patriarchal hierarchy (Payne-Mulliken and Renegar 69). My students consume one episode of *Buffy* after another in the first half of the semester without associating beloved characters with disconcerting feminist stereotypes. The series' tacit feminist underpinnings have made it possible for me to show students what feminism can look like in practice, before attaching a label to those practices.

The first time I taught the course I followed the "race through women's history" with scenes 12–15 of "I Was Made to Love You" (5.15) to illustrate the show's distinctly feminist viewpoint.[3] In this episode Warren designs and builds himself the perfect girlfriend, a robot named April who is beautiful, submissive, and loyal. Since this is the *Buffy*verse, April does not turn out to be perfect. What transpires next serves as a feminist comment on some women's misplaced desire to transform themselves in an effort to please a boyfriend. Warren soon finds April's ceaseless attention clingy and suffocating, while April is incapable of understanding why Warren rejects her in favor of Katrina. He has chosen a woman who in many respects is the opposite of April: one who is argumentative, independent and altogether human. Warren, who is at a loss as to how to control April, pits another strong woman, Buffy against her. Buffy defeats the robot only when April's batteries begin to run down. In one of the most poignant scenes in the series, Buffy sits with a dying April on a playground swing set and comforts her. April cannot even cry in her moment of grief, because "crying is blackmail, good girlfriends don't cry." When we discussed the scene afterward, students said it sent the message that it was not healthy or necessary for a girl to "live for a guy." This analysis echoes writer Jane Espenson's episode commentary that "if you try to make yourself perfect for a man, this is what you get" ("I Was Made to Love You"). "This" being rejection, heartbreak, and loneliness. Female students connected with April's plight more than male students, with several offering examples of former high school friends who turned away from their female friends in favor of one boyfriend or another. The combination of a brief women's history lecture, scenes from "I Was Made to Love You," and two articles about *Buffy* and feminism led to a fruitful discussion with students about the better choices young women can make in relation to men.[4] It did not seem however, to yield a clear redefinition of feminism on their part.

I have since traded Buffy and April's conversation for the pithy acceptance speech Joss Whedon delivered upon receiving an award from Equality Now, because his words suggest a contemporary and accessible definition of feminism. I show the speech directly after the "race through women's history" lecture. Lee Stearns, high school teacher, activist, and Whedon's mother, inspired her former student Jessica Neuwirth to create Equality Now which "work[s] for the protection and promotion of the human rights of women around the world." In 1992, these activists began to "[work] with national human rights organizations and individual activists [to] document violence and discrimination against women and mobilize international action to support their efforts to stop these human rights abuses." This organization honored Whedon in 2006 as a man "on the front lines" whose work counters "the negative stereotypes of women constantly presented by Hollywood" (Equality Now, *All for Equality Annual Report*). In his acceptance speech Whedon pretends to be on a press junket and takes on the personas of a variety of reporters who have asked him versions of the same question over the years, "Why do you write such strong women characters?" The audience finds an uplifting active definition of feminism in his answers. As they watch the speech, students take notes and write down the adjectives Whedon uses to answer the invisible reporters' question. Afterwards, students share their notes with the class and I make a new list on the board, right next to the original "Hillary Clinton" list. The Whedon list includes words such as "tough, cool, inspirational, extraordinary wit, strength, resolve, sexy, smart, funny, hot," and "power." They observe that Whedon writes "strong women characters" because his mother was such a woman, and his father and stepfather "understood recognizing someone else's power does not diminish your own." Students have asked me to define misogyny for them since Whedon argued it "is not a true part of the human condition." They are particularly moved and fascinated by his view that "equality is not a concept it's a necessity like gravity" (*On the Road to Equality*).

The students take his words seriously, because by this point in the semester his writing has earned their respect. As they watch the next two required episodes, "Surprise" and "Innocence," students write about and discuss the connections between love, torture, pain, death and power; how Buffy's life acts as a metaphor for the lives of all adolescents; the issues that inform Buffy's decision to have sex with Angel and how that decision reveals both her maturity and immaturity. Since students are now equipped with the knowledge that Whedon crafted *Buffy* as a feminist series, they are quick to point out that the viewer is seeing the decision to have sex from a female point of view, rather than a male's. One student commented that the episode made her cry, because Angel was so "mean to Buffy." Others noted that they sympathized with Buffy, because their female friends (never themselves) had dated men whose behavior toward them had "changed" after having sex. In this instance, students discussed the ramifications of teen sex, including the sexual double standard, in a classroom setting without discomfort or fear. They were talking about characters, not themselves. Once again, Buffy's "emotional realism" shines through and connects to its audience.

As I discussed earlier, students' acceptance of their own feminism and the label itself is a gradual process that the *Buffy* course puts in motion. Over the past four years I have kept in touch with most of my students and witnessed how their personalities and politics develop and change. Certainly not all of my former *Buffy* students embrace the feminist label, but some do. Several credit the show and Whedon's Equality Now speech for that transformation. For example, three years after having taken the course, Alex, a male student, wrote the following:

Buffy made me a feminist by making the ideology accessible. For people, like me, that grew up in a conservative, mid-west home this class and *Buffy* may be the only honest view of feminism that they ever get. *Buffy* essentially showed me the truth of feminism: how there is significant inequality and that accepting a woman's strength does not make a man weak. As a young man, I found Whedon's speech to be especially helpful in my acceptance of feminism. Whedon's speech showed feminism as logical, moral and sexy. It essentially showed me how backward, wrong, and ignorant it was not to be a feminist.

Alex also noted that the ease with which Xander "accepted and encouraged Buffy and Willow's strength" also appealed to him. Jennifer agreed with Alex that seeing Whedon's positive views of feminism persuaded her to reconsider the philosophy: "I never thought about men being feminists either, but knowing Joss Whedon is a feminist was actually pretty inspiring. If a man can recognize equality between genders then it's safe to say I can identify myself as a feminist." Another student, Laura, revealed that "taking the *Buffy* LAS expanded my view of feminism because before taking it, all I knew about feminism were the stereotypes associated with it. Once we addressed the stereotypes and were shown examples of real feminism, we all felt pretty silly for ever thinking differently." She went on to say, "I am [now] proud to call myself a feminist and share with others what real feminism is all about." These responses are gratifying, because part of my hope is that students will take from the course a positive representation of feminism. Even more gratifying is the response from Marlana who confirmed my belief in the value of teaching with popular culture. She wrote that after having taken the *Buffy* course, "I think that now I pay more attention to the television I watch. I notice on certain shows how women are portrayed as just sexual objects, or how on shows like *Castle* there are strong female figures who are both beautiful, strong and independent. I just think that now I do more than just watch: I actually decipher feminist ideas in the shows I watch."[5] As the title of the course suggests, Marlana learned first to "decode" *Buffy* and now she watches other television shows through an analytical and a feminist lens.

Watching and studying *Buffy*, alongside other texts and in conjunction with Whedon's own words about how and why he chooses to write those "strong woman characters" has the ability to transform student definitions of feminism. Some then take the next step and embrace the concept as part of their identity and realign their views of men, women, equality and popular culture as a result. Whedon once said that "If I made a series of lectures for PBS on why there should be feminism, no one would be coming to the party, and it would be boring. The idea of changing culture is important to me and it can only be done in a popular medium" (qtd. in Stuller 7). My own pedagogical goals include the creation of critical thinkers who carry what they learn about *Buffy*, feminism, and analytical questioning beyond the walls of the university. Evidence from my classroom experiences suggests that we are both accomplishing our goals, one viewer and one student at a time.[6]

NOTES

1. Scholars refer to the second phase of the U.S. women's movement as second wave feminism which took place during the 1960s and 1970s. First wave feminism focused on obtaining legal rights for

women, such as married women's property rights and the right to vote. Second wave feminism attempted to address multiple issues such as inequality in the workplace, reproductive freedom and the re-ordering of family relations. Third wave or contemporary feminism is pluralistic and concerned with issues of sexual orientation and equal rights, continues to challenge patriarchy and includes multiple perspectives from women of all ethnic, racial and religious backgrounds. See Sara Evans, *Born for Liberty,* bell hooks, *Feminist Theory,* and Ruth Rosen, *The World Split Open.*

2. See David Kociemba's article in this collection.

3. For another perspective on how to teach feminism with this episode see Rod Romesburg's essay in this collection.

4. Over the years I have assigned various combinations of Carolyn Cocca's "First Word Jail, Second Word Bait," assorted chapters from Lorna Jowett's *Sex and the Slayer,* and Sherryl Vint's "Killing us Softly: A Feminist Search for the Real Buffy."

5. Each of these students granted permission for their words to be used here. Alex Bednar, "Questions About *Buffy.*" E-mail to the author. 3 March 2010; Jennifer Wiederspan. "Questions About *Buffy.*" E-mail to the author. 6 March 2010; Laura Cejka. "Questions About *Buffy.*" E-mail to the author. 28 February, 2010; Marlana Randall. "Questions About *Buffy.*" E-mail to the author. 28 February, 2010.

6. The author would like to thank Alex Bednar, Kevin Bower, Tanya Cochran, Jodie Kreider, and Lisa Wilkinson for their thoughtful critiques of this article.

WORKS CITED

Casey, Bernadette, Neil Casey, Ben Calvert, Liam French and Justin Lewis, eds. *Television Studies: The Key Concepts.* New York: London: 2002. Print.

Cocca, Carolyn. "First World 'Jail,' Second Word 'Bait'": Adolescent Sexuality, Feminist Theories, and *Buffy the Vampire Slayer.*" *Slayage: The Whedon Studies Association Journal* 3.2 (n.date): n.pag. Web.

Cox, J. Renée. "Got Myself a Soul? The Puzzling Treatment of the Soul in *Buffy.*" *The Truth of Buffy: Essays on Fiction Illuminating Reality.* Eds. Emily Dial-Driver, Sally Emmons-Featherston, Jim Ford and Carolyn Anne Taylor. Jefferson, NC: McFarland, 2008. 24–37. Print.

Douglas, Susan. *Where the Girls Are: Growing Up Female with the Mass Media.* New York: Times Books, 1995. Print.

DeKelb-Rittenhouse, Diane. "Sex and the Single Vampire: The Evolution of the Vampire Lothario and Its Representation in *Buffy.*" *Fighting the Forces: What's at Stake in* Buffy the Vampire Slayer. Eds. Rhonda V. Wilcox and David Lavery. New York: Rowman & Littlefield, 2002. 143–152. Print.

Early, F. "Staking Her Claim: Buffy the Vampire Slayer as Transgressive Woman Warrior." *Slayage* 6 (2002): n.pag. Web.

Erickson, Gregory. "Sometimes You Need a Story: American Christianity, Vampires, and *Buffy.*" *Fighting the Forces: What's at Stake in* Buffy the Vampire Slayer. Eds. Rhonda V. Wilcox and David Lavery. New York: Rowman & Littlefield, 2002. 108–119. Print.

Espenson, Jane. "I Was Made to Love You" Commentary. *Buffy the Vampire Slayer: The Complete Fifth Season.* 20th Century–Fox. 2003. DVD.

Equality Now. *All for Equality: Annual Report.* 2006.

_____. Web. 5 April 2010. <http://www.equalitynow.org>.

Evans, Sara. *Born for Liberty: A History of Women in America.* New York: Free Press Paperbacks, 1997. Print.

Faludi, Susan. *Backlash: The Undeclared War Against American Women.* New York: Crown, 1991. Print.

Frankenstein, by Mary Shelley, *Dracula* by Bram Stoker, *Dr. Jekyll and Mr. Hyde* by Robert Louis Stevenson. With an introduction by Steven King. New York: Signet Classic, 1978. Print.

Heinecken, Dawn. *The Warrior Women of Television: A Feminist Cultural Analysis of the New Female Body in Popular Media.* New York: Peter Lang, 2003. Print.

Hibbs, Thomas. "*Buffy the Vampire Slayer* as Feminist *Noir.*" Buffy the Vampire Slayer *and Philosophy: Fear and Trembling in Sunnydale.* Ed. James B. South. Chicago: Open Court, 2005. 49–60. Print.

hooks, bell. *Feminist Theory: From Margin to Center.* Second Edition. Cambridge, MA: South End Press Classics, 2000. Print.

"I Was Made to Love You." *Buffy the Vampire Slayer: The Complete Fifth Season.* 20th Century–Fox. 2003. DVD.

Inness, Sherrie, ed. "Introduction," *Geek Chic: Smart Women in Popular Culture*. New York: Palgrave Macmillan, 2007. Print.

Jowett, Lorna. *Sex and the Slayer: A Gender Studies Primer for the Buffy Fan*. Wesleyan University Press, 2005. Print.

Levine, Elana. "*Buffy* and the 'New Girl Order'" Defining Feminism and Femininity." *Undead TV: Essays on* Buffy the Vampire Slayer. Ed. Elana Levine and Lisa Parks. Durham: Duke University Press, 2007. 168–189. Print.

Marinucci, Mimi. "Feminism and the Ethics of Violence: Why Buffy Kicks Ass." Buffy the Vampire Slayer *and Philosophy: Fear and Trembling in Sunnydale*. Ed. James B. South. Chicago: Open Court, 2005. 61–76. Print.

Miller, Jessica Prata. "The I in Team": Buffy and Feminist Ethics." Buffy the Vampire Slayer *and Philosophy: Fear and Trembling in Sunnydale*. Ed. James B. South. Chicago: Open Court, 2005. 35–48. Print.

Payne-Mulliken, Susan, and Valerie Renegar. "Buffy Never Goes It Alone: The Rhetorical Construction of Sisterhood in the Final Season." *Buffy Meets the Academy: Essays on the Episodes and Scripts as Texts*. Ed. Kevin Durand. Jefferson, NC: McFarland, 2009. 57–77. Print.

Pender, Patricia. "'I'm Buffy and You're ... History': the Postmodern Politics of *Buffy the Vampire Slayer*." *Fighting the Forces: What's at Stake in* Buffy the Vampire Slayer. Lanham, MD: Rowman Littlefield, 2002. 35–44. Print.

"Preparing for Global Citizenship" General Education Requirements and Faculty Declaration of Educational Intent. Nebraska Wesleyan University Course Catalog 2009–2011. 41–49. Print.

Rose, Anita. "Of Creatures and Creators: *Buffy* Does *Frankenstein*." *Fighting the Forces: What's at Stake in* Buffy the Vampire Slayer. Eds. Rhonda V. Wilcox and David Lavery. Lanham, MD: Rowman Littlefield, 2002. 133–142. Print.

Rosen, Ruth. *The World Split Open: How the Modern Women's Movement Changed America*. New York: Penguin Books, 2000. Print.

The Shriver Report: A Study by Maria Shriver and the Center for American Progress. 2009. Web.

Stuller, Jennifer K. *Ink-Stained Amazons and Cinematic Warriors: Superwomen in Modern Mythology*. New York: IB Tauris, 2010. Print.

Valenti, Jessica. *Full Frontal Feminism: A Young Woman's Guide to Why Feminism Matters*. Berkeley, CA: Seal Press, 2007. Print.

Vint, Sherryl. "Killing Us Softly?" A Feminist Search for the "Real" Buffy." *Slayage* 2:1 (n.date): n.pag. Web.

Whedon, Joss. "Innocence" Commentary. *Buffy the Vampire Slayer: The Complete Second Season*. 20th Century–Fox. 2002. DVD.

_____. *On the Road to Equality, Equality Now Award Show*. Unknown Location. 15 May 2006. Award Acceptance Speech. Web. 5 April 2010. <http://www.youtube.com/watch?v=cYaczoJMRhs>

Wilcox, Rhonda. *Why Buffy Matters: The Art of* Buffy the Vampire Slayer. New York: IB Tauris, 2005. Print.

Williams, J.P. "Choosing Your Own Mother: Mother-Daughter Conflicts in *Buffy*." *Fighting the Forces: What's at Stake in* Buffy the Vampire Slayer. Eds. Rhonda V. Wilcox and David Lavery. Lanham, MD: Rowman Littlefield, 2002. 133–142. Print.

Winthrop, John. "The Model of Christian Charity," *The Salem Witch Trials Reader*. Ed. Frances Hill. Cambridge, MA: Da Capo Press, 2000. 26–27. Print.

Buffy Goes to College:
Identity and the Series-Based Seminar Course

Rod Romesburg

As college teachers know, or anyone who experienced those turbulent college years remembers, students in college are obsessed with themselves. Recognizing this, many universities design first-year composition courses around writing about the self to teach students how to write and think critically about their favorite and most intimately experienced topic. Texts like *Buffy the Vampire Slayer* that treat seriously the development of identity in young adults can therefore be valuable to the university instructor, capturing students' interest by providing a world with which they easily identify while also allowing them the critical distance to critique the characters and events of that world without exposing their own personal insecurities to their peers. Although *Buffy* begins with a fantastical premise — that one female in the world becomes the vampire slayer, weighted with the responsibility of fighting vampires and demons until she is killed and destiny calls another — its realistically complex treatment of character and themes provide a depth belying the cavalier title. Additionally, because *Buffy* follows its central characters over seven seasons, from roughly sophomore year in high school into college and early adulthood, young adult students can recognize in these characters who they have been, who they are, and who they believe they may or may not be in the near future. Finally, the sheer number of episodes involved provides a broad range of themes addressed with great sophistication. *Buffy* thus provides rich material for a university seminar course examining three aspects of identity — stages of life, femininity/feminism, and masculinity.

Before discussing *Buffy* and identity, however, I need to explain the structure of the two *Buffy* courses I have designed. The first was a Freshman Seminar at The Ohio State University. The seminars are small classes exclusively for first-year students, one- or two-credits, based around a theme or research interest of the faculty member, such as the end of the world, nanotechnology, extraterrestrials, or the physics of baseball. Faculty members design their seminar to be both fun and academically-based — to introduce first-year students to the exciting possibilities of university education in a venue outside typical general education requirements and in some cases large, impersonal lecture courses. My second *Buffy* course was an Intersession course at Rollins College in Winter Park, Florida. Like OSU's Freshman Seminars, Intersession courses are intensive: one- or two-credit courses focused on a single theme or topic area, and offered for one week before Spring semester. Unlike the Freshmen Seminars, these courses accept students of all ranks and draw more upper- than lower-rank students.

Neither is a traditional college course, which brings advantages and disadvantages. First, their compressed nature, both in class time and credits offered, limits the out-of-class work expected of students. Reading assignments must be fairly brief and at a more general-audience level than in a regular course. In addition to select essays, a few of which I detail later, each course had a primary textbook. The first-year students read Rhonda Wilcox's *Why Buffy Matters*. Wilcox's book is both scholarly and accessible to a general audience, ideal for students new to college and perhaps unfamiliar with academic jargon. Additionally, she structures chapters around individual episodes, most of which I wanted to use in my Freshman Seminar. Wilcox covers ground not already explored by others, so while she addresses issues of identity, and especially femininity, feminism, and masculinity, it is not her focus. The more-experienced Intersession students possessed greater critical sophistication, permitting me to assign Lorna Jowett's *Sex and the Slayer*. Jowett writes well and clarifies complex ideas, but the density of her prose works better for advanced students than first-years.

As with the readings, the courses' compressed natures limited the amount of out-of-class work students produced. In both classes, students wrote response papers in which they had to choose a specific scene or few lines of dialogue from an episode, or a short passage from the reading assignment, and then perform a close reading of that limited selection.[1] By forcing students to focus on a smaller component of an episode or reading rather than a general review or reaction, they had to specify what they were thinking or feeling, how the specific language encouraged such reactions, how their own experiences influenced their reading, and what, critically, they had to say about the text. This worked especially well in my Freshmen Seminar because we met on Mondays and watched an episode. By Tuesday at midnight, students emailed me their response papers. When class gathered again on Wednesday to discuss the episode, I could say, "Jenna, you noted something interesting about Xander's attitude toward his car," allowing students to confidently enter our discussion. Frequently, too, students raised issues in responses that I had not considered and would open new avenues of discussion.

A second consequence of these non-traditional courses is their informality. While the limited amount of in- and out-of-class time sacrifices some depth in how much and how deeply the class can delve into *Buffy* and the criticism and themes surrounding it, it also permits some freedom in that those approving such courses do not expect it to meet the same standards as a typical course. I could build both courses around *Buffy* rather than merely using the show as a modern incarnation of a larger theme like vampires in literature, an illustration of a lesson, or material for an assignment. This structure, though, presents its own challenges. For example, I could not expect students to purchase the entire series to watch the handful of assigned episodes. Therefore, I had to use class time to view episodes. For the Freshman Seminar this worked fairly well, having students read before they watched, watch the episode, think and write about what they had seen, and then meet for discussion. In the Intersession class students read ahead of time but we then watched and immediately discussed what students had seen. This approach added freshness to the discussion, but sacrificed critical depth students may have uncovered had they more time to contemplate.

Another issue with basing an entire course around a single television show is the varying degree of familiarity students have with the show. Some students had never seen an episode, while others had created their own fan websites and/or written fan-fiction. Anticipating this, I avoided building the course around particular characters or plot points, which would leave less–*Buffy*-obsessed students out of the loop and perhaps bore those not requiring a lot of filling-in-the-background. To accommodate, I structured both courses so that each day had a broader theme. Organizing by themes helped those new to *Buffy* feel they were working on a single text rather than a chapter out of a novel they had not read. Additionally, in order to keep students focused on the details of the day's theme rather than where an episode fits in the series' progress I avoided relying upon any sort of chronological ordering of the episodes. Obviously, my approach sacrifices many layers of character development and season/series arcs — I spend only a few minutes of the first day of class introducing the major characters, their roles, and their relationships. Throughout the semester, however, the more-informed students tended to bring their deeper knowledge of the characters and their experiences into our discussions, anyway. On the whole, I have had more than enough student-evaluations expressing gratitude for not feeling "left out" to justify this strategy.

Beyond these nuts-and-bolts of the *Buffy* courses, the greatest moments of learning and enjoyment came in discussing the show's episodes and themes. Both courses shared a pedagogical goal of being discussion-based to encourage student interaction with the materials, teacher, and each other. Centering the course around *Buffy* also helped with student discussion. Those who loved the show were eager to discuss something about which they cared deeply. Those first-time viewers felt less intimidated discussing a television show than "real" literature because it is a medium with which they were intimately familiar and which they viewed as entertainment or pop-culture rather than as a "scholarly" text. Such a comfort level became especially important with linking identity-related themes and *Buffy*, because I deliberately asked students to reflect on how what we were reading and watching connected with their own experiences. In an environment that felt less comfortable, class discussions would be more confined and learning moments — those instances when students feel the ground of familiar assumptions slipping beneath them — less frequent.

One reason *Buffy* inspires such moments so well is because the show emphasizes how young people construct, and how others construct for them, their identity.[2] For students, college provides a crucial opportunity to break from a sense of self forged through family, friends, and past experiences. In interviews with 23 college-bound students, David Karp, Lynda Lytle Holmstrom, and Paul Gray reported that "students saw college as the time for discovering who they *really* were," characterizing "the importance of going away to college in terms of an opportunity to discard disliked identities while making a variety of 'fresh starts'" (258).[3] One possible approach to address the high school-to-college transition would be to focus on episodes from the beginning of Season Four, when Buffy Summers and her friend Willow Rosenberg graduate from Sunnydale High and move on to University of California-Sunnydale. Episodes such as "Living Conditions" (4.2) and

"Beer Bad" (4.5), turn common first-year experiences like bad roommates and binge drinking into supernatural challenges Buffy and her friends must address. However, rather than the type of shared experiences these episodes illustrate so well, my classes focus on more thematic issues of identity formation.

To foreground this, students began by reading two pieces addressing theories about the students' current stage of life and then watched episodes that illustrated the concepts and allowed the class to discuss both how the show addresses such issues and how they experienced the theories in their own lives.[4] To begin, students read an excerpt from Erik Erikson's classic work on psychology *Identity: Youth and Crisis*, detailing the stage of identity formation Erikson associates with adolescence. Erikson argues each stage of life confronts the individual with an "identity crisis" the individual must negotiate to progress to the next stage. For adolescents, the crisis comes in a battle to find larger ideas or people outside of themselves in which to believe, while at the same time being "preoccupied with what they appear to be in the eyes of others as compared with what they feel they are" (128). After reading Erikson, students watched the episode "Out of Mind, Out of Sight" (1.11), in which a Sunnydale High student Marcie, described in the shooting script as "so mousy she's the human equivalent of wallpaper," literally becomes invisible because the students and even teachers at Sunnydale High have ignored her presence.[5]

The episode, scripted by show creator Joss Whedon, explores multiple questions of identity: How do we define who we are? How do we build a sense of identity? How much do others control our own sense of self? What do we gain or lose through how others perceive us? Several characters in this episode struggle with who they are: Marcie; Buffy; Cordelia Chase, the seemingly ultra-confident queen bee of Sunnydale High; and even Angel, the 200-year-old vampire with a soul who fights beside Buffy and serves as her love interest. In discussion, students tended to quickly identify the episode's primary conceit of how Marcie, and by extension all adolescents, constructs a sense of identity by envisioning herself through others' eyes, and the implication that if that recognition is taken away, the self can disappear as well. They noted that Buffy, a newcomer to Sunnydale, struggles not only with her unwanted role of vampire slayer but also with how she fits with her friends and classmates. Students also identified a scene in which Cordelia, who seems to bear the confidence that wealth, status, and good looks provide, confesses to Buffy her own insecurities about whether or not people like her for herself or for her role as the alpha-female of Sunnydale High.

To focus the discussion, I re-screened a scene set in the girls' bathroom. Marcie is gazing at herself in the mirror when Cordelia, her friend Harmony, and two other "Cordettes" enter. The clique is mocking an alumnus' slideshow of his trip to Nepal. Marcie, physically positioned outside the group, laughs along and interjects that the man's toupee "looked like a cabbage," but her comment goes unacknowledged. As the clique continues the cut-downs, Marcie interjects a second time with the toupee comment, only to be rejected by Harmony's, "We're talking, okay?" Cordelia then makes the same toupee comment, same wording, to the delight of the Cordettes. As they leave, "the girl's eager smile slowly fades" and Marcie is left gazing "at the mirror, alone" ("Out of Mind, Out of Sight").

As shown in the response papers, having students concentrate their critical attention on this small segment encouraged them to look for details that might be overlooked when watching the entire episode. I asked in what ways the scene shows Marcie being denied a sense of identity. Students quickly pointed out the symbolism of the mirror that figures in the scene's opening and closing, emphasizing that the only one who really sees Marcie is herself. One *Buffy*-fanatic student connected this to the preceding scene, when Buffy's Watcher, a guide who trains the vampire slayer, speculates that being invisible would be powerful. Angel, who as a vampire casts no reflection, counters, "Looking in the mirror every day and seeing nothing there.... It's an overrated pleasure" ("Out of Mind, Out of Sight"). The other clear exclusion is the way Cordelia and her friends treat Marcie. This connects back to Erickson's observation that "Young people can be remarkably clannish, intolerant, and cruel in their exclusion of others who are 'different,' in skin color or cultural background, in tastes and gifts, and often in entirely petty aspects of dress and gesture arbitrarily selected as the signs of an in-grouper or an out-grouper" (132). The class discussed the Cordettes' cruel comments towards Marcie as well as how ignoring Marcie's comments became an equally effective means of exclusion. Students frequently compared this scene, and especially the importance of cliques in adolescence, to their own middle- and high-school experiences, empathizing with Marcie as the victim of emotional abuse delivered by the Cordettes. I then asked, if Marcie could join the Cordettes, would she? Obviously, she hungers for inclusion in their group, even though she recognizes how the Cordettes operate. Her attempted means of entry, after all, is to insult another person. Again, I connected what we have watched back to Erickson, who argues that adolescents suffering from identity crisis "temporarily overidentify with the heroes of cliques and crowds to the point of an apparently complete loss of individuality" (132). Marcie hopes establishing a Cordette identity will give her *some* sense of being rather than nothingness. If it worked, she would quickly proceed to exclude others the way she had herself been excluded, because that is the method most adolescents employ to survive this stage's identity crisis: to garner one's individual identity by surrendering individuality in favor of group identification. When I asked if they see elements of the broader American culture encouraging young people to situate themselves within a group identity, students pointed to elements of media — particularly advertising and television programs — as primary examples. Marcie is clearly the episode's antagonist, but the students' familiarity with her adolescent identity crisis complicates simple good-versus-bad categorization.

The second identity-centered essay the students read is by Jeffrey J. Arnett, Research Professor in Psychology at Clark University. Arnett theorizes that cultural shifts in Western industrial nations have created a new phase of life between adolescence and adulthood — emerging adulthood. Primarily because of the gap higher education provides from the late teens through the late twenties, this population experiences a period with few of the restrictions imposed in youth and none of the expectations associated with typical markers of adulthood such as marriage, children, and career.[6] When Arnett surveys such a group if they feel they have reached adulthood, nearly two-thirds respond "yes and no," showing their own ambivalence concerning where they fit into the culture's familiar categories of maturity (472). The same respondents do not identify those typical markers of adulthood (marriage, children, career) as threshold points but instead look to "individualistic qualities of character" (472–3), leading to an overall perception of "becoming a self-sufficient person" (473):

- Accepting responsibilities for one's self
- Making independent decisions
- Becoming financially independent

Arnett's essay focuses on how emerging adults use this time to explore possibilities and refine their identity concerning love, work, and worldviews.

Buffy provides a multitude of episodes that illuminate the exploration of identity associated with emerging adulthood. Students recognize the job versus career pressures that Buffy addresses in "Doublemeat Palace" (6.12), when she must take a job in a fast-food restaurant to pay the bills, even while her career as a vampire slayer continues. Another useful episode is "Selfless" (7.5), in which Anya, a demon-turned-human reverts back to being a demon after her fiancée leaves her at the altar. She constructs and deconstructs her sense of self through her romantic and career experiences.

The episode that generated the most lively student discussions concerning emerging adulthood is "The Replacement" (5.3), which focuses on Xander, one of Buffy's best friends and the fiancée who left Anya. The beginning of the episode emphasizes Xander's distance from "becoming a self-sufficient person," using Arnett's terminology. His clothing, a sloppy, un-tucked floral shirt, signifies his proximity to adolescence. His job as a construction worker (which provides its own sense of inferiority in comparison to all his college-attending friends) is soon ending. He still lives in his parents' basement, where he suffers uncomfortably as his friends try to ignore the shouts of his parents fighting upstairs. He is unable to afford the apartment Anya covets. Then a demon's magic creates a second Xander. After discovering the double, the "real" Xander cringes to see his twin handle Xander's life and challenges with ease. He dresses nicely, with shirt tucked-in and matching socks. He hears from the construction boss that not only is his work "first rate" but he is being promoted to a supervisory position with more responsibility and more pay. The attractive apartment manager comes on to him when they meet for the Xander-double to sign the lease. He even reassures Anya when she confesses fears about getting old and dying, having lost her demon-immortality in becoming human. Xander thinks he must destroy the new Xander, but, in actuality, the demon split Xander into two, creating a Xander bearing his strongest qualities and another with his weakest — the "real" Xander viewers have been following. The episode ends with the two Xanders merged once again.

"The Replacement" works well with Arnett because it provides students with a gap that encourages them not merely to recognize how they identify emerging adult qualities with themselves but also to critique why they desire these qualities over others. When I asked what they thought of Xander at the start, they pointed to the details listed above and agreed he is being portrayed as a failure. We then discussed why the students associate these qualities with failure — what does that say about their own expectations? Since the class was comprised of college students, they fell within the college-to-career young adults Arnett acknowledges as his focus. They therefore tended to share the values of the emerging adult classification, allowing us to question in our discussion why they treasure these values and how the episode expects its audience to agree. For example, I asked what they expected of Xander's double, and the students granted that, like "real" Xander did, they expected him to be evil. Unlike "real" Xander, who the regular *Buffy* audience knows is almost always at least one step behind the other characters and seems nearer to the qualities my students connect to adolescence, this twin bears the successful emerging adult qualities most students wanted to emulate. Eventually, Xander gets his happy ending, with the two halves remerged and Xander confident that he has the capacity to be a successful adult. This ending, however, allowed students to question whether he is happy because he improves as an individual or if he is happy because he now successfully conforms to a larger, societal ideal. This question led as well to a discussion about what the students were doing in college and how much they themselves may be conforming rather than forging their own path.

Both of these stages-of-life readings, Erickson's work on adolescence and Arnett's on emerging adulthood, provide students a means to understand their experiences and expectations. Linking Erickson to "Out of Mind, Out of Sight" and Arnett to "The Replacement" provides an example of the two concepts played before them and also provides material encouraging students to critique the episodes, the ideas, and how students' experience correlates with what they have read and seen. However, while students in both my first-year and Intersession classes did well discussing adolescence, the first-year students struggled more with emerging adulthood. Perhaps, for first-year students just entering college, Arnett's ideas seemed vaguely important for their future, but they identified more closely with adolescence. Fresh out of high school, the setting for "Out of Mind, Out of Sight," these new students' focus revolved more on adapting to college than what life after college will hold. Once they move past that first year, though, student discussions showed that they connect strongly with issues Arnett raised, confirming his findings through their past and current experiences as well as their trepidations concerning the future.

After addressing broad stage-of-life theories of identity, the courses shifted to explore gender and sexuality. Joss Whedon's desire to create a television show feminists would want their daughters to watch is well known (cited in Vint paragraph 6). In both courses, students watched clips from "Surprise" and "Innocence," (2.13–14) the two-part episodes in which Buffy loses her virginity to Angel, giving him the moment of perfect happiness that rips his soul from his body and transforms Angel into evil Angelus. The episodes encouraged students to discuss the oft-addressed fear of men turning into monsters after sex — why the fear exists, where it might stem from, what it says about male and female gender roles. A potent scene is the confrontation in "Innocence" in which Angelus, pretending to be Angel to an unknowing Buffy, belittles her naivety in treating their encounter as "a big deal." Particularly cruel is Angel's comment to Buffy that "it's not like I've never been *there* before" (emphasis added), reducing Buffy not just to any woman, or even to any person, but to a sexual organ. The scene opened a discussion about patriarchy in American culture and ways in which women's identities are tightly bound with their bodies.[7] The episodes also provided an entry to discuss Buffy's complicated role as a feminist icon.[8] I asked students to write, before they did any readings, their definition of a feminist role model and then if/how Buffy meets that definition.[9] When the class met, because students have such conflicted feelings regarding feminism, the discussion often became heated, provocative, and challenging to all viewpoints. To add historical perspective, I reviewed the three waves of feminism and asked the class to examine Buffy through the eyes of each wave. This review helped push students outside the bubble of their own assumptions and understand what is at stake in the Buffy/feminist argument.

In the Intersession course, with more time, students delved into these issues in greater depth. I began by asking students to identify "feminine" qualities. They started with the typical suspects: girly; soft; the right type of clothes; assertive, but not too much; physical, but not in a tough way; and helpful to others. I intended to ask if they thought of femininity positively or negatively, but they beat me to my question. My class included a majority of females, and they split about half-and-half, debating if femininity was empowering or demeaning to women. Most male students felt femininity was a positive attribute, which led to some females feeling confirmed and others arguing this was the problem — the term traps women, limiting their options. We discussed how powerful the idea was to the females' sense of identity, and most agreed it played a significant part, be it something they cleaved to or struggled against.

After discussing how femininity affects their own sense of identity, the class watched "I Was Made to Love You" (5.15), in which college-student Warren creates a robot, April, to worship him and satisfy his every need. Jowett identifies April as a "good girl," a "female constructed in relation to others" (44), and the episode is the best self-contained example of the social impact of femininity on identity. Buffy begins the episode wondering why she cannot maintain a healthy relationship — her "good-guy" boyfriend Riley has left her and Spike, a vampire with a computer chip in his brain that keeps him from attacking humans, has just confessed his love, to Buffy's repulsion. She worries her physicality attracts the wrong type (Spike) and muses, "Maybe I can change. You know, work harder, spend less time slaying, laugh at his jokes — Men like that, don't they? The joke-laughing-at?" ("I Was Made to Love You"). In other words, she wonders if the problem is her distance from traditional feminine qualities. The scene cuts to April arriving in Sunnydale, seeking Warren. She wears a pink, flowery sun dress. She has perfect make-up and an ever-present smile. When the man dropping her off asks what she is looking for in Sunnydale, she responds, "True love." The two scenes perfectly establish the contrast of the episode — both Buffy and April seek the same idealized constructions of femininity teach women a relationship is the goal of life. April is literally programmed to build her sense of self around the love of a man. Buffy worries her identity keeps her from achieving the goal of "true love" she believes she *should* desire, and therefore she must morph that identity to achieve the goal.[10]

In discussion, students, especially female students, empathized with both Buffy and April. They understood why Buffy would believe the "true love" goal, reflecting back upon the Disney princess movies of their youth. They recognized how the male characters — Xander, Warren, and Spike — all speak of April as "perfect" because April is built to serve a man: made to love *you*. Many female students acknowledged feeling such pressures to conform to a standard that ultimately erases individual identity in favor of an ideal that manifests male expectations. Students also accepted the weakness in April's "perfect" femininity. As April unknowingly admits, her happiness depends solely on Warren's approval. As soon as he tires of her she not only loses Warren, but her entire sense of being, confessing to Buffy, "I'm only supposed to love him. If I can't do that, what am I for? What do I exist for?" ("I Was Made to Love You"), which illustrates the weakness of perfect femininity by reducing April's reasoning to a series of aphorisms as her batteries run to zero. April has no individual sense of self to fall back upon and so can only echo the shallow "wisdom" of others. As students discussed April, however, they always distanced themselves from the extreme, aligning more closely with Buffy. Unlike the beginning of the episode, when April and Buffy seem to share an alignment of femininity and identity, at the end of the episode Buffy learns from April that she does not need or want to sacrifice her sense of identity to achieve the goal of "true love." Even when Xander reassures her that someday the right guy will come along, Buffy emphasizes that if so, okay, but what she really wants is to "get comfortable being alone with Buffy." In other words, Buffy rejects constructing a sense of self around another in favor of uncovering her own identity. Both male and female students tended to find this the more attractive mix of femininity and identity, which allowed me to tie this discussion back to Buffy's role as a feminist icon and push the students to debate how much femininity is too much femininity.[11]

Next, the courses shifted to analyzing the role masculinity plays in *Buffy's* characters and in the lives of the students.[12] Both courses began by discussing "masculine" qualities. As they brainstormed, I listed on the board: toughness, self-reliance, and dependability. Next, students listed archetypal masculine figures and discerned what those figures revealed about their expectations of males. Students then watched "The Zeppo" (3.13)—a Xander-centered episode in which the Scoobies (minus Xander) avert an apocalypse in the background while Xander stumbles through his own picaresque adventure. The episode dramatizes Xander's transformation from boy to man as he passes several typical rites of manhood and assumes some of the more distinctive qualities of masculinity. I opened the discussion by asking students how the episode's start shows Xander is *not* a man and why they find so many of these details cringingly funny. As students rattled through boy-Xander's qualities — his desperation for approval, flailing physical abilities, "geeky" pop-culture references — it helped them sharpen what they defined a man to be by what Xander is not. Students also pointed to Xander's antagonists in the episode, a group of high school bad boys raised from the grave by voodoo, as a masculine equivalent to the exaggerated femininity of April that served as a foil to Xander's lack of manliness. As with our discussion on femininity, I pushed students to critique the ways Xander "outmans" the bad boys by the end of the episode and what Xander may have gained and/or lost by taking on these masculine qualities.[13]

Both "I Was Made to Love You" and "The Zeppo" provide such gender-exaggerated antagonists that it seemed natural for my students to uncritically accept how Buffy and Xander identify themselves at the end of the episodes as a sort of middle-ground that felt "right" rather than an identity they are themselves performing, just like the antagonists.[14] Our discussions and readings, particularly Jowett's book in my Intersession course and Patricia Pender's essay, "I'm Buffy and You're ... History" in the Freshman Seminar, helped students question what appears "normal" to them. The episodes also helped students look back to the stages-of-life ideas and episodes and discuss how gender might affect those theories in ways Erickson and Arnett did not develop. For example, for male adolescent Xander in "The Zeppo" to find his identity he must defeat the episode's archetypes of masculinity. In contrast, female adolescent Marcie in "Out of Mind, Out of Sight" seeks her identity by submerging herself within the group of feminine archetypes. The classes discussed what such gender-based nuances might add to the stages-of-life, as well as what is gained or lost through any attempt to universalize the formation of individual identity.

This chapter merely touches on the surface possibilities of using *Buffy* as a text to help college students explore the nature of identity. Invariably, I received comments from students, both those who loved and those who had never seen the show, that they had no idea how rich *Buffy* is as a text. For this generation of college students *Buffy* provides a window, a way to witness characters address our students' own concerns, to discuss their reactions to the show and each others' experiences, and to explore how their culture influences their sense of self.

NOTES

1. The website <http://www.buffyworld.com/> is invaluable, providing full transcripts of all *Buffy* episodes.
2. For examples, see Lauren Schulz and Rhonda Wilcox "Buffy and the Monsters of Teen Life."
3. See Barbara F. Tobolowsky for broader discussion of college-age identity and television (including *Buffy*).
4. The two readings are an excerpt on adolescence from Erik Erickson's *Identity, Youth, and Crisis* and Jeffrey J. Arnett's essay, "Emerging Adulthood: A Theory of Development from the Late Teen through the Twenties."
5. All citations to scripts come from shooting scripts (or transcripts if shooting script is not available) located at <http://www.buffyworld.com/>.
6. Arnett notes such categorization applies primarily to part of the population — the educated class (470). His essay nods occasionally to those outside this group, but his main concern is those following the college-to-career path.
7. The episode "Dead Things" (6.13) also provides rich material for discussing gender, women's bodies, patriarchy, and identity.
8. See also Anne Millard Daugherty, Patricia Pender "'Kicking Ass Is Comfort Food,'" and Rachel Fudge.
9. I supplement the Wilcox or Jowett reading with Patricia Pender's essay, "'I'm Buffy and You're ... History.'"
10. For more on *Buffy* and femininity, see Sophie Levy, Gwyneth Bodger, and Elana Levine.
11. Additional relevant scholarship on feminism and femininity in *Buffy* can be found in Elyce Rae Helford, Gwyn Symonds, and Jessica Prata Miller.
12. I supplemented the main readings with Stevie Simkin's essay "'Who Died and Made you John Wayne?'"
13. Other discussions of Xander, masculinity, and "The Zeppo" include Marc Camron and Rhonda Wilcox's chapter "Laughter: For Those of Us in the Audience Who Are Me" in *Why Buffy Matters*.
14. "Performing" refers to Judith Butler's idea of performativity in gender, in which we all constantly and unconsciously act out our gender for an audience of those who observe us. By doing so, most people perform and validate what comes to be viewed as a norm — what Butler calls "true gender." It is a simple-on-the-surface concept and helps students understand how their own performances might or might not mirror the performances they see in *Buffy*.

WORKS CITED

Arnett, Jeffrey J. "Emerging Adulthood: A Theory of Development from the Late Teen Through the Twenties." *American Psychologist.* 55 (2000): 469–480. Print.

Bodger, Gwyneth. "Buffy the Feminist Slayer? Constructions of Femininity in *Buffy the Vampire Slayer*." *Refractory: A Journal of Entertainment Media* 2 (2003): n.pag. Web. 13 March 2009.

Buffy the Vampire Slayer: The Chosen Collection. Twentieth Century–Fox Home Entertainment, 2005. DVD.

Butler, Judith. *Gender Trouble: Feminism and the Subversion of Identity*. New York: Routledge, 1999. Print.

Camron, Marc. "The Importance of Being the Zeppo: Xander, Gender Identity and Hybridity in *Buffy the Vampire Slayer*." *Slayage: The Whedon Studies Association Journal* 6.3 (2007): n.pag. Web. 17 March 2009.

Daugherty, Anne Millard. "Just a Girl: Buffy as Icon." *Reading the Vampire Slayer: An Unofficial Critical Companion to Buffy and Angel*. Ed. Roz Kaveney. New York: Tauris Park, 2001. 148–65. Print.

Erickson, Erik. *Identity, Youth, and Crisis*. New York: W.W. Norton, 1968. Print.

Fudge, Rachel. "The Buffy Effect." *Bitch Magazine* No. 10 (1999): n.pag. Web. 16 March 2009.

Giddan, Norman S. *Community and Social Support for College Students*. Springfield, IL: C. C. Thomas, 1988. Print.

Helford, Elyce Rae. "'My Emotions Give Me Power': The Containment of Girl's Anger in *Buffy*." *Fighting the Forces: What's at Stake in* Buffy the Vampire Slayer. Eds. Rhonda V. Wilcox and David Lavery. Lanham, MD: Rowman Littlefield, 2002. 18–34. Print.

Jowett, Lorna. "New Men: 'Playing the Sensitive Lad.'" *Slayage* 4.1–4.2 (2004): n.pag. Web. 13 March 2009.

_____. *Sex and the Slayer: A Gender Studies Primer for the Buffy Fan*. Middletown, CT: Wesleyan University Press, 2005. Print.

Karp, David A., Lynda Lytle Holmstrom, and Paul S. Gray. "Leaving Home for College: Expectations for Selective Reconstruction of Self." *Symbolic Interaction* 21.3 (1998): 253–276. Print.

Levine, Elana. "*Buffy* and the 'New Girl Order': Defining Feminism and Femininity." *Undead TV: Essays on* Buffy the Vampire Slayer. Eds. Elana Levine and Lisa Parks. Durham: Duke University Press, 2007. 168–189. Print.

Levy, Sophie. "'You Still My Girl?': Adolescent Femininity as Resistance in *Buffy the Vampire Slayer*." *Reconstruction: Studies in Contemporary Culture* 3:1 (2003): n.pag. Web. 18 March 2009.

Miller, Jessica Prata. "'The I in Team': Buffy and Feminist Ethics." Buffy the Vampire Slayer *and Philosophy: Fear and Trembling in Sunnydale*. Ed. James B. South. Chicago: Open Court, 2003. 35–48. Print.

Pender, Patricia. "'I'm Buffy and You're ... History': The Postmodern Politics of *Buffy*." *Fighting the Forces: What's at Stake in* Buffy the Vampire Slayer. Eds. Rhonda Wilcox and David Lavery. Lanham, MD: Rowman and Littlefield, 2002: 35–44. Print.

_____. "'Kicking Ass Is Comfort Food': Buffy as Third Wave Feminist Icon." *Third Wave Feminism: A Critical Exploration*. Ed. Stacy Gillis, Gillian Howie, and Revecca Munford. Houndsmills: Palgrave, 2004. 164–74. Print.

Schultz, Lauren. "Concepts of Identity When *Nancy Drew* Meets *Buffy*." Buffy *Meets the Academy: Essays on the Episodes and Scripts as Texts*. Ed. Kevin K. Durand. Jefferson, NC: McFarland, 2009. 187–202. Print.

Simkin, Stevie. "'Who Died and Made You John Wayne?' Anxious Masculinity in *Buffy*." *Slayage* 3.3–3.4 (2004): n.pag. Web. 13 March 2009.

Symonds, Gwyn. "'Solving problems with sharp objects': Female Empowerment, Sex and Violence in *Buffy the Vampire Slayer*." *Slayage* 3.3–4 (2004): n.pag. Web. 1 April 2009.

Tobolowsky, Barbara F. "Beyond Demographics: Understanding the College Experience Through Television." *New Directions for Students Services* 2006:114 (2006): 17–26. Print.

Vint, Sherryl. "'Killing Us Softly?' A Feminist Search for the 'Real' Buffy." *Slayage* 2.1 (2002): n.pag. Web. 13 March 2009.

Wilcox, Rhonda V. "Buffy and the Monsters of Teen Life: 'There Will Never Be a *Very Special Buffy*.'" *Slayage* 2 [1.2] (2001) n.pag. Web. 13 March 2009.

_____. *Why Buffy Matters: The Art of* Buffy the Vampire Slayer. New York: I. B. Tauris, 2005. Print.

Ethics Homework from the Hellmouth: Buffy Stakes Her Claim in the First-year Composition Classroom

Keith Fudge

Approximately two years ago I recognized that using a conventional textbook for teaching Freshmen English II classes was not working. The majority of my students simply no longer seemed to care about writing on the typical social concerns such as politics, climate change, or an increasing dependence on technology. After reviewing new texts on the market I reached the conclusion that the majority seemed sterile when it came to opening the minds of students. Furthermore, I decided that if this was my perspective, there was a good chance that my students had probably reached that point as well, and after all, this course was for them and not about me. Consequently, I began to look for new and different mediums to engage students and teach them to write critically and clearly about those fundamental issues that affect the human condition. Speaking to colleagues across the country, I found many of them facing the same situation. Most told me that the only required text that they used was a writing handbook. Inspired by my findings, I proposed and received approval to use diverse texts that might better reach students, one of which was the television show, *Buffy the Vampire Slayer*.

At my institution, Freshman English II is the second offering in the composition sequence and is a general education requirement for all university students. The general objectives of the course are based on a series of university learning outcomes including mastery of analytical skills, communication skills, technological skills, ethics, quantitative reasoning, and deepening global and cultural perspectives. More specifically, the course is research-based, with critical and rhetorical methods used for argumentation and analysis. Classes are capped at 25 students and the prerequisite for admission is the completion of Freshmen English I with a grade of "C" or better. The students are traditional, for the most part, and drawn from a regional base. As expected, the non-traditional students have returned to school as a result of the recent economic downturn, desired a career change, or had taken time away from school to raise a family. Considering the makeup of my classes, the situations found in *Buffy* met several university learning outcomes in terms of what we wanted students to embrace. From there it was simply a matter of aligning department goals and objectives with episodes from the show that would address the moral dilemmas that faced Buffy and other characters. This essay recounts only one of

94

myriad approaches to teaching composition through *Buffy,* and while it has been successful with my students thus far, it is still a work in progress. Just as with any course, constant reflection and revision must be practiced as student needs and learning styles change, and we as educators must continue to adapt to them and not expect them to conform to us. While many topics in the *Buffy*verse could be addressed in the classroom, I chose ethics as *the* focus, for in addition to it fulfilling one of the University's learning outcomes, it was an area that I believed students would find engaging while enhancing their writing skills.

Launching into the *Buffy*verse as an instructor was walking on new ground. Even with a familiarity of Joss Whedon's work, approaching the show from the perspective of an instructor rather than that of a viewer was a learning experience. After watching the show for years, I recognized its rich potential to provide examples on some of life's most valuable lessons dealing with relationships, tolerance, as well as choices and their consequences. I had every confidence that *Buffy* would work well in the classroom. In addition, I was familiar with the scholarship written about the show and saw that it had a place in the classroom because students would not find it as dry and distant as traditional jargon-filled work. This opportunity to demonstrate to first-year students that scholarship could be produced about something other than classic literature would perhaps also put students at ease and more willing to read and write about their own ideas in a more confident and relaxed manner. In planning I allowed approximately four weeks on the syllabus for the work, but have since discovered that there must be flexibility depending upon how the students progress.

In the preparation of the unit on ethics within *Buffy,* several questions began to form concerning content such as what scenes or articles should be used, but soon more questions became apparent. First of all, would students remember *Buffy* if they even knew of the show at all? The series had not run in primetime for more than five years, a time period roughly comprising 25–30 percent of the ages of traditional college freshmen, and the chances were significant that many of the non-traditional students who might be enrolled in this class were busy with careers or families during the time when the show aired. After all, by the time students reach the level of university study one can almost safely assume that most know something about a work such as *The Adventures of Huckleberry Finn,* or *Hamlet,* but what about *Buffy?* Consequently, using *Buffy* might be a bit more problematic in terms of not having a strong understanding of my students' knowledge of the particular text. Yet, on second thought, I realized that this situation is not uncommon and is one that faces instructors with each text they teach, whether canonical or not. The fact is that teachers rarely understand what their students know unless they pre-assess students' knowledge. This method is sound pedagogy in recognizing a degree of familiarity or mastery concerning any work, whether it is *Buffy* or *Hamlet.* With that in mind, I decided to pre-assess students in terms of knowledge of the show as well as in writing ability which also provided me with a sample of their writing skills including punctuation, mechanics, and sentence structure.

After initial discussion of the unit, and after a brief question and answer session addressing any concerns they had, students wrote a one-page response about what they knew about the show, *Buffy the Vampire Slayer.* I encouraged students to write as if working on a journal. The only real criterion was that they had to write at least a page, and offer whether they had any knowledge of the show; or, if they claimed to know nothing, they were also to write about any pre-conceived ideas they did or did not have, or why they did not know anything about the series. The purpose of this requirement was to have a large enough sample to assess their writing abilities. I allowed students approximately thirty to forty minutes in class to complete the task. In addition, I informed students beforehand that this assignment would not be graded, but that comments concerning content knowledge and errors in grammar and sentence structure would be provided to them.

The papers were both predictable and startling in terms of both writing skills and summative knowledge of the show. Many of the writing problems encountered were anticipated in terms of sentence structure and usage, but it was surprising that only about 25 percent of traditional college students had any knowledge of the show. But, out of that minority, almost all had a strong understanding of not only *Buffy*, but of all of Joss Whedon's work. What was most revealing was that the non-traditional students were more knowledgeable about *Buffy*, and were more receptive to the analysis of the academic and social merits of the series. With this knowledge I could effectively evaluate the content to use and envision how to demonstrate the ethical circumstances that students might recognize. Much to my delight, after we began watching and discussing the show, I discovered that they were more than willing to embrace the opportunity to work on something unconventional, and were pleased to be given an assignment that offered a new venue to discover learning rather than having to discuss typical social issues or controversies. From that point the planning was simple:

Students would watch four episodes as a class.

1. Students would discuss ethical principles concerning choices and consequences.
2. Students would be given choices from a list of episodes to watch on their own.
3. Students would be introduced to doing research in the *Buffy*verse.
4. Students would begin the writing process including individual conferences with me.

As mentioned previously, pacing would be determined by student progress.

In choosing the content, given the limited scope of student knowledge of the show, I chose to bring the "non-watchers" up to speed by starting with "Welcome to the Hellmouth" (1.1). Just as with any text, this first episode provides a solid background in setting, theme, characters, and plot. It is also rich in context while introducing several of the key issues that the show addresses throughout its seven seasons. Issues regarding peer pressure, parental loyalty, romance, broken homes, education, popularity, responsibility, choices and their consequences are woven throughout a landscape of dusted vampires and witty dialogue. Observing the students as they watched the show, there was an awkward mix of giggly horror, fanciful amusement, and what seemed to be reflective silence. After watching the first episode, students were instructed to go online to find out more about the characters; however, I did not press this issue. I wanted them to come to the class with fresh eyes and ideas that could be discussed, and not simply with ideas restated from someone else's point of view. For the next class students watched "The Harvest" (1.2), thus receiving closure to episode one, and were now equipped with a cursory introduction to Buffy's new world at Sunnydale High School. After further discussion about the episodes, and with an assignment to research several new characters, we then moved on to watch "Becoming, Parts I & II" (2.21–22).

As we progressed, I introduced the role that ethics play in our everyday lives. It was easy to approach this topic from a "real life" perspective because traditional college freshmen are at an important time in their lives when personal conflicts arise, often when parental loyalty and new-found freedoms and values are at odds. It is a time when they are simply trying to figure out who they are as many are on their own for the first time. In contrast, most non-traditional students have already fought most of those battles. Consequently, as I prepared my list of supplementary episodes for student choices, and since ethical principles apply to a variety of situations, I provided a list of some of what could be considered key episodes in the series that students could choose and perhaps relate to their own experiences.

After students possessed a working knowledge of the show from watching the first two episodes from Season One and the last two episodes from Season Two, they also received some grounding in the study of ethics through discussion and preliminary research. By now they had also discussed the results of choices and consequences based on their own observations of the episodes. Next they were required to make connections to ethical decision-making. At this point, I gave the students a list of potential episodes to choose to watch outside of class: "Choices" (3.19), near the end of Season Three where several of the characters make decisions that will impact the rest of their lives, "Revelations" (3.7), where things are not always as they appear and trust must be earned, "The Wish" (3.9) where one should be careful what one wishes for, "Amends" (3.10), where there comes a time in one's life to try and right the wrongs of the past, and finally "Consequences" (3.15), where telling the truth is not as easy as it should be even when one knows it is the right thing to do. All of these episodes provide useful sources of discussion concerning ethics and allow students to make personal connections and observations. Ultimately, through viewing and critically discussing these episodes, students became more empowered to write about their lives and their beliefs in a manner that seems less "textbook" driven and more "process" driven, a methodology common to educators who understand the aim of any good curriculum or educational program. In addition, while the abovementioned episodes help students reflect on their past choices and the consequences that ensued, if instructors want traditional students to examine their present lives, episodes from Season Four, depict ethical choices and their consequences through Buffy's college experience. Beginning with "The Freshman" (4.1), a lesson in dealing with the adjustment to college life, "Living Conditions" (4.2), where tactics on how to deal with an incompatible roommate are explored, and the comical, but all too eerily accurate, "Beer Bad" (4.5), where the experimentation with alcohol is a bit more traumatic for college kids partying on the Hellmouth, students see just how the decisions are a bit more substantive and not as simple. As previously stated, the freedom that *Buffy* gives individual instructors is theirs for the taking. Additional avenues of study in ethics are abundant in Season Four and throughout the series including self-sacrifice, obligation, and deception. There are also personal ethical demons to be fought such as Dawn's bout with kleptomania shown in several episodes of Season Six, and the trickery and deception by the use of unnatural forces seen in Willow's use of magic to erase memories in the episode, "Tabula Rasa" (6.8), where a spell goes awry, affecting more people than she intended. *Buffy* also confronts issues of addiction and recovery as seen in Willow's dependence upon magic and her eventual breakdown in Season Six, as well as her rehabilitation in Season Seven.

But what cannot be stressed enough in teaching critical analysis and writing using *Buffy* is that at the end of the classroom unit and in our closing discussions, students not only learned about the series and how it is much more than a show for adolescents, they also began to discover a bit more about themselves in the process of watching and became empowered to talk and write effectively about their experiences. Soon, students began to note in their discussions, their drafts, and ultimately in their final papers, that all choices have consequences, and that they are faced with a variety of decisions every day that affect the lives of others. In this regard they also came to recognize that while consequences may not be immediate, and while they may not be positive for everyone involved, there are indeed burdens to bear because of the actions that one takes as well as from the decisions that one makes. By this time, students had actively watched, discussed, and questioned, and it is interesting to see how quickly the students vested themselves in the lives of Buffy, Angel, Spike, and the Scooby Gang.

To further demonstrate this point, in "Becoming-Part 2," Buffy makes a choice to leave home after her mother gives her the ultimatum that if she continues to be the Slayer then she would be on her own. Buffy walks away, choosing to leave; the ethical choice of following her destiny is placed in opposition to parental loyalty. As that scene played, there was a silence in the class that was particularly noticeable, and recognition among students that this subject matter is not foreign, but all too familiar for some. In short, as far as ethical concerns in relationships, the possibilities for viewing are virtually unlimited in the show. At this point, as student watched episodes outside of class, the class time was devoted to the introduction to the scholarship regarding *Buffy*.

Buffy as a unit of study provides an outstanding opportunity to introduce academic scholarship to freshmen through a venue where they are not intimidated or threatened. In fact, most of my students did not genuinely believe that writing about a show such as *Buffy* constituted legitimate scholarship, and when they discovered just how many academics wrote about *Buffy*, they were more than willing to read further and ask more questions. They researched articles and presented them to the class, particularly those pieces concerning the real-life ethical issues found in the series, and more importantly, about how those articles often connected to their own lives. Surprisingly, their discussions about personal experiences in relation to the characters or situations in the series were quite open and candid, ranging from engaging in illegal activities to experiencing difficulties in relationships to the death of a friend or a parent.

Two useful sources for class-wide readings of "freshmen-friendly scholarship" concerning the role of ethics are James South's *Buffy the Vampire Slayer and Philosophy* and Jana Riess's *What Would Buffy Do?*. South's text offers an outstanding collection of essays grouped into sections on feminism, knowledge, rationality and science, ethics, religion and politics, and the act of watching *Buffy* on television. While all the essays are quite good, concerning the discussion of ethics, I assigned one particular article, "Should We

Do What Buffy Would Do," by Jason Kawal. Largely playing on the recent, "What Would Jesus Do?" path of logic and reason wherein one places oneself as a moral compass seeking to emulate the actions of heroic figures, this piece was a helpful transition to the larger text *What Would Buffy Do?*, which is also a phrase ironically uttered by the character of Xander in the Fourth Season as he tries to make an important decision that he does not want to make on his own, and envisions himself as Buffy, trying to do the right thing. In this text, sections on "Personal Spirituality," "Companions Along the Way," and "Saving the World" are major issues that are not only addressed within the show, but also within one's life in attempting to better understand the ethical choices that people face each day. Paired with the more academic article by Kawal, these two sources complemented each other in moving students from the area of personal reflection to the "bigger picture." Not only do students recognize the effect that a decision has upon them, but they also begin to recognize their far-reaching effects upon the world and those around them. Riess's book moves in this pattern as well, beginning with a focus on the individual and moving toward a world perspective and ultimately puts readers in a position of, "here is the information — now do as you will." Students were assigned Kawal's article and several sections of Reiss's book as a class and then were expected to offer points they found interesting, or to pose questions regarding the issues they may not have fully understood. This process was also useful to students in learning to discuss scholarship and engage in critical discourse. These sources were also to be used in their papers, in addition to any other articles that they included from their independent research.

Another source that students were more than willing to use is the website, *Slayage*. Edited by David Lavery and Rhonda V. Wilcox, this site provides connections to all things *Buffy*, including twenty-seven issues of peer-reviewed scholarship containing articles published in their entirety, and features relevant links to other scholarly websites regarding the works of Joss Whedon. In addition, there is a complete and up-to-date academic bibliography that provides citations for a virtual library of articles on the *Buffy*verse. When students realized the amount of scholarship that has been written, and that it is seemingly "cool" to work in this field, many of them bookmarked the page immediately for future reference. Students chose many of the full-text articles on this site and used them in their own essays. At this point, students had approximately two weeks of watching, discussing, questioning, and now been assigned readings. It was now time for the formal writing process to begin.

Included below are a few of the prompts I used in previous classes. These topics are assigned approximately two weeks into the unit and students can then take the remaining two weeks to complete the essay. Students also have the opportunity to adjust their topics after they present their ideas for approval. The first week of writing consists of drafting and editing and the second week is comprised of individual conferences.

Essay Assignment

Choose one of the following prompts and in a clear and concise essay of 1,000–1,500 words, answer the prompt as thoroughly as possible using the strategies that we have discussed in class. Do not forget: if you use a direct quotation you must cite the source using parenthetical citations in MLA format (please refer to your handbook or consult me if you have any doubt at all).

A Reminder: You must use at least three secondary pieces of scholarship to reinforce your point of view. You need to use at least two of the articles that we have discussed in class, and you may consult <www.slayageonline.com> for links to additional essays and for further research.

Possible Topics:

1. Examine and discuss all aspects of ethics depicted in education, both formal and informal, in *Buffy*.

2. Discuss ethical behavior in relationships within the episodes that we have watched and how you may have had to deal with a similar circumstance in your own life.

3. Discuss the overall significance of ethics in *Buffy* and address how the decisions that Buffy (or any of the characters) make are similar to the decisions that you are faced with on a daily basis.

Now that students are provided with topics, they begin the writing process where they focus on a topic and on the direction of their papers. They are allowed to make personal connections to examples seen in *Buffy*, but they must include valid scholarship, including the article by Kawal, a selection from Reiss, and one other article of their choosing. Since this is the first essay of the semester, there is little wonder that by the end of the semester students always say that the *Buffy* paper was the toughest paper to write, and I tell them that is why we begin with it. Start them with high expectations and they will rise to meet them and continue to respond to them. As seen from the directions and the prompts, for the most part, the assessment is pretty conventional, particularly since the assignment is at the beginning of the semester. And even though the summative assessment is the formal essay, their notes and their class participation are weighted at 10 percent of their grade.

To offer some idea of the depth and scope of the papers that are received, often it is the case that one student who initially seemed uninterested by the assignment made the most significant connections, while on the other hand, those who seem enthralled by the content of the show often wrote the most superficial papers. In this regard, the results in terms of formal writing differ little than they would on any other topic. Of course, even though they write at least one or possibly two drafts prior to the final essay, there will still be comma splices and fused sentences, but for the most part at least they will be errors with analysis and reflection rather than writing about something they had no connection to or could reflect upon. Perhaps the biggest benefit discovered thus far toward the course objectives is that the students latched onto the scholarship; they wanted to read it and write about it, and I hope that they will continue that practice in other disciplines as well. Regarding their consideration of ethical decision making, as mentioned earlier, all we as instructors can do is open the door. Ethics and morality cannot be enforced. Besides, that is not our job. However, teaching writing and critical thinking is, and if using *Buffy* helps to make that more engaging for students, then it is a good approach. In fact, when their papers are returned, some of the students often asked, "Do you think I could publish this paper?" or "What would I have to do to get this published?" This bonus is just another benefit that was never considered at the onset of the unit.

While I enjoyed some extremely positive experiences as a result of teaching *Buffy* that is not to say there have not been some bumps along the way. After two successful semesters (and one summer session) of teaching the *Buffy*verse, two students confronted me after watching "Welcome to the Hellmouth." They told me that the show went against their religious beliefs. At first, I had no idea how to respond. I did not want to lose the students from the class, and although this was a university and I could have cited academic freedom and other issues of "professorial rights," the bottom line was that I never want a student in my class to be offended or uncomfortable in any way. I told the two students that I would try to find a compromise and we arranged to meet prior to the next class. That afternoon, I spoke with my department chair who told me that I had every right to tell them to drop or to stay: it was their choice. Asking whether I could offer an alternative assessment, I was told to do whatever I wished as long as the assignments and their respective assessments were equitable.

At the meeting with students, we discussed what bothered them about the show and quite frankly, I learned much. They spoke of issues I had not considered and I respected their opinions and beliefs. I dutifully offered much in the way of logic, of how the show was a clear depiction of good versus evil, and after our discussion, one of the students decided to remain, but the other declined. I offered the alternative assignment, the student accepted, and we worked out a schedule where the student would meet with me during office hours. Everyone left satisfied with the decisions that were made; in fact, the student who stayed with the *Buffy* unit now has a genuine interest in the scholarship.

The next semester, another circumstance occurred where a student was not comfortable watching the series due to the "fright factor." The show literally scared the student to the point of screaming at the slightest noise during each episode. I also gave this student the opportunity to complete an alternate assignment and the student accepted the terms. From that moment forward, I made sure that on the first day of class that we talk about the show in depth and I invite any and all students to voice their concerns in class, or privately thereafter. In other words, it only takes a few moments to issue a "disclaimer" where students can then make the decision to stay in this class or find a more traditional one. One other danger in teaching with *Buffy* or in using any other medium of popular culture is that one must be careful that the focus remains as a composition class and does not turn into a cultural studies class. Maintaining the focus on the writing process is the key.

Finally, from my experience, teaching the *Buffy*verse has great educational merit, but who am I kidding? It is also fun! And when students see a teacher who is interested in the subject, they are much more willing to ask, "What is going on here that is so good?" It is amazing how many students seem to talk to me about *Buffy* after the class is finished when I see them on campus one semester or a few semesters later. Often they want to know if I am still using *Buffy* in the class, or they will tell me that they recommended the class to their friends. They often cite that they purchased the seasons on DVD and shared them with others. More often than not, and surprisingly so, it is the non-traditional students who become the biggest fans, many of them also citing that they moved on to

Angel after finishing Buffy's adventures in Season Seven. Creating fans of the show was not my original intent, but it seems to have been another by-product of the experience. At the closing of these discussions, I asked them whether they thought their writing improved because of the subject, and almost all of them replied that they believe they now write better because their experience was fun and helped increase their confidence. Even more meaningful is when students tell me that the show made them think about their lives, the choices they make, and how they are more confident in expressing their thoughts, and reinforcing them with the ideas of others while addressing common issues through an unconventional medium: a high school girl and her buddies who dealt with their own issues and "saved the world ... a lot" ("The Gift" 5.22). These comments demonstrate to me that ultimately, they are now better thinkers and writers after leaving my class. After all, that's my job, and it helps to enjoy one's line of work.

WORKS CITED

Buffy the Vampire Slayer: The Chosen Collection. Twentieth Century–Fox Home Entertainment, 2005. DVD.

Lavery, David, and Rhonda V. Wilcox eds. *Slayage: The Whedon Studies Association Journal.* Web.

Riess, Jana. *What Would Buffy Do? The Vampire Slayer as Spiritual Guide.* San Francisco: Jossey-Bass, 2004. Print.

South, James B. ed. Buffy the Vampire Slayer *and Philosophy: Fear and Trembling in Sunnydale.* Chicago: Open Court Press, 2003. Print.

Whedon, Joss. "An Interview with Joss Whedon." By P. Ken. *IGN.* IGN, 23 June 2003. Web. 8 Feb. 2009. <http://movies.ign.com/articles/425/425492p1.html>.

College Isn't Just
Job Training and Parties:
Stimulating Critical Thinking
with "The Freshman"

Melissa C. Johnson

I incorporated the *Buffy the Vampire Slayer* episode "The Freshman" (4.1)[1] into the first week of the first semester of a general education core course for first-year students. I chose this episode as a text for my course because it works well as a stand-alone text for practicing the active learning skills of critical reading and collaborative group work, and is an ideal tool to initiate a conversation about the purposes of higher education and the ideas about those purposes prevalent in American culture. In addition, it depicts many of the challenges and adjustments my students experience in their first weeks of college.

In this episode, Buffy Summers, the titular vampire slayer, her best female friend, Willow Rosenberg, and Willow's boyfriend, Daniel "Oz" Osborne, are all beginning their first semester at UC Sunnydale. Willow is excited about the intellectual and magical opportunities and Buffy is apprehensive about her ability to find a balance between school and vampire slaying. In contrast to Willow and Oz, she is overwhelmed by the campus, the classes, and the challenges of the transition from high school to college. Buffy's new and annoyingly perky roommate, Kathy, and another freshman named Eddie are also introduced in the episode. Like Buffy, Eddie is worried about his ability to succeed academically and to acclimate to the new environment. Before he can begin to do so, he is attacked and killed by a gang of vampires led by a female vampire named Sunday who then strip his dorm room and leave a note indicating that Eddie has given up on college because it is too overwhelming. Buffy visits Eddie's room and begins to suspect foul play. From there, she goes to consult her former Watcher, Rupert Giles, only to interrupt his romantic visit from an old friend and to be told that she can handle the situation on her own. Patrolling the campus, Buffy runs into Eddie and discovers he has been turned into a vampire. She remorsefully stakes and dusts him, only to be confronted by Sunday and her gang who injure and beat her in hand to hand combat as well as mercilessly taunt her for being a clueless freshman. Upset by this defeat, she tries to go home for rest and comfort only to find that her mother has appropriated her room for storage. While Buffy is at home, Sunday and her gang strip Buffy's dorm room and leave a note indicating that she, like Eddie, has decided she cannot handle college. Unsure of what to do and desperate to return to the familiarity of her high school life, Buffy goes to The Bronze, a local club, and runs into her best male friend, Xander Harris, who helps restore her confidence and goes with her to track down and challenge Sunday. When he leaves to get weapons, Buffy falls through the skylight through which she has been watching the vampires and faces Sunday and her gang alone. Just as Xander returns with weapons and reinforcements, Buffy defeats Sunday. Walking back to her dorm room with her friends and all her belongings, she responds to Xander's query of "College not that scary after all, huh?" with "It's turning out to be a lot like high school. Which I can handle. You know, at least I know what to expect." Then the scene shifts and we see a vampire who escaped the battle, taken down by an armed paramilitary group.

Students in my Focused Inquiry I course watched this episode during one fifty-minute class period and discussed it during the next class period. Focused Inquiry I and II are the foundation of the core curriculum at Virginia Commonwealth University. These courses have taken the place of the previously required one semester of freshmen composition. The courses grew out of the VCU Compact, which is VCU's "pledge to create a shared undergraduate experience that enhances student engagement and learning, fosters a sense of community, and emphasizes the development of a set of skills essential for educational and professional successes and lifelong learning" ("VCU Compact"). Focused Inquiry is designed to develop five specific skill areas: communication (both written and oral), critical thinking and problem solving, information retrieval and evaluation, collaborative work, and ethical reasoning and civic responsibilities in the 21st century. Unlike many other introductory core courses at this large university, "Sections of the courses are intentionally kept small to allow students to get to know each other and learn in a small setting" ("Core Curriculum: Focused Inquiry"). The Focused Inquiry program is committed to the practice and development of an interdisciplinary curriculum and pedagogy which engage students and emphasize active learning and learner-centered teaching. For many students, this is an unfamiliar and even unwelcome concept of education and they have to be initiated and, in some cases, coaxed into engaging with active learning. Robert Leamnson and Maryellen Weimer offer persuasive arguments and helpful advice for creating a learner-centered course. While Leamnson offers biological and developmental rationales for the ways in which a learner-centered course increases learning and retention, Weimer's perspective is more feminist and constructivist and focuses on empowering students to take responsibility for their own learning. Both offer strategies and methods for initiating a learner-centered pedagogy including classroom practices, evaluation, assessment strategies, and even model syllabi and assignments. In my own teaching experience, I find popular culture, in general, and visual texts, in particular, to be useful in engaging students in discussion and debate. *Buffy* combines the attractions of popular culture with the characteristics of quality television to offer my students a rich and challenging text for critical reading and critical thinking.[2] My students' enthusiastic response to watching and talking about the show helped to establish an active-learning, student-centered classroom environment early in the semester.

The over-arching theme for the first two years of the Focused Inquiry program has been Cultural Identity. The theme for the first unit in which I used the "The Freshman" is Self, University, and Community and the focus is on Experience, Culture, and Text. My goals for this unit are to create an opportunity for students to think critically about the university as an institution in society, the purposes of higher education, the ways in which higher education is depicted in various communities and forms of media, and how this depiction has shaped their own ideas and attitudes toward college. As part of this thinking, I encourage them to analyze their own personal experiences of entering a new community and making the transition from high school to college through discussion and informal and formal writing assignments. Considering these questions and issues early in their college careers will help them more clearly understand the expectations and rewards of a university education. The specific skills introduced and exercised in this first unit are critical thinking and critical reading. "The Freshman" allows me to address almost all of these goals and skill areas in two fifty-minute periods. It also serves as a building block for the second major writing assignment of the semester. While all Focused Inquiry courses require a reflective essay for the second major writing assignment in the course, the particulars of this assignment are left up to individual instructors. For this essay, I asked my students to shift their focus from their own personal motivations for attending college which they had written about in the diagnostic essay, to the purpose college education serves in the larger society, while also interrogating how they arrived at their own ideas about the reasons to attend college and the public purposes college education serves. We launched our discussions and analyses of the purposes and perceptions of higher education with our viewing of "The Freshman."

When I announced to the students that we would be watching an episode of a television show called *Buffy the Vampire Slayer* several expressed excitement and surprise while a few were puzzled. VCU has a diverse student population with a large number of international students. The footnote on the handout below was intended primarily for those students who had no knowledge of the show, either because they had missed it when it was on the air or because they were new to the country. As I distributed the handout, I stressed that this activity was academic in nature and that I expected them to use their critical thinking and critical reading skills to respond to the episode, reminding them that we had previously done some reading about and practice of critical reading techniques with a printed text. Focused Inquiry employs a spiral curriculum which repeats and reinforces skills throughout the year. The rest of the period was spent watching the episode, which the students seemed to enjoy, even as they were taking detailed notes on their handouts (see handout below).

"The Freshman" (4.1)

You have been thinking about, discussing, and writing about the reasons you chose to pursue a college education (Essay #1) and the qualities of an effective classroom environment (Classroom of the Future Activity and Rights & Responsibilities Discussion Board). You have been experiencing the transition from high school to college in the past two weeks and we have discussed the stages of intellectual development of college students (Perry Game). Today, we are going to watch an episode of *Buffy the Vampire Slayer*[3] called

"The Freshman" which deals with many of these same issues. Please keep in mind that we are not watching this show for "entertainment," but in order to facilitate our discussion of these issues. We are "reading" this text in an academic environment and therefore should approach it critically and analytically. As you watch and reflect, consider the following questions:

1. How does this text reflect the transition from high school to college? In what ways does this depiction contradict or replicate your own experience of this transition?

2. How does this text depict or present a university community? In what ways does this depiction contradict or replicate your own experience of this community?

3. How does this text depict a university classroom environment? In what ways does this contradict or replicate your own experience of this environment?

4. How do the depictions of this transition and the University environment in this text compare to depictions in other popular culture texts such as movies, television shows, commercials, etc? What does this text emphasize? What do other popular culture texts emphasize? Give specific examples of other texts.

5. What generalizations can you make about depictions of the university experience in popular culture from this and the other texts you have considered?

6. How do these depictions reflect societal attitudes toward higher education?

7. How do these depictions shape students' ideas about and experiences of higher education?

Viewing the episode took the entire fifty-minute period and as students left the classroom, I urged them to expand their responses to the questions on the handout while the episode was still fresh in their minds and to bring the handout and their notes with them to the next class.

At the beginning of the next class meeting, I asked students to sit with their previously assigned small discussion groups (3–4 students) and to focus on sharing their answers to *one* of the discussion questions and trying to come to some kind of consensus about or summary of their responses. Then, each group presented the results of their discussion to the rest of the class, who were encouraged to add their own insights and viewpoints. This approach is a variation on Frank Lyman's Think/Pair/Share model for responsive class discussion, a pedagogical tool I use frequently throughout the year to facilitative active learning. A helpful discussion of the activity appears on Collaborative Learning Website of the National Science Institute for Science Education.[4] As the student groups reported, I asked follow-up questions and on occasion challenged some answers. In order to develop and exhibit critical reading skills, I often asked groups and individual students for specific evidence from the episode to support their conclusions.

In response to the first question, most student groups identified Buffy's transition to college as initially overwhelming and difficult, but ultimately successful. In our discussion, I encouraged students to think about and discuss the other transitions seen in the episode and to consider how they differ from Buffy's. Both Willow and Oz make much easier transitions than Buffy, but for different reasons. Willow's confidence in her intellect, love of learning and academics, and organizational skills make the transition a smooth one for her. She has selected her classes and acquired her student ID before Buffy and meets the same experience which Buffy finds "overwhelming" with confidence and great enthusiasm. Her almost sexual excitement about the learning opportunities available through the university is exemplified in her "spurty knowledge" speech at the beginning of the episode.[5]

> WILLOW: It's just in High School, knowledge was pretty much frowned upon. You really had to work to learn anything. But here, the energy, the collective intelligence, it's like this force, this penetrating force, and I can just feel my mind opening up — you know? — and letting this place thrust into and spurt knowledge into.... That sentence ended up in a different place than it started out in ["The Freshman"].

Oz is much calmer than Willow, but just as much at home in this new environment because of the social knowledge and connections acquired through his band's gigs on campus. As several of my students pointed out, Oz and Willow serve as character foils to Buffy in order to highlight her reaction to college. They defended focusing on Buffy's experience to answer the question because she is the protagonist and the focus of the episode. Once we began discussing other possible answers to how this transition was represented in the episode, students often pointed out that Eddie's difficult transition mirrors Buffy's, but has a much more tragic resolution. The students, both in their responses, and in their defense of those responses, were trying to pinpoint a single, correct answer. Our discussion of other possibilities highlighted the complexity of the text as well as the diversity of experience among the students in *Buffy* as well as the students in the classroom.[6] It also encouraged students to consider multiple perspectives before coming to conclusions.

Because VCU has the highest enrollment of any university in the state of Virginia and is an urban campus in downtown Richmond, many of the students identified with Buffy's inability to find locations on campus, being overwhelmed by the size of the library, paying a fortune for textbooks, being "ticketed" with flyers and information, and finding the campus unsafe at night. Several students mentioned that the flyers they received were not calls for activism and events on campus like those in "The Freshman," but offers from merchants in town — highlighting the urban nature of our campus. Many students were also struck by Buffy's incompatibility with her roommate — noting that this was one of the greatest challenges of adjusting to college. A few students in each class found Buffy's difficult adjustment over-exaggerated and drawn out, insisting that, after a few hours or days on campus, they felt perfectly at home. After some discussion and solicited responses from the rest of the class, they learned that their reaction might not be typical of all students — particularly those from small towns, rural environments, and other countries. This question was a success because it encouraged students to talk to one another about their experiences during the first week of college and allowed them to see that there was variety to those experiences.

During the discussion of this question, I challenged Buffy's confident final declarations that "college was a lot like high school" and that she knows what to expect, by reminding the students of the ending scene showing soldiers from The Initiative taking down a stray vampire and pointing out for those unfamiliar with the show that this was a new and mysterious development.

Later in the unit, we returned to the question of the similarities and differences between college and high school, both in terms of their public purposes and their methods and educational aims when we read Benjamin Barber's essay "America Skips School" about the failures of public secondary education. Barber argues that, despite rhetoric from all levels of society and both ends of the political spectrum to the contrary, Americans do not value education. He gives evidence of our cultural emphasis on wealth and materialism rather than citizenship and learning to support this claim. In questions 4–7 of this activity and throughout this first unit, students engaged in analysis of depictions of higher education in popular culture and their communities in an attempt to come to some conclusions about the origins of their beliefs about the purposes of higher education. Throughout the year, I encouraged them to avoid making judgments on limited information as Buffy does at the end of this episode when she is confident that she has college figured out after two days.

For the most part, students tended to initially interpret the second question on the depiction of the university community as being about the physical environment of the college rather than about the people who make up the community.[7] Several students pointed out that UC Sunnydale's campus was much more architecturally integrated, cleaner, and bucolic than VCU's and that Buffy's dorm room was luxurious compared to their own. When asked directly about who the students were and how they interacted with one another, they observed that the student population at UC Sunnydale was much less racially and ethnically diverse than at VCU and they noticed that students in the episode tended to be isolated or hang out with their friends from high school rather than branching out and making new friends. When asked about the Resident Advisor (RA) Buffy speaks to in Eddie's dorm, they characterized him as callous and unconcerned, unlike their own RAs who were always trying to encourage them to join in activities. The evidence they provided for this interpretation was the RA's speech to Buffy about Eddie: "Yeah, Eddie just took off, packed his stuff, left a note. Happens sometimes. People just can't handle it. There's always a few kids who lose it early in the first semester and just bail" ("The Freshman").

As they discussed the RA and the student body, they realized that despite the more welcoming physical environment, the students at UC Sunnydale tended to be somewhat anonymous and homogenous. This observation gave me the opportunity to highlight VCU's efforts to provide a more personalized educational experience for students through Focused Inquiry and other programs on campus and served as a nice transition into the questions about the way in which "The Freshman" represents higher education. Depending on the context in which one is teaching, this episode can be helpful to initiate discussion with students about life in the dorms, support services on campus, depression among college students and/or adjusting to being more independent and self-reliant. In any context, having a faculty member assign and then watching and discussing this episode in class lets students know that faculty are interested in and aware of the transition they are experiencing, thereby making it much easier for students to approach faculty with their concerns or to visit office hours.

In response to the third question, students quickly noticed that the classrooms shown in "The Freshmen" were large lecture halls with immovable seating where the Professor was "the sage on the stage" and students were the audience, although Professor Walsh's classroom was noticeably smaller and more intimate than the Popular Culture class in the episode. They found both, the Popular Culture Professor, Professor Reigert, and Professor Maggie Walsh, a Psychology Professor who viewers discover later in the season is the director of the covert government-sponsored demon-hunting organization called the Initiative, to be tough and somewhat frightening. In each of my three classes, at least one student noted that these characterizations of the tough professor verged into caricature. Surprisingly, this assertion was met in all three classes with an anecdote about a student having been ejected from a class at VCU in the first week of classes for various offenses by a tough and scary professor just as Buffy is ejected from Professor Reigert's class. This scene allowed students to discuss and process their own experiences and also gave us the opportunity to discuss some of the differences between high school and college — differences students need to become aware of to be successful in their first semester.

Most importantly, these two classroom scenes present a rich opportunity to discuss the differences between traditional lecture classes and active learning environments.[8] Almost all of my students had at least one class in a large lecture hall and had some experience with Teaching Assistants (TAs). The students identified the ways in which our classroom was different from the environments depicted in the episode, and thus gave me the opportunity to verbally reinforce the active learning philosophy of the Focused Inquiry program and the goals of the course as they are presented in the syllabus. Later in the unit, we discussed strategies for active learning and academic success in large lecture classes.

We did not have the time to discuss why Joss Whedon, who wrote and directed this episode, chose to depict college classrooms and college professors in these particular ways and why the depiction of the tough college professor ejecting students from class is so common in popular culture from *The Paper Chase* to *Legally Blonde*. However, these are questions worth pursuing.

For the fourth question, students generated numerous examples of college and university experiences on film from television's *Greek* and *Undeclared* to the quintessential college film *Animal House* and its numerous offspring including *Van Wilder*, *College*, *American Pie 2*, *American Pie Presents Beta House*, *PCU*, *Old School*, *Accepted*, *The House Bunny* and *Roadtrip*.

As discussion in all three classrooms quickly revealed, it was difficult for students to remember scenes in these films or television shows which focused on classroom interactions between faculty and students, college faculty as positive educational mentors, or college as a primarily academic environment. As they discussed these television shows and films and their emphasis on drinking, parties, relationships, sororities and fraternities, and subverting or gaming the academic system, they realized that "The Freshman" was somewhat unique in its emphasis on academics as central to college life and as a challenge to be seriously undertaken. None of the students brought up films such as *Mona Lisa Smile* or *The Paper Chase*, but it might be worth mentioning these as additional examples of the same themes. At this point, I reminded the students that a majority of them had, in their diagnostic essays, identified their primary motivation for attending college as a desire to get a good job while many had also mentioned the importance of the social aspects of college life while only a small percentage had focused on coming to college to learn. In a later class, we engaged in a think and write/group discussion/share activity in which students reflected on and discussed their preconceived ideas about the purposes of a college education and the sources of those ideas. Many of the students revealed that their parents, other relatives, and high school teachers had emphasized a college education as a necessary credential for obtaining a successful career while popular culture and their friends tended to focus on the social side of college life. Some students' parents also emphasized the social aspects of college as well in their discussions with them about college. When we read the Benjamin Barber essay which argued that creating citizens in a democracy was the primary purpose of public education, all of my students indicated that this was the first time they had considered this idea. We went on to encounter the idea that the primary purpose of higher education is civic in several more texts dealing specifically with university education and the students discussed it both in class and in their essays. We were not able to spend as much time on the last two questions as I would have liked, but we continued the discussion about these two questions throughout this unit as we approached new texts on the purposes of higher education.

We ended the class period with a brief full class discussion of the possibility that the vampires might serve as a metaphor for some aspect or aspects of college or university life. Students interpreted the vampires variously as representative of self-assured and disdainful upperclassmen, the fear and self-doubt that many freshmen feel upon beginning college, non-supportive friends and family members, and the materialistic and hierarchical values of the larger society outside of the "Ivory Tower" of higher education. In analyzing the vampires as a metaphor, the students expressed some of their own anxieties about college and discovered that they were not alone in feeling these anxieties. Because of its richness and its pertinent subject matter, "The Freshmen" is an ideal text to use with first-year students — particularly early in the year. A good scholarly article for collateral reading for students or instructor preparation for teaching *Buffy* in general, and discussing it with first year students in particular, Tracy Little's "High School is Hell: Metaphor Made Literal in *Buffy the Vampire Slayer*," traces the use of metaphor in the first three seasons of Buffy and analyzes the ways in which the series employs metaphor to move beyond folkloric and horror conventions to a postmodern hyper-reality. As Little observes:

> The writers and producers of *BtVS* have utilized this approach not just as an effective storyline motivator, but also as a valid way to appeal to viewers on several levels. In this context, such metaphors have the capacity to help viewers put their own fears and emotions into perspective, deal with such fears and emotions in a more effective way, to provide a point of comparison with the reality of the view and that of the show, to recognize that the fears and emotions played out by the show's characters may be similar to their own, and finally, to legitimize the feelings of the viewer. The complex nature of such metaphors also allows for multiple interpretations on the part of the viewer [284].

This was certainly true of my students' experience with "The Freshman."

The episode and our class discussion about it became a touchstone that the students returned to at various times throughout the semester. In one section, a group of students chose the activity as a springboard for a student-initiated and directed online discussion on Blackboard of the pros and cons of using television shows and films in the classroom as a learning tool. Comparing their high school experience with films in the classroom to their experience with *Buffy*, several students pointed out that engaging popular culture was much more useful if students engaged in explicit analysis as we had with *Buffy*, rather than just passively watching a show or a film, and if there were clear connections to the course goals and topics. Many offered stories about teachers using films to fill time or give the class a reward. Several students expressed the opinion that education could be made more entertaining through films and television shows, but that some of the "educational" films they had seen made them long to read a textbook instead. For the most part, they saw *Buffy* as entertaining, complex enough to warrant analysis, and relevant. However a few students expressed doubt that *Buffy* or any television show could be the focus of any sort of serious study and other students responded to this doubt with references to the fields of film and media studies as academic disciplines and provided links to resources on these disciplines. From there, the discussion board diverged into a debate about the value of watching films based on books as part of literary study and a discussion of the *Harry Potter* films. I was delighted that the students both saw the value of using *Buffy* in the classroom and continued to express and consider multiple points of view before coming to any conclusions without any guidance from me. They frequently replied directly to one another's posts and drew from other's posts when expressing their ideas.

The next time I use this activity, I will spend more time introducing *Buffy* to students before we watch the episode and assign Tony Daspit's article on education in *Buffy* for collateral reading. This article will help students make clearer connections between "The Freshman" and our discussions of liberal arts education and learner-centered pedagogy, as well as give them a context for and an example of viewing *Buffy* as a text worthy of scholarly study. While I made some cursory remarks about *Buffy* as quality television and the field of *Buffy* Studies, the discussion board showed some lingering skepticism about the value of watching television in class. I will also collect and comment on student responses to the questions on the handout, so that I have a clearer idea of how all students are responding and can follow up on any interesting observations that are not expressed verbally in the class discussion.

In addition to creating an environment in which students might express and share their anxieties about and experiences of beginning college, "The Freshman" allowed me to explicitly address the themes and goals of the course unit and to engage students in practicing critical reading, critical thinking, and collaborative work on a rich but approachable text. Most importantly, our in-class activities defined the ways in which the class would "work" throughout the semester by making students' voices and critical thinking central and getting students into the habit of think/pair/share. It also inspired students to engage in a critical inquiry and discussion about the value of using popular culture texts in the classroom — the type of engaged questioning and intellectual exploration that is the goal of the course.

NOTES

1. All quotations are from the shooting script of "The Freshman" available at <BuffyWorld.com>.
2. For discussions of *Buffy* as quality television, see the "Introduction" to Wilcox and Lavery xx–xxv; McKabe and Akass xviii and 37; and Wilcox.

3. *Buffy the Vampire Slayer* is an American television show broadcast for seven seasons from 1997 to 2003. The main characters went through high school and into college while fighting vampires and demons and "saving the world a lot." For more information on the show, see: IMDB <http://www.imdb.com/title/tt0118276/> and *Slayage: The Whedon Studies Association Journal* at <http://slayageonline.com/>.

4. <http://www.wcer.wisc.edu/archive/CL1/>.

5. See William Wandless's "Undead Letters: Searches and Researches in *Buffy the Vampire Slayer*" for a discussion of Willow's intellectual evolution in the series and James B. South's "My God, It's Like a Greek Tragedy": Willow Rosenberg and Human Irrationality" for a Freudian reading of this speech.

6. For the complexities and richness of *Buffy* as a text see, Wilcox's *Why Buffy Matters*.

7. Since my students were a little confused by the use of the term "community" in this second question, in the future, I will re-phrase it or preface it with a discussion about the possible definitions of community in order to ensure that students consider the participants in the community as well as the spaces they inhabit, particularly since the next few questions focus specifically on those spaces.

8. If an instructor had more time to spend discussing this episode and the depictions of teaching and learning in *Buffy* and wanted to assign collateral reading, Toby Daspit's article "Buffy Goes to College, Adam Murders to Dissect: Education and Knowledge in Postmodernity" offers an apt analysis of these scenes as examples of the banking model of education as defined by Freire and argues that they are the opposite of the kind of postmodern learning and education valued in the series as a whole. Other recommended scholarly articles written about this episode, education and learning in *Buffy*, and/or Professor Walsh include Madeline Muntersbjorn's from Buffy the Vampire Slayer *and Philo*sophy edited by James South, Daniel Clark's and Andrew Miller's article on the subversion of authority in *Buffy* published in *Slayage*, and two articles by Christine Jarvis focusing specifically on education and learning in *Buffy*.

WORKS CITED

Barber, Benjamin. "America Skips School: Why We Talk so Much About Education and Do So Little." *Harper's Magazine* 287.1722 1993: 39–47. Print.

Clark, Daniel A., and P. Andrew Miller. "Buffy, the Scooby Gang, and Monstrous Authority: *BtVS* and the Subversion of Authority." *Slayage: The Whedon Studies Association Journal* 1.3 (2001). n.pag. Web.

"Core Curriculum: Focused Inquiry." *VCU University College*. Virginia Commonwealth University, 30 Oct. 2008. Web.

Daspit, Toby A. "Buffy Goes to College, Adam 'Murder(s) to Dissect': Education and Knowledge in a Postmodern World." *Buffy and Philosophy: Fear and Trembling in Sunnydale*. Chicago: Open Court, 2003. 117–130. Print.

"Doing CL: Think/Pair/Share." *Collaborative Learning*. The National Institute for Science Education, 1 November 1997. Web. 8 June 2009.

"The Freshman." *Buffy the Vampire Slayer*. WB. 05 Oct. 1999. Television.

Jarvis, Christine. "Real Stakeholder Education?: Lifelong Learning in the *Buffy*verse." *Studies in the Education of Adults* 37:1 (Spring 2005): 31–46. Print.

_____. "School Is Hell: Gendered Fears in Teenage Horror." *Educational Studies* 27.3 (01 Sep. 2001): 257–67. Print.

Leamnson, Robert. *Thinking About Teaching and Learning: Developing Habits of Learning with First Year College and University Students*. Sterling, Virginia: Stylus, 1999. Print.

Little, Tracy. "High School is Hell: Metaphor Made Literal in *Buffy the Vampire Slayer*." Buffy the Vampire Slayer *and Philosophy: Fear and Trembling in Sunnydale*. Ed. James B. South. Chicago: Open Court, 2003. 282–293. Print.

Lyman, Frank. "The Responsive Classroom Discussion." *Mainstreaming Digest*. Ed. A.S. Anderson. College Park: University of Maryland College of Education, 1981. Print.

McCabe, Janet, and Kim Akass, eds. *Quality TV: Contemporary American Television and Beyond*. London: I. B. Tauris, 2007. Print.

Muntersbjorn, Madeline. "Pluralism, Pragmatism, and Pals: The Slayer Subverts the Science Wars." *Buffy and Philosophy: Fear and Trembling in Sunnydale*. Chicago: Open Court, 2003. 91–102. Print.

South, James B. "'My God, It's Like a Greek Tragedy': Willow Rosenberg and Human Irrationality." *Buffy and Philosophy: Fear and Trembling in Sunnydale*. Chicago: Open Court, 2003. 131–145. Print.

"Think/Pair/Share." *Collaborative Learning.* National Institute for Science Education, 1 November 1997. Web.

"The VCU Compact." *VCU University College.* Virginia Commonwealth University. n.d. Web. 10 March 2009.

Wandless, William. "Undead Letters: Searches and Researches in *Buffy the Vampire Slayer.*" *Slayage* 1.1 (2001): n.pag. Web.

Weimer, Maryellen. *Learner-Centered Teaching: Five Key Changes to Practice.* San Francisco: Jossey-Bass, 2002. Print.

Whedon, Joss. "The Freshman: Shooting Script." BuffyWorld. 22 July 1999. Web. 8 July 2009.

Wilcox, Rhonda. *Why Buffy Matters: The Art of* Buffy the Vampire Slayer. London: I.B. Tauris, 2005. Print.

_____, and David Lavery, eds. *Fighting the Forces: What's at Stake in* Buffy the Vampire Slayer. Lanham, MD: Rowman & Littlefield, 2002. Print.

"Can't Even Shout, Can't Even Cry" But You Can Learn! Non-Verbal Communication and "Hush"

Brian Cogan

The Joss Whedon creation, *Buffy the Vampire Slayer* is a television cult favorite and the object of much critical discussion and analysis. It is a text rich in interpretative value from a variety of angles. From semiotic analysis, to gender theory, queer theory and woman's studies, to analysis of the active audience and fan fiction, many academic fields have mined *Buffy*. As Josef Adalian noted (quoting J.J. Abrams), "Joss's storytelling is always that perfect fit of wit, deep emotion and passion for genre" (1). That is to say that Whedon's characters, created out of a passion for realness (albeit in a world with vampires, demons and the Hellmouth), are closer to reality than most traditional television. This dichotomy between the fantastic and the realistic help make *Buffy* an effective tool for analysis and teaching. Because of the polysemic nature of the show and the richness of its story and universe (often called the *Buffy*verse or Whedonverse) *Buffy* lends itself to numerous uses in the classroom. This chapter will recount my own use of *Buffy* in teaching, and how I used it to spark critical examination and discussion among students.

My field of study and most of my published work is in the field of popular culture and communication, therefore I find it natural to try and work popular culture texts into many classes. When I teach non-verbal communication, I usually teach it as a component of either a larger class on intercultural communication, or in the introductory session to the general communications class. Early on in my career, I felt that I relied too much upon the suggested exercises in the texts and not enough upon my own background in popular culture studies. After starting to add innovations of my own (such as students interviewing students they did not know well without spoken words or writing), I realized that what had led to success in many other classrooms, incorporating popular culture texts in ways that were both rigorous and engaging, would also be a way to revive the students' (and sometimes my own) flagging interest in the topic of non-verbal communication. I realized that often students are not invested in the subject matter if teachers are not invested in the subject matter. It is easy to rely on a pre-packaged model or free exercises that are provided by the textbook publisher, but harder to demonstrate passion for something when the teacher is relying on outsiders to determine class content.

Since *Buffy* was released on DVD, I have used various episodes in classroom discussions in numerous courses and found that many episodes are both relevant for classroom discussion and effective teaching tools. As a teacher accustomed to using popular culture texts for analysis or lecture aids in my classes, I successfully used episodes such as "Welcome to the Hellmouth" (1.1) and "The Harvest" (1.2) regularly in gender communication classes, as well as using the musical episode "Once More, with Feeling" (6.7) to examine issues of post-modernism. As a matter of fact, almost any *Buffy* episode can be used in gender communication classes, and in explanations of feminist analysis as evidenced by the numerous books and academic articles that have examined *Buffy* from a feminist or queer theory perspective.[1] However, one of the most effective episodes to use as a teaching tool is the fourth season episode "Hush" (4.10). "Hush" is the famous episode where horrific fairy tale creatures, the Gentlemen, steal the Scooby gang's voices. It is fascinating in and of itself, but the unique nature of the episode facilitates explaining and discussing non-verbal communication. When using "Hush" in the classroom I have applied through student exercises, group activities and reaction papers, non-verbal analysis of haptics (the way people communicate through touch), territoriality (our sense of possession of personal space), kinesics (body language and expressions and gestures), power relations and other aspects of non-verbal communication. *Buffy* serves not just as an icebreaker, but as a powerful text to analyze the ways in which gender differences help influence non-verbal communication and symbolize issues of power and control. It is effective to use a text that the students, especially freshman and sophomores can relate to. Whedon's central thesis that high school is literally "hell" is something they can understand having recently survived that experience themselves. This connection is especially true at a college that demographically has a higher number of female students than male students. In addition, the idea that non-verbal communication is often more easily understandable than verbal communication rings much truer to students that age.

For many reasons, "Hush" is considered by fans and scholars alike to be one of the best episodes in the *Buffy* series.[2] The episode was written and directed by Joss Whedon, and when originally aired on December 14, 1999, was quickly noted by critics as being an unusual examination of the concept of communication and the inherent difficulties in communicating among friends and lovers. The episode was the highest rated of the fourth season and was nominated for an Emmy award for Best Writing for a Dramatic episode. The plot hinges on the arrival of the sinister Gentlemen, a cabal of evil demons who seek to collect seven human hearts in order to complete a nefarious ritual. Accompanied by their gruesome straight-jacketed servants, they weave a spell of silence, capturing the town's voices as they sleep, leaving the residents fearful and apprehensive. Naturally Buffy and the Scooby gang investigate. Riley, Buffy's budding love interest and a member of the Initiative (a secret government organization involving professors and graduate students who are really capturing demons and experimenting on them) both look into the occurrence, while Anya and Xander squabble over their relationship and Willow meets and befriends the shy but powerful witch Tara. Buffy and Riley's worlds collide as they both discover each other's secrets while fighting the Gentlemen. As a result, evil is defeated, goodness triumphs, peace is restored, and nothing will ever be the same in Sunnydale. As the inhabitants of Sunnydale, and soon my students discover, it is often when things are quietest that the most is "said."[3]

"Hush" is not only a pivotal *Buffy* episode; it is probably the most effective episode in terms of pedagogy. In teaching a class on non-verbal communication, it is often difficult to come up with new and innovative ways to not only fully teach the implications of non-verbal communications, but also to use popular culture texts that are sometimes familiar to the students in innovative ways that not only fulfill the curricular requirements, but also engage the students. As Di Gregorio put it, "the substance of what we read out of an audiovisual text such as *Buffy* can be just as stimulating as a study of Shakespeare's *Romeo and Juliet*, as well as exposing us to material that is relevant to the lives of young men and women today" (92). To use a text such as "Hush," is to try and have students see a scenario that is familiar to them and one which they spend endless time talking about, the problems inherent in human communication and relationships. Although *Buffy* came out of left field to some of the students, including a small minority of the class who found it difficult to relate to *Buffy* for various reasons, many remarked in both their reaction papers and in their classroom responses that they noticed in the episode sometimes subtle and profound connections to their own lives. Di Gregorio notes about "Hush" that "while the scenario is straight from a horror film, the sub-text of the episode is the lack of communication between Buffy and her friends, and the difficulty of saying what you mean in a relationship" (93), something that most students can relate to. Through "Hush" students can see fictional, but realistic interactions that make sense to them in terms of their own exchanges. The added benefit of "Hush" is that the episode, with its lack of sound for 29 minutes, almost begs to be used to dissect non-verbal communication. Like Jules Dassin's 32 minute soundless heist in his classic film *Riffifi* the lack of sound activates other perceptual methods the students, in some cases the teacher, had not considered before. [4]

In "Hush" Buffy is perplexed by a chant she heard in a prophetic dream, one that made her aware that a new menace was coming to Sunnydale. In her dream, a little girl holding a small wooden box sings:

> Can't even shout, can't even cry,
> The Gentlemen are coming by
> Looking in windows, knocking on doors
> They need to take seven and they might take yours....

This rhyme is itself not only important, but is a crucial moment in the episode for students' exercises where I make them aware that what they are watching is not shown to simply entertain them, but that this scene has meaning. Before even showing the video, or explaining what the lesson is about, I start the class by writing the chant on the board and asking the class what it means. After some puzzled looks, some suggest that it is a nursery rhyme of some sort, possibly one they have forgotten or one in a story that they have not heard before. When I explain that their guesses are not far off, I ask them to sound it out, and soon the entire class agrees that it must be a forgotten rhyme. It is usually at this point that I announce to the class that the nursery rhyme, (a good guess on their part) is actually not old, but comes from a specific episode of a television program about a girl who is chosen to slay vampires and her groups of friends. At this moment, the make or break point in the class comes, when I explain the concept behind *Buffy*, the basic characters, and a little back-story. I considered throwing them head-first into the episode, but realized that some larger context would be lost without some basic explanation. I tell them that we will be watching this episode in order to understand non-verbal communication better, but do not initially tell them why I chose this particular episode, nor about the lengthy silent sequence. This omission gives them freedom of possible interpretation without too many restrictions or guidelines at first. Sometimes (although certainly not always) too much direction is as bad as no direction at all, as it might spoil the overall experience. After giving them a written list of examples of nonverbal communication, including haptics, territoriality, kinesics and expressions of gender related nonverbal communication I begin showing the episode. They watch the episode straight through, pausing only for quick questions about clarity, and after a moment's break, we go over what had seemed most relevant about class material from the episode. I write these thoughts on the board, and then ask what they found to be confusing. After going over the episode in general, I then add an initial list under the headings haptics, kinesics, territoriality, and gender relations to the board. With these numerous instances listed, I ask them, in smaller groups, to see what kinds of on-screen behavior fit into these categories, as well as what kind of hidden or submerged meanings could be below the surface.

Many students brought up the point that without knowing the characters, they were interested by the awkward arrangements of the various relationships and how their body language explained those relationships. As Trenholm, an expert on non-verbal communication wrote in the textbook we use for the class, "Managing territory and distance is an important aspect of nonverbal behavior" (120). The body's territory is the most important, and the most significant right or privilege in any kind of relationship is the right to be touched or not touched. Sociologist Edward Hall in his book *The Silent Language* noted that, "people have developed territoriality to an almost unbelievable extent. Yet we treat space as we treat sex. It is there but we don't talk about it" (Hall 159). Even though many students had not seen the show before, it seemed as though they had no major difficulties in figuring out the gender and power dynamics in these relationships. Despite the fact that characters were talking constantly, arguing, debating and even shouting at each other, no one seemed to really "get" what the other person was saying. This behavior was easy to elaborate for the students in terms of space and nonverbal communication. In the first moments in the opening dream sequence, Buffy and Riley naturally feel quite awkward as Buffy lies down on the desk and Riley approaches her, after she utters the line "fortune favors the brave" he, for the first time, breaks her personal space and kisses her. Students, who later put this down under the category of territoriality interpreted how personal space was managed, also remarked how often talking, or the difficulty in articulating relationships, came up in the next few minutes of the episode. An example of this lack of articulation is the scene between Xander and Anya, who are also are having an awkward conversation about their relationship, or the relative lack thereof. When pressed by Anya as to how he feels about her, he simply replies, "I ... You ..." before lapsing again into silence. This tension is broken by Anya's annoyed rant that Xander does not care about her, but simply wants "lots of orgasms," saying the line as they enter Giles's house, interrupting his concentration.

Just as the Scooby gang has problems in communicating among themselves, the same difficulties are happening outside Giles' house as well. An example occurs with Willow, whose Wicca group is a juxtaposition of language specific to the religion, mixed with banalities, culminating in a debate about a potential "bake sale" with the club leader asking, "who left their scented candles dripping all over my women power shrine?" Students noticed power relations in the Wicca group, revealed in terms of who has the power to speak and who is symbolically, or literally, silenced. Many of the students, particularly the female students mentioned that they felt bad for Tara. Tara is represented as shy and symbolically feminine, not really able to articulate what she wants to say or alternately, not allowed to talk, while Willow is presented as having more symbolically masculine characteristics, more assertive and outspoken. She defies the leaders of the "wanna-blessed-bes" while Tara is silenced. Many female students noticed that this was typical not only of feminine power dynamics, but also of male-female power dynamics, and even classroom dynamics. As several students indicated under the territoriality section, the body distance had changed for several characters, most notably Willow and Tara.

The topic of talking is recurrent during the first scenes in the episode and students pointed out that in describing her interactions with Riley, Buffy refers to him as being "all talk." They described their efforts at verbal communication as being a conversation where nerves take over, Buffy starts to babble, and it becomes a "babblefest." Many students also noticed multiple emphases on the topic of verbal communication, such as when Riley's friend and fellow Initiative member Forrest tells him that he talks too much and to "get to the kissing," when the tied up Spike imitates Anya to Xander and is then told by Xander to "shut up," and when Olivia tells Giles after she arrives "that's enough small talk." The students were deeply involved in the class discussion at this point. Many thought they had figured out what was going on, that the episode was a meta-commentary on communication was apparent. Many of them figured that the episode was designed almost as a classroom aid, one that made points on what we talk about, when we talk about communication. Now they only had to take notes on the non-verbal attributes while the characters talked and fought during the rest of the episode. But what most did not know was that the real assignment was about to begin. Studying verbal communication is relatively easy, while non-verbal can be much more complex.

While "Hush" is about communication, there is a paradigm shift in the episode, one that took many students by surprise. When the Gentlemen's spell takes effect suddenly all of the characters lose the ability to speak. As there is essentially silence for the next 29 minutes of the episode, students find themselves watching closely, not distracted or engaged in digesting dialogue, but instead looking for alternative means of understanding the dynamics of the situation. The town wakes up unable to speak, leading to scenes of varying intensity in reaction, from Willow thinking she has lost her voice, to Xander's anger at Spike, to a young woman who walks by Buffy and Willow's dorm room sniffling, confused as to exactly *how* they are going to survive without talking. Xander and Buffy realize the absurdity of trying to communicate over the phone without a voice and others find new ways to communicate such as through white boards and computer modulated voices. Characters must attempt new forms of communication, as older forms prove to be unusable.

One commonly used exercise in any class involving a non-verbal component is the interview without words, in which students are asked to gain information as to a fellow student's age, name, job status and family without speaking or writing. In this way they realize a powerful aspect of the communicative process, and one that they rely upon too often, only when verbalization has been taken away. Naturally, trying to communicate almost solely through non-verbal communication can lead to misunderstandings. I point out that just as Riley learns that not having a voice can be literally dangerous, such as when the elevator activates a "lethal countermeasure" when he and Forrest cannot use a voice activated code, so it is also dangerous in terms of student's assumptions about their peers. Often they need to concentrate on what appear to them to be small or even trivial details about each other. This advice is echoed in "Hush" when Professor Walsh ironically points to the sign next to the elevator, warning that in case of emergency, "use the stairs." Students learn that the obvious is sometimes right before their eyes; they only have to look more closely to see it. In addition, non-verbal communication can lead to gross mis-interpretations. Buffy's nonverbal references, and their inherent misinterpretations, such as when Buffy mimes 'staking" the gentleman and Xander misinterprets this action as a reference to masturbation, are understood by students who have never seen the program before and appreciated in more depth by students who are *Buffy* fans.

Instructors in non-verbal classes teach the importance of paralanguage and paralin-guistics; sounds that accompany, and sometimes replace words. Lack of spoken words does not mean a lack of sound. "Hush" demonstrates that just as students learn that they can communicate without words, sound without words can often take on even more prominent a role, as when the sound of a bottle breaking in the dorm common area is jarring to the characters and to the audience. As an example, I ask student to make notes of what "language" is being used initially in the episode, without telling them that I am looking for paralinguistics. While some students analyze the episode carefully, looking to see if any words are spoken inadvertently, many take note of smaller cues, such as the fact that people can still cough (as in the case of Riley and Forrest in the elevator, and sniffle (as does the young women in the hallway who walks quickly by Buffy and Willow). Many students do not realize that silence itself is a form of paralanguage. Trenholm noted, "an often overlooked aspect of paralanguage is silence. Just as sounds create meaning, so too does the absence of sound" (117). The lack of sound itself is the foundation of many key scenes in "Hush," one that the students need to learn to be quiet and watch closely to find the hidden meaning.

In "Hush," a world without words is a world without recognizable order, one where the banks and other businesses are closed, church services take place silently on the street, and liquor stores prominently advertise that they are still available for those that need the release of alcohol.[5] The Scooby gang eventually uses small white boards for writing, but they turn out to be of limited use, good for only short declarative sentences and without much meaning or nuance. For example, Willow simply uses hers to write "Hi Giles," illustrating that a world without sounds is somewhat akin to the limited character count of Twitter, where often the banal and the vital compete for limited space. Professor Walsh, on the other hand, while talking to the members of the Initiative, uses a voice modulation unit like Stephen Hawking's, where her typing is translated to a computer voice. As one or two students noted, in her dual role as professor and leader, Walsh can still use technology for control and to maintain her position as head of the Initiative. Some students in the class also mention that this symbolic level of control also connects to her instructions to the members of the Initiative to wear civilian clothes as they patrol the streets of Sunnydale, as military outfits might be misinterpreted as something more sinister by the populace. The fact that many students pick up on this point in both class discussions and in their papers without me asking explicitly demonstrates that once they start looking for paralinguistic or other symbolic clues, they start to make more connections and relate it to the assigned texts.

According to my students, when Buffy and Riley meet in chaotic downtown Sunnydale they find that non-verbal communication is often easier than the awkwardness of their earlier conversations. When they kiss they realize that there is no need to verbalize how they feel. Most students found this scene fairly easy to relate to, with some joking that "it was about time that they kissed," or wondering aloud why Buffy and Riley were so "shy" around each other. They had noticed the duo's body language during the dream sequence and afterwards in the flirtatious way in which Buffy and Riley talked to each other at the start of the episode. Perhaps this observation was based on more personal experience than application of theory, but students were able to understand through their movements, eye contact and lack thereof, that something "was going on." Many students added this observation under their notes for haptics. While not all students noticed this as well, the majority were able to properly categorize the ways in which the characters touched each other under haptics. Some even took difference in culture into account. As Trenholm has noted, haptics (or touching), is often related to cultural differences which are regulated by cultural norms (125); touch defines relationships as romantic or non-romantic. Therefore, many in the class interpreted Buffy and Riley as a potential couple, while others were unsure whether Willow and Tara were potentially a couple or simply friends.

While it is important that students watch television shows that use music as a means of communicating how characters feel, and often "comment" on how they are acting by adding dramatic cues, or more romantic musical interludes, the sound design in the episode itself is extremely important in terms of interpretation and it often influences how students are supposed to interpret a scene or scenes.[6] The Gentlemen have a unique presentational style. They are tall, slim to the point of emaciation, bald and pasty white, but strangely enough, meticulously dressed in elegant suits and expensive shoes that need never touch the ground as the men simply float along. They also have a unique sound design all their own. Christopher Beck's soundtrack indicates themes now open for audience interpretation. A quick example of this is the sound of a heartbeat under the music in the clock tower where the Gentlemen store their captured hearts. The Gentlemen, who cannot speak and apparently disdain loud noises, give each other only a mild "golf clap" at the success in capturing three hearts in jars in a night's work. Usually during the next class, I play parts of the soundtrack to ask students to associate music with memories of particularly evocative scenes. Most students are able to replicate almost exactly where both romantic and suspense-indicating cues were in the episode they had watched a few days ago, illustrating the power of the score in communicating the meaning of such scenes.[7]

There are several other important uses of sound in the episode that help to create meaning for students. The classroom scene, where Giles gathers the members of the Scooby gang to explain as best he can the nature of the Gentlemen's threat, is familiar to any professor who has used projections, videos or even PowerPoint to conduct a lesson, and no doubt evokes some painful memories. In the classroom that Giles is using to explain the Gentlemen's plan, some "students" are attentive like Willow offering suggestions, some make crass jokes (accidentally or not) such as Buffy and Xander, some ask pointed questions and some are merely there to be amused, like Anya who sits eating popcorn. Giles, the over-eager teacher has a lesson plan that anticipates most questions, but to the amusement of many of the students, he has overdone the lesson with increasingly bloody pictures for emphasis. Students not only found this demonstration similar to some of my own teaching methods, but also mentioned that they were able to "get" what Giles was trying to communicate, even before Buffy did. This indicates not only the way in which students pick up on the teaching methods of their professors, but also the way in which "Hush" so keenly elaborates on communication principles.

Another aspect of the episode, one that does not involve directly nonverbal communication, is the use of diegetic versus non-diegetic sound. Diegetic sound is that which is actually present and can be seen to be created by something, such as a visual symphony orchestra or even a small cassette player, as opposed to sound that does not come from any given source onscreen, and therefore is sound that is simply designed to be accepted by the audience as background music.[8] After researching in a large book labeled *Fairy Tales,* Giles calls the Scooby gang together to discuss what he has found out about the Gentlemen. As he starts a projector, he also pushes the start button on a cassette player, providing background music for the nonverbal "lecture" that he is giving to a seemingly attentive class. Without this music the class presumably would not be able to focus on his "lesson." They seemingly needed the music to provide context for his visual aids. This is the only time in the episode where the background music has a source, coming from Giles' tape player, and this time the music is different than at any other time in the episode, changing the way that we the viewer are supposed to understand and follow the score. Most students do not notice that Giles was providing the music, but when prompted can tell the difference between the regular non-diegetic score of the show, and the diegetic music that accompanies Giles' lesson. Not only are the slight noises of the episode important, but also that music serves in two different ways to highlight and communicate vital information throughout the episode.

While the students increasingly noticed the way in which sound helped move the narrative along, they also picked up on visual clues. One revealing and teachable scene towards the end of the episode that can be read by students in multiple ways is when Tara, seeking a solution to the problem, goes through a book, literally looking for spells "of speech and silence." Students who have taken courses on critical theory and cultural studies suggest in discussion that it could be read as perhaps an invocation of the Marxist and semiotic idea that words contain literal power and that those who are symbolically voiceless are symbolically powerless.[9] Tara, who is almost voiceless to begin with due to a stutter, finds that she can contribute through the (literal) power of words, instead of using words as ways to control the weak, as did the Wicca group members. Tara can cast a spell to find literal strength and to try and solve the mystery of the Gentlemen.

In terms of another important aspect of the non-verbal lesson, the study of kinesics, these scenes are ripe for close analysis of body language. As Trenholm noted, "Body movements that convey emotional states are called affect displays" (113) and can express even what the face does not express. The literally trembling Tara reaching out to Willow, was noticed by some in the class as a foreshadowing of the attraction the two women soon feel for each other, and by others as simply signals of raw terror. Their body language alone, even without an emphasis on facial expression, conveyed the gravity of the situation. Students, after discussing these concepts previously in class, increasingly identified body language as they watched the episode. Facial expressions are also a key component of kinesics. As Trenholm also notes, "Regulators are nonverbal behaviors that act as 'traffic signals' during interaction" (112). This metaphor indicates that we use regulators as indications of what meaning it conveyed. She goes on to note that facial expressions "intensify certain emotions and de-intensify others, also eye behavior, indicates positive and negative emotions (116). Examples of these, some of which involve direct facial expressions, include head nods and eye movements. An example that most students found particularly amusing was the scene when the captured Buffy rolls her eyes at Riley when he smashes the wrong box and looks very pleased with himself. Many women in the class indicated that this was a condition observed only too well in male non-verbal communication. The use of humor, such as Giles's increasingly bloody representations of the Gentlemen's harvest in his overhead projections, or Buffy's outrage at the size of the hips that Giles has drawn in his version of her, are some of the more easily explainable and understandable demonstrations of applied theory for students. *Buffy* has always included healthy dollops of humor in-between extreme violence and teen angst. It has possessed since the start what Mary Magoulick called "playful humor and wry wit" (Magoulick 729). As silent movies have shown, the audience does not need verbal expression for humor, what is equally important is body language. Kinesics are some of the easiest ways to convey humor nonverbally.

Emblems, or nonverbal signs that have verbal representations, are often a key cause of humorous misunderstandings and can lead to conflict resolution, in a way the students can understand and appreciate. This concept is illustrated by Xander mistaking Spike's bloody face and Anya's body lying in repose for the results of a vampire attack, leading him to viciously pummel Spike. This misunderstanding goes on until Anya corrects Xander and rewards him for his presumptive heroism by indicating with her finger that they should go and have sex. Many students in their notes and in class discussions correctly defined this as an example of emblems, which are "kinesic behaviors whose direct verbal translations are known to all the members of a social group. Emblems are like silent words" (Trenholm 111). An example as many in the class noticed was that holding hands could be taken as a sign of affection, but also a sign of connection. Willow and Tara needed to hold hands in order for the spell to work, and once they connected, they turned their heads simultaneously, and magically moved the soda machine through the air to block the door. In teaching, this particular aspect of the episode was perhaps the easiest point to get across, as most students were able to both understand and elaborate on the concept of emblems.

By the end of the episode most students seemed to have grasped the basic concepts and to have relate them in both comments and on worksheets. When the "scream by the princess" kills the monsters, bringing the audience back to spoken dialogue after 29 minutes, many students were startled, as if they had gotten used to the lack of dialogue. Just as the town of Sunnydale symbolically awakens, so too do the students, and as several indicated, it was jarring for them to return to spoken language, just as it was for the characters. After the scream, the scenes shift to the next day where various characters "talk over" what has just happened and what has changed in their relationships, much as my students did at the end of the episode. In the end even while talking, body language remains more important for Willow and Tara who flirt awkwardly, and glance shyly at each other. The feelings they are developing for each other are obvious, even if they cannot verbalize them yet.

For Buffy and Riley, things are even more awkward. When Riley enters Buffy's room and sits down on the bed across from her, he ventures, "I guess we have to talk": she responds, "Yeah, I guess we do" and the rest is silence as the episode ends without further explanation or resolution. Although many students found the lack of resolution to this relationship to be disappointing (I urged them to rent the boxed sets, after all, I can't show them *all* of the episodes in class!) many others thought that the ending perfectly summed up the ways in which non-verbal communication was *less* difficult than actually verbalizing feelings. Although many had not seen the characters before the screening in my classroom, students could understand the dynamics as if they had watched the series from the start.

"Hush" is a subtle episode, and makes an excellent teaching tool in a communications class of any variety. While the episode is about communication (as Buffy's psychology professor, Dr. Walsh explains in the classroom dream at the start of the episode) it is also about what Richards calls a "rhetoric of identity with some consistency across all of its seasons" (124). The characters in *Buffy* do not remain static; they grow and evolve as distinct individuals from season to season. *Buffy* reveals that in communication and in the show, there is always much more below the surface than meets the eye. An ordinary girl is the chosen Slayer; a seemingly innocuous town hides a portal to the world of demons below it and so on.

In adopting "Hush" as a teaching tool, I convey two key concepts. One is that students understand the subtle and often complex way in which non-verbal communication is a vital and primary part of human communication. The second and equally important skill for them to obtain is the capacity for critical thinking and the ability to challenge authorities. A critical examination of "Hush" helps me to teach the students that while academic experts (such as Professor Walsh, or Watcher Giles) can analyze a situation and offer advice, at the end of the day the slayer, like my students, must learn to improvise. Like Buffy, students need to also take the lesson that critical analysis, the use of interpretative skills, constantly questioning one's surroundings, and looking for meaning are central to analysis of all media and texts, and to communication. These skills cannot be learned in one class, much less in one lesson, yet "Hush" provides a unique way to look below the surface and read a text or scene with new skills they are unaccustomed to applying, interpreting in ways that seem on the surface, but much more difficult than they had initially imagined at the start of class. As Neil Postman and Charles Weingartner argue, "the critical content of any learning experience is the method or process by which the learning occurs" (19). In analyzing *Buffy*, students are not there merely to identify what kinds of non-verbal communication various characters are using, but to ask what it is to communicate, to ask what importance things such as language, sound, territory and space occupy in the pantheon of the human learning experience. This lesson asks students to decode emotional resonance and meaning based upon clues without their usual safety net of easy explanation, and also asks the students to think deeper and more critically about what lies below the surface of a text or show. If teaching "Hush" to students inculcates one primary lesson, it is that no matter what they have to say, both as students, and as human beings, they should never be silenced.

NOTES

1. An example of critical analysis of *Buffy* and queer theory is found in Allison McCracken. One of the best feminist critiques of *Buffy* is by Yael Sherman.
2. Two books that deal with the episode in great detail include Paul Attinello, Halfyard, and Knights, eds., and Jowett, (2005).
3. For further reference, see also Overbay and Preston-Matto.
4. See also Cogan (2008).
5. See also Wilcox (1999) and Wilcox (2005).
6. See Graeme Turner.
7. For a recent book length discussion of this see Attinello, Halfyard, and Knights eds.
8. For a more in-depth discussion on music and *Buffy*, see also Wilcox (2005).
9. For one of the most compelling arguments about power and society see Stewart Hall.

WORKS CITED

Adalian, Josef. "Joss Whedon Returns to Television After Dr. Horrible." *Televisionweek* February 2, 2009: 1–23. Print.

Attinello, Paul, Janet Halfyard, and Vanessa Knights, eds. *Music, Sound and Silence in* Buffy the Vampire Slayer. United Kingdom: Ashgate, 2010. Print.

Cogan, Brian. "Film and Television Portrayals of Organized Crime." *Organized Crime: From Trafficking to Terrorism*. Ed. Shanty Frank. Denver, CO: ABC-CLIO Press, 2008. Print.

Cover, Rob. "'Not to Be Toyed With': Drug Addiction, Bullying and Self-Empowerment in *Buffy the Vampire Slayer*." *Continuum: Journal of Media & Cultural Studies* Vol. 19 No.1 (March 2005): 85–101. Print.

Di Gregorio, Luciano. "*Buffy the Vampire Slayer*: Using a Popular Culture Post-Modern Text in the Classroom." *Screen Education* 42 (n.date): 90–93. Print.

Hall, Edward. *The Silent Language*. New York: Doubleday, 1990. Print.

Hall, Stewart, ed. *Representation: Cultural Representations and Signifying Practices*. London: Sage Publications, 1997.

Howell, Amanda. "'If we hear any inspirational power chords...': Rock Music, Rock Culture on *Buffy the Vampire Slayer*." *Continuum: Journal of Media and Cultural Studies* 18.3 (September 2004): 406–422. Print.

Jenkins, Alice, and Stuart Susan. "Extending Your Mind: Non-Standard Perlocutionary Acts in 'Hush.'" *Slayage: The Whedon Studies Association Journal* 9 (n.date): n.pag. Web. 5 April 2009.

Jowett, Lorna. *Sex and the Slayer: A Gender Studies Primer for the Buffy Fan*. Connecticut: Wesleyan University Press, 2005. Print.

Kromer, Kelly. "Silence as Symptom: A Psychoanalytic Reading of 'Hush.'" *Slayage* 19 (n.date): n.pag. Web. 5 April 2009.

Magoulick, Mary. "Frustrating Female Heroism: Mixed Messages in *Xena, Nikita* and *Buffy*." *The Journal of Popular Culture* 39.5 (2006): n.pag. Print.

McCracken, Allison. "At Stake: Angel's Body, Fantasy, Masculinity and Queer Desire in Teen Television." *Undead TV: Essays on* Buffy the Vampire Slayer. Ed. Lisa Parks and Elana Levine. Durham: Duke University Press, 2007. Print.

Overbay, Karen Eileen, and Lahney Preston-Matto. "Staking in Tongues: Speech Act as Weapon in *Buffy*." *Fighting the Forces: What's at Stake in* Buffy the Vampire Slayer. Ed. Rhonda V. Wilcox and David Lavery. Oxford, UK: Rowman and Littlefield, 2002. 73–84. Print.

Postman, Neil, and Charles Weingartner. *Teaching as a Subversive Activity*. New York: Delta Books, 1969.

Richards, Chris. "What are We? Adolescence, Sex and Intimacy in *Buffy the Vampire Slayer.*" *Continuum: Journal of Media & Cultural Studies* 18.1 (March 2004): 121–137. Print.

Shade, Patrick. "Screaming to Be Heard: Reminders and Insights on Community and Communication in 'Hush.'" *Slayage* 21 (n.date): n.pag. Web. 5 April 2009.

Sherman, Yael. "Tracing the Carnival Spirit in *Buffy the Vampire Slayer*: Feminist Reworkings of the Grotesque." *Thirdspace: A Journal of Feminist Theory & Culture* (Special issue on Representation and Transgressive Sexualities). 3.2 (March 2004): n.pag. Print.

Trenholm, Sarah. *Thinking Through Communication*. New York: Allyn & Bacon, 2005. Print.

Turner, Graeme. *Film as Social Practice*. London: Routledge, 1988. Print.

Wilcox, Rhonda V. "There Will Never Be a 'Very Special' Buffy": *Buffy* and the Monsters of Teen Life. *Journal of Popular Film and Television* 27.2 (1999): 16–23. Print.

_____. *Why Buffy Matters: The Art of* Buffy the Vampire Slayer. London: IB Taurus, 2005. Print.

"Show, Don't Tell": Teaching the Elements of Film Production

Jane Martin

Over the last five years I have integrated *Buffy the Vampire Slayer* into almost all my courses in filmmaking. The series exhibits excellent production values which illustrate the techniques of filmmaking effectively to any audience. Content, execution and originality are the three basic concepts I promote and *Buffy* excels at each. The series adds creativity and excitement to my curriculum and my classroom experience. *Buffy* works as a text because of the challenges it demands of its audience. Students are required to become active rather than passive viewers to gather the content as well as the production values of the show.

I am a tenured Associate Professor of Communication at a small Catholic University in the Midwestern United States. My curriculum includes courses and topics in Film and Video Production, Film Editing and Writing for the Screen. During the first 10 years of my career, I have to admit, I stayed with the classic films for examples in the classroom. To illustrate exemplary filmmaking I utilized canon such as *Citizen Kane* for sound, lighting, cinematography and editing, *Rear Window* for mise-en-scène and *Un Chien Andalou* for experimental filmmaking. My students responded fairly well to these examples, but with each passing year, they were less inclined to engage with these historic examples without a lengthy lecture on how each was significant to filmmaking and an explanation on black and white cinematography. It was also necessary to show the entire film to give the student context to understand the examples or at least to give the film its needed reference.

Sue Turnbull's lecture at the first *Slayage* conference on *Buffy*, "'Enough *Buffy*': Towards an Aesthetics of Television" led me to understand that everything I was doing had to change. Her discussion on the aesthetics of television and her concluding argument that: "This is the crucial moment in Television Studies: the moment when the history of the text and the experience of the viewer come together in a potentially productive intellectual and emotional encounter" spoke to me. She called that moment the aesthetic moment, and suggested that as teachers and fans we can "share this moment, explore it and extend it through an exchange of knowledge and experience in which there should be no hierarchies of cultural values since all forms of knowledge (including knowledge of the classics, history and the popular) are of equal importance in the quest for understanding how meaning is produced and how texts are experienced." Her lesson continued, "this moment, with this quest, that a revised notion of Television Studies should begin since, as the myriad fans of *Buffy* have already demonstrated, it is in this moment of shared understandings, shared knowledge and shared aesthetic experience that we all stand to learn from each other." (Turnbull) It was clear that I was holding back as a teacher, not truly integrating myself into my instruction. During this time I was also reading a number of books on classroom instruction and my experience at the Slayage Conference reinforced a concept conveyed by Maryellen Weimer in her book *Improving Your Classroom Teaching*. She observes that when you share your passions and your interests with students, "Your vulnerability touches theirs and they respond. They decide to take a second look — to follow your lead and take risks of their own." (Weimer 22). I had never been a risk taker in my classroom, but if ever there was a time, this was the moment to embrace risk.

According to Weimer, the components of effective instruction include: enthusiasm, preparation and organization, ability to stimulate student thought and interest, and clarity and knowledge (7). The combination of examples from *Buffy* and an increased enthusiasm for my classes has contributed to a more successful classroom experience for both my students and me. That was over five years ago and now I am a complete convert to teaching with *Buffy*. Not only do I share my passion for *Buffy* with students, but also *Angel, Firefly* and the series, *Supernatural*. My course evaluations have improved greatly over the last five years and so has my rapport with students. They are more willing to share their interests in television, graphic novels and film. This self-disclosure has improved my understanding of their involvement with the public arts and expanded my opportunities for more relevant classroom examples. Adopting *Buffy* across my curriculum allows me the opportunity to integrate my personality into the classroom. Just as Joss Whedon invites us to bring our subtext to his work, my subtext has infiltrated my teaching. Sue Turnbull was correct, this is "the moment of shared understandings, shared knowledge and shared aesthetic experience that we all stand to learn from each other. It is time to take television and popular culture seriously and in a good way." My course preparation and instruction are more effective and admittedly, more enjoyable.

Outlined in the following pages is the use of specific episodes and segments (DVD chapters) used to teach visual production, screenwriting, setting, content, props, costumes, sound and theme. I provide either before or after each viewing a selection of questions/topics for students to write about that guide the classroom discussion. The students receive the handout prior to the viewing and we go over the specifics of theme, content, execution, and visual thinking. For originality and creativity, students are asked to relate the watched clip or show to others in their viewing experience. Here is a sample of the guided worksheet that I introduce and use with the viewing of shorts and movies.

- What is the intended message/theme of the show?
- How is the theme presented visually?
- How is the theme presented in the dialog?
- Briefly discuss how the show meets the following criteria:

o Originality

o Creativity

o Content

o Execution

o Visual Thinking

o Other observations?

Course: Introduction to Audio/Video Production
Selection: "Welcome to the Hellmouth: A Demon in Sunnydale" (1.1)
Topic: Developing setting and content.

"Introduction to Audio/Video Production" is a perfect fit for *Buffy*. Utilizing a forty minute television show for classroom example allows me to play an entire episode during a class period and still have time for a discussion. Full length films prohibit this opportunity and use much more time in class than I have available for this type of instruction.

Storytelling is the most important element of film and video production. Many of my students are well versed in the standard Hollywood filmmaking style which stresses spectacle, but most have spent little time recognizing how the story is conveyed to the audience. The same concepts which they used to analyze literature in their English course can be used to analyze film. These same elements; plot, character, setting and theme are used to tell a film story with one major difference. Film is a visual medium, so we "show, don't tell" the audience the story. *Buffy* excels in the film concept of 'show the audience, don't tell them' and it is successful not only in production but in storytelling and craft.[1]

The first day of the course begins with the first scene from the series. The showing of this scene establishes a tone for my course and some insight about me as the instructor. I explain my interest in the show and why I think that the series is quality television worthy of study. The students are either intrigued or roll their eyes. They realize that both this course and this professor are unique. Immediately, I challenge them to think about something they never have before or to take an academic look at something that they like or may even love. This approach changes their perspective about watching television. Most people are passive television viewers; this assignment requires them to become active participants in the media and to pay attention to detail.

The student's critical viewing begins with the opening chapter of the pilot "A Demon in Sunnydale" and it wakes the class up on the first day. The scene begins with a long shot of Sunnydale High School, moves into the school, down the hallways, through the spooky skeletons of a biology lab and quickly to a window as we hear glass break. A teenage couple comes in through the window and it appears that they are in the high school for a romantic encounter. The girl nervously and somewhat fearfully asks if the young man hears anything and if anyone is there. When he says "no," she turns into a vampire and bites him. The students analyze the potential message of the series and examine the lighting, sound, cinematography, acting, editing, props, sets and editing. These elements are essential to discuss the success of the director to "show" the audience the information. They are able to articulate that this is a show about high school, teenagers, that there is an element of horror and that *Buffy* was not at all what they expected. They expect the blonde girl (Darla) to be the victim and yet she is the predator. The students note that the show is going to be full of surprises and work outside the expectation of the genre (horror). Another point that they are quick to communicate is that none of the major characters in the show are in the opening sequence. The absence of these characters also indicates that something will be different about this series. After dealing with this content information, we review the scene again and discuss their observations about the execution of the lighting, shot composition, sound construction and editing in more detail. Since this is the first day of class, students are instructed to simply discuss what they see and hear. This discussion sets the stage for the development of these components throughout the semester. Repeated viewing is essential for students. They develop a much more active viewing style from exercising their critical viewing skills. We watch this scene at least three times and have a short discussion between each.

Course: Introduction to Audio/Video Production
Selection: "Storyteller: Masterpiece television/Main Titles" (7.16)
Topic: Sets, Props and Costumes for character development.

"Storyteller" is particularly successful in establishing the concept of mise-en-scene. Mise-en-scene used literally means "putting onto the stage" and for the purposes of film describes the lighting, action, costumes, sets, props and any other elements contained in the shot. "Storyteller" opens with a shot of a bookcase. The books are hardback and beautifully bound. Two titles clearly in focus are Nietzsche and William Shakespeare. All the other volumes on the shelves are intentionally out of focus. After a subtle dissolve the camera pans left across relics, artifacts, and what appears to be the skull of a vampire (teeth prominently displayed). Lying atop the antique table is a comic book or graphic novel open to a layout starring the Silver Surfer. Another dissolve and pan leads us to a beautifully framed poster for *Star Wars*, Episode Four prominently displaying Luke and Leia. On the bookcase in front of the poster there are additional relics including what looks to be a magic lamp. The pan continues to a fireplace where another *Star Wars* poster rests above the mantel. The pan moves left past the fireplace to reveal the character Andrew wearing a smoking jacket, holding a pipe and reading a book in an oversized leather chair. Andrew is a member of a trio of inept villains who try to destroy the slayer in Season Six. His character is immersed in comic books, fantasy fiction and *Star Wars*. He breaks the fourth wall and says to the viewer, "Oh hello there, gentle viewers." After this sequence of events, which is only twenty-one seconds into the program, students are asked to discuss the character presented and the concept for this show. Students get the point quickly. The setting and props tell the audience about Andrew and his desire to see the world from his own viewpoint, which is far from reality. The film makers use the visual media quite effectively. Once again, the rule of "show the audience, don't tell them" establishes this scene as highly successful. As Andrew addresses the audience, the objects surrounding him illustrate his character and establish his identity. Also, the *Star Wars* fans love the references. As the years pass the one film that does not seem to fall out of fashion is the original *Star Wars*. A majority of my students are male and for the most part, are genre fiction fans. This particular scene is relevant to them and from their participation in class it appears that they feel they can speak more freely in my courses after a bit of *Star Wars* banter. Students often share how many times they have seen the film, their collections of *Star Wars* memorabilia and the merit of Episodes Four, Five and Six over One, Two and Three. Most everyone feels free to discuss what they are passionate about because I am sharing my passion for *Buffy*. This modeling or mentoring gives the students the opportunity to more openly discuss their media passions.

As Andrew documents the story of "Buffy: the Slayer of the Vampires," he is interrupted by Anya — who would like to come into the bathroom. The viewer discovers that Andrew's sets, props, costumes and lighting have all been part of his story, his imagination. When Anya asks Andrew what he is doing, he points to the camera and says, "Entertaining and educating." This dialogue develops an additional topic of discussion. I ask students, "Do they think this will be a theme in Whedon's work?" Another conversation that can develop from this moment is about entertainment and content. While visual media can either invoke an intellectual or emotional response, it is at its best when it accomplishes both. To develop content that works both intellectually and emotionally, filmmakers should develop a theme and structure the story and visual elements to illustrate and support that theme. Students are asked to produce the themes for their projects before they begin any pre-production development. The theme directs the elements of their storytelling and keeps the production unified. I suggest they strive to produce quality productions and that their themes/content will lead them to the same goal as Whedon, "entertaining and educating." As stated by Matthew Pateman, "Though Andrew may have other things in mind in "Storyteller," his assessment is absolutely true: *Buffy*, in ways that are already becoming apparent and in many which remain to be seen, is spectacularly, wonderfully, culturally and aesthetically "a legacy for future generations." (211) The goal for the students is to challenge their audience; try to have some ambition in their work, to follow the guidelines that "Storyteller" illustrates about quality programming.

Courses: Writing for the Media
Selection: "The Body" (5.16)
Topic: Integrating theme in all production aspects.

In "Writing for the Media," "The Body" provides a unique example for discussing theme and dialogue. In this course, we watch the full episode for content and execution of story and dialogue. This episode clearly illustrates how visual elements support the theme throughout a plot line.[2] The use of the body or bodies and physicality can be seen throughout the episode. Students search for the "bodies" in the episode and discuss how visual bodies contribute to the meaning of the piece. This episode opens with Buffy finding her mother, Joyce, dead on the sofa in their home. Buffy, Dawn and the other characters must deal with their loss and their grief over her death. It is a difficult episode for many students to watch. We discuss moments in the dialogue that are particularly well crafted.

The tone of "The Body" is not the same as the majority of the series and the lack of horror elements is surprising to those who are unfamiliar with the show. Students are fascinated with the fact that the series kills off one of the main characters, since this happens so rarely in television. This adds to the students' understanding that *Buffy* aimed for a higher quality of television production.

Prior to the class discussion of "The Body" students wrote a general paragraph discussing their impressions of this episode as a whole and a paragraph on anything that they found either remarkable or troubling about the episode. One student recorded the following as his impression of what he found compelling:

> The character I found most interesting on the surface was Anya. She follows in a long line of television science fiction characters, "learning to be human." This theme is common throughout all science fiction, though — a non-human — learning to be human represents what humans go through every day ... in a sense we are all learning to be human. This idea is crystallized when Anya asks what is happening and how she should feel. Willow, speaking for all humans, for all those who have ever felt, and for all those who have ever lost responds: "I don't know." The death of Buffy's mother has taught them all a little more of what it means to be human.

This commentary was particularly insightful and suggested this student's understanding not only of the episode but the "learning to be human" concept from other references in his reading and viewing experience. His knowledge and expertise helped to guide the others in the class discussion on the episode.

"The Body" is one of the richest episodes from the series. It can be used to teach screenwriting, theme, dialogue and the elements of visual and sound production as I outline in my course preparation for Advanced Audio/Video Production in the next section. Students identify with the loss that Buffy feels at the death of her mother and her need to protect her younger sister. Also, since this show has little of the violence or horror elements that are present in most episodes it is a good introduction to the series for those who are not interested in or troubled by horror films.

Course: Advanced Audio/Video Production
Selection: "The Body" (5.16)
Topic: Sound

For the Advanced Audio/Video Production Class I show this episode to explore the use of sound-or lack of sound in visual production. The lack of music or sound effects really intensifies students' physical reaction to the show. In the episode, Buffy comes to school to get Dawn and let her know of their mother's death. Dawn is in art class, drawing a figure (a body), the class has glass walls which look out into the hallway. Buffy and Dawn are outside the classroom in the hallway when she tells Dawn. Dawn breaks down and cries. Her cries are muffled, we only see and hear what the students in the classroom can see and hear. This approach is an effective way of making the viewer an observer who must witness Dawn's public display of grief. It is very moving and as a student stated, "difficult to watch." This sequence provides another effective demonstration of "show, don't tell" for the audience. Students are asked to evaluate how the sound establishes a feeling or mood for the piece. One of the most intriguing aspects about using this episode is the silence that usually overtakes the viewing experience. Each time I show the episode, the students remark that they did not want to make any noise while watching. They did not even want to move in their chairs for fear that they would spoil the mood of the piece. They are apprehensive about making any noise; they want to keep the atmosphere of the piece consistent in their viewing. Students often fidget, text, or check their phones for the time during classroom viewings of other media. This does not happen during "The Body." They are captivated by the silence. It is a good lesson in filmmaking that less can be more.

After the episode students are asked to write a paragraph discussing their impression of how sound is employed to involve the viewer. One student commented after viewing the episode: "I must confess the nature of the episode kept me in a constant state of waiting for some horrible payoff, which only heightened the powerful silence." Another student commented about the sound:

> The lack of music allows the visual and how we feel about them to take over — there is no soundtrack to give us a sense of hope or despair — it is left entirely up to where the visuals take us. We are allowed to hear every sound of what's going on, and told nothing about where the scene is going to end up. We find out what happens when she does, while normally the soundtrack would lead us there before hand.

This episode demands active viewing, which is a viewing strategy I suggest that students develop to become more observant. The discussion focuses on the difference between active and passive viewing and how the use of soundtrack guides the viewer through and instructs the viewer how to feel. Without a soundtrack as a device, this episode involves the audience much more intensely in the character's world.

Course: Editing Processes and Theory
Selection: "The Body" (5.16)
Topic: Editing

"The Body" is also a reference for Editing Processes and Theory class. Students are asked to evaluate the editing techniques; examining what is shown, not shown, heard or not heard. This exercise is designed to utilize critical viewing skills. After watching the episode students are asked to write two comments on what they specifically saw and heard during the production. Here are two comments from students in this course:

> The editing also really lets the performers tell the story. The best example is how we didn't have to hear Buffy say — that their mother had died, we knew that already. What was important was Dawn's reaction to it and the surrounding she was in, which was also clearly shown since the camera was still in the classroom looking at her through the glass. This pulled her classmates into the moment as well as the audience.
> That Buffy telling Dawn their mother had died happened in such an uncompromising

way—we saw them through a window and heard Dawn's voice crack from a distance—really exposed us, the audience, for what we are ... observers. And seeing such an emotional scene unfold in that way as compared to giving us close-ups where we can hear their voices, made it all the more difficult to watch.

Students relay that this scene continues to support the concept of "show, don't tell." The staging of the scene in this fashion is more effective than actually hearing the dialogue. The episode clearly illustrates the editor's choices in how to effectively convey the information to the audience.

Course: Advanced Audio/Video Production
Selection: "Once More, with Feeling" (6.7)
Topic: Cumulative Final Exam

In the "Advanced Audio/Video" course students take a final exam, and each year I state that we will end the class exactly where we began. The students know that they will be evaluating a scene from *Buffy*. I often show the opening scene from "Once More, with Feeling" at the end of the course. This selection allows them to analyze a genre piece (the musical) complete with titles and special effects. With the written instructions for the final, they are given the following quote by well known director Sidney Lumet (*Network*, *Twelve Angry Men* and *The Verdict*):

> What the movie is about will determine how it will be cast, how it will look, how it will be edited, how it will be musically scored, how it will be mixed, how the titles will look, and, with a good studio, how it will be released. What it's about will determine how it is to be made.

Lumet's comment reminds them of the content for our class; that whatever a production is about (the theme) will instruct the director on how it should be made. All the elements of production: lighting, sound, cinematography, props, setting, acting and editing should be executed to convey the theme and that our goal is to show, not tell the audience. The final exam instructions are as follows:

> Students will analyze a scene from *Buffy the Vampire Slayer*. It will be shown once for you to watch, then again for you take notes, and one more time so you do not miss anything. Please answer the following questions. You may answer them in any order you like. Structure your answer as you wish as long as it is in essay form with complete sentences and paragraphs. Make sure that you complete all the questions. Have fun, you know how to do this.
>   1. How does the tone of the piece support the genre it imitates?
>   2. How does editing effectively guide our thoughts, associations and emotional responses from one image to another so that smooth continuity and coherence are achieved? How does the cutting speed (which determines the average duration of each shot) correspond to the emotional tone of the scene involved? What types of editing styles are used?
>   3. Is the lighting of the scene (a) direct, harsh, and hard; (b) medium or balanced; or (c) soft and diffused? Does high-key or low-key lighting predominate? How do the lighting decisions fit the scene's story?

4. Does the cinematography create clear, powerful, and effective images in a natural way, or does it self-consciously show off the skills and techniques of the cinematographer? Explain.

5. How effectively does the music support the visual? Does the selection of music further the plot?

6. How would you describe the acting technique? Does it fit the tone of the piece?

7. How are special effects used to support the scene?

8. Is the piece effective, why or why not? Include the title sequence in your response.

The students' evaluation of the scene is usually thoughtful and well processed. They enjoy the scene and can evaluate all the elements of production from it. This exercise also ends the class on such a high note. "Once More, with Feeling" is the musical episode of *Buffy*. The opening sequence is used for the exam. The scene opens with Buffy in a graveyard singing about her lack of enthusiasm for slaying. She is supported by a host of backup singers; the vampires and monsters she is hunting. The scene ends with a spray of vampire dust and a big musical finish. Students evaluate all the elements listed above and the overall effectiveness of the piece. Since this has been supported throughout the course, they are usually quite well prepared for this analysis.[3]

After five years of integrating *Buffy* and other popular media into my coursework my teaching has become more effective. My institution utilizes the IDEA Center course evaluations which give an overall rating in four areas (along with a multitude of information): progress on relevant objectives, excellent teacher, excellent course and an average of excellent teacher and excellent course. In my "Introduction to Audio/Video" course the scores were usually 4.4–4.5 out of a 5 scale in the categories listed above. After the integration of *Buffy* the evaluations improved to a 4.7–4.9 in the categories outlined. In the "Advanced Audio/Video Production" course the evaluations were initially 4.4–4.8 and after integrating *Buffy* they increased to 4.8–5.0. The last time I taught the class, I received 5.0 in each category, which never happened before bringing *Buffy* into the classroom. The most encouraging input that reflects my improved instruction came in the comment section of one of my evaluations. A student stated, "I feel that you are really in this with us, that you are a part of what we are doing and learning and working with us in every way." Integrating *Buffy* into my curriculum improved my teaching performance specifically because I enjoy the classroom experience. Sharing *Buffy* and my enthusiasm for the excellent technical and writing execution of the show gave the students concrete examples of successful production.

The inclusion of *Buffy* or any other piece of popular media in the classroom must be accompanied by thorough preparation and organization for each episode or clip. Use worksheets or questions to guide the learning, without these students get bogged down in the plot and what happened in the story, which is usually not what is wanted unless the exercise is on plot. Guide students on what to evaluate before they watch the episode. Review the criteria with them and answer any questions. Often students have questions about the plot that need answers before a thorough discussion can begin. Explain clearly why they are watching and what they are to get from the episode or clip. If instructors do not, students will just watch it passively and not look beyond the entertainment factor. Also, be sure to review scenes multiple times. Students get much more information from a selection after several viewings. The series has the ability to stimulate student thought and interest. Many of the students watched the show when they were much younger and did not consider the themes or messages for the viewer. Those who have not seen the show had often dismissed it due to its name; these students develop a new appreciation for a television series they had misjudged.

After the integration of *Buffy* into my curriculum, I am more connected with students and their interests. The students and I are truly in this together. I am not the sage on the stage nor the guide or the side. I am the co-learner, the mentor-the mentored-I am a fan, they know that I love what I teach and have great passion for it. Bringing my subtext to my teaching has improved my course instruction, my course assessment but most of all my love for teaching. I enjoy the classroom experience more than I did five years ago. The integration of *Buffy* into my course instruction has added to my enthusiasm to teach and created a more conducive learning environment for my students.

NOTES

1. For insight into the effects of *Buffy* on quality television refer to Robert Moore's essay, "When TV Became Art: What We Owe to *Buffy*."

2. For an excellent analysis of "The Body" please refer to "'They're Going to Find a Body': Quality Television and the Supernatural in "The Body"" by Rhonda Wilcox in her examination of the series, *Why Buffy Matters*.

3. For additional information and potential teaching resources for "Once More, with Feeling," refer to Richard S. Albright's essay "Breakaway pop hit or ... book number?": "Once More, with Feeling" and Genre." *Slayage* 17, (June 2005).

WORKS CITED

"The Body." *Buffy the Vampire Slayer*. WB. 27 February 2001. Television.
"Once More with Feeling." *Buffy the Vampire Slayer*. UPN. 6 November 2001. Television.
"Storyteller." *Buffy the Vampire Slayer*. UPN. 25 February 2003. Television.
Turnbull, Sue. "'Not Just Another Buffy Paper': Towards an Aesthetics of Television." *Slayage* 13/14 (2004): n.pag. Web.
Weimer, Maryellen. *Improving Your Classroom Teaching*. Newbury Park, London Sage Publications,1993. Print.
"Welcome to the Hellmouth: A Demon in Sunnydale." *Buffy the Vampire Slayer*. WB. 10 March. 1997. Television.
Wilcox, Rhonda. *Why Buffy Matters: The Art of* Buffy the Vampire Slayer. London: I. B. Tauris, 2005. Print.

Television, Violence and Demons: Discussing Media Effects with the Vampire Slayer

Rosie White

This essay discusses the process and experience of employing an episode from *Buffy the Vampire Slayer* as a means to engage second year undergraduate students in debates about violence and television. At Northumbria University (United Kingdom) I teach a module called *Quality and Popular Television* which is a second year option for single honors English Literature students. This module is designed to expand students' understanding of the discipline as applicable to other media as well as literary texts, in addition to developing their skills in independent analysis and interpretation. Issues regarding the notion of "quality" are addressed in relation to a variety of television genres, including documentary, reality series, lifestyle programming, crime drama and soap opera. Information distributed to students via the module guide in electronic and printed form includes the following.

Module Synopsis

This module approaches the medium of television with some of the critical tools which have been developed in cultural studies and media studies over the last forty years. Through detailed examination of some of television's most critically acclaimed productions you will be encouraged to analyze the assumptions upon which judgments about "quality" television are based. Close attention will be paid to the manner in which quality television represents and addresses issues of gender, race and class, with the aim of questioning ideas about television as a medium and, in the process, developing a critical awareness of its role in contemporary culture.

AIMS OF THE MODULE

1. To enhance students' understanding and knowledge of twentieth century cultural theory in relation to television.
2. To consider a range of approaches which will enrich and inform their study of textual and visual media.

3. To encourage students to interpret and discuss complex academic writings about culture and value in an independent manner.

4. To expand students' understanding and knowledge of the range of academic debates around gender, sexual, and ethnic difference.

LEARNING OUTCOMES

Upon successful completion of this module, students will have gained

1. An enhanced knowledge of 20th century cultural theory.

2. A developed understanding of the debates regarding quality and value within contemporary television studies.

3. An increased ability to understand and discuss complex academic writings.

4. The enhanced ability to select relevant primary and secondary materials and to deploy this evidence in answers to conceptual issues and questions.

5. Enhanced analytical and interpretative skills in presenting an argued case in written form.

ASSESSMENT

Presentation (40 percent) and 2,000 word essay (60 percent).[1]

The *Buffy* session occurs in Week 6 of a 12 week program and invariably proves both popular and lively. In the module guide each week's topic is accompanied by some questions to consider in preparation for seminar debate, and further reading on the subject. These titles have been starred in the works cited section following this essay.

WEEK 6: TELEVISION AND (REAL) VIOLENCE— BUFFY AND COLUMBINE

1. To what extent does watching television affect our behavior?

2. Why is violence on television perceived to be bad for us?

3. Why is there so much violence depicted on television programs?

For many current students *Buffy* invokes a certain nostalgia, as many of them watched it when it was initially broadcast on terrestrial television in the UK from 1998 to 2004. In this sense the material reminds them of their younger selves. Some students can consequently be dismissive of *Buffy* as a program which they connected to in their early teens, and from which they wish to now distance themselves. In each group, however, there is invariably a student or a few students who have continued to watch *Buffy*, *Angel* and other fantasy adventure series with similarly complex storylines. The tension between those who are dismissive and those who are knowledgeable creates a useful dynamic within the seminar group and produces much debate about the value and status of particular forms of television.

The module is taught to a group of approximately 25 students over 12 weeks, via one two-hour session followed by a one-hour session a day or two later in the week. This structure gives both tutor and students a great deal of flexibility regarding how the material is delivered and how much time is spent on small or large-group debate. The schedule varies from week to week depending on the type or duration of the television program which is being studied. During the week which addresses *Buffy* and violence the sessions run as follows: I begin the first, two-hour session with a brief overview in the form of a mini-lecture, sketching a few of the debates around violence on television, and some of the background to the series and the episode that we are about to view. This introduction is followed by a screening and group debate. Students lead the subsequent one-hour session of presentations on set texts and then hold another group debate.

While giving a lecture is not always the most effective way of conveying information, this background is necessary for students who have only just begun studying visual media in this manner. A few students in the group may have taken Media Studies at "A" Level (high school or college pre-degree qualifications), and can bring this prior knowledge to bear on the sessions. Many pre-degree qualifications in media as an academic subject address the question of violence as it remains one of the most problematic and contentious issues across all forms of visual media. My introductory remarks are thus designed to make students who have not done media studies before aware of the variety of debates within academic work on the subject. The introduction is also designed to establish a questioning approach to "common-sense" ideas about violence and the media — effectively to raise the level of subsequent seminar debate beyond a "moral panic" approach.[2]

Briefly, my introduction notes the different academic accounts of the effect of television as a popular medium and violence on television in particular. I begin by outlining what is popularly known as the "hypodermic effect" model, which is based on the broad assumption that television and other popular media have a controlling effect on their consumers, almost to the extent of brainwashing. Work by members of the Frankfurt School, particularly Theodor Adorno, has endorsed this view, arguing that popular forms of entertainment such as television are an opiate of the masses; dope for dopes. Having presented this perspective I quickly move on to argue its limited viability in the light of scientific study of the effect of television viewing upon specific audiences, particularly children. David McQueen cites the infamous experiment by Bandura where a number of children were allowed to observe an adult attacking an inflatable clown and then left to play in a room containing a similar toy.[3] The results showed that the children who had seen the adult attacking the clown were more aggressive than those who had not, appearing to endorse a simple "hypodermic" scenario in which children (or other viewers of visual media) potentially imitate aberrant behaviors (McQueen 181). Subsequent academic studies have questioned the interpretation of the findings and the evident artificiality of the scenarios (Gauntlett 59; Davies and Houghton). Studies which appear to endorse the "hypodermic effect" model have not been able to find conclusive proof of a direct relation between violence on television and violent behavior, despite popular belief that the two are connected in a cause and effect manner.[4] I end by citing David McQueen's overview of the media effects debate, with the conclusion that studies have shown that television, like other media, tends to be "an agent of reinforcement rather than an agent of change"

(McQueen 182). As a counterweight to the "hypodermic effect" model, I then outline the "uses and gratifications model," which privileges the ability of viewers/consumers to use the media to gratify particular needs (McQueen 183). The "uses and gratifications model" posits a more active viewer (itself a problematic assumption) who is alert to potential manipulation by television but also able to deploy particular forms of a program as a means of gratifying a desire for entertainment, cultural identity and even social networking. Henry Jenkins' work on the active fan-base around *Star Trek* is a notable example of this. This overview gives students a taste of the variety of academic responses to popular and political debates about the potential effects of violent scenarios in visual media. Violence onscreen — and specifically in *Buffy*— is thus contextualized within a discursive framework that undermines and destabilizes over-simplified or "common-sense" accounts of violent effects.

The remainder of my introduction offers the student group a brief overview of the background to *Buffy* within contemporary television studies. In particular, I situate *Buffy* as one of a range of American television series that have been called "new television" (Moran). More specifically, for those students who have not watched *Buffy* before, or have not followed it at any length, I stress the intricate nature of its story arcs, the multiple references to other media through dialogue and plotlines, and the conscious fostering of a knowing and media-literate fan-base by its production team.[5] This introduction thus describes *Buffy* as a sophisticated form of cult fantasy drama which is both popular and critically lauded.[6] I also indicate the challenge of Buffy herself, as a young woman who employs violent tactics in her profession as vampire slayer. Students are encouraged to reflect upon the wider, allegorical implications of Buffy's role as a young female professional and as an account of feminism or post-feminism. While the session's primary focus is on issues around television representations of violence, the wider remit of the session within the module is to make students fully aware of the complexities of television series such as *Buffy* as contradictory sites for multiple debates regarding contemporary society and culture.

Students are subsequently shown one of the two episodes "Earshot" (3.16), which was withdrawn from the schedules in the United States in the aftermath of the Columbine incident. On April 20, 1999, two students from Columbine High School in Colorado entered school buildings armed with pipe bombs and guns. They killed 12 students and one teacher, injuring many others before committing suicide. Eric Harris was eighteen and Dylan Klebold was seventeen. In the media frenzy that followed it was alleged that these two students had been influenced by the violence depicted on television, computer games and in popular music. Michael Moore's 2002 film, *Bowling for Columbine* argued that, contrary to popular opinion, the Columbine shootings had not been facilitated by violent media. Students are often familiar with Moore's film, if not with the original details of the Columbine shootings. Before beginning the *Buffy* episode they are asked to take notes and each student is given one of the following questions to consider as they watch:

1. What (implied) audiences is this program targeting? Who do you think is watching and why?

2. What kinds of violence are visible in this episode? Grade them 1–10 (10 being extreme)

3. What reasons or justifications does the episode offer for acts of violence?

4. Might this program encourage people to commit acts of violence (and if so, how) or is this simply entertainment?

5. How else (other than violence) might *Buffy* have a negative influence on viewers?

6. How is *Buffy* "quality" television — are there aspects of the series that are not "quality?"

Question six is standard for each week in order to bring the debate back to the overarching theme of the module; quality television. In the preceding week students addressed the *CSI* franchise as an example of American quality television; that session consequently informs discussion regarding the "quality" aspects of *Buffy*. The cinematic production values of the *CSI* franchise, together with its complex storylines and stellar guest list, epitomize what has come to be known as American quality television (Jancovich and Lyons; Wilcox and Lavery xx–xxv).

Following the screening of the episode the students are given five minutes or so to discuss their findings with the other students assigned the same question and then each small group is invited to feedback to the larger group. Some of the questions invite a range of responses and that, in itself, is part of the exercise; to emphasize the diversity of possibilities in interpreting such an apparently straightforward drama. For example, responses to the first question regarding the implied audiences are invariably diverse and divergent — a number of students tend to regard *Buffy* as a children's series, perhaps because they themselves or their friends watched it in their younger years. Nevertheless, without fail there has so far always been a *Buffy* fan present in these sessions, ready to assert the range of audiences around the series and Joss Whedon's subsequent work. Even if this were not the case, the responses themselves raise questions about how the implied audience and the real audience may differ, and also begins to touch upon issues of audience response and the difficulties (a) of ascertaining who the audience actually is, (b) of ascertaining what those audiences' responses might be, and (c) the difficulty of assessing why different audiences view the same program. The latter issue frequently leads to some debate about the spectacular pleasures *Buffy* offers, both in terms of its action/adventure plots and sequences, and in terms of its attractive cast.

The second session of the week is timetabled for one hour and is designed to accommodate an element of assessment for the Quality and Popular Television module. Two or three students each week are scheduled to give an assessed presentation to the seminar group. This assignment constitutes 40 percent of the overall grade for the module so it has relatively high stakes. In their first year, students on the BA (Honors) English program experience speaking in small and large groups, presenting work in small groups and so on. This module, like its equivalent options on the second year of the program, requires that students offer a brief presentation to the group; a quite different form of seminar engagement, which students are often anxious about. While this activity takes students out of their "comfort zone" and places them in front of an audience, students have historically responded well to the activity, providing support for each other and recognizing the value of the presentation as a transferable skill for the wider world of work beyond the university.

I introduced a high-stakes presentation as part of the assessment for this module based on discussion with my colleague, Dr Victoria Bazin. Dr Bazin is a Fellow of the Centre for Excellence in Teaching and Learning at Northumbria University (CETL), which has a particular focus on Assessment for Learning. Following work with the CETL and Dr Bazin, I became an Associate member of the project. The CETL Assessment for Learning project, funded by the British government, asserts that the following conditions are necessary for assessment to contribute to the learning experience.

1. emphasizes authenticity and complexity in the content and methods of assessment rather than reproduction of knowledge and reductive measurement

2. uses high-stakes summative assessment rigorously but sparingly rather than as the main driver for learning

3. offers students extensive opportunities to engage in the kinds of tasks that develop and demonstrate their learning, thus building their confidence and capabilities before they are summatively assessed

4. is rich in feedback derived from formal mechanisms e.g., tutor comments on assignments, student self-review logs

5. is rich in informal feedback e.g., peer review of draft writing, collaborative project work, which provides students with a continuous flow of feedback on "how they are doing"

6. develops students' abilities to direct their own learning, evaluate their own progress and attainments and support the learning of others (*What is CETL AfL*)

The 40 percent weighting means that students cannot dismiss the presentation as an element of assessment (as could sometimes occur where assessments were lightly weighted at 10 percent or 20 percent). In order to pass the module students have to pass the presentation element.[7]

This emphasis on the presentation is also designed to underpin the importance of the presentation as a means of students' engagement in their own learning. On this module the week begins with a lecture from the module tutor (described above) and it ends with a session led by the students' own (assessed) presentations and the subsequent seminar debate is guided by questions which the student presenters provide. The idea is thus that, if only momentarily, the students become "experts" within the seminar, having read an academic paper or chapter on a relevant topic. During the seminar debate that follows, I often call on students who have just delivered a presentation to elaborate on what they have said or to clarify particular points. To date, this method has worked well; while the process of presenting may be stressful (to a larger or lesser extent depending on individual student's predilections) students enjoy being called upon to provide further information during more informal discussion.

Buffy lends itself to this shift in discursive authority, because it is a text embedded in popular culture and saturated with media references. Even if they are not regular viewers, students are able to employ their own cultural expertise in recognizing and interpreting the range of references which the series employs. While this may be said of much contemporary popular television drama, *Buffy* may be regarded as meta-television in its overt pleasure in referencing television history and popular culture both visually and verbally.[8] Students doing presentations for the *Buffy* session are often avid viewers or fans, so the informal discussion allows them (and other students in the group) to exercise their expertise and knowledge of the series. Such interchange adds to students' sense of confidence and is unusual within a university curriculum which often presents them with material of which they have no prior knowledge or expertise.

Students have access (via the university e-learning portal, Blackboard) to the list of academic essays/chapters on which their presentations will be based in advance of the first seminar. Following an introduction to the module in the first week, students sign up for particular weeks and essays/chapters.[9] For the week on *Buffy* students are offered the following texts to choose from: Chapter Three, "Media Effects" from David McQueen's *Television,* David Gauntlett, "Ten Things Wrong With the Media "Effects" Model," and Lisa Parks, "Brave New *Buffy*": Rethinking "TV Violence." The sequence of presentations is designed to take students from a broad overview of debates about violence (McQueen), through a critique of the "effects" debates (Gauntlett), to a detailed reading of debates about violence on television through an examination of *Buffy* (Parks). In effect, the content of the essays (and hopefully the students' accounts of them), replicate the process of the preceding two-hour session — from my brief introductory lecture (in which I quoted McQueen), to the students' viewing and discussion of an episode of *Buffy*. Lisa Parks' essay addresses "Earshot" in some detail, offering a sophisticated reading of the use of violence in *Buffy* and its self-conscious address to the debates around television violence:

> Ironically, with its cache of parental warning labels, *Buffy* is exactly the kind of TV violence that teens and parents need to see. The show's spectacular displays of physical aggression often function as a means of exposing and de-naturalising invisible and institutionalised forms of violence that affect youth especially.... I use *Buffy the Vampire Slayer* to complicate the meanings of "TV violence," and I explore how its generic hybridity, gendered physical aggression, racial/ethnic representations and discourses on social alienation provide new paradigms for thinking about TV violence.... Rather than encouraging violent behaviour, *Buffy* has become an important pedagogical tool, providing opportunities for adult and teen viewers alike to unravel and discuss the complex meanings of violence [119].

Parks thus advocates *Buffy* as a means of *learning about* violent representations rather than arguing for or against its classification as a dangerously violent series. This analysis offers an important contribution to the week's seminar work, as it makes clear the complexity of the issues at stake in debates about television violence without closing down further discussion.

The content of the student presentations and the process that they go through to produce them places an emphasis on the acquisition of knowledge as a discursive process. As with all the presentations on the module, students can approach the assignment in a variety of ways, and the most successful candidates engage in discussion with their peers and their tutor before, during and after the event. The presentation and the subsequent group debate is a visible piece of assessed work and offers a different assessment experience to the private and closed text of the standard essay or examination. An examination of

Buffy in this context is entirely appropriate, as it opens up the debate about media violence *as* a debate, rather than a concrete and "finished" argument. Like the complex narratives and characters within *Buffy*, the debate about the effect of representations of violence in the media is not simple or easily resolved.

The sessions on *Buffy* work well, as the students rapidly become engaged in discussion of *Buffy* in general or the "Earshot" episode in particular. Once they have viewed the episode, debate centers around the set questions provided before the episode was screened in class. Students who wish to distance themselves from *Buffy* as non-viewers — for whatever reason — often attempt to deride the series as aimed at a younger audience, or a primarily young female audience. By assigning the question about target audiences to a small group of three students the discussion has to move beyond a derisory dismissal. Students note the sexualized aspect of the program, particularly its visual appeal to male and female viewers who may identify with or desire the attractive cast of characters: Buffy, Cordelia, Angel, Xander, Willow, Oz, and others. It is useful to look at the merchandizing around the series at this point, as advertisements and commercial poster images of Sarah Michelle Gellar, David Boreanaz and Charisma Carpenter are noticeably more overt in their sexual appeal in these peripheral media than in the series itself. This leads to discussion regarding the impact of the static, photographic studio shot (such as those used in magazine and billboard advertising) when it does not fit with the complexities of an ongoing televisual narrative like *Buffy*.[10] Where the static shots represent idealized and conventionally sexualized images, *Buffy* itself often works to compromise or even ridicule such stereotypes. Students also note the complex and humorous dialogue; denoting "quality" scriptwriting and thus another characteristic of quality American television. This discussion leads to a wider account of the variety of markets/viewers for this form of television; the group acknowledges the spectrum of potential audiences for *Buffy*; they also note the difficulty of assigning a "target audience" without relying heavily on stereotypical assumptions regarding gender or age.

Despite the debates around *Buffy* as an example of violent media — often predicated on the assumption that *Buffy* is aimed at younger viewers — and the withdrawal of the episode in the wake of Columbine, "Earshot" contains little explicit violence. Students note the *lack* of violence and this leads to discussion about the definition of violence, cultural contexts and censorship. There is a short fight sequence in the opening minutes and the threat of violence from one character, Jonathan, who has retreated to the Sunnydale High School bell tower with a rifle. This aspect of the episode was the reason "Earshot" was withdrawn following the Columbine shootings (Parks 120). The assumption that he is about to shoot his fellow students or staff is shown to be false, as his intention was to commit suicide, but Buffy talks him out of it by arguing that all Sunnydale students have their own problems. The final sequence involves a comic fight scene between a school lunch lady, Xander and Buffy. As a whole, students note the low level of violence; that the violence is not explicit — there is no visible blood or gore — and also that violence in *Buffy* is often made comic, as in the final sequence with the lunch lady, or fantastic, as in the opening sequence where Buffy is fighting demons. This leads to a discussion of violence and realism in visual media. Many students are familiar with recent styles of cinematic violence from directors such as Quentin Tarantino and John Woo, where depictions of combat draw upon martial arts traditions and the use of "wire-work" in Hong Kong cinema, producing a fantastic and hyper-real spectacle. The fight sequences in *Buffy* clearly refer to this tradition and thus represent a form of combat that is explicitly non-realist (West). Employing *Buffy* as a means of addressing debates around media violence enlivens group debate and demonstrates that issues around violence and representation are not simple or straightforward. Students' responses to the presentations, the episode and the set questions lead to a spirited and informed discussion of a complex topic.

NOTES

1. This information is also available to students via the university website before they make their option choices for their second year. General information about the module is also publicly available via the Northumbria University website at: <http://nuweb.northumbria.ac.uk/live/webserv/module. php?mcr=UUFENLI&code=EL0503>.

2. The term "moral panic" was first coined by Stanley Cohen, the British sociologist, in his 1972 book *Folk Devils and Moral Panics*. A "moral panic" refers to an overreaction by the media to a particular issue, event or "deviant" social group which is perceived as challenging social norms.

3. For an elaborated account of the original experiment, see Albert Bandura, Dorothea Ross and Sheila A Ross.

4. David Gauntlett's essay "Ten Things Wrong with the Media 'Effects' Model" (2006) offers a concise account of this debate.

5. See, for example, Larbalestier 2002.

6. One indication of the critical and academic status of *Buffy* is its inclusion in the British Film Institute's series "TV Classics": Anne Bilson, Buffy the Vampire Slayer: *A Critical Reading of the Series* (2005).

7. In some second and third year modules presentation work was only weighted at 10 percent of the overall assessment. Following debate regarding the second year single honors options the English division at Northumbria agreed that a more substantial weighting would give the presentations more importance within the module and also reward the efforts of students who perform well in oral forms of assessment.

8. For example:
> BUFFY: Sorry to interrupt, Willow, but it's the Bat-signal. ("Some Assembly Required" 2.2)
> WILLOW: [Of Buffy] She couldn't have dressed up like Xena? ("Halloween" 2.6)
> BUFFY: It was terrible. I moped over you for months. Sitting in my room listening to that Divinyl's Song, "I Touch Myself." [suddenly sheepish] Of course, I had no idea what it was about. ("Lie to Me" 2.7)
> WILLOW: [Playing the game, "Anywhere but Here"] I'm in a little restaurant [in Florence], having ziti, and there're no more tables so they have to seat this guy with me, and it's John Cusack. ("The Dark Age" 2.8)
> XANDER: If Giles wants to go after the fiend that killed his girlfriend, I say, "Faster, pussycat, kill, kill" ("Passion" 2.17)
> XANDER: Swim team. Hardly what I call a team. The Yankees. Abbott and Costello. The A's. Those were teams. ("Go Fish" 2.20)
> SPIKE: The truth is—I like this world. You've got dog racing, Manchester United, and you've got people. Millions of people walking around like Happy Meals with legs. ("Becoming, Part 2" 2.22)

9. Students who are absent or do not make a choice are given a deadline to submit their choice to the tutor via email. If they do not meet this deadline I allocate material to the student(s). The schedule of presentations and presenters is then posted on Blackboard for future reference.

10. See Diane DeKelb-Rittenhouse and Elisabeth Krimmer and Shilpa Raval on sexual desire in *Buffy*; see also Mendlesohn on how queer sexualities are contained in the series—all in Wilcox and Lavery (2002).

WORKS CITED

Bandura, Albert, Dorothea Ross, and Sheila A Ross. "Imitation of Film-Mediated Aggressive Models." *Critical Readings: Violence and the Media.* Eds. C. Kay Weaver and Cynthia Carter. Open University Press, 2006. Print.

Bezin, Victoria. *"Presentations" Center for Teaching and Learning.* Northumbria University, n.d. Web. March 12, 2010.

Bilson, Anne. Buffy the Vampire Slayer: *A Critical Reading of the Series.* London: British Film Institute, 2005. Print.

DeKelb-Rittenhouse, Diane. "Sex and the Single Vampire: The Evolution of the Vampire Lothario and Its Representation in *Buffy.*" *Fighting the Forces: What's at Stake in* Buffy the Vampire Slayer. Eds. Rhonda V. Wilcox and David Lavery. Lanham, MD: Rowman & Littlefield, 2002. 143–152. Print.

*Gauntlett, David. "Ten Things Wrong with the Media "Effects" Model." *Critical Readings: Violence and the Media.* Eds. C. Kay Weaver and Cynthia Carter. Open University Press, 2006. Print.

*Helford, Elyce Rae, ed. *Fantasy Girls: Gender in the New Universe of Science Fiction and Fantasy Television.* Lanham, MD: Rowman & Littlefield, 2000. Print.

*Inness, Sherrie A. *Tough Girls: Women Warriors and Wonder Women in Popular Culture.* Philadelphia: University of Pennsylvania Press, 1999. Print.

Jancovich, Mark, and James Lyons, eds. *Quality Popular Television: Cult TV, the Industry and Fans.* London: British Film Institute, 2003. Print.

Jenkins, Henry. *Textual Poachers: Television Fans and Participatory Culture.* New York: Routledge, 1993. Print.

Krimmer, Elisabeth, and Shilpa Raval. ""Digging the Undead": Death and Desire in *Buffy.*" *Fighting the Forces: What's at Stake in* Buffy the Vampire Slayer. Eds. Rhonda V. Wilcox and David Lavery. Lanham, MD: Rowman & Littlefield, 2002. 153–164. Print.

Larbalestier, Justine. "*Buffy's* Mary Sue is Jonathan: *Buffy* Acknowledges the Fans." *Fighting the Forces: What's at Stake in* Buffy the Vampire Slayer. Eds. Rhonda V. Wilcox and David Lavery. Lanham, MD: Rowman & Littlefield, 2002. 227–238. Print.

*McQueen, David. *Television: A Media Student's Guide.* New York: Bloomsbury USA, 1998. Print.

Mendlesohn, Farah. "Surpassing the Love of Vampires; or, Why (and How) a Queer Reading of the Buffy/Willow Relationship is Denied." *Fighting the Forces: What's at Stake in* Buffy the Vampire Slayer. Eds. Rhonda V. Wilcox and David Lavery. Lanham, MD: Rowman & Littlefield, 2002. 45–60. Print.

Moran, Albert. "Configurations of the New Television Landscape." *A Companion to Television.* Ed. Jane Wasko. Wiley-Blackwell, 2005. Print.

*Owen, Susan A. "*Buffy the Vampire Slayer*: Vampires, Postmodernity and Postfeminism." *Journal of Popular Film and Television,* 27.2 (Summer 1999); 24–31. Print.

*Parks, Lisa. "Brave New *Buffy*: Rethinking 'TV Violence.'" *Quality Popular Television.* Eds. Mark Jancovich and James Lyons. London: British Film Institute, 2003. Print.

West, Dave. "Concentrate on the Kicking Movie: *Buffy* and East Asian Cinema." *Reading the Vampire Slayer: An Unofficial Critical Companion to Buffy and Angel.* Ed. Roz Kaveney. New York: Tauris Parke Paperbacks, 2001. Print.

"What Is CETL AfL?" Northumbria University, n.d. accessed March 12, 2010. Web.

Wilcox, Rhonda V., and David Lavery, eds. *Fighting the Forces: What's at Stake in* Buffy the Vampire Slayer. Lanham, MD: Rowman & Littlefield, 2002. Print.

Weeding Out the Offensive Material: Beauty, Beasts, "Gingerbread," Television, Literature and Censorship

Leith Daniel

Over the decade I have been teaching English, I learned that choosing a successful text to teach students in a secondary English classroom is an art in itself. In my experience, a classroom text should be accessible for the students, but academically challenging. It must be aesthetically and technically advanced, but still be representative of other texts. The text must also be full of themes, issues and moral lessons, but not so overtly polemical that it will put off the average teen. That same experience has led me to believe that this combination — whilst on the surface appearing contradictory — can be fulfilled by the right choice of text. *Buffy the Vampire Slayer* is one of the few texts I have found that not only achieves this successfully but also inspires me and the students to explore concepts (such as representation) not immediately accessible and new ways of assessing student knowledge. This chapter will use two specific episodes, "Beauty and the Beasts" (3.4) and "Gingerbread" (3.11) to demonstrate my use of *Buffy* as a text in my Australian secondary level English classroom.

The unit that I designed began in a standard manner — it was meant to simply be a textual analysis of a television drama of my choice. As I progressed however, I discovered new angles and approaches to take. What is more, the students were willing to go there with me, thereby enhancing their overall educational experience. In this chapter, I explain those ideas I know work, but I will indicate ideas that are so far untested; I do not plan to leave them untested for long.

The unit is designed around the use of art as a political tool — how it can be used to push certain values, but also how it is used as a device to justify censorship. The unit tested the students' knowledge of social issues — most prominently censorship — the nature of television drama, and multiple readings of texts. To test their skills and knowledge, I encouraged students to display them via both written and oral formats. To teach the concepts effectively I had to devote a full term (ten weeks) to them; since I was able to cover so many outcomes (viewing, speaking and listening, reading, and writing) with this unit, focusing on one text was not a problem.

Before we began watching the episodes below, we discussed the difference between serialized and episodic television. Whereas episodic shows are easily introduced to a new audience, serialized shows which develop not just an immediate plot, but a continuing extended narrative, are increasingly difficult to simply begin watching at any place beyond the beginning. To combat the disorientation that is bound to occur, the first handout I distributed was the following.

Buffy *Cheat Sheet*

Buffy Summers: A high school girl who has become "The Slayer," a young girl chosen by unknown forces to fight the demon world. She is blessed with superhuman strength and fighting skills. She is joined by a number of friends who form the "Scooby gang."

THE SCOOBY GANG

Willow: A young nerd who in later episodes becomes a powerful witch.

Xander: A dopey young man who has a crush on Buffy.

Giles: Buffy's Watcher. The man trained to train Slayers. He is a father figure to Buffy.

Angel: Buffy's first boyfriend, a vampire cursed with a soul. During the second season, he experiences "one true moment of happiness" and reverts back to Angelus, his evil self. To save the world, Buffy has to kill him and send him to Hell. "Beauty and The Beasts" (3.4) takes place after his mysterious return.

OTHER CHARACTERS

Oz: Willow's high school boyfriend; Werewolf.

Tara: Willow's university girlfriend.

Riley: Buffy's university boyfriend. Part of a secret government organization.

Spike: A cruel vampire, who, in later episodes, gets a chip put in his head that stops him from attacking humans.

Anya: An ex-vengeance demon who turns into a real girl and falls in love with Xander.

Faith: Another slayer.

Cordelia: The high school cheerleader bully of the Scooby gang; used to date Xander.

The first three seasons are set when the characters are in high school.

The fourth season is set primarily at university.

The fifth and sixth seasons are set around the town of Sunnydale.

The sheet is designed to give as brief detail as possible, and yet provide an idea of the major players — which is why the descriptions appear in order of significance, rather than alphabetical order.

The first episode we view together is "Beauty and the Beasts." This episode revolves around the issue of male/female relationships, something that Whedon's work represents often and well. It serves as a great introduction to the concept of intertextuality (the theory that all texts and their interpretations are based on and can be linked to all other texts. (Quinn and Rayner),[1] opening and closing as it does with extracts from *Call of the Wild*, the classic tale of savagery and civilization by Jack London. It also beautifully illustrates, along with the pilot, "Welcome to the Hellmouth" (1.1), the intentional confusion of archetypes and stereotypes that is the source of much of *Buffy's* quality.[2] But first I must prepare students for viewing with a number of tasks.

Task One involves an introduction to the concept of archetypes and stereotypes. In short, archetypes are the Jungian notion of recurring characters appearing in all forms of literature. Stereotypes are social assumptions based on prejudices and simplified knowledge of a certain type of person. Archetypes are character roles that recur throughout narratives (Stewart; Schafer).[3] I have found that teaching the etymologies of both words go some way to helping the students understand the differences between the two. (Harper) After defining these concepts with the class, I drew up a two columned table on the board, one labeled "archetype" and the other labeled "stereotype." In the first column I led the class in brainstorming as many types of characters as possible, and placed these ideas into the column labeled "archetypes." The archetypes I was aiming for in particular were *hero, villain, mentor, sidekick, love interest, villain's flunky,* and *comedy relief.* It does not matter if you get suggestions which are specific to particular genres (such as *the hooker with the heart of gold*) as these are sometimes useful and can be drawn on for genre studies. Nor does it matter if you get more or variations on the names (for example, "wise old man" for *mentor*) as sometimes (for non-standard jargon at least) it is better to use the terminology invented by the class, than a word imposed upon them.

The next step is to collect stereotypes in society and culture that the students are aware of. This part of the lesson is fraught with danger, as it can slip dangerously into offense. As with any of these potential classroom minefields, how you as the teacher deal with this is entirely up to you. While I let the students provide ideas for themselves, colleagues of mine occasionally provide stereotypes for discussion, thereby avoiding any racial comments. This is a decision that, of course, must be left up to the individual teacher depending on their temperament and students' personalities. I prefer to give the students ownership of the terms and make it clear that stereotypes are harmful and generally have no basis in reality before I begin any detailed studies of stereotypes. The stereotypes I steer towards (for the purposes of the task) include *woman, man, blonde, cheerleader/prom queen/popular girl, jock/All American boy/beefcake, Briton, geek/computer nerd/squid* (the current Australianism for a student who actually turns up to school to do school work). When writing these descriptions, I ensured that the students included gender for stereotypes where the genders were not instantly clear.

When this task was complete, I linked items in the two lists together by having the students decide which stereotypes were most appropriate for which archetype. Of course, my expectation was that the action roles were filled by male stereotypes and the more passive roles were filled by females. What actually happened, in the post–*Xena*, post–*Buffy*, post–*Dark Angel* world, was that the students were commendably reluctant to tie gender roles to the more action-related archetypes (hero, for example), although the love interest and damsel in distress were still tied, almost indelibly so, to female stereotypes. I suspect, however, that in the post–*Twilight* world, these more active roles may shift back (*Cracked*; Gabriel). But that is just personal prejudice.

I then hand out a series of question and answer sheets that are set up in a standard "before-during-and after" format. I ask questions asked about the issues and techniques the students will confront in the episode to help orient their viewing; questions designed to keep them actively watching by looking for specific moments in the episodes; and finally questions are asked of them to consolidate their knowledge of the episode and how the overall images are put together to communicate the meaning of the episode. In the case of "Beauty and the Beasts," the questions are designed to elicit understandings of three key concepts of English. The first — archetypes and stereotypes — has been discussed above.

The second is intertextuality: when one text makes an overt or subtle reference to another, the audience takes the knowledge and the feelings associated with the original and transfers them to the new text. In teaching "Beauty and the Beasts," I concentrated mainly on the issue of the omnipresent possibility of redemption in the "Beauty and the Beast" fairy tale, and the plot detailing the inevitability of a descent into savagery in *The Call of the Wild*. What the students picked up, via the questions and open discussion in class, is that these are two antithetical views of human behavior (although in this episode only men are featured as savage) and both views are addressed in the episode. Those views are neatly summed up by Giles, ever the source of wisdom, who tells Buffy: "In my experience, there are two types of monsters. The first can be redeemed, or, more importantly, want to be redeemed.... The second is void of humanity: cannot respond to reason ... or love." The following handout guides the students as they watch the episode.

"Beauty and the Beasts" (3.4) from Buffy the Vampire Slayer

Before you watch:

> There are many themes, one social analogy and two major literary allusions in this episode. The first allusion is referred to in the title. It refers to the classic children's tale "Beauty and the Beast."

> What was the story of Beauty and the Beast about? (include its plot and theme)

> The other major allusion made in this show is to Jack London's classic story *Call of the Wild*. This is a story about a dog taken from comfortable surroundings to Alaska. Eventually he submits to 'the call of the wild,' becomes a savage, and ends up the leader of a wolf pack.

> How do you think these references relate to the episode?

> One of the reasons that *Buffy* has been so successful is due to its reversal of traditional action-show gender roles. Below list the traits and the character roles that are typical for action roles:

> Males:
> Females:

While you are watching:

Describe the main characters, in appearance, personality and actions.

What does Buffy say about the villain at the end of the episode? How do you think these references could relate to the episode?

After you have watched:

How do the portrayals of the gender roles in the show compare to what is traditional?

How do you think the two allusions related to the episode? What do you notice about the physical, and personality aspects of the characters? Is there a link between the two? (Think about the fairy tale allusion)

The plot of the villain and his relationship to his girlfriend is an analogy to a social problem. What is it?

Considering Buffy's judgment of the villain, the allusions, the analogy, and the portrayal of genders in this episode, what do you think the theme of the episode is?

I also provide a number of quotes from *Call of the Wild* in particular the quotes used by Buffy in the opening and closing of the episode. It is because of these references that this episode can open up even more intertextual links.[4]

The other key learning foci are the identification of issues, values and themes mainly through representation. A quick glance through websites devoted to assisting English teachers soon reveals English teachers all over the world have slightly different definitions of these terms. The concepts themselves, however, are ubiquitous so replace the terms as you see fit.[5]

The discovery of these elements in "Beauty and the Beasts" leads to another concept in English: that of the 'allegory.' This *Buffy* episode, as with many in the first four seasons, are allegorical tales. The strength of *Buffy* is that it is not horror for the sake of horror. It, as with all good horror, does something termed "externalizing the internal."[6] Where horror texts have a tendency to go wrong is that they forget this and instead go for visceral thrills over interesting characterization. *Buffy* takes the fears of teenagers (in particular teenage girls) and gives them a physical form for the characters to face and overcome. By providing a physical representation of these fears, the audience can vicariously experience triumph over of the problem through the recognition of the metaphoric quality of the episode. These fears include (but are not limited to)—losing one's virginity ("Surprise/Innocence" 2.13–2.14); not being accepted and being treated as invisible ("Out of Mind, Out of Sight" 1.11); bullying ("The Pack" 1.6); steroid abuse ("Go Fish" 2.20); Internet stalking ("I, Robot, You Jane" 1.8); step-parent relations ("Ted" 2.11); and the stresses of graduating from high school ("Graduation Day" 3.21–3.22). "Beauty and the Beasts" is about domestic violence (that bit of beast in all men) and alcohol abuse. Buffy's assessment at the end of the episode is a categorical condemnation of the villain of the piece, therefore illustrating the filmmaker's condemnation of all men who beat their significant others and use the excuse of being under the influence of alcohol:

CORDELIA: You mean he wasn't under the influence of anything?

BUFFY: Just himself.

The next episode to show the students is the underrated "Gingerbread" (3.11). This episode, in part, is about paranoia and the tendency of humans to succumb to mob mentality — putting gut instinct above intelligence — and the danger and destruction that this leads to. It involves a demon that thrives on human hate by disguising itself as Hansel and Gretel of the fairy-tale (thus the episode's title). This episode is dialogue heavy, with one gratuitous fight pre-opening credits, and an easily dispatched bad guy. The director of the episode, James Whitmore, Jr., attempts to film all the dialogue scenes in a way that avoids the static two-shot, over-the-shoulder, over-the-shoulder, two-shot style of the soapies. One particularly effective scene that showed the strong link between cinematography and meaning was the adults' raid on the lockers. I also asked students to concentrate on the dialogue and how it is shaped to emphasize characterization. After all, since there was so much dialogue in the episode, I was able to point out how it was filmed, rather than simply what was said, and how these techniques contribute to the characters' personalities and the tone of the episode.

As with any progression of textual analysis, I did not provide the same amount of scaffolded questions as the previous worksheets, but instead asked the students to arrive at the major conclusions.

"Gingerbread" (3.11), from Buffy the Vampire Slayer

Activity: Identify:

(a) Major issues;

(b) Representation;

(c) Themes;

(d) Film language used to emphasize certain emotions in specific scenes;

(e) Any historical events that the plot can be read as an allegory for; Any current events that the plot can be read as an allegory for;

(f) Any intertextual allusions and the effect of this.

After viewing and discussing the two episodes there were two ways I found useful for consolidating them. For my Year 11 and 12 classes (upper school, 16–17 years of age) essay writing was sufficient (and, with the Western Australian curriculum being as it is — obligatory). The essay questions ranged from general statements about texts to questions that specifically referenced *Buffy*. Each question was conducted in a standard style for the Australian curriculum. That is, each was designed to be an analytical essay of 1,000 words each. The students were required to choose from the following list of essay questions and complete one over the course of a week and one had to be conducted during an hour of class time in examination conditions.

Discussion/essay topic:

Texts do not need to resemble the real world to make effective comments on it.

Intertextuality is an effective method of transferring complex concepts from one text to another. How true is this in your experience?

Intertextual references enrich our experiences of texts.

Does art reflect or influence society and what is the responsibility the audience has in either accepting or rejecting these assumptions?

Horror texts contain certain qualities that make the text identifiable as a horror. What are they, and how have they been used in a text you have studied?

Texts are only truly effective if they challenge society-held beliefs about social roles.

Discuss how the television show *Buffy the Vampire Slayer* subverts traditional gender roles and assess its effectiveness.

Even as I was teaching these texts to my Year 11s, I could not help but feel that it seemed a waste of the creativity of *Buffy* to end it in such a banal manner. When I taught this unit later in Year 10, I experimented somewhat with how to assess their knowledge. To do this, I decided on a freeform task.

Freeform is a style of live role-playing where each member of the participating group is given a role, a brief description of that role, and an objective. Then the participants are let loose. With a boisterous group, an exercise such as this can be extremely entertaining. While "entertaining" is not a curricular goal, any assessment that the students enjoy is likely to be more successful. A past supervising teacher for me when I was training as a teacher called it the "*Karate Kid* school of teaching" in which the students engage in a task that seems somewhat unrelated to learning, and only realize its full benefit when all is complete. At first glance, this task may seem more appropriate for a drama class. However, there is no script, and each participant has their own goal which they must use speaking and listening skills to achieve as best they can.

There are required roles and some extra roles that are optional (they are marked with "**") depending on class size. This also means with a class size of 30 one can run all three scenarios, with the non-participating groups watching. I used the non-participants as assistant markers; I handed out marking sheets with performing students' names written on them. These names are kept secret from the performers, since they have no idea which students are marking them. This keeps the performers from changing their performance based on who is marking them; it also keeps the markers away from bullying issues.

I came up with Scenario One during a Banned Books Week exercise that mushroomed into a term-long program.[7] We began by looking into the history and reasons for censorship, then studied a book of the students' individual choice from the list. The length of the unit required a task that allowed the students to let off a little steam. This scenario fit nicely, especially with the issues presented in "Gingerbread." Scenario Two is also based on censorship and requires the students' knowledge of the same episode. While there are characters who appear in the episode in the scenario, the three main members of the "Scoobies" are absent, to avoid *Buffy* fans squabbling over the portrayal of the characters. The students were not to be punished for inaccurate portrayals of characters, particularly when they had limited knowledge of the show. (For example, a student who does not know the mayor is the "Big Bad" of the season should not be penalized for portraying him as an uptight bureaucrat who ultimately cares for his constituents.) Instructors may have to rein in some of the more enthusiastic members, however. I once had a student playing Amy who attempted to "win" by turning the school board into mice. Instructors should also be careful using Larry Blaisdell as a character, since he is gay and this might lead to some bullying. That said, I found it a good chance to deal with that issue, as the character does not follow the assumptions many of the students had for a gay character.

Scenario Two is a play on an issue that has been plaguing Australian English teachers for a while now. The two major newspapers in Western Australia, the cleverly named *West Australian* and *The Australian*, have been criticizing the English curriculum for supposedly spending more time on texts such as television shows and pop music than classics like Shakespeare and Dickens. I often bring these ideas up, drawing in articles and opinion pieces, and talk about the nature of classics and socially-imposed, value-laden censorship. This one requires students to consider just what makes a text "canonical" and works best with "Beauty and the Beasts." It requires an in-depth knowledge of that text and preferably knowledge of a couple of canonical texts from Western culture. In future years I plan to use this after I have done a classic study that I alluded to earlier. This scenario also allows for interjections from the audience, which not only involves the participants, but also the members of the other, previously passive, groups.

Scenario One: BAN IT!

You are a member of the school board of Sunnydale High. The recent murder of two small children in what appears to be a witchcraft ritual has made everybody in town jumpy. It has been brought to the attention of the school's administration that certain students have been dabbling in the practice of witchcraft, aided partly by the odd number of occult-themed books in the school library. It is the school board's job to come up with an appropriate response to the crisis.

Scenario Two: BAN IT!

You are part of a panel discussion at an English Teachers' Conference. The topic is "Dumbing Down English: From the Bard to *Buffy*." The argument is about the legitimacy of texts currently taught in English classrooms. Obviously, the main focus will be on *Buffy*. Each member of the scenario must try to get their point of view heard above all others. This, however, does not mean they need to yell louder than everybody else.

Answer the following questions based on the role you have been given and the information you have assumed about the character.

Who are you?

What is your background? (As provided by your role sheet) Is there any more important background information about you?

What are your relationships like with the other participants?

What is your role in your meeting?

What is your objective?

What type of language would you use?

What are your favorite words and expressions?

How do you stand? How do you sit?

What is your body language like?

What will you being wearing to the meeting?

Do you have any habits? What are they?

What other information you need to know before the meeting?

Scenario One Roles

Mayor Richard Wilkins, III: The mayor of the city of Sunnydale. The consummate politician; you always know what to say to calm people down without ever committing to anything. You know that directing everybody's attention to the school as the cause of the trouble will mean that they stop looking at you to stop the rising crime rate.

Principal Snyder: Students are vermin. And you are the exterminator. Your job is to make every student quake in fear so they go out into the world frightened of authority figures and therefore become complacent, productive members of society. This is the perfect opportunity to give the toilet of a school a decent flush and expel as many children as possible in one go.

Joyce Summers (President of MOO): You are truly concerned about what is going on in your town. Your daughter, Buffy, is going through a rough time at school and this does not help things. She cannot look after the town on her own and you are going to give her as much help as possible by eliminating all the negative influences at her school — whether she asks you to help or not.

Sheila Rosenberg: You are a psychologist so you are more familiar with what is truly going on than anybody else (but it is not like you say that to anyone — much). You know that a fascination with the occult is a typical response of many teens who feel like they are outcasts — like your daughter, Willow. The best response to this is to set clear boundaries, because whether they know it or not, that is what these children really crave.

Rupert Giles: You are the wise old (but not that old) man of the school. You also know that the occult is real and you need all the books they are preparing to confiscate. On the other hand, you also know that if you say any of this you are bound to not only lose, but be thrown into the loony bin for good measure. You are also against book banning on general principle anyway.

Amy Madison: A practicing witch, but no one is to know that. You have to do your best to stop any kind of persecution without giving away who you are.

Larry Blaisdell: You are captain of the football team. You are one of the most popular students at school, but you know what it is like to be an outsider, since you are gay. You came out last year, which surprised everybody since you do not act 'typically' gay at all. You are not in favor of any persecution, and are very open about that.

Science Teacher: You are a member of the board primarily because you wanted to be on the offense against any moves to introduce Intelligent Design into the science classroom. You cannot understand anyone's fascination with things like the occult, since it is clearly not real and therefore harmless. You cannot even see what the big deal is. You have not decided which way you are going to go yet. But you will probably go against whatever Snyder says.

School Board President: You have been told what to do by Snyder your entire career. You have been told what to do by the Mayor. And now there is a new organization called MOO which is trying to tell you what to do now. Well, no more, damn it!

Student Council President Nancy Doyle: Stereotypical over-achiever. There is nothing stopping you from winning the top student of the school award, other than possibly the unusually high mortality rate of the students. But your goal will be helped by fully supporting Principal Snyder in whatever he does. And hey, the Mayor's coming. If you are known by him, you are sure to get an internship with City Hall when you graduate.

Scenario Two Roles

Eli Hylton (Panel Member): Education reporter for the *Daily News*. You have hated English teachers ever since *that* incident with your English teacher back in Year 12. You are going to trap the teachers into saying as many stupid things as possible so you can take them out of context for tomorrow's paper.

Andy Arrow (Panel Member): Opinion column writer for *The National Cryer*. You have long been a critic of the way the English curriculum has been going nationally. It seems no one has any respect for the Classics and the Masters of the English Language. What is wrong with teaching Shakespeare and Dickens and Chaucer? And what is with this critical literacy thing? Some kind of left-wing conspiracy?

President of the English Teachers of Australia Organization (Panel Convener): Expert in pedagogy and the concerns of such. You have been published in international journal after international journal. Some accuse you of being out of touch, but is it your fault your lexicon is out of the grasp of the common hoi polloi? You have never seen *Buffy*, but you are a great believer in beginning any piece of work by starting from what the students know.

President of the Western Australian English Teachers' United Front (Panel Member): An experienced English teacher who has published many text books for the English classroom. You are always looking for new things to use in your latest books, so whenever something new is being used it is a good thing. It seems Eli has had a vendetta against you since you took up the role. You are told you had Eli in your Year 12 class years before, but you cannot remember him/her at all.

President of the English Teachers' Front of Western Australia (Audience member): You are the head of a splinter group of English Teachers who feel the WAETUF are new-age, left-wing nut-bags who are taking English away from the real reason for English: novels and grammar. You are sick of being treated like a dinosaur because you do not think that websites should be studied, and believe not enough novels and poetry are being studied, having been pushed aside for songs, television drama and political studies.

Lee Rouge (Panel Member): You are a relatively young teacher who loves your job passionately. You cannot see what all the fuss is about. You accidentally began this controversy by teaching the *Buffy* episode "Beauty and the Beasts" (3.4) in the classroom and then writing about it for the English Teachers' Journal.

Robin Ringer (Audience member): You are an English teacher with a future. In that future, you see published books, paid appearances and a position as president of the WAETUF. A good appearance at this event will let you become known to as many people as needed. And there are reporters here! However, you cannot get over the fact that the president gave that little idiot Lee Rouge a panel position — but not you! You believe that English teachers should worry about texts which are relevant to kids today. And that means films, websites, television shows and computer games. Anything else should be left to those over-intelligent weirdos who do English Literature.

Gerald Healton: You are a concerned citizen (retired) who has been eagerly following this debate in the papers for a long time. You miss the good old days when they learned to read by repeating the alphabet day in, day out, they had the cane, and young people knew respect. That is what's missing today, and that is why young people are so disrespectful. How can you know who you are and what you need to honor, when you have no idea about what made this culture so great (Shakespeare, Wordsworth, Dickens, et al.)?

Mrs. Healton: You are a concerned citizen (retired) who has been reluctantly following this debate in the papers for a long time. You do not understand what all the fuss is about. You remember back when you were in high school just how boring everything was. You also chuckle about this since you know that some books that were frowned upon back then are now considered to be classics (*On the Beach, A Clockwork Orange, Sons and Lovers*). You have seen a couple of episodes of this *Buffy* and think it is quite clever.

As I mentioned at the beginning of this chapter, *Buffy* is the ultimate boon for English teachers. It is replete with everything an English teacher — or this English teacher, at least — could possibly need in a text. Using this unit description as a guide, the teacher could find the following curricular goals covered:

Knowledge of film language (arguing why a text is worth learning for its skill in construction).

1. Knowledge of broader concepts
2. Knowledge of characterization/stereotypes/archetypes
3. Speaking and listening skills (particularly negotiation)
4. Knowledge of outside issues (censorship/"Culture Wars")

The students were able to understand the more detailed concepts through the medium of a text that they were able to enjoy, and as there were different options open to them, I found myself using a form of differentiated learning where the students were able to extend themselves to whichever level they felt most comfortable.

Of course, not all of the students felt entirely comfortable watching *Buffy*. Finding a text that all students enjoy is ultimately impossible. One student memorably criticized its "graphics" leaving me entirely flummoxed. However, I found even those students who did not feel drawn into the world of *Buffy* were still able to address issues they were previously unable to grasp. And I cannot help but feel that part of my success in teaching issues like censorship and concepts like allegory, while at the same time pepping up my classroom and engaging my students was due to *Buffy*.

NOTES

1. See also Woofter and Grzanka in this collection.
2. While the language may be different, the representation of female and male characters permeates throughout the articles available on slayageonline.com.
3. See also Morris in this collection.
4. The most obvious is *The Strange Case of Dr Jekyll and Mr Hyde*. Oz is after all, a werewolf, a key plot point of the episode, and as Stephen King once noted *Dr Jekyll...* is the prototypical werewolf novel. (*Danse Macabre* King, S). *Frankenstein* can even be used at this point as it plays with the idea of the inventor's creation becoming uncontrollable. In fact, one year I decided to focus on classic texts for a year 10 class (middle high school, 15 years of age); this entire introduction through *Buffy* was completely advantageous as the students were less reluctant to take up the challenge of reading classics, since they had already been introduced to not just the plots, but the entire themes through a much more accessible text beforehand.
5. According to the way I have been teaching it for the past decade (Quin, R.). *Readings & Responses*. Melbourne, Victoria, Australia: Pearson Education Australia Pty Limited.:

Issues: The social problems that are dealt with in a text.
Values: What the author of a text demonstrates to be important.
Themes: The author's take on life and the world — essentially, what he or she is saying about the issue.
Representation: The concept that the characters constructed in a text are meant to be what the author feels about the real world equivalent. For example: if all males in a text share the same trait, that trait is what the author feels all males possess.

6. In fact the psychiatrist Buffy is sent to in this episode to "convince him [she's] little Miss Stable" spells this out beautifully. He describes the trials of the teen years using language such as "demons," encourages her to "fight" them, and succinctly summarizes the entire plot of the second half of Season Two almost perfectly. The irony comes from the fact that he thinks he is being metaphorical; Buffy and the audience know that he is inadvertently speaking literally.
7. Banned Books Week is an initiative of the American Library Association. It occurs in the last week of every September. See www.bannedbooksweek.org

WORKS CITED

"Cracked Topics: *Twilight*." *Cracked.com*. Cracked, n.d. Web. June 2009.
Gabriel, N. H. "*Twilight* Makes for the Best Fanwank Ever." *i09.com*. io9, Nov. 2008. Web. June 2009.
Harper, D. *Online Etymology Dictionary*. Nov. 2001. Web. June 2009.
King, S. *Danse Macabre*. USA: Everest House, 1981. Print.
Quin, R. *Readings & Responses*. Melbourne, Victoria, Australia: Pearson Education Australia Pty, 2008. Print.
Rayner, R. Q. *Contexts & Conventions: TEE English*. Perth, WA, Australia: Pearson Education Australia Pty, 2000. Print.
Schafer, E. D. *Exploring Harry Potter*. London, UK: Beacham, 2000. Print.
Stewart, K. *A Glossary of Literary Terms: second edition*. Perth. WA, Australia: Batavia Press, 1997. Print.

"Best Damn Field Trip I Ever Took!" Historical Encounters In and Out of the Classroom

Jodie A. Kreider

Students in my history classes never find *Buffy the Vampire Slayer* on their syllabi. Historians discuss *Buffy* only among friends over beverages, not at professional history conferences or in their classrooms. Yet, when asked to prepare an interdisciplinary first year seminar in 2007 based on "my passion," *Buffy* seemed an outstanding choice for a variety of reasons. *Buffy* provides abundant source material for analysis from multiple disciplinary perspectives. The length, complexity and quality of the text itself, as demonstrated by a significant body of literature, references and represents multiple historical incidents and themes, including the role of cemeteries in society, witchcraft, and feminism, to name but a few. *Buffy* also provides ample material for students to explore current issues encountered in their transition to adulthood and daily college experiences. In addition to the episodes representing the difficulties of transition to college, including roommates, dating, and first-time independence, the literature of *Buffy* Studies provides an accessible introduction for students at multiple levels to what scholars and teachers do as part of a larger academic community. The variety of themes, references, and literature, combined with the accessibility of the *Buffy* text, accomplishes the goals of a course aimed at introducing students to academia, the college classroom experience, sophisticated critical analysis, and how their classes and texts address relevant issues whether produced in the 1790s, 1890s, or like *Buffy*, the 1990s. Studying *Buffy* models for the students the connections between education, "intellectual passions," and lifelong learning, meeting several of the goals of the Freshman Seminar program at the University of Denver.

My first year seminar *Gender, Feminism, Power & Pop Culture in Buffy the Vampire Slayer,* uses a variety of texts and assignments to focus on multiple historical, cultural and literary themes, including witchcraft and power in 17th century Britain and on the Hellmouth, Romanticism, discourse and power, masculinity, femininity, feminism, Fairy Tales, and others. I rely heavily on scholars who analyzed *Buffy* in relation to these themes from different disciplinary perspectives in the pages of *Slayage* or elsewhere in the *Buffy* literature.[1] Students read that literature alongside literary texts and watch *Buffy* as part of the class. My course contains different types of assignments that break up the traditional seminar format based primarily on discussion and writing of response papers.[2] Intended to encourage active-learning among the students, these assignments include an off-campus field trip to a local historic cemetery and asking students to prepare and present their own unit for the course as their final project. This chapter will outline these different assignments, alongside the more traditionally organized seminar unit on witchcraft, and thereby demonstrate the utility of *Buffy* as an ideal text to examine historical themes.

The University of Denver organizes a week-long orientation program for incoming first-year students, during which I act as mentor and guide through the mysterious rituals of registration, book buying, academic honor codes, and most importantly, how to watch *Buffy* episodes as texts full of symbolism, representation and meaning, rather than simply as entertainment. The program requires that after three days of meeting with my students to discuss student life, advising, and academic skills, I cap the end of the week-long orientation by taking students off-campus on a trip that relates to the theme of the course, includes a meal, and familiarizes them with the city of Denver. Although stymied at first about what type of trip one could relate to gender and *Buffy*, I struck upon the idea of taking my students to the historic, yet still active, Fairmount Cemetery in Denver. I then had to reason out the connections between an historic cemetery, the discipline of history, and the modern text of *Buffy*.

The cemetery occupies a central place in the geography and action of *Buffy* as a show and Sunnydale itself. The first episode "Welcome to the Hellmouth," (1.1) sees a young male vampire tempt and dare Willow into entering the cemetery, which she recognizes as a dangerous space, as a shortcut on the way to the ice-cream parlor. He then ushers her to a crypt as an offering for the Master, the "big-bad" vampire of the season. She then runs into her friend Jesse, who is in the same position, but his young female vampire captor Darla snacked upon him before arrival. The crypt and the cemetery act as doorways between the surface and the underground tunnels, and for the characters, a threshold between life, death and "unlife." As Jesse discovers, if taken underground into the vampire's lair, victims are transformed into food, new members of the vampire ranks, or both. As the Slayer, Buffy faces innumerable battles in the various cemeteries of Sunnydale killing vampires as they rise from the dead. The cemeteries are literally her workspace and her office, her hunting ground, just as they are for the vampires and other monsters. In Season Four she identifies herself to her boyfriend Riley Finn as "She who hangs out a lot in cemeteries" ("Doomed" 4.11). Buffy also takes advantage of Sunnydale's multiple cemeteries as places to make out with her first serious boyfriend Angel, both before and after she realizes he is a vampire, as well as a place to study for her SAT exams, and pick her college schedule ("Band Candy" 3.6; "The Freshman" 4.1). Buffy's friends, the Scooby Gang, bring snacks and mock the vampires as Buffy fights them, her Watcher Giles uses cemeteries as training and testing grounds, and Spike the vampire literally sets up house in an abandoned crypt where he watches the soap opera *Passions* in his recliner eating snacks from the fridge. These cemeteries are not quiet places occupied only by the dead and mourners, although they are present as well.

Cemeteries in Sunnydale fail to fulfill their designated function. Designed as places of eternal rest, the Sunnydale cemeteries contain a population of dead citizens who refuse to stay underground, rising as vampires, and then threatening the well-being of the entire community. Numerous funerals take place throughout the series, often as background to the action, with the cemeteries fulfilling their traditional functions. However multiple episodes feature newly-made vampires rising from their graves. And it is not only the monsters that refuse to stay buried. The most significant example of the dead refusing to stay dead is Buffy, who, after sacrificing herself, is buried for several months under a headstone that reads, "She saved the world. A lot." She digs herself out of her grave, alive once more due to Willow resurrecting her with a spell. ("The Gift" 5.22; "Bargaining" 6.1–6.2) She rejoins society traumatized, not as a monster, though she is different. The cemeteries of Sunnydale also act as sites of human predation, failing to protect and contain the non-vampires, as graves are robbed of numerous body parts for scientific experimentation ("Some Assembly Required" 2.2; "Revelations" 3.7).

Buffy creator, writer, and often director Joss Whedon thus turns the horror genre on its head, acknowledging cemeteries as dangerous spaces which contain the horrors created by death, both violent and peaceful, yet presents them as places where that threat is rewritten. The vampires rise from their graves hungry and ready to feed, only to be met by Willow and Xander eating popcorn while mocking their wardrobe, fashion sense, strength and techniques, and by Buffy wittily quipping as she slays them verbally as well as physically.[3] Buffy scorns Dracula's reputation and Xander his accent while drinking a mocha, neither believing that he is the real Dracula or a real threat ("Buffy vs. Dracula" 5.1). Willow and Xander eat chips while annoying Riley on patrol in Season Five ("Fool for Love" 5.7). The cemetery is presented as a place of death, tragedy, humor, and life. Jack O'Toole raises his friends, the corpse named Bob, and his buddies from their graves as zombies, repeatedly. Thus death and burial represent no barrier to the knowledgeable. When the zombies arise from their graves, their first goal is to party. Rather than immediately hunting for brains or human flesh to eat, Bob asks Jack if he had taped the television show *Walker Texas Ranger* while he was dead ("The Zeppo" 3.13). In addition to demonstrating the combination of horror and humor in *Buffy,* this example also reveals that Jack himself is a zombie, moving back and forth between the cemetery and the town at will, raising his own friends as companions. He is not under the control of another human or monster, but self-aware and driven to restore himself to his old life, hanging out at the high school, clubbing at the Bronze, and terrorizing the nerds and geeks of Sunnydale High in a fashion indistinguishable from his habits while alive. The show represents cemeteries as places of both life and death, movement and rest, violence and peace, but in all ways central to existence on the Sunnydale Hellmouth.

Beyond their narrative function, cemeteries and headstones provide the scenic backdrop for the series. Whedon filmed the first season and a half of *Buffy* on location at various cemeteries in California.[4] Chosen for their aesthetic appeal, the monuments through which Buffy bounds, flips, and slays, and the Scoobies perch, were real. Cemeteries and headstones also appear as the tools through which the viewer accesses the menu items on the Season Two DVDs. To access the world and text of *Buffy* the viewer must flip through various levels of the cemetery to enter crypts and click on certain gravestones, monuments, or statuary. Thus the audience is forced to interact with the representation of the cemeteries, making them part of the world of the dead, and of the show. Both the menu "cemeteries" and those in the series then represent the liminal space, the threshold where the living, the dead, and the undead interact, and where the fictional and real worlds intersect.

Visually, and physically, and with regard to narrative, the cemeteries in *Buffy* represent the complex and changing roles of cemeteries in both historic and modern society. This realization gave me a way to link a cemetery visit into my course, and a historical theme for the students to wrestle with throughout orientation week as an introduction to academic analysis and during the rest of the quarter.

To introduce this theme I assigned an article by James A. Hijiya, "American Gravestones and Attitudes toward Death: A Brief History" for students to read prior to their arrival on campus. They had to respond in both written and verbal discussion formats during our orientation week meetings. This article examines three-hundred years of Northeastern United States gravestone design and outlines how these stones, whether they are carved in Plain Style, a Death's Head, an Angel, an Urn and Willow, or representations of the deceased, reflect changing American attitudes towards death, as well as their social and cultural contexts. Hijiya, in a style accessible for new first-year students, articulates the difficulties and issues that arise when analyzing these representational artifacts, noting that symbols have multiple meanings that change over time, that viewers examining such symbols decades or centuries later find it difficult to identify the figures, let alone the meanings, as is true with all artistic interpretation. This article provides the students, many of whom have never experienced the death of a loved one or ventured into a cemetery, with a basic understanding of cemetery functions and their historical context, as well as the issues that arise trying to definitively analyze visual images and art.

I assess their completion of this reading assignment, and their reading, comprehension, and writing skills through a written three page paper that they bring to the first orientation session. I asked them to read the article critically, not just for its basic information, but to "evaluate its strengths and weaknesses, present the questions and issues you [the student] would like to discuss further, and inform the reader of its accessibility, difficulty and usefulness." I also asked them to specifically address in their papers the following:

1. Why should anyone study gravestones? What do they have to tell us?
2. What are some of the difficulties or issues that arise when analyzing gravestones?
3. What is Hijiya's overall purpose in writing this paper? What is his argument? Do you think he supported his assertions well?

During our meetings over the course of the week we discuss this article. Based around their papers, students have already thought and written about it, and this provides them a comfort zone for their first class discussions at the college level. They tend to do a good job discerning the author's self-confessed geographic limitations and speculation based on limited evidence. But they also respond well to the article with its relatively jargon-free discussion of the subject which makes it an appropriate article to use to introduce them to academic writing as well as to cemetery functions prior to their trip to the real thing.

After they are familiar with the patterns of cemetery art and burial identified by Hijaya as the norm in America, I challenge their belief in a simple model applicable to the entire country. On the second day I present a slide lecture on the significance of location, artistic inspiration, and interpretation in understanding how cemetery art reflects its historic and cultural context, as well as how people dealt with death, summarizing the work of Annette Stott. Based on her research across Western states from Montana to New Mexico, Stott argues that the images traditionally used to represent the Old West such as Frederic Remington sculptures, Albert Bierstadt paintings, and others were in fact imagined and created using props in the studios of the East. She asserts that the authentic art of the West is located in cemeteries, where markers and mausoleums were commissioned by local residents, created by local artists, and used as teaching tools in their local communities. She also details the role of cemeteries in Western life, where they acted as parks and gathering places for towns and residents to hold not just funerals, but picnics, rallies, band concerts and escape the bleak Western prairies for an artificially lush landscape of mature trees, green grass, and flowers created by architects and enabled by irrigation.[5] After this lecture, I ask the students to reconcile the two different scholars' arguments, what issues this raises for understanding a piece of art, the significance of context for the artist as well of the viewer, and so on. Students then are also cued to observe the role of the cemetery in *Buffy* overall, as well as the episodes we then watch during the next two meetings during orientation week, "The Freshman" (4.1) and "Living Conditions" (4.2). Combining all of these images and texts during the first week of orientation helps train students to view critically and carefully how cemeteries are represented in a fictional text as well as encountered in their locality, yet both must be analyzed to understand the intent of the artist, the function of the text, and how the text reflects or reframes reality.

These assignments and discussions are capped off with a tour of historic Fairmount Cemetery the following day. I begin the day by showing "Welcome to the Hellmouth" and "The Harvest" (1.1–1.2), in order to familiarize the students with the series, its characters, and setting. Both of these episodes feature significant action in the cemeteries of Sunnydale, including long scenes within crypts and mausoleums used by vampires and Buffy as access ways to the sewer system below the town.[6] Afterward we venture to the cemetery, where we take an historic tour of the grounds, with a guide from the Fairmount Heritage Foundation, who specializes in Denver and Colorado History.[7] Students get to peek into real crypts and explore mausoleums, comparing them to those depicted in the episodes they had watched that morning. After the tour we eat a picnic lunch in the lush and often surprisingly pleasant setting, which also reminds them of how people used cemeteries as parks and recreational spaces, spending Sundays relaxing, eating and socializing. I then set them free to wander the cemetery for over an hour, analyzing symbols and images, aided by their copies of Douglas Keister's *Stories in Stone: A Field Guide to Cemetery Symbolism and Iconography*.[8] To assess that analysis I tried a number of different assignments, including having students draw three interesting images they find in the cemetery, or photograph a variety to put on a course web page, and the most effective, to write a response paper about what they learned from the cemetery tour and how that is reflected in their own lives as well as *Buffy*. Although that is the end of the formal assignments on this topic, throughout the rest of the quarter students point out examples of the complex role of cemeteries when discussing various *Buffy* episodes, characters, and arcs.

Based on these class discussions, this unit successfully teaches students that in real life, as well as in *Buffy*, cemetery functions include both the social — as gathering places for individuals, groups, and cities; the educational — places of art to teach moral and aesthetic lessons; in addition to their role as places to inter and remember the dead. Cemeteries may seem relatively quiet, but still buzz with life; human, plant, and animal. Over the past four field trips students encountered preparations for public band concerts, groundskeepers maintaining the flowerbeds and trees in the cemetery which remains the largest outdoor arboretum in the state, as well as family members visiting tombstones. The Colorado Division of Wildlife recently designated Fairmount as a Colorado Wildlife viewing location. This assignment reveals that Whedon's depiction of the cemetery as a liminal space between life and death, full of transitions and life among both the living and the dead, reflects the current role of cemeteries in American culture and society. Yet it also highlights the historical and cultural aspects of cemeteries found in *Buffy* and introduces other themes that are discussed throughout the course including death, life after death, memory, representations of gender in art and in text, and significantly, the use of a canonical quality television series to explore such issues.

Building on the non-graded foundational structure of orientation week, I designed the ten week course around thematic units such as Gender, Feminism, Masculinity, Witchcraft, *Dracula*, Vampires as Brooding Gothic Heroes, *Frankenstein,* Parenting, Language and Silence in "Hush" (4.10), Death and "The Body" (5.16) and finally music. Each unit combines several required episodes for students to view on their own time, several articles from *Buffy* scholarship, and a literary text or scholarly monograph, and recommended episodes that also pertain to that theme. Occasionally a unit is based around one specific episode, which we then view in class. To assess their completion of the assignments, comprehension of the theme or issue, and critical response to the materials, students turn in a four page reaction paper for every unit. These papers ask students to respond to the common theme of the episodes and readings, as well as to articulate how those materials and their creators speak to each other. As time went on and the students grew more comfortable with the course and university level work, they grew increasingly willing to evaluate, challenge, and critique the authors, as well as the episodes. By the end of the quarter students began building on information from other courses and their own experiences and interests in their papers and discussions. This is an important step in encouraging them to integrate the various types of knowledge discovered through a liberal arts education and to transfer that knowledge and accompanying analytical skills to multiple college situations, and also to the rest of their lives, both now and in the future.

My own interests and training in gender studies, British and European history impact how I teach the course.[9] One example is apparent in the unit on witchcraft, "'It Could Be Witches, Some Evil Witches': Young Women, Witchcraft & Power," taught midway through the course. This unit explores historical witchcraft cases in comparison with the version depicted in *Buffy*. Most of the first-year students that I encounter in the United States read Arthur Miller's *The Crucible* in high school and are familiar with it as a commentary on the McCarthy hearings as well as a discussion of the Salem witchcraft trials in 17th century North America. Rather than tread that ground again and to break students out of the mind-set that everything must be discussed in relation to the modern United States, I chose to contrast the representation of witchcraft practices and their social repercussions found in *Buffy* with a specific witchcraft case in 17th century England, and European witchcraft cases on a larger scale. The course explicitly deals with gender and feminism in England, Europe and the USA, in the past, today, and finally in *Buffy*, often to the dismay of some of the students. Although the connections may not seem obvious at first, particularly among many disciplinary perspectives, the quality and broadly referential nature of the *Buffy* text allow scholar-teachers to integrate the show into a variety of classroom situations, and a variety of topics and interests into the teaching of the show itself.

Although *Buffy* abounds with witches and wiccans, the difficulty of how to approach the issue of witchcraft becomes obvious when one confronts the variety of representations of the phenomena in the series. Throughout the seven seasons characters such as Willow, Amy, Amy's mother Catherine, Jenny Calendar, Tara, the Wicca group at UC–Sunnydale, Ethan Rayne and Giles wrestle with the moral, social and personal power issues involved with choosing to engage in a wide variety of witchcraft or wiccan practices, as well as the problems associated with being labeled a witch. For this one-week unit of the course, students are required to view the episodes "The Witch" (1.3), "Bewitched, Bothered and Bewildered" (2.16), "Something Blue" (4.9), and "Gingerbread" (3.11), on their own. Other episodes are listed as recommended viewing, including "Tabula Rasa" (6.8), "Smashed" (6.9), and "Wrecked" (6.10).[10] These episodes span the entire series and thus can "spoil" some of the major plot and character developments.[11] Alongside these episodes, students read their first scholarly monograph, James Sharpe's *The Bewitching of Anne Gunter: A Horrible and True Story of Football, Witchcraft, Murder, and the King of England* (2001). Sharpe traces a single, well-documented witchcraft case from early 17th century England that James I, the King of England eventually settled. The case involved a young woman, Anne Gunter, whose father encouraged and then forced her to accuse other women in the village of witchcraft by claiming to be bewitched and faking the vomiting of pins, seizures, visions, and other signs. Notably, the book allows students to explore gendered power relations at multiple levels of society, ranging from the Gunter family, the elites as well as the female outcasts of the village of Moreton, up through the Privy Council to the monarchy. Although they complained about Sharpe's detailing how the Privy Council worked and other aspects of reading a historical monograph on a history they knew little about, in their papers and in class discussion students demonstrated that the text worked well and they understood the crucial elements of Anne's story and Sharpe's argument. Students compared villager reactions to accusations against the witches to those of Buffy's mother Joyce leading her organization MOO to attempt to burn her daughter, Willow, and Amy at the stake in "Gingerbread." They discussed the attraction of becoming wiccan or literally practicing witchcraft for Willow, Amy and Goth boy Michael in contrast to women, usually outcasts, falsely accused in early-modern society, who often confessed to being witches to scare, threaten, or gain rare power against those that oppressed them. Although the 17th century women of Anne's world were not really witches, and witchcraft itself was primarily regarded in England as a relationship with the devil rather than a religion, the function of witchcraft accusations in the social relationships of Moreton and Sunnydale reflect historical phenomena. Assigning Sharpe also allows me to highlight the difference between disciplines like human communications, gender studies and history, in this case the significance of historical context, the use of documentation, and the style of writing. In addition to Sharpe's historical analysis students read two articles that explore the depiction of witchcraft in *Buffy* including Tanya Krzywinska's "Hubble-Bubble, Herbs, and Grimoires: Magic, Manichaeanism, and Witchcraft in *Buffy*" and Jason Lawton Winslade's "Teen Witches, Wiccans & "Wanna-Blessed Be's' Pop-Culture Magic in *Buffy*."[12] Student response papers revealed that these articles help link the historical aspects of early modern English witchcraft from Sharpe with the 20th century development of Wicca as a modern religion, and the representations of witchcraft in modern popular culture to that of *Buffy*. The series' creators and artists produced a text that effectively represents major aspects of gender, power, and religion in both early modern and modern, political and popular Western culture for students to explore in a classroom setting.

After the cemetery field trip, and multiple, traditionally-structured units like the witchcraft unit, the final assignment asks students to actively construct their own unit for the course. I encourage them by promising to credit them on future syllabi should I adopt one of their units for the course in the following years. The assignment description states the following:

> This paper can be based on a topic you wish we had covered, revising a unit with different texts and episodes that you feel would be better selections, or coming up with something completely different based on the work of literature in the field of *Buffy* Studies. You will present your unit to the class in a 5–10 minute oral presentation, and also write the unit up in a formal typed, double-spaced, five page paper.
>
> **I. Requirements:**
> A. Your unit must include multiple readings, sufficient to occupy four hours of classroom discussion. You may include other works of literature, and if sufficient size they make up the majority of the reading. Think at least 30 pages per class day, minimum! Remember also that you cannot assign too much reading, or your students will simply not do the reading, and resent you forever! You may not repeat the readings I have assigned in this course unless they make up a minimum of the total for the week. Consider things you have read in other classes or seen mentioned in the literature that would be useful to read alongside the show.
> B. Your unit must include a list of episodes for required viewing over the weekend prior to the week's classes. You may also add a list of recommended episodes.
>   You may view ONE episode during the week's unit in class. I would encourage you to consider not doing so to avoid simply "workshopping" an episode.
> C. Your paper must assert the significance and weight of the topic, outline the major themes of the unit, the arguments of the various readings, and how you see them fitting together into a valuable unit for the course. Include a daily schedule of how you would organize the material, and what you would have students do in class. The paper should demonstrate that you did the readings and have thought this out.

As a final assessment of the quarter, this assignment requires students to demonstrate the skills that they developed and practiced all quarter, figuring out how the various assigned texts and materials interacted and "spoke to" each other, evaluating the quality and significance of each text, and articulating their ideas in both written and verbal formats.

Beyond its value at assessment of their skill level in critical thinking, presenting and writing, the assignment works well because it reveals what they want to investigate in relation to *Buffy*, what they bring to the text, and that they can justify those interests based on their value to the other students. Over the last three years the units proposed by students continue to surprise me. Several students argued that expanded time be given to certain issues discussed in class but not explored in any detail, including death, specific relationships, and the repercussions of sex and sexual assault amongst young people in both *Buffy* and real life. Others suggested focusing on the role of technology and science in the show, arguing that the unit on *Frankenstein* spent too much time on the literary and historical themes of Romanticism. Every year several students propose a vampire unit comparing vampire myths across time and various media, particularly *Twilight*, and *True Blood*, alongside *Dracula*. This past year one student incorporated these same texts into her proposed revision of the feminism unit by analyzing Buffy, Sookie Stackhouse and Bella, from *True Blood* and *Twilight* respectively, as feminist characters. Students often revise the feminism unit to exclude Lorna Jowett's *Sex and the Slayer* due to its theoretical discussions and binary-structured organization, replacing it with articles by Sharon Ross and Patricia Pender among others. One student creatively suggested a comparison between Los Alamos, New Mexico where the atomic bomb was developed, and Sunnydale as Hell-mouths, one on television, and one in reality, and emphasized the danger and silence that surrounded both. Every year students suggest a new unit on female heroism and how it alters Joseph Campbell's monomyth or Buffy as a female superhero. One student suggested a unit that focused on fashion in the show as a way to track character changes across seven seasons, while others focused on representations of insanity, disillusionment, or politics in the show. Not all of these units and pairings were equal in quality or validity, but reveal what intrigued the students about the series, particularly those who were not fans when the course began.

The best units have integrated non–*Buffy* readings from other fields and disciplines into their lesson plans. Students suggest works by prominent authors like Ray Bradbury, J.K. Rowling, Ernest Hemingway, Charlaine Harris, Anne Rice, Sigmund Freud, William Wordsworth, and Friedrich Nietzsche be read alongside a wide selection of articles from *Buffy* literature as well as other disciplines. The relatively large number of units using other authors as avenues into the show demonstrates that even fan-students seem to prefer to analyze *Buffy* as a text in relation to other aspects of their lives, and other texts or concepts encountered in their own education or recreational reading and viewing. Students tend to use *Buffy* to illuminate or explore themes they already find interest in, rather than focus solely on the series.[13] Students, like myself and many viewers, integrate *Buffy* into their existing knowledge-base and understanding of their world using familiar and classic historical and literary themes, as well as popular culture references. This type of assignment is successful because it forces students to use different kinds of thinking and skills to identify their own cultural influences and interests, justify the theme, text or angle into what specifically about *Buffy* they want to research, write their assignment, and then articulate verbally how to theoretically teach it to their fellow students. Essentially, to successfully transfer their learned knowledge and cognitive skills between different experiences, courses, and contexts, defined by Perkins and Salomon as educationally valuable forward and back-ward reaching "high-road transfer" (25). This type of assignment and thinking forces them to use their liberal arts education to analyze the show and what it reflects about society and culture. This then, is a successful active-learning and student-centered class-room assignment.

These varied types of assignments, from field trips, to discussions, to planning out pedagogical units, successfully teach to understand, evaluate, and enjoy *Buffy* in relation to the larger Western canon of literature, history, and culture that it references. They also facilitate active engagement with the material, teaching students how to "read" and analyze a canonical television text like *Buffy* within its larger cultural framework. Rather than just receiving information in a lecture, watching the television, or reading a book, these assignments force them out of their usual roles in the classroom, asking them to literally leave the classroom, and later, to approach the classroom as a teacher. These assignments break down the binary structure of teacher and students in the classroom, at least briefly, just like Buffy as a character, and *Buffy* as a series have always done on screens and written pages across the globe. These assignments also demonstrate that historical themes, events, and patterns, can be explored and made relevant to students' lives and experiences through a popular, non-explicitly historical genre television show. Hopefully, that experience resonates with students enough so that when their parents and peers ask them about taking a cemetery field trip and "the Buffy class" they can look back fondly and report, as one potential slayer did in Season Seven of *Buffy,* that it was the "Best damn field trip I ever took!" ("Potential" 7.12). And should I ever teach a history class that deals with early modern witchcraft or a similar theme, *Buffy* will be prominent on my syllabus.[14]

NOTES

1. See the larger listing at the Academic *Buffy* Studies and Whedonverse Bibliography http://www.alysa316.com/Buffyology/ This is also linked through the *Slayage* website http://slayageonline.com See a complete compilation in Don Macnaughtan, *Bibliography of* Buffy the Vampire Slayer *and* Angel, (tentative title; McFarland, forthcoming).

2. The course meets for two hours at a time, twice a week, for ten weeks on the quarter system. This structure both facilitates in-depth classroom discussion and in-class episode viewing, but also creates the need to break up the rhythm and length of the period to maintain student attentiveness.

3. For more on the creative wielding of language as a weapon see Adams; Wilcox (2005); Wilcox (2009).

4. Joss Whedon, Commentary, "The Harvest" (1.2). After that a mock up cemetery was created on the parking lot of the studio where the show was filmed.

5. Conveniently for the class, one of the major cemeteries discussed in the book is Fairmount Cemetery in Denver.

6. This is also when Willow is endangered by her attraction to a vampire who draws her into the cemetery as a short-cut on the way to get ice cream.

7. Patricia Carmody heads the non-profit Fairmount Heritage Foundation and both Gary O'Hara and Tom Morton have acted as excellent tour guides, assisting us in numerous ways. For more information see http://fairmountheritagefoundation.org

8. Keister provides an easy to use guides to the multiple meanings and history of most symbols found in cemeteries, definitions of various styles of monument design, a key to acronyms used by organizations, clubs and societies, and famous graves of note accompanied by pictures for most entries. I use my course budget to purchase copies for my students, and most of them keep them to use again.

9. My original 2007 syllabus for this course was inspired by panels at the Slayage conference in Barnesville, GA, and constructed in collaboration with Meghan Winchell and our discussions of her own syllabus. I owe her a great deal. However my course quickly changed to suit the goals of the University of Denver curriculum and my own interests. For more on her Liberal Studies course on *Buffy* see her chapter in this volume.

10. For instructors not familiar with the show, short summaries of these episodes can be found online at various sites, but I recommend Roz Kaveney ed., *Reading the Vampire Slayer,* new edition, (2004).

11. In my experience, attempting to maintain a "spoiler-free" experience for students is difficult,

if not impossible, particularly in a ten-week course. For an in-depth and insightful discussion of the issues surrounding "spoilers" and teaching with *Buffy* and other television texts, see David Kociemba's chapter in this volume.

12. I found a number of texts helpful in familiarizing me with American and British witchcraft. For the debates around the issue, and particularly the invention and development of modern Wicca see Gibson (2007). For a larger contextual discussion of 17th Century English "witchfinders" and cases, see Gaskill (2005), and for a contrast with European witchcraft and how it both limited and empowered women, see Roper (2003).

13. This is intriguing, as it gives hope for the longevity of *Buffy* scholarship and courses as the series is studied in relation to other disciplinary issues and canons, rather than simply as an isolated television show.

14. This article owes a great deal to feedback from several colleagues and friends including Elizabeth Escobedo, Shannon Brence, Laura Shelton, and most significantly Meghan Winchell who read numerous drafts. Audience response to the initial presentation of these ideas at the SC3 conference also helped me refine my ideas and my position on multiple issues. Jennifer Fish Kashay accompanied me to many historic cemeteries along the Front Range and guided me through the basics of public history. My thanks go out to all of them.

WORKS CITED

Adams, Michael. *Slayer Slang: A* Buffy the Vampire Slayer *Lexicon.* Oxford: Oxford University Press, 2003. Print.

Gaskill, Malcolm. *Witchfinders: A Seventeenth-Century English Tragedy.* New York: Harvard University Press, 2007. Print.

Gibson, Marion H. *Witchcraft Myths in American Culture.* New York: Routledge, 2007. Print.

Hijiya, James A. "American Gravestones and Attitudes Toward Death: A Brief History." *Proceedings of the American Philosophical Society* 127.5 (1983): 339–63. Print.

Jowett, Lorna. *Sex and the Slayer: a Gender Studies Primer for the Buffy Fan.* Middletown, CN: Wesleyan University Press, 2005. Print.

Kaveney, Roz. *Reading the Vampire Slayer: The Complete, Unofficial Guide to "Buffy" and "Angel."* New York: Tauris Parke Paperbacks, 2004. Print.

Keister, Douglas. *Stories in Stone: A Field Guide to Cemetery Symbolism and Iconography.* Layton, UT: Gibbs Smith, 2004. Print.

Krzywinska, Tanya. "Hubble-Bubble, Herbs, and Grimoires: Magic, Manichaeanism, and Witchcraft in Buffy." *Fighting the Forces: What's at Stake in* Buffy the Vampire Slayer. Lanham: Rowman and Littlefield, 2002. 178–94. Print.

Perkins, D. N., and Gavriel Salomon. (1988) "Teaching for Transfer," *Educational Leadership* 46, No. 1 (Sept 1988): 22–32. Print.

Roper, Lyndal. *Oedipus & the Devil: Witchcraft, Sexuality and Religion in Early Modern Europe.* London: Routledge, 1994. Print.

Sharpe, James A. *Bewitching of Anne Gunter: A Horrible and True Story of Football, Witchcraft, Murder and the King of England.* London: Profile, 1999. Print.

Stott, Annette. *Pioneer Cemeteries: Sculpture Gardens of the Old West.* Lincoln: University of Nebraska, 2008. Print.

Whedon, Joss. *Commentary.* "The Harvest." *Buffy the Vampire Slayer: The Complete First Season.* DVD.

Wilcox, Rhonda V., and David Lavery. *Fighting the Forces: What's at Stake in* Buffy the Vampire Slayer? New York: Rowman & Littlefield, 2002. Print.

_____. "Set on This Earth Like a Bubble: Word as Flesh in the Dark Seasons." *Buffy Goes Dark: Essays on the Final Two Seasons of* Buffy the Vampire Slayer *on Television.* Eds. Lynne Y. Edwards, Elizabeth L. Rambo and James B. South. Jefferson, NC: McFarland, 2009. 95–113. Print.

_____. *Why Buffy Matters: The Art of* Buffy the Vampire Slayer. London: I. B. Tauris, 2005. Print.

Winslade, J. Lawton. "Teen Witches, Wiccans & "Wanna-Blessed Be's": Pop-Culture Magic in *Buffy the Vampire Slayer.*" *Slayage: The Whedon Studies Association Journal* 1 (2001) n.p. March 10, 2010.

Little Red Riding ... Buffy?
"'Buffy vs. Dracula"
in Explorations of Intertextuality
in Introduction to College English

Kristopher Karl Woofter

I teach at Dawson College, a preparatory college in Montréal, Québec, and I often find it a challenge to introduce my students, whose ages generally range from 17 to 22, to the more sophisticated level of critical thinking and analysis required of them at university. The first major obstacle occurs with getting students to see literary studies as its own discipline, worthy of study on an aesthetic level, and not justifiable solely as a means toward practical applications such as critical thinking and communication skills. The second major obstacle comes with making students aware of two questions regarding media that I believe are never mutually exclusive, no matter how simple or complex the subject matter: that is, the degree to which artistic works are entertainment, and the degree to which popular entertainment is artistic. To this effect, positioning popular entertainment in the context of the study of literature has proven to be an effective pedagogical method in my teaching experience. The *Buffy the Vampire Slayer* television series — because it is familiar to my students, and because it is decidedly a textually porous, allusive and self-referential body of work — thus becomes an enormous resource in helping students to make the transition from the personal responses they are taught to produce in high school to the more critical analyses they can expect to produce at the college and university levels.[1]

I have used episodes of *Buffy* extensively for a number of pedagogical goals: to show evidence of the continued influence on contemporary entertainment of literary sources such as Robert Louis Stevenson's *Strange Case of Dr. Jekyll and Mr. Hyde* (in episodes like "The Wish" [3.9]) and Mary Shelley's *Frankenstein* (in episodes like "Some Assembly Required" [2.2]); to illustrate concepts such as the doppelganger in my "American Gothic" course.[2] I have also used "Wrecked" in my "Horror in Popular Culture" course as an example of a contemporary "social problem film," much like those that had their heyday in 1930s Hollywood. In my "Introduction to College English" ("Intro") course, implementing *Buffy* has proven to be among the most effective ways of introducing critical thinking regarding literary allusion, allegory and intertextuality. I use the episode "Buffy vs. Dracula" (5.1) as a key component to the course's final unit, which gradually develops students' analytical skills through a comparative approach, encouraging them to think through connections with respect to a bevy of sources related by their status as pastiche, parody, revision or abstraction of the traditional "Little Red Riding Hood" fairy tale. *Buffy* proves especially useful in this context of artistic works that replicate, gesture to, or critique problematic fairy-tale paradigms in that the series so clearly aligns itself with a revisionist discourse in which a female hero is not only born to fight monsters instead of running from them, but is also shown to be variously tormented and invigorated by the power that such a birthright bestowed upon her. The responses from my students to my use of *Buffy* in this course and context in particular have been compelling. Four years of positive results with the unit on fairy tales in the "Intro" course have convinced me that, given sufficient context — whether formal, sociological, or theoretical — individual episodes of *Buffy* can be useful tools to introduce students to complex concepts such as "discourse," "normativity," "ideology" and "critique."

Entitled "From Fairy Tale to Revisionist Tale: Narrative, Motif, Theme," the unit in which I use *Buffy* is the last of four major divisions in the overall structure of the "Intro" course, each division designed according to specific cumulative goals. The first of these divisions, entitled "Reading Critically," shows students how to look for important textual and visual cues in both fiction and film, how to properly annotate a text with their observations, how best to record their observations on a film, how to turn their observations and annotations into statements, and how to avoid mere speculation in their arguments. The second division, entitled "The Literary Elements and the Short Story," has a twofold purpose: first, it is a review of essential literary terms, using short fiction to reintroduce students to typical narrative components such as setting, conflict, and focalization (point of view); second, it considers the short story as a narrative form. The third division, entitled "The Form and Function of the Novel," focuses on a short novel (I most recently used both Shirley Jackson's *The Haunting of Hill House* (1959) and *We Have Always Lived in the Castle* (1962) because of their gestures to fairy tale motifs) to show students how the literary elements they have reviewed translate to a longer narrative form. The "Fairy Tale to Revisionist Tale" unit concludes the course with a focus on the permutations of fairy tale narrative structures, motifs and themes in fiction, film and television. This final unit serves as both a synthesis of all that the students have learned so far in the course, and an introduction to later core English courses they will take at the junior college level that explore a single literary theme, genre or form. The unit is, in essence, a mini-course within a course.

I have taught the "Fairy Tale" unit five times in the "Intro" course since the fall of 2005. I created this unit (and much of the course in general) as a response to several factors that I noticed in Dawson students: first, they are not excited about reading, let alone analysis, but they become more inspired when they have their eyes opened to material that they *think* they know inside and out (fairy tales, comics, genre fiction, television); second, the way they process information is becoming increasingly visual as television, graphic novels, comic books, the cinema and video games draw their attention away from traditional literature (even though these visual media incorporate myriad literary forms in often sophisticated ways); third, they respond more enthusiastically to a variety of materials and methods in the classroom; and, fourth, they respond best to learning modules of about three-weeks in length, with clear-cut goals. This "Fairy Tale" unit has six pedagogical goals: (1) to enable students to differentiate between subject matter (content) and theme; (2) to enable students to differentiate between moral and theme; (3) to illustrate literary terms such as "motif," "metaphor" and "allegory"; (4) to help students to establish a clear basis of comparison for writing about more than one source; (5) to help students to understand narrative as variably original, inherited, allusive, and revisionist; and (6) to help students situate artistic works of various media in a discourse. Like the structure of the course in general, this unit is broken down into sub-units that increasingly evolve outward from the fairy tale proper to show the diversity and influence of fairy tale motifs and themes: we move through a number of variations, abstractions, appropriations and extrapolations of the traditional "Red Riding Hood" tale. "Buffy vs. Dracula" ends the unit as a potential extrapolation of a fairy tale narrative. I include the most recent version of this unit below, followed by an explication of the subdivisions of the unit. At Dawson College, each class meets twice per week for one hour and 45 minutes. I ask students to prepare readings for the class on which they appear; I screen all visual material in class.

Unit IV — From Fairy Tale to Revisionist Tale: Narrative, Motif, Theme

Class #1 — Red Riding Hood: Moral versus Theme

READING:
Anonymous. "The Grandmother's Tale."[3]
Grimm, Jacob and Wilhelm. "Little Red Cap."
Perrault, Charles. "Little Red Riding Hood."

VIEWING AND DISCUSSION:
"Little Red Riding Rabbit." Dir. Friz Freleng.

Class #2 — Variations on a Theme I

READING:
Dahl, Roald. "Little Red Riding Hood and the Wolf."
Strauss, Gwenn. "The Waiting Wolf."

Class #3 — Variations on a Theme II

READING:
Sexton, Anne. "Red Riding Hood."

VIEWING AND DISCUSSION:
"Red Hot Riding Hood." Dir. Tex Avery.

Class #4 — Variations on a Theme III

READING:
Lee, Tanith. "Wolfland."
or,
Carter, Angela. "The Company of Wolves."

VIEWING AND DISCUSSION (of selected clips from):
Company of Wolves, The. Dir. Neil Jordan.

Class #5 — Abstraction of a Theme

VIEWING AND DISCUSSION:
"Down to the Cellar." Dir. Jan Svankmajer.

Class #6 — Appropriated Structure

READING:
Lovecraft, H. P. "The Outsider."

Class #7 — Narrative Motifs and Extrapolated Theme, I

READING:
Phillips, Robert. "After the Fact: To Ted Bundy."

VIEWING:
clip from *Cold Case Files* featuring an interview with Ted Bundy

Class #8 — Narrative Motifs and Extrapolated Theme, II

READING:
Jackson, Shirley. "Jack the Ripper."

Class #9 — Narrative Motifs and Extrapolated Theme, III

VIEWING AND DISCUSSION:
"Buffy vs. Dracula." *Buffy the Vampire Slayer.* Dir. David Solomon.

Class #10 — Review

Class #11 & #12 — In-Class Writing of Final Essay

The ultimate goal of this unit is to position "Buffy vs. Dracula" in a context of texts that appropriate and/or open a dialogue with fairy tale motifs derived from the "Red Riding Hood" tale. I define the traditional fairy tale as resting formally between the oral folktale and the literary tale. I resist the idea that the fairy tale exists in a vacuum, but instead make it clear to students that even popular fairy tales as recorded by Charles Perrault and Jacob and Wilhelm Grimm are neither the "original" form of the tale, nor bastardizations of some "purer" form that has been lost to time. In other words, they are just as much a *version* of the already-diasporic folktale as the revisions and abstractions in form that we will discuss throughout the "Fairy Tale" unit. This focus on transmutations of form, motif and theme shows the degrees to which the myriad variants of the tale are successful in both illuminating and working to counter the persistent historical, cultural and aesthetic norms their authors may see as confining or oppressive.

I designed this unit to develop notions of intertextuality gradually, and I take great pains to emphasize with the students that each new text adds to a knowledge base on which to consider future texts in the unit. The unit uses traditional fairy tale morals, themes, iconic imagery and narrative structures as bases for identifying more complex variations and revealing juxtapositions. We work specifically with fairy tale traditions as formulated by scholars like Jack Zipes and Maria Tatar. Referring to the "Red Riding

Hood" tale specifically, Zipes and Tatar both stress its formal adaptability to cultural concerns as they develop and evolve over time. Zipes sees the tale as "indicat[ing] real shifts, conflicts, and ruptures in the Western civilizing process," especially in its "male-dominated" focus on the "discipline and punishment" of the Red Riding Hood character (31). And Tatar identifies the "arbitrariness" in the tale's generic formulation, where "strength confronts weakness, and any predatory power can be substituted for the wolf, with any innocent standing in for the heroine" (51). With these basic formulations about the traditional tales in mind, students develop an approach based upon a hypothesis to be tested and debated. Not all of the works fit snugly into the traditional fairy tale themes and motifs that the students track over the course of the unit, and that potential for divergence from what students come to see as a normative mode encourages them to think through possible ideological differences in the works, or to recognize possible breaks from, or criticisms of, the dominant discourse set out by the fairy tale proper. Thus, students approach "Buffy vs. Dracula" looking to test its adherence to, or divergence from, the traditional fairy-tale themes, such as those that link innocence with the feminine, experience with impurity and corruption, and salvation with a reestablishment of patriarchal power — and to make their conclusions about the episode accordingly.

I begin the unit with three different versions of "Little Red Riding Hood" (one by Charles Perrault, one by the Grimm Brothers, one anonymous) to set up a basic critical foundation, and to distinguish the terms, "subject matter," "moral," and "theme." Students contribute their ideas to a chart of themes, messages and motifs in the traditional "Little Red Riding Hood" tales; this chart forms a typological template that we can augment and revise as we encounter the different incarnations of the traditional tale in the rest of the unit. I then move on to explicit variations on, and reinterpretations of the tale by authors such as Anne Sexton, Roald Dahl, Tanith Lee and Angela Carter, all of whom focus on its implications of experience and power gained through victimization and violence. I follow these specific variations of the tale by an "abstraction" of the "Red Riding Hood" theme — a short film by surrealist Czech animator Jan Svankmajer, entitled "Down To the Cellar," which readjusts the tale as a child's nightmare journey to the basement potato bin in her coal-blackened, decaying apartment building. The final part of the unit focuses on works that appropriate the structure and themes of "Red Riding Hood" in less obvious ways. Works by H. P. Lovecraft, Shirley Jackson, and "Buffy vs. Dracula" are all extrapolations of the "Red Riding Hood" theme that do not at first appear to be in any way related to the tale, but offer revealing looks at the issues of identity, gender and power that arise in the tale proper. As the works grow more revisionist, complex and abstract, students can refer to that original foundation — the traditional fairy tale — to anchor themselves in the newer material. This anchor also brings up a variety of bases of comparison that the students can then choose to take up in their writing. The final essay topics ask students to address "Buffy vs. Dracula" in this now quite diverse context.

To give a stricter sense of the context that develops throughout this unit, I give more detail on the sources I have chosen, and how I work with those sources to build confidence in the students that they are gradually becoming "expert" at picking out the developing themes and motifs in the sources. The first thing students notice is how unexpectedly different the three traditional versions of the tale are. The anonymous "Grandmother's Tale"

(France; Louis & Francois Briffult, 1885; Achille Millien, date unknown; recorded in 1951 by Paul Delarue), tends to be the most surprising with its focus on bodily functions and fleshly corruption. In it, the wolf tricks the girl into drinking the blood and eating the flesh of her grandmother before the girl realizes his true nature (while naked in bed with him). The girl then outwits the wolf by claiming the need to defecate. The wolf tells her to do it in bed, but the girl suggests he tie a string to her so that she can go outside. She then ties the string to a tree, tricking the wolf and buying herself time to escape to safety. The idea that the girl must somehow be sullied as a symptom of gaining experience comes up again and again, here tinted with both incest and religious undertones of the ritual taking in (and expulsion) of sacrificial blood and flesh. Charles Perrault's "Little Red Riding Hood" (France, 1697) eschews notions of cannibalism but keeps intact the suggestive sexuality. Most surprising to my students who do not remember this version of the tale is Perrault's decision not only to have the girl be devoured without rescue, but to blame her for her own predicament in a caveat-in-verse that warns young women to beware of slick seducers. Perrault's ending generates rich discussion in the classroom around the problematic fairy tale motif of blaming the victim for being inexperienced. The Brothers Grimm's "Little Red Cap" (Germany, 1812) removes all references to sexual seduction and focuses on forbidden knowledge—specifically, curiosity with respect to the unknown and the dangers of overstepping boundaries. The girl, like her granny, is devoured by the wolf, and later rescued by a woodsman in what Anne Sexton calls "a kind of caesarian section" in her poetic revision of the tale, emphasizing the ostensible rebirth of the girl into a world of experience learned through violence (272). Students identify in the traditional tales such elements as spiritual and fleshly corruption, a consistent reinforcement of patriarchal power, limited degrees of resourcefulness in the female figure, a linking of curiosity to transgression, and a multitude of functions and meanings for the wolf as the tale's monstrous unknown. Pairing the traditional tales with Friz Freleng's Bugs Bunny cartoon, "Little Red Riding Rabbit" (1944) allows us to explore parody as a way of drawing out stereotypical fairy tale motifs that other authors in the unit present with varying degrees of satire, playfulness, seriousness or ire.

The works I categorize as "variations on a theme" treat the "Red Riding Hood" tale explicitly to offer alternative takes on the tale's themes. Roald Dahl's "Little Red Riding Hood and the Wolf" and Tex Avery's "Red Hot Riding Hood" fall in the tradition of parodying "tired" fairy tale traditions. Dahl's eponymous protagonist refuses to go through the motions of revealing the wolf, despite his pleas, and she ends up shooting him and turning him into a fur coat. Avery's characters, beginning the tale traditionally, break the "fourth wall" to express their boredom with the tale and demand that it be updated. The recourse to parody in these two works offers students a point of entry into the quite complicated fairy tale revisions by other artists. More serious revisions of the tale occur in Gwen Strauss's poem "The Waiting Wolf," Anne Sexton's poem, "Red Riding Hood," and Tanith Lee's short story, "Wolfland." Strauss's poem, for example, places the reader uncomfortably inside the mind of an abuser, and Sexton's revision of "Little Red Riding Hood" takes up the subject of self-deception to focus on the continuing cycle of violence and victimization of women. Because Strauss's and Sexton's poems alter focalization to raise notions of subjectivity, I ask students to consider carefully how each work addresses its audience to keep the students focused on the importance of perspective as it frames power relations in such texts. For the third class on "variations" on the traditional fairy tale, I alternate between Tanith Lee's story "Wolfland" and Angela Carter's story "In the Company of Wolves," along with clips from Neil Jordan's sophisticated 1984 film version of the latter tale. Both Carter's and Lee's revisions focus on pubescent girls coming into their own role both socially and sexually in a world of violence, and both feature lycanthropic predators. Carter playfully subverts Perrault's tale of ill-fated seduction by having her heroine flaunt her sexuality and welcome the embrace of the werewolf who seduces her while in the form of a man.[4] Lee's grim take on "Little Red Riding Hood," like her other gothic revisions of classic fairy tales,[5] focuses on the burdensome heritage of abuse and self-loathing passed on from one generation of women to another. Here, "grandmother" is a werewolf who must pass on her curse to her granddaughter so that the former may be released from a cycle of her own violence caused by horrendous past abuse.

Power relations once again are at issue in these works, and students are quick to notice in Lee's story the damaging effects of a legacy of brutal male violence. These works' specific engagement with recovering female (and literary) agency in the wake of long-term abuse, introduce key concepts for the presentation, later in the unit, of "Buffy vs. Dracula." The *Buffy* series is critical of configurations of the feminine as imperiled and/or victimized, particularly those beleaguered, breathless horror "heroines" in films like *Halloween* (1978) and *Friday the 13th* (1980) who literally stumble into positions of power as a result of their having confronted monstrosity (which *Buffy*'s characters repeatedly — and tellingly — term, the "Big Bad"). Accordingly, "Buffy vs. Dracula" is a useful final text, bringing students back to Sexton's, Strauss's, Carter's and Lee's critiques of the innocent, ignorant fairy tale heroines found in the tales of Grimm and Perrault. Like these reevaluated Red Riding Hoods, Buffy Summers is a female hero conflicted by a power to which she *already* has access, but that nonetheless manifests itself through her (sometimes intimate) contact with monstrosity.

With Sexton's, Strauss's, and Carter's or Lee's specific formulations of "power" in place, we move from the "variations" subsection to works that I consider to be either "abstractions" or "appropriations" of the "Red Riding Hood" tale. These works either appropriate the tale's narrative structure, or they subtly evoke the tale's themes and symbols to play on notions of innocence and experience. I typically assess the students' perspectives and analytical capabilities throughout the unit by way of short writing assignments at the beginning of class, or by questions and topics that I hold up for discussion and debate. It is with these more abstract works that I begin to see students broadening their analytical capacity through attempts in both writing and discussion to locate connections where there seem to be none, and, in some of the stronger students, a willingness to challenge my inclusion of the works at all. A work such as Svankmajer's "Down to the Cellar" (1982) gives students pause. In this short film, Svankmajer offers a surrealist-fantastic take on the "Little Red Riding Hood" tale, where a girl's simple quest to fill a basket with potatoes becomes increasingly nightmarish: she must navigate a corridor filled with ravenous, animated shoes; must fend off the advances of a salacious old man in a bed of coal; must resist an offer of coal-biscuits from a haggard old woman; and, on her journey back, must evade a monstrous black cat. The power of the girl to fill the unknown void ahead of her with elements of her everyday world magnified by her fear places her in a liminal state between a world of innocence and experience, like a meeker (though perhaps more imaginative) version of Dahl's gun-toting Red. Because Svankmajer's short film makes no obvious gesture to the tale proper, students have the opportunity to test and debate its adherence to narrative and thematic codes developed by the more clearly linked variations mentioned above.

Similarly implicit (or debatable) in their possible appropriations of the tale's components are H. P. Lovecraft's classic short story, "The Outsider," Robert Phillips's epistolary poem "After the Fact: To Ted Bundy," and Shirley Jackson's disturbing short story, "Jack the Ripper." In "The Outsider," Lovecraft's titular narrator, an innocent sufferer, trapped in the gloomy halls of his ancestors, embarks upon a quest to explore the outside world. At the end of his journey, he confronts what he thinks is a monster, but is instead revealed to him as his own mirror image — which he has never seen. Lovecraft explores issues that are instantly recognizable to students who have come thus far in the "Fairy Tale" unit. These include the stretching of mind and body to their limits in the search for forbidden knowledge, the burning curiosity that far outweighs the fear and dread of new experience in the unknown, and the protagonist's conflicted condition — the outsider's ignorance of a world to which he is inextricably linked, his dual role as a pure innocent and a figure in whom a greater darkness lurks. Many students remark in our discussions that Lovecraft, like Perrault, seems to blame the story's titular victim for his own limited exposure; others see a protagonist that combines the girl and the wolf— innocence and monstrosity — into one conflicted figure, emblematic of a much more complex way of looking at identity than the traditional "Red Riding Hood" tales manifest, and once again suggestive of the way that the character will be configured in "Buffy vs. Dracula."[6]

Two more works further complicate the traditional tales' simple binaries with respect to victim and victimized, innocent and evil: "After the Fact: To Ted Bundy" by Robert Phillips and "Jack the Ripper" by Shirley Jackson draw upon serial killers, putting the reader into the mind of a victim in the former, and the villain in the latter. In Phillips's poem, the female voice has been so marked by her contact with Bundy that she sees all attractive men as vile predators and becomes physically ill with even the suggestion of intimacy. After we have discussed Phillips's poem to some extent, I show a clip of an interview with Ted Bundy from Bill Curtis's *Cold Case Files* to emphasize the unsettling real-world inspiration for the poem. Student responses are mixed with respect to the poem's success at wresting some power for the female voice appropriated by Phillips. They frequently are troubled by this vision of a woman who remains obsessed with her tormentor, to the point of addressing her words to Bundy after he has been executed. Many students are even more troubled by Shirley Jackson's story, "Jack the Ripper," which pointedly gives the female victim no voice whatsoever. The focus in both works is on the violence that lurks beneath deceptive surfaces — quite potent in "Ripper," where the potential rescuer of a drunken woman passed out in the streets turns out to be the infamous title character: the Grimms' kindly woodsman as a wolf in disguise. Written responses by students to Jackson's story invariably address the problematic doll-like passivity of the female character in the story, compared with the violent active nature of the male figure, noting that such oppositions may be only a disguised version of the traditional tale's simple binary.

"Buffy vs. Dracula" is the final work that we discuss in the unit and the course. For students who have been actively engaged in our discussions of fairy tale appropriations, revisions and abstractions, writer Marti Noxon's complex treatment of an innocent in "thrall" confronting the monstrous tends to meet expectations rather than defy them. Buffy Summers' attraction to, and connection with, that most famous of monsters, Dracula, reveals both a potential weakness in, and a sense of purpose for, the television hero. Buffy begins the episode showing her hunger to explore her own power, leaving hunky boyfriend, Riley, behind in bed in the middle of the night to go on a "hunt" for vampires. An offer to tap into her own darkness comes in the seductive form of Dracula himself. As in Bram Stoker's 1897 novel, Dracula invites his most desired victim — in this case, a red-leather-pants-clad Buffy — to taste his blood, and thus to share a bit of his power. Buffy's tapping into and claiming of the monster's darkness to discover her own identity and power indicates a key parallel between the "Little Red Riding Hood" source narrative and the overall narrative arc of the *Buffy* series, for in the intermingling of protagonist and monster lies the catalyst for the protagonist's transformation, or the seeds of her destruction. Students are quick to note how much the *Buffy* viewer's pleasure is caught up in the vampire's act of meshing with his victim — that his act of sullying, like the wolf's in the traditional "Red Riding Hood" tale, brings us pleasure because it brings Buffy closer to full knowledge of herself. The invocation of the hero's own darkness brings up an important question for both the tale and the series, which I pose to the students directly after we screen "Buffy vs. Dracula" together in class: How close can one come to the darkest part of oneself, or one's world, and still remain sane, intact and healthy, let alone heroic? The traditional fairy tale's rote pairing of an innocent female against a monstrous male as part of her struggle for individuation provides another of many discursive possibilities through which students consider the episode. Here, I point students back to the beginning of the unit, suggesting that they make comparisons with respect to notions of power in "Buffy vs. Dracula," the traditional fairy tales, and the revisionist fairy tales by Sexton, Strauss, Carter and Lee. Students notice that, though Buffy is a born fighter, there is a strain of negativity and torment in her discovery of that power in the episode, which, like that of the revisionist works, manifests through violence and has as part of its legacy a link to the monstrous and patriarchal. Dracula's summons to Buffy to taste his blood as a way of locating the origins of her power, for example, emphasizes that power's connection to a monstrosity that is configured as male and fatherly. Thus Buffy Summers inherits a power that she finds both invigorating and burdensome, connected as it is to the very trauma it seems intended to overcome. I encourage students to explore such notions by asking questions that elucidate the episode's position in the debates we have raised in class: To what degree is Buffy figured as innocent or monstrous, "pure" or "tainted" even before she meets her adversary? To what extent is Buffy's "darkness" related to her sexuality? Does the episode escape or perpetuate the traditions of female transgression and male aggression we find in fairy tales?

As I suggest here, by the time the students reach the end of the unit — and "Buffy vs. Dracula" — they have been primed to explore a number of ways in which the fairy tale can be transformed, from parody of form (and formula) to serious critical engagement. I notice a surprising degree of sophistication in student responses: most neither reduce the episode to its fairy-tale components, nor rest upon what the episode or its creators "intend" to do. I have found that placing works in such a context opens up students' analyses to considerations of ideology—that is, how these works create a dialogue on issues such as gender dynamics, power relations, moral arguments, physical and psychological manifestations of monstrosity, and other larger cultural foci that serve to *position* these texts in a tradition, rather than isolate them for a study of what they "mean." A pointed example of this is that many of the analyses I present here on the works in the unit are derived from class discussions. Certainly, there is a degree of prompting here: the organizing principle of the "Fairy Tale" unit encourages a developing argument, but I do not dictate that argument to my students. I presume that the implications of presenting the material in the same context are enough of a cue to students that there are connections to be found. In this way, I leave such connections open to the possibility of debate and disagreement. Only if I encounter a weaker dynamic in a class do I offer stricter guidance in the form of leading questions, possible assumptions, and suggested arguments. More typically, the questions I ask about the works (in quizzes, reading guides, and discussion) challenge students to consider potential connections amongst the works, but rarely assign those connections. A common strategy for both in-class writing and group work, for example, is to select a passage and ask students to discuss the significance of that passage to the work under consideration, to other works in the unit, or to our considerations of the unit (or the course) as a whole. Assigned the passage, "I might not have gone further, / but then nothing ever remains / innocent in the woods," for example, students might situate the wolf's voice from Gwen Strauss's "The Waiting Wolf" into a discourse of blaming the victim for transgressing moral boundaries that exculpate him from any wrongdoing (328). Thus, I can extrapolate from this, in further discussion with the students, Strauss's possible critique of the male-dominated, hegemonic nature of many such folk narratives.

In what follows, I give a sense of the handouts and assignments I use that are specifically related to "Buffy vs. Dracula" as the episode, by design, serves as a springboard for a retrospective critical look at the unit by the students. I first use a viewing guide, discussed below, to encourage careful viewing of, and later reflection on, the episode during an in-class screening. The episode runs 45 minutes, which allows us to discuss the viewing guide for another 45 minutes before students go off to think more about the questions raised. I begin the next class period (Class #10 on the sample unit) with a brief discussion of the students' responses to the remaining questions on the viewing guide, followed by an exercise in class, which asks them to create an outline for a critical discussion of the episode.

I divide the viewing guide into two sections: topics to consider while viewing the episode, and questions to answer after the viewing for future discussion. In the first section, I ask students to trace the evolution of the issues introduced in the episode's opening segment, in which Buffy stirs from sleep to engage in a violent hunt, where she first meets Dracula. I also ask them to pay close attention to themes arising from other confrontations between Buffy and Dracula, as well as to how the secondary characters, Willow, Xander, Giles and Anya, react to Dracula insofar as their reactions help to define him, or to clarify Buffy's response to Dracula. I intend these viewing cues to draw students' attention to key elements in the episode without coloring their responses. In the second section, I ask students, first, to identify the episode's surface and deeper conflicts; second, to consider the degree to which the episode re-envisions the characters of Red Riding Hood and the wolf; and, third, to explore what connotes "power" in the episode. The first post-viewing question cues a literary term that students can use to explore the episode's themes; the second brings in the fairy tale element; and the third raises a concern that is made quite clear in the episode — the nature of power — leaving the students to draw their own conclusions on that issue. The questions are designed to guide students to think critically about key issues in the episode and its place in the context of the other works we have discussed — that is, *conflict* within the episode (question 1) leads to placing the episode in the context of the unit (question 2), which leads to the episode's conclusions about power inside and outside that context (question 3).

The viewing exercise during the next class operates on a more transparent schema of leading questions to direct students to specific fairy-tale comparisons while also taking them through the steps (and proper questions) for creating an argument. I include this viewing exercise below, along with a sampling of the responses from a single class of 40 "Introduction to College English" students. Students completed the exercise in groups of about five using their viewing guides from the previous class, during which we screened the episode. Their responses follow each question.

Viewing Exercise

You have been asked to prepare an abstract for a conference on fairy tale motifs and themes in popular entertainment. The text you will be discussing is "Buffy vs. Dracula," episode 1, Season Five of *Buffy the Vampire Slayer*. Use the following questions to develop your thesis and main points, and be prepared to present your abstract to the class in outline form.

1. What general fairy tale motifs and themes can you locate in the episode?

   Deception of an innocent: the vampire puts thoughts into her mind, tempts her

   Potential knowledge: the vampire forces her to learn through experience

   Weakness of women: Buffy is easily controlled at first by the vampire's seduction

   Ignorance of one's true identity

   Seduction used to cause heroine to physically and mentally diverge from her goals

   Acquiring knowledge leads to wider worldview but also to loss of innocence

   Ignorance leads to conflict

2. What motifs and themes specific to the individual traditional "Red Riding Hood" tales surface in the episode?

   "The Grandmother's Tale": the vampire taints Buffy by biting her and later allowing her to drink his blood so that she becomes less pure and less innocent.

   Idea that knowledge about oneself may lead to corruption of mind and body

"Not a killer but a Slayer": Buffy is hiding behind a curtain of illusion; she cannot face the naked truth about her identity

Sexual vulnerability and temptation

Dracula is like the wolf in Charles Perrault's version, where "sweetest tongue has sharpest tooth"

3. Does the episode offer any important variations on, or criticisms of, the "Little Red Riding Hood" motifs and themes?

Roald Dahl's "Little Red Riding Hood" because Buffy meets the monster prepared to fight.

While Red Riding Hood has no idea of any danger related to the wolf, Buffy enters with some knowledge; while Red Riding Hood is a symbol of weakness, Buffy has both weak and dominant sides.

Knowledge corrupts the mind, but Buffy uses it to her own advantage to beat the wolf (and her own weakness)

Buffy needs to fight her own demons

In the traditional story, the girl doesn't know the wolf is evil; Buffy and all her friends know Dracula is evil and are attracted to and seduced by his fame

The episode equally criticizes and supports the idea that women are the weaker gender; Buffy breaks the thrall on her own, but she still allows herself to be corrupted by a seductive male

Buffy wants to learn more about herself throughout the episode, while Red Riding Hood just wants to pursue beauty

4. Based on your notes above, what will the main points of your article be? List them here:

The pursuit of knowledge about one's identity

Corruption of the heroine by the villain; corruption of an innocent

Harm and danger may lurk behind beauty, fame and temptation

Experience and knowledge lead to possible corruption, but also to self discovery

Experience and resistance of temptation will break the world of illusion and ignorance

Manipulation

Victimization of Women

5. Academic articles are known for having long, involved titles, like "Buffy and the Deceptive Allure of the 'Big Bad'": Slayer as Contemporary Red Riding Hood in 'Buffy vs. Dracula.'" Try your hand at it. What will the title of your article be, based on the main points you have brought up?

Dracula's Manipulation of Buffy: A Modern Day Reflection of the Traditional "Little Red Riding Hood" Tale

Buffy's Thirst for Knowledge when Seduced by a Symbolic Wolf Figure in "Buffy vs. Dracula"

The Seduction and Manipulation of Buffy: The "Little Red Riding Hood" Motif in "Buffy vs. Dracula"

Note that the answers to #4 show some students are thinking on a strictly moral level, while others refrain from exploring that dimension of the story, choosing instead to get the question answered with a simple identification of an issue to be explored. This particular aspect of the responses — a reversion to superficial interpretations of fairy tale messages — gave me the opportunity to address the importance of an arguable and clearly expressed thesis statement, as well as to remind students that they needed to make sure that addressing the episode's moral nature was, indeed, what they set out to do. We had a brief review of the difference between moral and theme at this point. More encouraging are the stronger points brought up in #2 and #3, where the students' engagement with the traditional "Red Riding Hood" tale and the episode's potential variations and revisions of that tale prompted more sophisticated responses based upon their awareness of a context in which to fit the episode. I pointed this out to them, of course, encouraging them to trust their abilities when it came to holding the episode up to the context provided by the unit.

Exercises such as the above prepare students for the more complicated responses expected from them in the final essay written in class over two two-hour periods during the final two classes. Together, the viewing guide and exercise encourage students to situate the episode in the context of the traditional fairy tale; they do not directly address the other works in the unit. I expect and encourage these comparisons to arise through my questions and guidance of the discussion. After we complete this exercise, I review the topics they are expected to handle on the final essay, a 750- to 1,000-word comparative critical analysis. Included below is a selection of essay topics that I have used in the past. While I usually provide students with only three topics, I offer an additional example here to show the variety of approaches I asked students to take over five semesters.

Final Essay Topics

1. Many of the works we discussed in this unit, including Sexton's poem, "Red Riding Hood," Strauss's "The Waiting Wolf," and Lee's short story, "Wolfland," have taken issue with the traditional representation of gender in the "Red Riding Hood" fairy tale. Discuss the *Buffy the Vampire Slayer* episode, "Buffy vs. Dracula" as another attempt to evaluate such traditional views of gender. You may refer to other works in the unit if you wish, but your primary analysis should be the episode.

2. In a past essay, one student concluded that Buffy Summers' comment that she is "not a killer, but a Slayer," shows her to be "hiding behind a curtain of illusion, unable to face the naked truth about her identity." With reference to one of the traditional tales and two relevant variations, discuss the notion that the "Little Red Riding Hood" tale is ultimately about fighting one's own demons to get at "the naked truth" of one's identity.

3. Which two of the following variations of "Red Riding Hood" are most similar with respect to how the author envisions monstrosity?

    Lovecraft's story, "The Outsider"

    Jackson's story, "Jack the Ripper"

    Svankmajer's short film, "Down to the Cellar"

    "Buffy vs. Dracula" from *Buffy the Vampire Slayer*

    Explain your answer with appropriate references to both works you discuss. Be careful not to focus on superficial (obvious) similarities.

4. Choose a version of the traditional "Little Red Riding Hood" tale, and analyze which of the following variations offers the most radical revision of that tale's themes, symbols and/or conflicts.

    "Wolfland" by Lee

    "The Outsider" by Lovecraft

    "Jack the Ripper" by Jackson

    "Buffy vs. Dracula," written by Marti Noxon, from *Buffy the Vampire Slayer*

    Be careful not to focus on superficial (obvious) differences.

While these topics are specific in the directions they lead students, as well as suggestive in their juxtapositions of selected works, they still leave the questions open to the students' original ideas as much as possible. Topics 1 and 2 offer a critical setup and ask the students to follow it through using a number of possible choices that are open to them; thus, despite the setup, there are still options for creative thinking and the students' own revealing juxtapositions. Topic 3 is perhaps the most limited in its focus on a single concept — "monstrosity" — though it, too, allows students options with respect to which works they will draw upon to make their argument. In a variation on this topic, I replace "monstrosity" with "power" and realign the choice of primary texts to draw students' attention to works that, along with "Buffy vs. Dracula," explore notions of power more fully: Lee's "Wolfland," Lovecraft's "The Outsider" and Jackson's "Jack the Ripper." Topic 4 is arguably the most open-ended of the choices, cueing students only to the degree of variation of a selection of works from the traditional "Red Riding Hood" tale, and leaving the focus, approach and choice of text up to the student. While I leave open the degree to which students address the *Buffy* episode in their final essays, most students choose to focus on the episode significantly, and the intellectual results are impressive. My students' final essays have touched upon subjects as diverse as the titillation of fairy-tale audiences with respect to taboo issues, notions of feminine strength as exotic fantasy, and the possible limitations of feminist revisions of fairy tales because of their essentially reactive, not proactive, nature. The test that a pedagogical method is working is, for me, indicated by the students' ability to stretch beyond the topics in their writing, and to point to considerations that push the boundaries we have set up in our class discussions. The stronger students certainly do so, and come up with such angles on the topic as I listed above. But even weaker students have been able to draw convincing and often surprising comparisons between texts simply because "Buffy vs. Dracula" is an already rich text made the richer by virtue of the context we have set up over the three weeks prior to the writing of the final essay.

The feedback received from students with respect to this unit has been extremely positive. When presented with the syllabus on the first day of classes, students are unsure at first how an episode of *Buffy* could help them understand transcendent themes and intertextuality, but once the giggles, eye-rolling and subtly encouraging smiles from diffident *Buffy* fans have faded, I typically observe a high degree of diligence in the students' approach to the unit. When I surveyed my most recent group from Fall 2008, I asked them questions ranging from their first impressions of a unit involving an episode of *Buffy*, to which issues were most interesting to them through their study of the episode. One student was "intrigued" and "pleasantly surprised" to see a popular television show represented on the syllabus; another observed, rather cannily:

> I often write off shows like *Buffy the Vampire Slayer* as just another dumb half-hour, so, no, it never occurred to me as something you could analyze and discuss seriously. However, I did have an open mind to it because I had heard of entire serious university courses built upon television shows like *The Simpsons*! ["Teaching *Buffy the Vampire Slayer* Survey"].

There are, of course, entire courses focusing on *Buffy*, as well, though I have often found myself deflecting criticism when discussing the show (or any television show, for that matter) as a pedagogical tool with my colleagues. Few and far between are comments like a recent one from a colleague who teaches courses on Cyberpunk and "Surviving Overload": "keep doing what you're doing!" I appreciate the encouragement, but I also find sufficient encouragement in practice. Prior to adding *Buffy* to my courses, I struggled with how best to leap from textual analysis to touch upon the more complicated theoretical notions around literature and culture and not see forty sets of eyes glaze over, or forty sets of arms fold in resistance. Based upon the students' enthusiasm for the subject matter and the degree of critical sophistication I have seen develop in them as a result of this pedagogical approach, I am reinventing this unit to include other episodes of *Buffy* in a variety of contexts, from narratological explorations of the show's complex allusiveness, to the show's focus on apocalypse and renewal. And then there is that entire course on *Buffy*....[7]

NOTES

1. Much has been written about *Buffy*'s allusiveness and intertextuality, or, as Matthew Pateman argues, its aesthetic quality of "involution" (2006: 111). I see my pedagogical approach to *Buffy* as a contribution to this larger dialogue on the reflexive nature of the series, as well as its spinoff, *Angel*, and their universe-expanding comic incarnations. Recommended studies in this vein include:

Callander, Michelle. "Bram Stoker's *Buffy*: Traditional Gothic and Contemporary Culture." *Slayage: The Whedon Studies Association Journal*. 3 (June 2001) Web. http://slayageonline.com/essays/slayage3/callander.html.

Chandler, Holly. "Slaying the Patriarchy: Transfusions of the Vampire Metaphor in *Buffy the Vampire Slayer*. *Slayage*. 9 (August 2003) Web. http://slayageonline.com/essays/slayage9/Chandler.htm.

Fritts, David. "Warrior Heroes. Buffy the Vampire Slayer and Beowulf." *Slayage*. 17 (June 2005) Web. http://slayageonline.com/essays/slayage17/Fritts.htm.

Jarvis, Christine. "'I Run to Death': Renaissance Sensibilities in *Buffy the Vampire Slayer*." *Slayage*. 27 (Winter 2009) Web. http://slayageonline.com/essays/slayage27/Jarvis.htm.

Mukherjea, Ananya. "'When you kiss me, I want to die': Gothic Relationships and Identity on *Buffy the Vampire Slayer*." *Slayage* 26 (Spring 2008) Web. http://slayageonline.com/essays/slayage26/Mukherjea.htm.

Pateman, Matthew. *The Aesthetics of Culture in* Buffy the Vampire Slayer. Jefferson, NC: McFarland, 2006. Print.

Wilcox, Rhonda. "T.S. Eliot Comes to Television: *Buffy's* 'Restless.'" *Slayage* 7 (December 2002) Web. http://slayageonline.com/essays/slayage7/Wilcox.htm.

_____. *Why Buffy Matters: The Art of* Buffy the Vampire Slayer. London and New York: I.B. Tauris, 2005. Print.

2. Using the episode "Bad Girls" (3.14); and to expose them to applying a methodology to a text (for example, pairing James B. South's "'My God, It's Like a Greek Tragedy': Willow Rosenberg and Human Irrationality" and the episode "Wrecked" (6.10).

3. Full bibliographical entries for the works listed on this syllabus appear in the Works Cited.

4. See also Carter's other baroque, bawdy and often metafictional revisions of traditional fairy tales in the collection, *The Bloody Chamber* (1979).

5. In her collections *Red as Blood, or Tales from the Sisters Grimmer* (1983) and *White as Snow* (2000). See especially "When the Clock Strikes," Lee's dark retelling of "Cinderella," in the earlier of the two collections.

6. My approach in this study can be situated within a substantial body of work on how the *Buffy* series works consistently to disrupt binaries, especially around gender, morality, monstrosity, sexuality, genre, heroism and villainy, and power and responsibility. Exemplary studies among these include:

Battis, Jess. "'She's not all grown yet': Willow as Hybrid/Hero in *Buffy the Vampire Slayer.*" *Slayage* 8 (March 2003). Web. http://slayageonline.com/essays/slayage8/Battis.htm

Braun, Beth. "*The X-Files* and *Buffy the Vampire Slayer*: The Ambiguity of Evil in Supernatural Representations." *Journal of Popular Film and Television.* 28.2 (Summer 2000) 88–95. Print.

Burr, Vivien. "*Buffy* vs. the BBC: Moral Questions and How to Avoid Them." *Slayage* 8 (March 2003). Web. http://slayageonline.com/essays/slayage8/Burr.htm.

Early, Francis. "Staking Her Claim: Buffy the Vampire Slayer as Transgressive Woman Warrior." *The Journal of Popular Culture.* 35. 3 (Winter 2001): 11–27. Print.

Jowett, Lorna. *Sex and the Slayer: A Gender Studies Primer for the* Buffy Fan. Middletown, CT: Wesleyan University Press, 2005. Print.

Loftis, J. Robert. "Moral Complexity in the Buffyverse." *Slayage* 27 (Winter 2009) Web. http://slayageonline.com/essays/slayage27/Loftis.htm.

Owen, A. Susan. "*Buffy the Vampire Slayer*: Vampires, Postmodernity and Postfeminism." *Journal of Popular Film and Television.* 27.2 (Summer 1999) 24–32.

Pender, Patricia. "'Kicking ass is comfort food': Buffy as Third Wave Feminist Icon." *Third Wave Feminism: A Critical Exploration.* Ed. Stacy Gillis, Gillian Howie, and Rebecca Munford. New York: Palgrave-McMillan, 2004: 164–174. Print.

Reiss, Jana. "The Monster Inside: Taming the Darkness Within Ourselves." *What Would Buffy Do?: The Vampire Slayer as Spiritual Guide.* San Francisco: Jossey-Bass/Wiley, 2004. Print.

Spicer, Arwen. "'Love's Bitch but Man Enough to Admit It': Spike's Hybridized Gender." *Slayage* 7 (December 2002) Web. http://slayageonline.com/essays/slayage7/Spicer.htm.

Stevenson, Gregory. *Televised Morality: The Case of* Buffy the Vampire Slayer. Lanham, MD: Hamilton Books, 2003. Print.

7. I would like to thank Cory Legassic and Papagena Robbins for their indispensable comments on earlier drafts of this essay. I would also like to thank the nearly 200 Dawson College students who have made contributions to this study via their insightful commentary in writing and class discussion.

WORKS CITED

"Buffy vs. Dracula." *Buffy the Vampire Slayer: The Complete Fifth Season.* Twentieth Century–Fox Home Video, 2003. DVD.

Carter, Angela. "The Company of Wolves." *Burning Your Boats.* New York: Henry Holt, 1995. 212–220. Print.

The Company of Wolves. Dir. Neil Jordan. Perf. Stephen Rea, Angela Lansbury, David Warner. ITC Entertainment, 1984. Hen's Tooth Video, 2002. DVD.

Dahl, Roald. "Little Red Riding Hood and the Wolf." *Little Red Riding Hood Uncloaked.* Ed. Catherine Orenstein. New York: Basic Books, 2002. 157–9. Print.

"Down to the Cellar." Dir. Jan Svankmajer. *The Collected Shorts of Jan Svankmajer, Vol. 2: The Later Years*. Slovenská Film, 1982. Image Entertainment, 2003. DVD.

"The Grandmother's Tale." *Little Red Riding Hood Uncloaked*. Ed./Trans. Catherine Orenstein. New York: Basic Books, 2002. 65–7. Print.

Grimm, Jacob, and Wilhelm Grimm. "Little Red Cap." *Little Red Riding Hood Uncloaked*. Ed. Catherine Orenstein. Trans. Rainer Braun. New York: Basic Books, 2002. 41–5. Print.

Jackson, Shirley. "Jack the Ripper." *Stranger: Dark Tales of Eerie Encounters*. Ed. Michele Slung. New York: Perennial, 2002. 266–272. Print.

Lee, Tanith. "Wolfland." *The Trials and Tribulations of Little Red Riding Hood*. Ed. Jack Zipes. New York: Routledge, 1993. 295–323. Print.

"Little Red Riding Rabbit." Dir. Friz Freleng. Warner Bros. 1944. Warner Home Video, 2004. DVD.

Lovecraft, H. P. "The Outsider." *Lovecraft: Tales*. Ed. Peter Straub. New York: Library of America, 2005. 8–14. Print.

Perrault, Charles. "Little Red Riding Hood." *Little Red Riding Hood Uncloaked*. Ed./Trans. Catherine Orenstein. New York: Basic Books, 2002. 19–21. Print.

Phillips, Robert. "After the Fact: To Ted Bundy." *Telling Stories*. Ed. Joyce Carol Oates. New York: Norton, 1998. 355–357. Print.

"Red Hot Riding Hood." *Tex Avery's Screwball Classics*. Dir. Tex Avery. MGM, 1943. MGM Home Video/Turner Entertainment, 1989. VHS.

Sexton, Anne. "Red Riding Hood." *The Complete Poems*. New York: Mariner, 1999. 267–273. Print.

Strauss, Gwen. "The Waiting Wolf." *The Trials and Tribulations of Little Red Riding Hood*. Ed. Jack Zipes. New York: Routledge, 1993. 328–330. Print.

Tatar, Maria. *The Hard Facts of the Grimms' Fairy Tales*. Princeton, NJ: Princeton University Press, 1987. Print.

"Teaching the Vampire Slayer." Survey of "Introduction to College English" Students, Fall 2008. Dawson College. Montréal, Québec. 10 March, 2009.

Zipes, Jack. *The Trials and Tribulations of Little Red Riding Hood*. New York: Routledge, 1993. Print.

Buffy the Black Feminist?
Intersectionality and Pedagogy

Patrick R. Grzanka

Efforts to treat race, gender, sexuality and other "dimensions of difference" as separate and isolated variables of human experience, as Black feminist theorist Patricia Hill Collins has argued, elide the *reality* of human experiences (5). In actuality, lived experiences are framed by the *intersections* of social identity categories, or "intersectionality."[1] All people have a race, gender, sexual identity, and social class status; comprehensive understanding of an individual's life experiences — much less the experiences of larger social groups — requires a substantive recognition of the ways in which identity categories and oppressions interact. This chapter explores how *Buffy the Vampire Slayer* is a productive text for teaching intersectionality in college-level courses across the disciplines. This discussion is based on four years of teaching *Buffy* in an interdisciplinary honors seminar on contemporary social issues and empirical research on students' attitudes about *Buffy* as a text. Various scholars have argued that representations of race, gender, sexuality and other dimensions of identity in *Buffy* are neither wholly progressive nor universally essentialist (Jowett 2; Kellner 16). This ambivalence creates the pedagogical utility of the series, because it facilitates moving beyond reductionist discussions of "positive and negative images" that conceal the complexity of representational politics and the connections between identity categories and binaries (Jowett; Hunt 15). *Buffy's* narrative structure lends itself to a similarly sophisticated treatment of identity, power and discourse in the classroom. In other words, the complexity of *Buffy* makes it well suited to demonstrate what Leslie McCall calls "the complexity of intersectionality" (1772; see also, Wilcox).

Fostering an intersectional lens among students of the humanities and social sciences is integral to promoting more comprehensive and democratic perspectives on social inequality and systems of oppression, such as racism, classism, sexism and heteronormativity (Dill, McLaughlin, and Nieves 630; Zambrana and Dill 283). This chapter begins with a brief, selective review of intersectional research and the various approaches to intersectionality developed largely by Black feminist scholars, artists and educators. Next, I explicate specific teaching methods, assignments and student responses that illuminate the effectiveness and limits of *Buffy* as both intersectional *text* and *pedagogy*. Finally, I conclude by reflecting on how my students have reacted to *Buffy* and intersectionality; this discussion is informed by survey-based data from three cohorts of students' reactions to *Buffy* that reveal potential correlations between prejudicial attitudes and perceptions of *Buffy*. Ultimately, despite the representational limitations of the series, particularly in terms of race and class, *Buffy* is an especially pragmatic text for teaching how to make visible and destabilize otherwise invisible identities and taken-for-granted assumptions about identity, power and difference. Though Buffy herself might not be an exemplar of Black feminism, *Buffy*'s complicated representations encourage critical investigations of power and identity at the intersections of race, gender, sexuality and other dimensions of difference (Mittell 33; see also Jowett).

Courses that use television to teach any topic must address one fundamental issue in the study of media: *appreciation* for a television series is not the foundation of substantive, critical reflection. This may be commonsense to most teachers and even those outside the academy, but should not be underemphasized. When attempting to promote critical thinking, student *enthusiasm* should not be mistaken for *learning*. Enrollment for courses on popular culture tends to be high at least in part because students expect to have a good time. But the fun students may have with *Buffy*, for example, is not indicative of anything other than enjoyment of a course; it certainly is not evidence of intersectional thinking. Criticizing a television series from an academic position, however, does not foreclose enjoyment of the series. Instructors have an opportunity to model such behavior by identifying as fans *and* critics. When assigning readings that are especially critical of *Buffy* (e.g., Kellner, Jowett or Gill), make sure that students recognize that these authors are fans of the series. I discourage instructors from using prompts that begin, "Select your favorite episode..." or "Pick your favorite television series and write about..." because talking about one's "favorite" anything does not spark critique. Television is entertainment; critical cultural studies are not designed to minimize entertainment, but substantive analyses of television series do qualify this pleasure with a critical lens. Moreover, academic criticism should be framed as complementary to everyday viewing practices, because being able to critically engage with a text only heightens the depth of a viewer's connection to the text.

Similarly, teaching intersectionality should not be equated with merely addressing cultural diversity in the curriculum.[2] In *Black Feminist Thought*, Collins posits intersectionality as *critical* social theory because of its commitment to social justice for U.S. Black women as a collectivity and for similarly oppressed groups, globally (9). Intersectionality helps to ground and locate experiences of marginalization within the "matrix of domination," a term which Collins uses to refer to how intersecting oppressions are organized structurally (18). This process of situating lived experiences is dependent upon the complexity of intersectionality as *theory* and the rigor of intersectional analysis as *method*. "Reclaiming Black women's ideas also involves discovering, reinterpreting, and analyzing the ideas of subgroups within the larger collectivity of U.S. Black women who have been silenced," said Collins (13). Despite their silencing within Black communities and the dominant cultures of the United States, U.S. Black women have generated significant intellectual work throughout centuries of oppression — complex, shifting intersections of race, class, gender, sexuality, age, ability and nation.

Intersectional analyses are purposefully distinct from additive models that simply incorporate multiple axes of difference and treat identity categories as discrete variables.[3] Moreover, Dill argues that Black women's knowledge about their social worlds may at best not easily fit into existing models of race, gender and class; at worst, such paradigms "essentialize" or reduce Black women's lived experiences into one-dimensional narratives that deny the inter-related meanings of race, class and gender for the very people being studied. In the late 1970s, before intersectionality had been fully articulated, Dill and others were arguing for a new paradigm — for and by Black women — that could rely on Black women's experiences (i.e., histories) to unsettle supposedly given or static categories (e.g., race, gender) and racial formations. By the 1990s, scholars had asserted that dimensions of difference could no longer be treated merely as variables: "Race, class, gender and sexuality are not reducible to individual attributes to be measured and assessed for their separate contribution in explaining social outcomes ... where a woman's identity consists of the sum of parts neatly divisible from one another" (Zinn and Dill 327).

Though the genealogy of intersectionality begins in race, class and gender studies, intersectional theory and methods have ushered transformations in areas of research and teaching across the social sciences and humanities. Teaching about intersectionality can happen in virtually any course that studies human beings, including the natural sciences. Intersectionality, though grounded and originating in the experiences of U.S. Black women, has proven to be a potent critique across diverse areas of study and policy projects.[4] In other words, though social justice is always at the center of it, intersectionality is not exclusive to the study of Black women's issues (Collins 9). Indeed, intervening in the discourses of racism, sexism, heterosexism and other systems of oppression requires uncovering and challenging injustices throughout human experience. Accordingly, teaching intersectionality with *Buffy* is possible from a variety of disciplinary perspectives and with a wide range of topics.

Centering intersectionality in one's teaching presents unique pedagogical challenges to both the selection of course content, delivery of material and the politics of the classroom itself. In fact, it may seem easier to avoid intersectionality in the classroom, particularly in lower-level courses in which students are just beginning to grapple with individual categories of identity and inequity. One might ask: "How can I possibly address race, gender, sexuality and all these aspects of difference in a single semester, much less do so with any depth and substance?" The solution is both difficult and easier than one might expect. The traditions of Black feminism and critical pedagogies assert that intersectional teaching about any aspect of oppression is not "optional." Think of it this way: would it not be considered irresponsible to teach medical students the inner workings of every organ in the body but never mention how they interact to keep a person alive? Does it make sense to teach physics students about what happens inside a nuclear reactor but not how these processes result in the production of energy and radiation? We do not expect students to understand the interactions between concepts unless we provide them with the skills and content necessary to comprehend such relationships. To make *Buffy* meaningful in the classroom is to connect the representations in *Buffy* to the "real world" and to explicate how the representations in *Buffy* matter. Fortunately for scholars who use the series to interrogate any range of social, historical, literary and cultural issues, *Buffy* interfaces seamlessly with intersectional topics and pedagogy. The remainder of this chapter is dedicated to outlining the various ways in which intersectionality can be incorporated into courses that use *Buffy* as a primary text. This discussion will move from intersectional analyses that focus on within-group differences, such as the diversity of experiences contained within the social category of "White women," to between-group differences, such as variations in privilege and oppression as experienced by Black women and White men.

Across seven seasons, other spinoff television series (e.g., *Angel*) and several graphic adaptations (e.g., *Buffy: Season Eight, Tales of the Slayer, Fray*), the "*Buffy*verse" provides boundless opportunity for the investigation of how multiple, shifting axes of difference shape human experiences. Much has been written in this and other volumes about the richness of individual character development and storytelling that makes the series compelling as televisual text.[5] My attention here is oriented toward the social and structural elements of the series and a mode of analysis that is made possible by the narrative complexity of *Buffy* (Mittell 33; Bacon-Smith xiii; see also Wilcox). *Buffy* is a multi-faceted series based in a self-referential continuity. As a result, the series lends itself to teaching intersectional analyses that interrogate how power is negotiated and exchanged across time and space within the series, which can be figured both as a text and a social world unto itself. Furthermore, these analyses can help forge connections between the series and the cultural context(s) in which it was produced, disseminated and engaged, illuminating the ways in which *Buffy* both reflects and subverts intersecting forms of oppression. In order to promote intersectional thinking, one must be prepared to help students view *Buffy* not only as sophisticated and interesting, but as potentially problematic.

Sociologist Leslie McCall explicates how intersectionality can highlight "...the socially constructed nature of gender and other categories and the fact that a wide range of different experiences, identities, and social locations fail to fit neatly into any single 'master' category" (1777). As a reality unto itself, the *Buffy*verse presents representations that challenge *and* reinforce assumptions that gender is stable and binary (i.e., man/woman, masculine/feminine). Analytic attention should be directed toward the complex terrain of femininity and masculinity in *Buffy*. Below, I offer some guiding, thematic questions for both in-class discussions and writing assignments that help students understand what it means to "trouble" taken-for-granted categories.

- What is femininity in the *Buffy*verse? What are the primary markers of femininity? Who possess it? Is there an idealized version of femininity in the series, and if so, which character "best" represents femininity? (The same can be asked of masculinity.) (Jowett 70)

A major learning outcome of most introductory courses in feminist, women's, gender, sexuality and cultural studies is that gender is everywhere and is constantly being "performed."[6] The questions above highlight two concepts that are constantly but invisibly cited in everyday life: masculinity and femininity. Instructors may choose to use these prompts early in the semester, when the concepts are relatively new to students; at this time, it can be helpful to pair these questions with an episode or group of episodes that obviously centralize gender role issues, such as "Surprise" (2.13) and "Innocence" (2.14), when Buffy first loses her virginity, or "The Zeppo" (3.17), in which Xander questions his manhood. However, revisiting such questions in unexpected contexts can illuminate the pervasiveness of gender politics. Consider having students analyze a climactic fight scene in any episode for its representation of idealized gender performance (Marinucci 69).

- Which characters are both masculine and feminine? How do we know their gender if they "perform" their gender in multiple ways? Which male characters are most feminine, and on what basis do we make this judgment? Which female characters are most masculine? Do these characters confirm or challenge stereotypes about gender?

Either in class or for homework, students should consider whether or not there is a continuum of gender performance in *Buffy*. If so, which characters represent the poles of the continuum? To facilitate students' analyses, I have assigned DeKelb-Rittenhouse's essay, "Sex and the Single Vampire," as well as the introduction to Lorna Jowett's monograph that introduces gender studies through *Buffy*. With these readings and exercises, I encourage students to draw upon their lived experiences. Does *Buffy* reflect norms about gender? Students should concentrate on how their own lives are similar to and different from the *Buffy*verse in terms of gender politics. The point here is to connect the theoretical insights of gender studies to everyday life, which promotes learning and retention of the material, as well as helps students apply knowledge from the classroom to the proverbial "real world." Because the focus should be on the intersections of social categories, instructors should consistently ask students to consider how assumptions about gender are challenged by its sites of intersection with other identity categories, such as sexuality and class. For example, how are Faith and Buffy's performance of femininity distinct? What do we learn about social class when we examine how Buffy's middle-class sexuality diverges from Faith's? In all cases, students should be asked to justify their conclusions by considering how it is that we arrive at these assumptions about gender.

- How are nonhuman characters gendered? Must all living things have a gender and, if so, why? What about non-living things?

The fantastical elements of *Buffy* are pedagogical goldmines for exploring how identity seeps into all facets of social life. Students from all backgrounds, but especially those who occupy multiple positions of privilege, are often skeptical of readings, lectures and course content that asserts the persistence of sexism, racism and other forms of oppression in American culture — and they receive messages from dominant entertainment and news media that reinforce these notions of a so-called post-racial or post-gender society. With its general elision of identity issues beyond sexuality, *Buffy* can also be read as supporting these notions (see Kellner; also Jowett). However, students should be prompted to examine how difference can be seen literally everywhere in *Buffy*, even in nonhuman elements of the series ranging from demons to various forms of technology.[7] Especially in courses about culture, science and technology, *Buffy* is helpful for investigating how nonhuman actors and actants (i.e., *things* in social interactions) are gendered, raced and sexualized.[8] Episodes featuring the Initiative storyline in Season Four can facilitate conversations about how human interactions with technology imbue cultural values into technologies, which are, of course, created by humans. Any scene with Initiative members or in the Initiative complex itself involves pervasive representation of advanced communication technologies, biomedical interventions, technologies of surveillance and confinement, or tools to facilitate violence.[9] Students should be asked to create a list of 5–10 prominent technologies (e.g., computer-assisted speech in "Hush," 4.10) and try to indicate the valence of their gender, allowing room for androgyny or absence of gendering. The point here is not to reinforce prevalent stereotypes or gender binaries, but to illuminate how seemingly meaningless interactions produce gender *norms*. This is a key point of intersectionality, which attempts to historicize and situate identity categories within cultural contexts and to promote a sense of the contingency of these exclusionary categories that structure social life. To further connect *Buffy* to our everyday lives, one should also ask:

- How are gender norms in the Buffyverse reflective of gender norms in our culture(s)? Are gender norms more or less flexible in the Buffyverse?

Through these macro-level questions about the texts, teachers can introduce *and* destabilize three primary and intersecting concepts/categories: sex, gender and sexuality. Jowett, for example, posits *Buffy* as an exemplar of "postfeminism" (3). Postfeminism and "postfeminist" refer both to academic perspectives (theory) and actual socio-historical contexts, i.e., the conditions of postmodernity. Resisting a simplistic reading that might deem its depictions of men, women and their interactions as empowering *or* (hetero)sexist, *Buffy* is viewed by postmodernists as a discursive site of struggle: a representational space in which power, identity and inequalities are being worked through, made and re-made (Jowett 4). Put simply, Jowett observes, "[*Buffy*] treats identity as inherently unstable" (4). Accordingly, a course in the psychology of women might pair readings from Anne Fausto-Sterling's *Sexing the Body* with episodes that feature Willow Rosenberg as both "Dark Willow" ("Two to Go," 6.21) and Vampire Willow ("Doppelgangland," 3.16).[10] In both of these storylines, we see a central woman character constructed as mentally pathological. In one case, Buffy's best friend, Willow, is driven mad by vengeful rage over the death of her lover, Tara; her insanity is also fed by addiction to magic, which had previously been under control through an abstinence approach to addiction. In the "Vampire Willow" storyline, viewers learn that in the absence of inhibition, Willow's latent or repressed sexual desires manifest themselves; furthermore, it takes the lack of a soul and a literal thirst for blood to reveal these aspects of Willow's sexuality. How do these episodes represent assumptions about "woman nature?" How do they challenge or affirm our expectations of women's sexuality? How is lesbian sexuality constructed when Willow "goes bad," and what are the implications of Willow's sexuality for her gender performance? How does Willow's body itself become something that must be contained, cured or fixed? *Buffy* episodes can be paired with recent television and print advertisements for pharmaceutical drugs that feature women seeking chemical help for depression, menstruation, pregnancy, weight loss, mood, aging and body image. In class discussion and writing assignments, students should investigate how the female body — especially the White female body — is constructed as a site of crisis in *Buffy* and biomedical discourse. For courses that allow for creative writing exercises, students might be asked to re-write episodes of the series to reflect what they have learned in class, or to compose an original teleplay for a *Buffy* episode that tackles these and related issues about gender, sex and sexuality.

Individual characters offer case studies for exploring the relationships between gender and sexuality, which further destabilizes the notion of gender or sexuality serving as one-size-fits-all categories. For example, villain-turned-Scooby Andrew's ambiguous sexuality becomes a source of humor throughout the series' seventh season. Though Andrew is never explicitly partnered with any character—woman or man—and we do not witness him engage in sexual contact with any other characters, his sexuality is consistently being constructed through his gender performance. A question for students becomes: In the absence of sexual behavior, how do we know or "read" a character's sexuality? Through interrogation of how we as viewers come to know the sexual orientation(s) of fictional characters, we can see how gender performance becomes a primary marker of sexuality in everyday life. Useful readings to pair with episodes such as "Storyteller" (7.16), include Erving Goffman's classic *Presentation of Self in Everyday Life* or his influential *Gender Advertisements*; Judith Halberstam's landmark *Female Masculinity*; or Eve Kosofsky Sedgwick's innovative *Epistemology of the Closet*. Goffman's use of a protracted theatre metaphor to describe everyday life is especially helpful in the context of *Buffy*, because students can explore how the series' actors construct their characters' identities using subtle and largely unnoticed practices, including fashion, gestures and vernacular (Shuttleworth 213). Halberstam's text transformed queer studies because of how it unhinged masculinity and femininity from their supposedly fixed location in men and women's bodies, respectively. Finally, Sedgwick's foundational work moves discourse on sexual identity beyond reductionist narratives of repression and toward a critique that asks how "the closet"—as a subjective space and a cultural concept—is productive of meaning about sexuality and social norms. *Buffy*'s characters experience ongoing transformations of self, so the series can be figured as a kind of archive of identity performances in the late 20th and early 21st century.

Because Willow's sexuality shifts most pointedly over the course of the series, her character exemplifies how sexuality is dynamic over the course of an individual's life history and is shaped by other dimensions of identity. Through Willow's identity formation, students can ask challenging questions about the ontology of "the closet" and sexual identity labels, such as "lesbian," "homosexual," and "bisexual." Discussion and essay prompts include: Is it appropriate to describe someone as being in the closet if they are unaware of their queer desires? How is Willow both a lesbian and someone who has loved men; what is "homosexual" about her identity? How does Willow's shifting sexual orientation reinforce stereotypes about the flexibility of women's or feminine sexuality? How might different audience members, including us, react if Xander or Oz had undergone similar transformations? The emphasis in these questions is on the moves and shifts of sexual identity, which disturb dominant rhetoric about sexual orientation based on concepts such as "natural," "essential," and "permanent."[11]

As a discursive space, *Buffy* features over-represented social groups that come to constitute "normal," namely middle-class, able-bodied, heterosexual, White people. By both exploring what these identities actually *mean*—rather than allowing them to remain "commonsense"—and focusing attention on those characters who do not fit neatly into this "normal" space, teachers can aid students in their understanding the diversity of experiences that happen within unquestioned, unmarked and invisible social locations.

Buffy, for example, is fixated on being "normal." Several episodes centralize this pre-occupation, including "Becoming, Part 1" (2.21), "Becoming, Part 2" (2.22), "Tabula Rasa" (6.8), "Normal Again" (6.17) and specific interactions throughout Season Seven, including a notable argument with Willow and Xander in "Selfless" (7.7). What Buffy actually thinks constitutes normal is up for debate, but Buffy and her friends do have certain expectations of normalcy that are framed by culturally contingent values. During many of Buffy's more prominent monologues, we hear her articulate normalcy with specific examples: having a boyfriend, driving her own car, going to college, wearing nice clothes, being homecoming queen, and so on. Actually tapping into these values is challenging because they often go unspoken and unnamed; this is at least partially because the audience of *Buffy* is assumed to be aware of—if not *share*—these expectations of normal (and thereby, what constitutes *abnormal*). Students should disturb these expectations and name them even as the characters of the *Buffy*verse let these values remain unarticulated. Deep, thick description of a specific character's personality and identity is a pragmatic assignment that cultivates students' skills in observation and ethnography while helping promote intersectional thinking. Students can be guided in their writing by the following questions:

- Besides being the Slayer, what motivates Buffy? What about her identity and her experiences have shaped her sense of self, as well as her morality and judgment?

- In "Inca Mummy Girl" (2.4), Ampata says that she wants to be like Buffy; she wants to be a normal girl. What is "normal" about Buffy? What counts as normal in the Buffyverse and how is Buffy representative of normal?

- If Buffy is normal, then who is her foil? Who is Buffy's "Other"?

- What about Buffy's identity is shared by both slayers Faith and Kendra? How are they different, and how does the audience learn about these differences? What are the consequences of these differences?

In each of these questions, emphasis is placed on those aspects of Buffy that might go unnoticed because they are based in stereotypes (i.e., a generic, thin, blonde, teenage girl from California) (Kellner 16). By bringing these aspects of her identity forward, the differences in women's experiences in the series can be made explicit and meaningful.

By investigating how multiple dimensions of difference constitute identities in the Buffyverse, students have the opportunity to turn the intersectional lens inward and engage in self-reflexive feminist analyses. In other words, the overall question posed to students is: "Once we have seen how race, gender, sexuality and class together influence Buffy's sense of self, how do race, gender, sexuality and class shape *my* sense of self and others?" By first providing content-based knowledge about these dimensions of difference, instructors can then begin the process of helping students to unpack these categories and investigate how they shape their own perspectives on the world around them. How do their identities influence their reception of the series? Jhally and Lewis's classic study of White people's reactions to *The Cosby Show* demonstrates how race can shape how a person literally "sees" a television series. Begin with group discussion of 'neutral' topics: ask students to discuss as a group how their collective social location influences their reception of *Buffy*? How might the show appear different to them ten years in the past, in a different part of the country, or in another country?

The responsibility for this introspection falls not only on the students' metaphorical shoulders, but the instructor's as well. We cannot ask our students to put themselves out there, so to speak, if we are not willing to do so ourselves. Creating a safe learning community in which to investigate the complexity of intersectionality, particularly for those students for whose subject positions are defined by multiple oppressions, translates into substantive disclosure of one's own standpoint. An intersectional standpoint, moreover, should articulate the contradictory ways in which we all are simultaneously privileged and disadvantaged. Before any given semester, instructors should devote time to considering which aspects of themselves they are willing to reveal — and which they are not. Ask oneself: "Is this demonstrative of a learning outcome or goal for my students? How does this offer a tangible example of intersectionality in everyday life? How might my disclosure help those students whose identities are marginalized?" Instructors should model constructive disclosure for their students so that students are better prepared to do the same.[12]

Though people of color constitute a small minority of characters in *Buffy*, their presence and relative absence is especially meaningful. Black characters such as Mr. Trick, the First Slayer, Robin Wood, Kendra, Forrest and Rona represent the deployment of persistent stereotypes about Black people that inform representation of and discrimination toward African Americans (Edwards 85, 88). Critical theorist Douglas Kellner argues that *Buffy*'s diversity is largely limited to superficial multiculturalism that represents difference without interrogating it (16). He asserts that both Whiteness and middle-class ideals are privileged throughout the series, particularly in the juxtaposition of tragic slayers Kendra and Faith against the backdrop of Buffy's flawed-but-ultimately-triumphant hero. "On the level of the politics of representation," concludes Kellner, "*Buffy*, like most television, reproduces much dominant ideology." (17). For example, Buffy and the all–White Scoobies' values consistently serve as the litmus for goodness and integrity, and these heroes are offered redemption when they falter in their path toward self-actualization. As part of the representational landscape of *Buffy*, the Black characters demonstrate the dynamic nature of power relations and the diversity of experiences within the broad identification of "Black;" though most Black characters are villains and/or killed, not all are represented as poor or working class (Gill 244; Edwards 91). On the other hand, these characters' shared experiences can also serve to highlight the common oppression of Black people — and the privileges of Whiteness that other characters enjoy. These contradictions highlight one of the most palpable challenges of intersectionality: despite the diversity of experiences within a given social group, the power of certain social identities links people in oppression and privilege. Though individual lived experience is central to intersectional theory, the commonalities and shared experiences of privilege and oppression expose systemic inequality. As Tim Wise reflects on the trouble of Whiteness and intersectionality, "...despite the fact that white privilege plays out differently for different folks, depending on those other identities, the fact remains that when all other factors are equal, whiteness matters and carries great advantage" (x). While grasping the complexity of identity is paramount, students should also understand the relative simplicity and determinacy of certain forms of oppression, namely racism and White privilege. Likewise, race in *Buffy* is neither simple nor impenetrable. With pedagogy oriented toward intersectionality, instructors are better prepared to balance the continuities and discontinuities of race and intersecting social identities categories. Sometimes, however, analytic simplicity is necessary to communicate complex relations of power and to illuminate injustice; we will explore the instances in which this is appropriate in the following section.

Some intersectional analyses provisionally adopt social identity group categories in the interest of explaining macro-level forms of inequality (McCall 1784–1785).[13] By emphasizing the similarities between individuals in a social category — and even downplaying within-group differences — we can see the ways in which particular social groups face greater inequity than others. When looking at *Buffy* through this lens, the instructor is most concerned with establishing how identity categories influence the outcomes of characters and groups of characters who share common identities, and connecting these narrative elements to the real world and other course content. The emphasis, in this instance, is less on the destabilization of identity categories and more on clarifying the *effects* and *consequences* of identity on macro-level social relations.

To illuminate macro-level social issues through *Buffy*, one might consider teaching *Buffy* alongside other primary sources, including economic datasets, such as U.S. census data or local demographics; ethnographic studies, such as life histories or cultural anthropologies; and even other television series or art forms. These forms of comparison are best at demonstrating the large social effects of inequity, as opposed to anecdotal interactions between individuals. Comparisons between *Buffy* and representations from other series are effective in making transparent unequal distribution of wealth and resources. For example, pair *Buffy*'s representation of fictional Sunnydale High School with Baltimore City public schools in Season Four of *The Wire* and ask students to consider what these representations connote about urban versus suburban public education. With this approach, *Buffy* may become the space in which to actually *see* the topics being discussed in other materials, such as the plight of working class American women in Ehrenreich's *Nickel and Dimed*[14] or differences in the roles and screen time of people of color as analyzed by sociologist Darnell Hunt in his essay "Black Content, White Control."[15]

For example, one strategy involves asking students to work in groups to investigate how class status is constructed along race and gender lines in *Buffy* story arcs. Assign a season or set of episodes and ask students to chart the social class status of each main, recurring or significant guest character and to label each character's gender and race, as well. The process of being "forced" to label a character's class status (as poor, working, middle, upper class.) elucidates the subjective nature of social labels and the importance of perception versus self-identification. Depending on the instructor's goals, students can define these categories as a group before or during the exercise; but in any case, students should be asked to justify their choices so that their coding methods are made evident. Relevant questions include: which visual and verbal cues did you use to determine a character's social class status? By mapping these data across a group of episodes, students gain methodological skills that are central to empirical social science, such as content analysis. And by examining the results of these mappings, students identify trends in the representation of certain social groups (working-class women), as well as differences between social groups (middle-class White men and middle-class White women). Additional variables, such as nationality or ethnicity, can be added to investigate how subtle differences in identity may correspond with representations of different social groups. The goal here is not to causally link the narrative fate of certain characters to their race or gender (e.g., Kendra dies *because* she's a Black, Third World woman), but to explore how these social groups are differentially *represented* (e.g., how does Kendra's character fit with other representations of non–U.S. women in the series and within popular culture generally?).[16]

Comparisons between seasons may also demonstrate how the representations of certain groups may shift, such as the arguably increased visibility of working-class men in later seasons (i.e., five through seven) when Xander is unemployed and then starts a career in construction, Buffy meets several characters while working at a fast food burger joint and Spike becomes a more central character. Ultimately, these exercises facilitate learning by requiring students first to look beyond individual interactions within single episodes in the interest of exploring over-arching trends, and then to see how these representations may reflect actual macro-level issues of social inequity.

Once students have mapped out several episodes worth of characters along specified dimensions of social group membership, analyze seasons in relationship to one another. Ideally, students should cultivate their own research questions, but they can also be guided by general topics introduced and explored through supplemental readings. If *Buffy* is the primary course text and time allows, season-based analyses might focus on outcomes of character storylines with questions such as: are there particular dimensions of identity that link characters who die or leave the series? Are members of a particular social group (e.g., White, working-class, straight women) more likely to be represented as villains than heroes? Which social groups are completely absent from a given season; does a social identity-based group, such as White queer women, appear and then disappear?

On the other hand, analyses of individual episodes might be oriented toward more micro-level analyses of episodic content. For example, in a unit on gender, work and family, students could be instructed to select an episode, identify the multiple social identity group memberships of each character, and then examine how various aspects of domestic life are represented in the episode (e.g., who is performing unpaid household labor?). Topics such as cultural geography or demography might utilize an episode set at Sunnydale High School or UC–Sunnydale to explore the racial and ethnic makeup of the fictional town. Who lives, works and goes to school in Sunnydale, and how is this cultural landscape different from the "real" southern California? These exercises train students in how to conduct sophisticated textual research, to "see" and explore issues of inequality through representations, and consider these inequalities along multiple axes of difference that constitute social groups. This approach, like all forms of intersectional pedagogy, present challenges in addition to myriad opportunities.

My discussion thus far has focused on pedagogical approaches that instructors might take to centralize intersectional issues when using *Buffy* in any courses that deal with identity and inequality. I conclude by shifting my focus from cognition (i.e., teaching and learning) to affect by sharing some of my experiences with teaching intersectionality using *Buffy*. Intersectionality is a serious academic pursuit, but its status as a complex approach to social and cultural research does not mean that intersectionality is divorced from feelings. One should also be prepared for a diversity of reactions from students that may range from joy over finally hearing their life experiences validated in a classroom space, to anger, resistance and frustration over first grappling with the concepts of identity-based privilege and systemic inequality (Tatum 5).

For four semesters at a large public university in the northeastern United States, I taught a freshman honors seminar on social issues in popular culture that used *Buffy* as the primary course text. Each week, we would screen a different episode of *Buffy* and explore a variety of social issues through the series' narrative; examples include suicide and sacrifice in "The Gift" (5.22), which was paired with Gregory Sakal's essay "No Big Win: Themes of Sacrifice, Salvation, and Redemption," and teenage sexuality in "Surprise" (2.13) and "Innocence" (2.14). During three of these semesters, I conducted exploratory research with my students using questionnaires administered at the beginning and end of the course. These surveys were each designed to assess students' attitudes, namely opinions about and emotional responses to issues of race and racism, before and after exposure to a course on social issues. This research involved relatively small groups of students (ranging from 14 to 22 each semester) and was not experimental; one does not need training in social science research to imagine the variety of uncontrollable variables that might influence students' attitudes over 15 weeks of a semester.[17]

Though it might seem counter-intuitive, fans of *Buffy* are not necessarily the students most willing to critique the series or accept that certain representations in the series are limited, regressive, or stereotypical. My data suggest that those who identified as fans of the series prior to enrollment in the course tended to be more willing to positively endorse statements such as "People of color are fairly and accurately depicted on *Buffy*" than students who were not fans. Similarly, students who identified less with *Buffy* and who indicated that they were not a fan of the show tended to indicate that they saw more problematic racial imagery in *Buffy* than students who highly identified with the series and considered themselves fans. Simultaneously, students who scored higher on a standard measure of racism were also less likely to perceive racist representations in television generally and *Buffy* specifically.[18] The converse was also true: students with less prejudicial attitudes tended to perceive more racist imagery in *Buffy* and indicate lower levels of identification with Buffy and other characters in the series.

Managing students' responses requires a flexible pedagogy. For students who are reacting to and resisting ideas about structural privilege and inequity, the best approach may be initially to move away from anecdotal examples from the series and toward convincing data, such as statistics on employment, incarceration, labor inequity, or domestic abuse that denote macro-level trends. However, de-personalization of the course content might be exactly the wrong approach to take with another student who is feeling deeply connected to the issues discussed in your course, such as sexual violence. In less than a decade of teaching, I have interacted with at least a dozen young women and men who have disclosed that they have been the targets of sexual violence, and we know statistically that a staggering proportion of female students have been the victims of sexual assaults on campus that will never be investigated. So when talking about the infamous attempted rape scene between Spike and Buffy in "Seeing Red" (6.19), instructors should make sure not to speak about sexual violence as a purely systemic phenomenon, because it affects our individual students — whether we know it or not. Finally, instructors should not assume that they understand a student's experience based on an observed aspect of the student's identity. Though instructors undoubtedly develop assumptions about types of students, it would be a mistake to presume, for example, that students of color are always going to be better prepared to talk about the personal effects of racism; that White students are not equipped for discussions of White privilege; or that women students are automatically feminists of any kind.[19]

As I have argued throughout this essay, the polysemic and complex identities and relationships in *Buffy* facilitate intersectional teaching and learning. My essay title poses a question that is meant to help us think about how a White, straight woman's fictional adventures as a vampire slayer can possibly illustrate the philosophies of Black feminism and the perspective of intersectionality. Buffy, like the series itself, is quite complicated. Her gender performance, social class and sexuality, as well as her intimate, professional and interpersonal relationships, are constantly in flux. As a fan and critic, I assert that the complexity of Buffy herself makes *Buffy* such a compelling series.[20] Buffy is not a Black feminist at all, but Buffy is messy — and this is what makes her story so powerful when teaching about the messiness of life. Messiness signifies complexity, and it also connotes uncertainty, confusion, borderlands, contact zones and transformation — the stuff that happens at the intersections of identity and difference. This is also what happens when our students learn that, because of inequality and diversity, life is much more complicated than they had ever expected. By embracing the fantastic, extraordinary, consciousness-altering elements of metaphor, allegory and fictional narratives endemic to *Buffy* the series, we can empower students to wrestle with the ordinary complexity of our real lives.

NOTES

1. Collins, a sociologist, first defines "intersectionality" as a concept: "particular forms of intersecting oppressions," such as race and gender, or race and nation (18). Intersectional teaching and scholarship explore how intersecting oppressions shape society. Intersectionality, "remind[s] us that oppression cannot be reduced to one fundamental type, and that oppressions work together in producing injustice" (18). Analyses that privilege race *or* gender at the expense of other organizing categories of social experience obfuscate the ways in which race and gender and co-constitutive, as well as shaped by other meaningful identities. See: Dill, Bonnie Thornton, Sandra Murray Nettles, and Lynn Weber. "Defining the Work of the Consortium: What Do We Mean by Intersections?" *Connections: Newsletter of the Consortium on Race, Gender and Ethnicity.* Spring 2001. 4 Jan. 2009.

2. As an academic concept, intersectionality has a specific lineage that is most closely associated with Black feminists, including Collins, as well as legal scholars working in "Critical Race Theory," such as Patricia Williams and Kimberlé Williams Crenshaw. Crenshaw is credited with coining the term "intersectionality": Crenshaw, Kimberlé Williams. "Race, Reform, and Retrenchment: Transformation and Legitimation in Antidiscrimination Law." *Harvard Law Review* 101 (1988): 1331–87.

3. For example, Cole offers an accessible discussion of the differences between intersectionality and the practice of simply using identity categories as variables in psychological research. See: Cole, Elizabeth. "Intersectionality and Research in Psychology." *American Psychologist* 64 (2009): 170–80.

4. Scholars of color working in sexuality studies have used intersectionality to expose how much of what came to be known as "queer theory" was biased toward the experiences of White, middle-class, gay men; a "queer of color critique" has emerged. See: Ferguson, Roderick A. *Aberrations in Black: Toward a Queer of Color Critique.* Minneapolis: University of Minnesota Press, 2004. Johnson, E. Patrick and Mae G. Henderson, eds. *Black Queer Studies: A Critical Anthology.* Durham: Duke University Press, 2005. Print. Similar critiques have occurred in disability studies; see: Thomson, Rosemarie Garland.

Extraordinary Bodies: Figuring Physical Disability in American Culture and Literature. New York: Columbia University Press, 1997.

5. Mittell identifies *Buffy* as a quintessential example of "narrative complexity," because of its protracted story arcs, self-referential scripts and blending of genre-based conventions (33). *Buffy* became compelling to critics because it represented a seemingly limitless variety of multifaceted social issues in metaphorical structures (Little 283). Early anthologies of "*Buffy* Studies" scholarship and academic meetings, such as the *Slayage* conferences featured some sophisticated analysis. Much of this early scholarship in *Buffy* Studies was celebratory, but critiques soon emerged which highlighted those aspects of the series that reinforced hegemonic and oppressive ideas, particularly along lines of race and class.

6. For a thorough and canonical treatment of gender as performance, see: Butler, Judith. *Gender Trouble: Feminism and the Subversion of Identity.* 2nd Ed. New York: Routledge, 1999.

7. For how these issues relate to theories of knowledge, see: Wall, Brian, and Michael Zryd. "Vampire Dialectics: Knowledge, Institutions and Labour." *Reading the Vampire Slayer: An Unofficial Critical Companion to* Buffy *and* Angel. Ed. Roz Kaveny. London: Taurus Parke, 2002: 53–77.

8. History, philosophy and sociology of science instructors especially should refer to: Muntersbjorn, Madeline M. "Pluralism, Pragmatism, and Pals: The Slayer Subverts the Science Wars." Buffy the Vampire Slayer *and Philosophy: Fear and Trembling in Sunnydale.* Ed. James B. South. Peru, Illinois: Open Court Publishing Company, 2003: 91–102. Also: Aberdein, Andrew. "Balderdash and Chicanery: Science and Beyond." Buffy the Vampire Slayer *and Philosophy: Fear and Trembling in Sunnydale.* Ed. James B. South. Peru, Illinois: Open Court Publishing Company, 2003: 79–90.

9. For the *Buffy* studies perspective, see: Marinucci, Mimi. "Feminism and the Ethics of Violence: Why Buffy Kicks Ass." Buffy the Vampire Slayer *and Philosophy: Fear and Trembling in Sunnydale.* Ed. James B. South. Peru, Illinois: Open Court Publishing Company, 2003: 61–75.

10. See: Fausto-Sterling, Anne. *Sexing the Body: Gender Politics and the Construction of Sexuality.* New York: Basic Books, 2000. Fausto-Sterling's work brings the insights of science studies to a multidisciplinary audience; this book explores how cultural assumptions have influenced the science of gender and sex differences.

11. Questions about individual characters' identity development can always stretch across seven seasons, but instructors with limited real estate in their syllabi should select two or three key episodes for viewing outside of class. Online resources such as Hulu and iTunes provide legal and affordable viewing options for students and can maximize in-class time for discussion and lecture — rather than episode screening.

12. For a philosophical exploration of standpoint, see: Haraway, Donna. "Situated Knowledges: The Science Question in Feminism and the Privilege of Partial Perspective." *Feminist Studies,* 14 (1988): 575–599. For a pedagogical discussion, see: Romney, Patricia, Beverly Tatum, and JoAnne Jones. "Feminist Strategies for Teaching about Oppression: The Importance of Process." *Women's Studies Quarterly* XX (1992): 1–10.

13. The provisional adoption of social categories is reminiscent of DuBois' racial essentialism and what postcolonial feminist Spivak calls "strategic essentialism." For further discussion see: Spivak, Gayatri Chakravorty. *In Other Worlds: Essays in Cultural Politics.* New York: Routledge, 1988.

14. Ehrenreich's personal investigation of life as a minimum wage worker is popular among college teachers because it is both accessible and shocking, especially for middle class students who have had little contact with working class life or issues.

15. Hunt's investigation of television in the early 2000s demonstrates that, perhaps surprisingly for some viewers, Blacks were actually "over-represented" on television during the first part of this decade, while Whites retained executive positions and control of networks.

16. See Edwards' discussion of Kendra as "tragic mulatta," and Gill's work on the racial(ist) logic of violence in *Buffy.* See also the chapter titled "Bad Girls" in Jowett.

17. The results of these studies were designed to inform future research, not to serve as the basis for any formal claims about attitudes, the effects of my teaching, or learning about identity through *Buffy.* Regardless, some of my findings and observations were intriguing and merit a brief discussion here. Most of my students were White women, but each group included at least three students of color and more than five men.

18. Saucier and Miller's "Racial Argument Scale." See: Saucier, Donald A., and Carol T. Miller. "The persuasiveness of arguments as a subtle measure of racism." *Personality and Social Psychology Bulletin* 29 (2003): 1303–15.

19. Reflexive pedagogy is the first antidote to deconstructing how teaching can reinforce inequalities.

Analyze your own teaching and ask: How can I avoid using ableist language, such as "paralyzed" and "crippled" when I really mean "hindered" or "challenged"? Is my syllabus written in an Americans with Disabilities Act (ADA)-compliant font? Do I presume heterosexuality by referencing husbands and wives or boyfriends and girlfriends? What percentage of my syllabus is composed of readings by women and non–White authors? See: Lynn, Marvin. "Inserting the 'Race' into Critical Pedagogy: An analysis of 'race-based epistemologies.'" *Educational Philosophy and Theory* 36 (2004): 154–165. See also: Tatum, Beverly Daniel. "Teaching White Students About Racism: The Search for White Allies and the Restoration of Hope." *Teacher College Record* 95 (1994): 462–476. And finally: Friere, Paolo. *Pedagogy of the Oppressed*. New York: Continuum, 2000.

    20. For a succinct defense of *Buffy*'s academic merits, see: South, James B. "And was there a lesson in all this?" *Fear and Trembling in Sunnydale:* Buffy the Vampire Slayer *and Philosophy*. Ed. James B. South. Peru, Illinois: Open Court Publishing Company, 2003. 1–3. Print.

Works Cited

Bacon-Smith, Camille. "Foreword: The Color of the Dark in *Buffy the Vampire Slayer*." *Fighting the Forces: What's at Stake in* Buffy the Vampire Slayer. Eds. Rhonda V. Wilcox and David Lavery. Lanham, MD: Rowman & Littlefield, 2002. xi–xiii. Print.

Collins, Patricia Hill. *Black Feminist Thought: Knowledge, Consciousness, and the Politics of Empowerment*. 2nd ed. New York: Routledge, 2000. Print.

DeKelb-Rittenhouse, Diane. "Sex and the Single Vampire: The Evolution of the Vampire Lothario and Its Representation in *Buffy*." *Fighting the Forces: What's at Stake in* Buffy the Vampire Slayer. Eds. Rhonda V. Wilcox and David Lavery. Lanham, MD: Rowman & Littlefield, 2002. 143–52. Print.

Dill, Bonnie Thornton, Amy E. McLaughlin, and Angel David Nieves. "Future Directions of Feminist Research: Intersectionality." *Handbook of Feminist Research: Theory and Praxis*. Ed. Sharlene N. Hesse-Biber. Thousand Oaks, CA: Sage Publications, 2007. 629–38. Print.

Edwards, Lynne. "Slaying in Black and White: Kendra as Tragic Mulatta in *Buffy*." *Fighting the Forces: What's at Stake in* Buffy the Vampire Slayer. Eds. Rhonda V. Wilcox and David Lavery. Lanham, MD: Rowman & Littlefield, 2002. 85–97. Print.

Ehrenreich, Barbara. *Nickel and Dimed: On (Not) Getting by in America*. New York: Metropolitan Books, 2001. Print.

Gill, Candra K. "'Cuz the Black Chick Always Gets It First: Dynamics of Race in *Buffy the Vampire Slayer*." *Gender Relations in Global Perspective: Essential Readings*. Ed. Nancy Cook. Toronto: Canadian Scholars' Press, 2007. 243–51. Print.

Goffman, Erving. *Gender Advertisements*. New York: Harper, 1979. Print.

_____. *The Presentation of Self in Everyday Life*. New York: Overlook Press, 1959. Print.

Halberstam, Judith. *Female Masculinity*. Durham: North Carolina Press, 1998. Print.

Hunt, Darnell M., ed. *Channeling Blackness: Studies on Television and Race in America*. New York: Oxford University Press, 2005. Print.

Jhally, Sut, and Justin Lewis. "White Responses: The Emergence of 'Enlightened' Racism." *Channeling Blackness: Studies on Television and Race in America*. Ed. Darnell M. Hunt. New York: Oxford University Press, 2005. 74–88. Print.

Jowett, Lorna. *Sex and the Slayer: A Gender Studies Primer for the Buffy Fan*. Middletown, CT: Wesleyan University Press, 2005. Print.

Kellner, Douglas. "*Buffy the Vampire Slayer* as spectacular allegory: A diagnostic critique." *Douglas Kellner's personal Web site*. 2004. Web. 9 Mar. 2009. <http://www.gseis.ucla.edu/faculty/kellner/essays/buffy.pdf>.

Little, Tracy. "High School Is Hell: Metaphor Made Literal in *Buffy the Vampire Slayer*." *Buffy the Vampire Slayer and Philosophy: Fear and Trembling in Sunnydale*. Ed. James B. South. Peru, Illinois: Open Court Publishing, 2003. 282–93. Print.

McCall, Leslie. "The Complexity of Intersectionality." *Signs: The Journal of Women in Culture and Society* 30 (2005): 1771–1800. Print.

Mittell, Jason. "Narrative Complexity in Contemporary American Television." *The Velvet Light Trap*. 58 (2006): 29–40. Print.

Romney, Patricia, Beverly Tatum, and JoAnne Jones. "Feminist Strategies for Teaching About Oppression: The Importance of Process." *Women's Studies Quarterly* XX (1992): 1–10. Print.

Sedgwick, Eve Kosofsky. *Epistemology of the Closet.* Berkeley: University of California Press, 1990. Print.

Shuttleworth, Ian. "They Always Mistake Me for the Character I Play: Transformation, Identity and Role-Playing in the *Buffy*verse (and a defense of fine acting)." *Reading the Vampire Slayer: An Unofficial Critical Companion to* Buffy *and* Angel. Ed. Roz Kaveny. London: Taurus Parke Paperbacks, 2002. 211–36. Print.

Tatum, Beverly Daniel. "Talking About Race, Learning About Racism: The Application of Racial Identity Development Theory in the Classroom." *Harvard Educational Review* 62 (1992): 1–24.

Wilcox, Rhonda. *Why Buffy Matters: The Art of* Buffy the Vampire Slayer. New York: I. B. Tauris, 2005. Print.

_____, and David Lavery, eds. *Fighting the Forces: What's at Stake in* Buffy the Vampire Slayer. Lanham, MD: Rowman and Littlefield, 2002. Print.

Wise, Tim. *White Like Me: Reflections on Race from a Privileged Son.* 2nd ed. Brooklyn, NY: Soft Skull Press, 2008. Print.

Zambrana, Ruth E., and Bonnie Thornton Dill. "Conclusion: Future directions in knowledge building and sustaining institutional change." *Emerging Intersections: Race, Class, and Gender in Theory, Policy, and Practice.* Eds. Bonnie T. Dill and Ruth E. Zambrana. New Brunswick, NJ: Rutgers University Press. 274–90. Print.

Zinn, Maxine Baca, and Bonnie Thornton Dill. "Theorizing Difference from Multiracial Feminism." *Feminist Studies* 22 (1996): 321–331. Print.

Slaying Shakespeare in High School: Buffy Battles *The Merchant of Venice* and *Othello*

Julia L. Grant

High school is hell. This is the metaphor made literal[1] for the first three seasons of *Buffy the Vampire Slayer*, a metaphor which contributes to the continuing popularity of the show because it rings true: for many, high school is, or was, hell. And more often than not, part of that hellish experience for students and teachers alike, is Shakespeare. As Whedon notes in the commentary to "Innocence" (2.14), "the show only works if it resonates." For many young people, Shakespeare no longer resonates; his magic remains hidden behind antiquated language and four centuries of cultural and historical change and negative expectations. By providing a modern basis of comparison to Shakespeare in a work like *Buffy*, a work which explores many of the same themes as Shakespeare but makes them new again, students are able to get past the diction and the difference to appreciate the brilliance of Shakespeare, while gaining a new respect for *Buffy* in the process.

Like their real-world peers Buffy and her friends must face the complexities of Shakespearean drama. In "Out of Mind, Out of Sight" (1.11) Buffy's class studies *The Merchant of Venice* and in "Earshot" (3.18) her class tackles *Othello*. Shakespeare's presence in *Buffy* should not seem unusual. Buffy Summers is in some respects a typical teenager and Shakespeare is typical high school fare; at Sunnydale High she and her fictional contemporaries study the same subjects that actual high school students study. But the time restrictions of a television series often limit depictions of Buffy's high school experience to lunch, short breaks between classes, and after school in the library. When classes are in session they often involve Buffy, Xander and Willow discussing the new beast in town or their romantic entanglements, thereby maintaining the narrative pacing while setting expository scenes in a likely and relatable location. When a scene actually focuses on an instructor teaching, it either means that the teacher is in some sort of danger, or that the content of the lesson holds thematic resonance for the show itself.[2] In the commentary to "Earshot," writer Jane Espenson explains the presence of *Othello* in the episode:

> This is a scene that Joss rewrote.... I recently looked back at my first draft and in my first draft it was a history class and they were talking about Henry VIII and Anne Boleyn and it didn't have any thematic resonance with the rest of the show. Joss said how if what they

are discussing in this class actually relates to Buffy's situation and how she feels about Angel, and so I changed it so it was an English class and they were discussing *The Catcher in the Rye* and I found some interesting connection ... and Joss rewrote it so that now it's a discussion about *Othello* [Espenson "Earshot"].

The use of *Othello* or by extension, the earlier use of *The Merchant of Venice* is not accidental; Whedon deliberately chose these references for their relevance to the show. By making episodes of Shakespeare derivative, the show gets the maximum use of a classroom scene by situating Buffy, apart from her Slayer abilities, as a typical teenager faced with classes and homework, while providing a foil for Buffy's adventures outside the classroom. On a grander scale, using Shakespeare establishes *Buffy*'s indebtedness to literary classics, consequently aiding in the elevation of the series into a work of artistic merit in its own right. But far more importantly for the high school teacher, Shakespeare's presence in *Buffy* has practical applications: the added bonus of making *Buffy* a viable teaching resource in real high school classrooms.

The adaptation of *The Merchant of Venice* in *Buffy* is entirely contained in "Out of Mind, Out of Sight." In this episode an invisible entity of some sort is attacking students. Buffy discovers that it is Marcie Ross, a student who is literally invisible because she has been ignored by everyone around her. Marcie seeks revenge for this wrong, and she aims all of her hatred at Cordelia Chase, the beautiful and popular girl whom everybody (including Buffy) loves to hate.[3] Buffy is put in the unlikely position of protecting Cordelia from harm, but she cannot slay this enemy, because it is not a demon, but human.

In this lesson the class views "Out of Mind, Out of Sight" before reading *The Merchant of Venice*. This structure provides students with a foundation for future analysis which eases them into more daunting territory. Before viewing the episode, encourage students who are fans of the show to offer a brief introduction to the series for those students unfamiliar with *Buffy*. With instructions to pay close attention to the characterization of Buffy, Marcie and Cordelia, play the episode. After viewing the episode, re-view the classroom scene. This scene, which occurs before the opening credits, serves as the real-world students' introduction to *The Merchant of Venice*:

> Ms. MILLER: "If you prick us, do we not bleed? If you tickle us, do we not laugh? If you poison us, do we not die? And if you wrong us, shall we not revenge?" OK, so talk to me people, How does what Shylock says here, about being a Jew, relate to our discussion — about the anger of the outcast in society?... Cordelia, what's Shylock saying?
>
> CORDELIA: How about, "color me totally self involved."
>
> Ms. MILLER: Care to elaborate?
>
> CORDELIA: With Shylock it's whine, whine, whine, like the whole world is about him! He acts like it's justice, him getting a pound of Antonio's flesh. It's not justice, it's yicky [1.11].

This conversation provides the perfect segue for a class discussion about differences in interpretation. One should ask how Cordelia's selfish nature causes her to believe that Shylock is selfish, whereas Willow is more likely to pity his position as outcast because she is not popular. Discussing how interpretations can be wildly different and still be valid if they are supported by the text allays students' fears about sharing their ideas and shows them that independent thought is encouraged.

The invariable precursor to instruction of *The Merchant of Venice* is a discussion of religious persecution and stereotyping. This conversation can occur before or after the class views "Out of Mind, Out of Sight" but in either case should immediately follow the class being informed that it will use the episode as a basis of comparison to the play, and should include some points of comparison between the two works, in order to dispel any fears that such a comparison is mocking the struggles of the Jewish people. Comparing the plight of a girl made invisible because she is ignored by her peers in an episode of *Buffy* to that of Shylock does not seem so absurd when one understands the attitudes towards Jews in Shakespeare's England: "Jews had been officially banished from England for three centuries, since the reign of Edward I. In the popular imagination they figured almost as mythical beasts: strange, evil beings who had once crucified Christ" (Barton 250). In *Shakespeare and the Jews*, James Shapiro notes how "generations of English children were exposed to stories of how Jews abducted, mangled, and cannibalized Christian children" (91); Jews were portrayed as monsters or bogeymen who would come get you if you did not behave. The basic concept behind *Buffy* is that Buffy must protect society from vampires and demons, consequently making the appearance of monsters a routine occurrence in the series. Also, though Jews were banished from England does not mean that there were no Jewish people living in England, but that they lived quiet secretive lives. Fearing arrest, persecution and exile, they made themselves as invisible as possible.[4] That Marcie is an unpopular teen made invisible because everyone ignores her rather than the victim of religious persecution provides teachers, after viewing, with the opportunity to discuss the consequences of bullying that is not religiously motivated.

As "Out of Mind, Out of Sight" is the starting point for future analysis of *The Merchant of Venice*, students must have a full understanding of the main characters before continuing with the play.[5] This can easily be handled through Think-Write-Pair-Share exercises.[6] These exercises may take a class session to complete, but in actuality they will save future class time, as a fuller understanding of the episode will enable the students to grasp concepts at work in the play more swiftly. While reading *The Merchant of Venice* students are urged to refer back to "Out of Mind, Out of Sight" and think about the similarities and differences between the characters in each work. Teachers can easily incorporate this activity into their current instruction method. For example, if the students keep reading journals they should be asked to write entries on differences and similarities between the main characters as they read the play over the following weeks. If the class is discussion-based the play can be discussed in groups or as a class. After the play is read in its entirety, the comparisons gleaned over the course of reading *The Merchant of Venice* are to be reconstituted first by the individual student and then by the class into complete comparative character studies. Venn diagrams are useful in constructing these comparisons and can easily be supplemented with evidence from the text(s).

For the benefit of the instructor what follows is a detailed, but by no means exhaustive, comparative analysis of Marcie, Buffy, and Cordelia to characters in *The Merchant of Venice*. This can be used as a master copy when evaluating student work or aiding in the construction of Venn diagrams.

The comparison of Marcie to Shylock is the most straightforward; the majority of students should be able to identify multiple similarities between the two characters. Both characters base their actions on how others have historically treated them. The students and teachers of Sunnydale ignored Marcie, which causes her to become invisible. Being invisible is detrimental to her psyche, as Giles succinctly stipulates: "The isolation, the exile she's endured ... she has gone mad" (1.11). Similarly, Antonio habitually treats Shylock like an animal, thus Shylock reacts as an animal would; "Thou call'dst me dog before thou hadst a cause, / But since I am a dog, beware my fangs" (III.iii.6–7). Both Shylock and Marcie want revenge against those who have wronged them. Shylock directs his vitriol at Antonio:

> I hate him for he is a Christian;
> But more, for in that low simplicity
> He lends out money gratis, and brings down
> The rate of usance here with us in Venice.
> If I can catch him once upon the hip,
> I will feed fat the ancient grudge I bear him [I.ii.42–47].

For Shylock, Antonio is representative of a Christian society which constantly imposes its power over his existence. Like Antonio, Cordelia is a likely scapegoat for the sins of many because she embodies everything that Marcie has grown to despise; she is popular with both her peers and her teachers and she stands out due to her beauty and wealth. Though Cordelia is her main target, Marcie also attacks members of Cordelia's circle in order to heighten Cordelia's terror and punish her followers.

When Shylock seizes the opportunity to exact revenge against Antonio, it is his business as a money lender which enables him to put Antonio in his debt. Usury was one of the few businesses Jews were allowed to partake in, so one could say that his Jewish identity is the quality that has caused Shylock to be abused which gives Shylock the chance to get even. Although Marcie's invisibility is more of a punishment than a power, she wields it like a weapon. Marcie's plans for revenge, like Shylock's, are surgical, but instead of a pound of flesh she intends to disfigure Cordelia so people will stare at her due to her grotesque visage rather than her beauty. In the execution of their gruesome plans for revenge Shylock and Marcie intend to teach the societies which will not accept them a lesson. Shylock initially directs this lesson at Antonio: "The villany you teach / me, I will execute, and it will go hard but I will / better the instruction" (III.i.71–73). Shylock believes that this will get his pound of flesh because he has a notarized document which legally entitles him to it. By seeking justice in the courts Shylock's lesson becomes a lesson for an entire city. Marcie times her revenge to correspond with Cordelia's coronation as May Queen, using the mock court (and the one word messages left at her crime scenes) to teach a lesson to everyone at school. And like Shylock, who refuses to hear the pleas of Antonio, his friends, or even of the authorities to show mercy upon Antonio, Marcie will not be swayed from quest for revenge.

After Marcie is subdued by Buffy, she is taken away by two FBI agents who say that they can rehabilitate her. In the last scene Marcie enters a special FBI school for invisible teenagers, where the class is hearing a lesson on Infiltration and Assassination. Although Marcie will never again be a full member of society, the government will exploit her invisibility for its own purposes. The segregation of the outcast with others of her kind, their abilities being used to suit the needs of the government, is comparable to the long-standing, economically beneficial role of Jewish money-lenders in Europe. Both Marcie and Shylock are the tools of the societies which do not recognize them as members.

As the Slayer, Buffy is a tool of a society within which she does not completely belong. Marcie knows Buffy's secret identity and thinks that Buffy might understand her "vision" because of her outcast status. According to Cordelia, Buffy is a member of a "social leper colony" (1.11). She even has problems relating to her friends Willow and Xander, as they have a history together that she does not share. At Buffy's former school she was May Queen; in Sunnydale she is the strange girl who hangs out in the library and carries weapons in her purse. Her outcast status is something she shares with Marcie and Shylock. And like Shylock, Buffy is asked to help her enemy. Shylock is shocked by Bassanio and Antonio's request, as Antonio is opposed to usury and has treated Shylock with contempt (1.iii.106–129). When Cordelia asks Buffy for help (and manages to insult her while doing so) Buffy is also surprised: "So you're coming to *me* for help? There's a Why? Inside me screaming to get out" (1.11). But while Shylock lends money to Antonio because it holds the possibility of him getting revenge, Buffy helps Cordelia because it is the right thing to do. Understanding that the episode casts Buffy as an outcast in society who does not seek vengeance allows students to consider whether Shylock and Marcie's bloodlust is not wholly the fault of others, but perhaps part of their natures.

Buffy's behavior in "Out of Mind, Out of Sight" shares some strong similarities with that of Antonio, Bassanio, and Portia. When Antonio lends money to Bassanio he risks everything, including his life, to help a friend. Buffy risks her life on a regular basis fighting demons and vampires to keep the people of Sunnydale safe. When Marcie leaves three one-word messages at her crime scenes ("LOOK," "LISTEN" and "LEARN") Buffy chooses to listen, since by listening to the movement of her invisible opponent, she can determine her location and fight her. Like Bassanio, who correctly chooses the leaden casket and wins Portia's hand, Buffy chooses the correct cryptic message. In using Marcie's own lesson to defeat her, Buffy is also like Portia. Portia understands that Shylock is demanding justice and that he is relying on the law to give him his pound of flesh. Portia initially asks Shylock to be merciful, which he refuses. Buffy initially tries to reason with Marcie, but Marcie is beyond reason, as Buffy comes to realize: "You know, I really felt bad for you. You've suffered. But there's one thing I didn't factor into all of this. You're a thundering loony" (1.11). Portia then finds loopholes in Shylock's contract with Antonio, his "lesson" with which to defeat him. Shylock and Marcie both intend to teach a lesson, but it is Portia and Buffy who end up getting the final word.

As mentioned earlier, Cordelia takes on the role of Antonio. In the opening scene of *The Merchant of Venice* Antonio is surrounded by friends who are attempting to cheer him up. Antonio is the center of attention. The opening scene of "Out of Mind, Out of Sight" shows Cordelia with her friend Harmony and her boyfriend Mitch. The conversation revolves around Cordelia; the others look to her for approval. This is echoed in a flashback scene: when Marcie repeatedly tries to be included in a conversation by remarking on a lecturer's toupee, she is ignored. When Cordelia repeats Marcie's comment that the toupee "looked like a cabbage" (1.11), everyone listens and laughs. Cordelia is depicted as dismissive, even cruel, toward Marcie's attempts at friendship by being rude to her or by ignoring her completely. Antonio may have many friends, but he treats Shylock miserably, as Shylock attests repeatedly. Even Antonio admits to treating Shylock badly, and, when Shylock asks why he should lend money to someone who has been so cruel to him, professes that he is likely to do so again: "I am as like to call thee so again, / To spet on thee again, to spurn thee too"(I.iii.130–131). When Cordelia asks Buffy for help she attempts to be nice, but still manages to insult Buffy and her friends. After thanking Buffy for saving her life, Buffy gets only a quick thank you from Cordelia before Cordelia reverts back to her popular persona.

Cordelia also shares characteristics with Portia. In the first scene Bassanio describes Portia as a prize worth possessing:

> In Belmont is a lady richly left,
> And she is fair and, fairer than that word,
> Of wondrous virtues...
> Nor is the wide world ignorant of her worth
> For the four winds blow in from every coast
> Renowned suitors, and her sunny locks
> Hang on her temples like a golden fleece...
> And many Jasons come in quest of her [I.i.161–163,167–170,172].

Mitch, though less eloquent, also seeks to possess Cordelia: "It's not her arm I'm looking to be on" (1.11). Like Portia, bombarded by suitors dazzled by her wealth and beauty, Cordelia is surrounded by hangers-on:

> You think that I'm never lonely, just 'cause I'm so cute and popular? I can be surrounded by people and be completely alone. It's not like any of them really know me. I don't even know if they like me half the time. People just want to be in the popular zone. Sometimes when I talk, everyone's so busy agreeing with me, they don't hear a word I say [1.11].

Portia's suitors fail the riddle test because they judge the exterior rather than the interior; Portia can dismiss the suitors who fail her father's test, while Cordelia is left feeling alone in a crowd.

When Cordelia learns that an invisible girl trying to hurt her, her response is: "I don't care what it is, just get rid of it!" (1.11) She refuses to cancel her coronation at the dance because "then Marcie's won" (Whedon et al., 33). Cordelia does not care about Marcie's motivations; she wants Marcie dead or in prison and her life to go on as before. Her summary judgment of Marcie is similar to Portia's less than judicious treatment of Shylock. Portia is not satisfied merely with insuring that Antonio is not required to provide a pound of his flesh to Shylock, but absolves Antonio of any debt to Shylock, divests Shylock of his fortune and at Antonio's request forces Shylock to become a Christian. Portia punishes Shylock in order to not have her happiness with Bassanio disturbed by the death of Antonio.

Unlike the classroom scene in "Out of Mind, Out of Sight," where the entire episode was a loose adaptation of *The Merchant of Venice*, the class discussion of *Othello* in "Earshot" correlates directly to one portion of the episode: the lingering doubt Buffy feels about Angel's fidelity after he pretends to turn evil, or lose his soul, in order to get information from Faith in the episode previous, "Enemies" (3.17). But *Othello* seems to be at work in many episodes of *Buffy*: Buffy and Angel's "classic star-crossed romance" (Whedon

Interview "Surprise" 2.13), a romance more akin to that of Othello and Desdemona than Romeo and Juliet, runs its course from Season One to Season Three, with Buffy kissing him ere she kills him in the Season Two finale; Faith plays Iago to Buffy's Othello throughout Season Three; and the themes of jealousy, love, adultery and revenge so intrinsic to *Othello* are also vital to *Buffy*.

These comparisons to *Othello* are both a blessing and a curse: the material enriches the teaching of *Othello* in high school English classes, but there is insufficient class time to view all of the relevant episodes and study the play. The following is a more piecemeal approach: two short lessons (half a class to a full class in length) which address specific issues in *Buffy* and *Othello*, and suggestions for further study for the more adventurous instructor.

In "Earshot," Buffy is infected with an "aspect of the demon" she has touched; the power of telepathy. Initially her ability seems like a positive tool, which Buffy uses to her advantage in her English class on *Othello*. Because Buffy has the ability to read her teacher's mind, she gives the teacher the "right" answers, but she does so without providing evidence from the text to support them.

This activity is little more than an open book, written test wrapped in a bit of *Buffy*. Since this activity tests reading comprehension and retention it must occur after students have read the play. This is an excellent time to review how to footnote source material. The students view the classroom scene twice:

BUFFY: Jealousy.

MS. MURRAY: Buffy. Right Very good. Jealousy is clearly the tool that Iago uses to undo Othello.

NANCY: (I knew that.)

MS. MURRAY: But what's his motivation? What reason does Iago give for destroying his superior officer? (Cassio has my place. Twixt my sheets he's done my office.)

BUFFY: Well, he was passed over for promotion: Cassio was picked instead. And people were saying that Othello slept with his wife ...

MS. MURRAY: Any other reason?

NANCY: Race!

MS. MURRAY: Uh, good Nancy. Can't overlook that.... Is there something else at work here?

BUFFY: Well he um, he sort of admits himself that his motives are, spurious? He does things because he enjoys them. It's like he's not really a person. He's a, the dark half of Othello himself.

MS. MURRAY: Buffy, really, very astute.... And doesn't that also explain Othello's readiness to believe Iago? Within seconds he turns on Desdemona, he believes that that she's been unfaithful. And we're all like that. We all have our little internal Iagos that tell us our husbands or girlfriends or whatever don't really love us. You can never really see what's in someone's heart [3.18].

The students are then asked to find the evidence which supports Buffy's hypotheses, with the understanding that finding the right answer without evidence in an English class is like solving an equation in math without showing your work, only worth partial credit.

The "Prove Buffy Right" test consists of the following questions:

1. According to Buffy/Ms. Murray, jealousy is the tool Iago uses to undo Othello. What evidence is there in the play to support this hypothesis?

2. Buffy posits three motivations for Iago's actions. What are they? What evidence in the text supports these assertions?[7]

As there is a wealth of evidence of Iago's use of jealousy to manipulate Othello, the students should limit their response to three specific examples. The evidence of Iago's three possible motivations is more specific, and therefore harder to find. A student who locates two out of three within the test time ought to receive a high score. After the teacher evaluates this activity, students should be given the opportunity to learn from each other by forming small groups to review their findings.

Build upon this lesson by asking the students why *Othello* is part of the episode "Earshot." To aid in their understanding, provide Espenson's explanation from the commentary to "Earshot." Then play the episode from the beginning and concluding with the scene following the classroom scene.

When the classroom conversation turns to the nagging doubts that cannot be proven, Buffy is reminded of her doubt concerning Angel's fidelity. Even though Angel declared his love for her the night before, Buffy is still plagued by doubt. Realizing that with her gift she can "see what is inside someone's heart" she leaves school to find Angel and attempts to read his mind. It does not work:

ANGEL: You can't get into my mind.

BUFFY: How did you — why not?

ANGEL: It's like the mirror — the thoughts are there, but they create no reflection in you [3.18].

When Angel asks Buffy why she did not just ask him what he was thinking she replies, "but that would have made sense." Buffy understands that her doubt has caused her to act irrationally.

After viewing this section of "Earshot" have the students compare the treatment of doubt and jealousy in the episode to their use between the characters in *Othello*. Some important points to look for would include the illogical nature of jealousy, and whether or not it is possible to prove fidelity, as Buffy tries but fails to do with her powers and Othello swears he will do: "I'll see before I doubt; when I doubt, prove; / And on the proof, there is no more but this- /Away at once with love or jealousy" (III, iii, ll.190–2). These comparisons can be made in Think-Pair-Share exercises or in class discussion, and should take no more than fifteen minutes of additional class time.

The *Othello* classroom scene's pertinence is not limited to the episode which contains it but speaks to the Buffy/Faith dynamic at work throughout Season Three. If, as Buffy states, Iago is "the dark side of Othello" (3.18), Faith could be construed to represent the dark side of Buffy. In this expansion exercise students view the episode "Enemies" and compare and contrast Faith's motivations and actions to Iago's and describe how, assuming she is a modern version of Iago, they would expect her to behave in other episodes.[8] This would make an excellent essay topic.

The second lesson takes a portion of the Season Two episode "Innocence" (2.14) to discuss the importance of setting, in particular, the setting of Desdemona's murder at the hands of Othello. As this exercise relates to the final scene of the play, it must take place after the entire play is read. With viewing time under five minutes,[9] and the entire exercise length at about twenty minutes, this exercise is an excellent way to incorporate *Buffy* into the classroom, and to see if this approach meshes with your teaching style.

Open with a brief synopsis of the storyline which has led to this point: Buffy and Angel are a couple. She is a Vampire Slayer; he is a vampire, but he has a soul. Not realizing that the gypsy curse which restored Angel's soul has a proviso that if he experiences one moment of perfect happiness, his soul will be lost and he will be evil again, Buffy and Angel succumb to a night of passion. He loses his soul, and decides to seek revenge against Buffy. Then, show the class the "Innocence" interview with Joss Whedon, which will contextualize the viewing of the bedroom scene, entitled, "Buffy Gets Hurt," immediately after.

In "Innocence" Angel goes missing after having sex with Buffy for the first time and Buffy is extremely worried about him. In the bedroom scene Angel returns. At first Buffy is relieved, but their conversation leaves her hurt and confused, as Angel belittles the significance of their intimacy. Angel debases their first shared (and her first) sexual experience, ending their conversation with an "I'll call you" which comes across as a joke. Although Angel is now evil, and could easily take Buffy by surprise and kill her, he chooses cruelty instead. In the interview Whedon explains that this scene was originally set outside, but as that location did not hold the right emotional resonance it was moved to Angel's bedroom: "we had to play this in the bedroom where they had made love, that he had to be, you know, semi-nude, and it had to be as intimate as it possibly could. When we came back to it both actors just hit it out of the park" (Whedon Interview "Innocence"). As outlined by Whedon, the proper setting is crucial for creating the appropriate atmosphere. One should ask their students what the bedroom represents; what moods they associate with being in their bedrooms. Then turn the focus to Whedon's explanation of how this scene is a bedroom scene. Why does this scene "work" in the bedroom? Angel betrays Buffy in his bedroom; the site of their first and only sexual encounter. This creates a sense of intimacy, but it also heightens the betrayal, as it sullies the memory of that shared moment.[10]

In *Othello* the bedroom is the setting of the murder of Desdemona at the hands of her husband. The importance of the setting of Desdemona's demise is often overlooked perhaps because it seems like such an obvious choice or because it is so well known, but setting the climax of the play in the bedroom was calculated and brilliant in its simplicity. Shakespeare starts setting the scene early; the second scene of Act Two solely consists of the Herald proclaiming the celebration of Othello and Desdemona's nuptials. This reminds the audience that Othello and Desdemona were separated immediately after they were married, and have not had their "wedding night." Othello and Iago both reaffirm this fact in the next scene (II.iii.9–10 and II.iii.16–17). After establishing how Desdemona is to die, Shakespeare builds up the horrific nature of a murder in such an intimate location by having Desdemona ask Emilia to put her wedding sheets on the bed (IV.ii.105); sheets which represent Desdemona's purity and innocence and the sacredness of the wedding vows, and which the audience associates with the bedroom in the citadel where Desdemona is to die. In the next scene Emilia tells Desdemona that she has done as she was asked

(IV.iii.21); Desdemona's reply is macabre: "If I do die before [thee], prithee shroud me / In one of those same sheets" (IV.ii.24–25). Repeatedly referring to the sheets builds up the audience's anticipation and anxiety; the murder of Desdemona becomes more heinous, and the audience's sympathy for her plight more intense.

Following Desdemona's murder the intimacy of the bedroom is sullied further by having such a private room made public. Emilia, Montano, Gratiano, Iago, Cassio, Lodovico, and assorted officers all enter this private sanctum; Othello attempts to kill Iago, Emilia is murdered by Iago, and Othello kills himself. Although it is practical to keep the action in the room both as a means to trap Othello and to maintain narrative pacing, it also means that the audience and Othello are left with the stark reality of the crime. Desdemona's lifeless body remains in view, for all to see. The bedroom has become the site of her brutal murder, not her happy marriage.

The location of Desdemona's murder is intrinsically connected to the method with which Othello chooses to kill her: Desdemona is smothered in her bed. Othello had opportunity to kill her earlier, but he waits for this moment. It is Iago's suggestion that he kill her in the bedroom: "Do it not with poison; strangle her in her bed, / even the bed she hath contaminated" (IV.i.207–208). Iago dismisses poisoning Desdemona because it is too easy; too impersonal; Othello cannot "chop her into messes" (IV.i.200) because that would be impossible to stage, but strangling is intimate and violent. By having Othello strangle Desdemona, Iago's revenge is complete; Othello is no longer the virtuous warrior, but a monster. After examining the bedroom scene in Othello, students complete a take-home creative assignment in which they choose a new setting for one of these texts, or one of the scenes in the texts, they studied that year. They then must explain why they chose the new location or time period and how this change will alter the story. This activity gives students a better insight into the creative process by allowing them to engage their own imaginations.

Due to issues of race and religion *Othello* and *The Merchant of* Venice are problematic to teach at the high school level. *Buffy* helps the class see past these issues so that students can appreciate the universality of their themes and the brilliance of their construction; they can learn to appreciate, if not love, Shakespeare. And in the process the next generation of young people, who at best only thought of *Buffy* as entertainment and at worst were not familiar with *Buffy* at all, have been exposed to the depth of the text. High school is hell, but Shakespeare does not have to be.

NOTES

1. For a detailed analysis of this and other pertinent metaphors in *Buffy*, please see Rhonda V. Wilcox's article, "There Will Never Be a 'Very Special' *Buffy*: *Buffy* and the Monsters of Teen Life" and Tracy Little's article, "High School Is Hell: Metaphor Made Literal."

2. Or in the case of Ms. Miller, both: in "Out of Mind, Out of Sight" she gives the lesson on *The Merchant of Venice*. She is later attacked for favoring Cordelia.

3. Thompson and Emmons-Featherston provides comparisons between the Cordelia in *Buffy* and the Cordelia in Shakespeare's *King Lear*.

4. For a more detailed history, see Shapiro.

5. This lesson focuses on character analysis, but another class activity would be to have the class (in small groups, then as a whole) create a detailed plot summary of the episode. This summary would

ideally be kept on the wall, next to a matching blank sheet. As *The Merchant of Venice* is read over the following class periods, the plot summary would be filled in and discussed in reference to "Out of Mind, Out of Sight."

6. Randomly assign each student one character (either Buffy, Marcie or Cordelia). After thinking about the character and writing down observations, each student pairs up with another who had the same character to review their findings, and then share their conclusions with the class as a whole.

7. As a bonus question you can ask the students if Iago gives any other reasons for his actions, or if any other reasons are implied. Students should remember that Iago also states that he thinks that Cassio has slept with his wife: "For I fear Cassio with my night-cap too" (II.ii.307).

8. For further discussions on Buffy and Faith see Rhonda Wilcox's *Why Buffy Matters* and Lorna Jowett's *Sex and the Slayer*.

9. Instructors with more time or sufficient resources are encouraged to have their students watch the whole episode (or, preferably, view both "Surprise" and "Innocence") in or outside of class. These episodes offer an excellent basis of comparing and contrasting Buffy and Angel's relationship to that of Othello and Desdemona.

10. Angel/Angelus is a character who understands how violating the bedroom increases the magnitude of the attack. In later episodes he breaks into Buffy's bedroom to draw her while she sleeps, he breaks into Willow's bedroom to kill her fish, and, after murdering Miss Calendar at the high school, he transports the body to Giles' bedroom in order to augment Giles' anguish.

WORKS CITED

Barton, Anne. "Introduction." *The Merchant of Venice. The Riverside Shakespeare*. Boston: Houghton Mifflin, 1974. 250–253. Print.

"Earshot." *Buffy the Vampire Slayer: The Complete Third Season*. WB Network. 21 Sept. 1999. 20th Century–Fox, 2003. DVD.

"Enemies." *Buffy the Vampire Slayer: The Complete Third Season*. WB Network. 16 Mar. 1999. 20th Century–Fox, 2003. DVD.

Espenson, Jane. Commentary. "Earshot." *Buffy the Vampire Slayer: The Complete Third Season*. 20th Century–Fox. 2003. DVD.

"Innocence." *Buffy the Vampire Slayer: The Complete Second Season*. WB Network. 20 Jan. 1998. Television.

Little, Tracy. "High School is Hell: Metaphor Made Literal." Buffy *and Philosophy: Fear and Trembling in Sunnydale*. Ed. James B. South. Chicago: Open Court, 2003. 282–293. Print.

"Out of Mind, Out of Sight." *Buffy the Vampire Slayer: The Complete First Season*. WB Network. 19 May 1997. 20th Century–Fox, 2002. DVD.

Shakespeare, William. *The Merchant of Venice. The Riverside Shakespeare*. Boston: Houghton Mifflin, 1974. 254–285. Print.

_____. *Othello. The Riverside Shakespeare*. Boston: Houghton Mifflin, 1974. 1203–1248. Print.

Shapiro, James. *Shakespeare and the Jews*. New York: Columbia University Press, 1996. Print.

"Surprise." *Buffy the Vampire Slayer: The Complete Second Season*. 20th Century–Fox. 2002. DVD.

Thompson, Gregory J., and Sally Emmons-Featherston. "'What Shall Cordelia Say?': Buffy as Morality Play for the Twenty-First Century's Therapeutic Ethos." *The Truth of* Buffy: *Essays on Fiction Illuminating Reality*. Eds. Emily Dial-Driver, Sally Emmons-Featherston, Jim Ford and Carolyn Anne Taylor. Jefferson, NC: McFarland, 2008. 158–172. Print.

Whedon, Joss. Interview. "Innocence." *Buffy the Vampire Slayer: The Complete Second Season*. 20th Century–Fox. 2002. DVD.

_____. Interview. "Surprise." *Buffy the Vampire Slayer: The Complete Second Season*. 20th Century–Fox. 2002. DVD.

_____, et al. "Out of Mind, Out of Sight." *Buffy the Vampire Slayer The Script Book: Season One, Vol. 2*. New York: Pocket Books, 2000. 265–327. Print.

Wilcox, Rhonda V. "There Will Never Be a 'Very Special' Buffy: *Buffy* and the Monsters of Teen Life." *Journal of Popular Film & Television* 27.2 (Summer 1999): 16–23. Rpt. in *Slayage: The Whedon Studies Association Journal* 2 (2001).

_____. *Why Buffy Matters: The Art of* Buffy the Vampire Slayer. London: I. B. Tauris, 2005. Print.

About the Contributors

Tanya R. Cochran is an associate professor of English and communication at Union College in Lincoln, Nebraska, where she teaches first-year writing and rhetoric and coordinates the Studio for Writing and Speaking. With Rhonda V. Wilcox, she co-edited *Investigating* Firefly *and* Serenity: *Science Fiction on the Frontier* (Tauris, 2008). Past chair for the Science Fiction and Fantasy Area of the Popular/American Culture Association, Cochran currently holds editorial board positions for the online journals *Slayage* and *Watcher Junior.*

Brian Cogan is an associate professor and chair of the department of Communication Arts and Sciences at Molloy College in Long Island, New York. He serves on the editorial board of the *Journal of Popular Culture* and on the editorial board of ABC-CLIO's Popular Culture project. He has also written about these topics for publications such as the *New York Post, Chunklet, Go Metric,* and Punknews.org.

Leith Daniel is a secondary teacher with more than a decade's experience teaching English. He is a regular speaker at English teacher conferences across Australia and a writer of professional journal articles which cover a range of topics, from using popular culture in English classrooms to etymology as a specific area of study for high school students.

Keith Fudge is an assistant professor of English at the University of Arkansas–Fort Smith, where he teaches classes in writing, American literature, and popular culture. He has published articles on William Faulkner and eighteenth-century studies, and his current research interests are now in American popular culture, including the history of rock music.

Julia L. Grant holds a B.A. in Spanish and English from the University of King's College and an M.A. in comparative literature from the University of Western Ontario. An independent scholar, she lives in Toronto.

Patrick R. Grzanka is the associate director of the Honors Humanities Program at the University of Maryland–College Park. His teaching and research investigate the intersections of race, gender and sexuality in contemporary American life and culture, particularly the ways in which identity influences emotions.

Melissa C. Johnson is an assistant professor in the University College of Virginia Commonwealth University, where she serves as the curriculum coordinator for the Focused Inquiry Program. She is the co-author of a textbook for first-year writing and cultural studies courses, *Uncommon Threads: Reading and Writing About Contemporary America.*

David Kociemba is the editor-in-chief of *Watcher Junior,* an online, peer-reviewed journal devoted to publishing undergraduate scholarship on the work of Joss Whedon. He has previously written for *Slayage, Buffy Goes Dark, Battlestar Galactica: Finding the Way Home, Buffy and Angel Conquer the Internet,* and *A Dragon Ate My Prom* (forthcoming).

K. Dale Koontz makes her home in western North Carolina, where she teaches at Cleveland Community College. The author of the book *Faith and Choice in the Works of Joss Whedon*, she is fascinated by the intricacies of Whedon's work and has incorporated episodes into her classes — efforts that have converted more than a few students into Whedon fans.

Jodie A. Kreider is a lecturer in the arts and humanities at the University of Denver. She holds a Ph.D. in modern European, British, and comparative women's history from the University of Arizona and a master's in teaching from Washington University in Saint Louis, Missouri. She teaches courses on Celtic identities and British and Irish history, and has taught a first year seminar on *Buffy the Vampire Slayer* for the past four years.

Jane Martin is a professor in the Communication Program in the School of Creative Arts at the University of Saint Francis, Fort Wayne, Indiana. Martin received an MFA from the University of North Carolina at Greensboro in film and video production. She has taught at the University of Saint Francis for 16 years and greatly appreciates the contributions of her students to her course instruction and her life.

Barry Morris is the chair of Communication Studies at Pace University. His primary research program is the rhetorical analysis of political rhetoric and popular culture. He has published articles on subjects ranging from Wall Street as American synecdoche to the drive-in movie reviews of Joe Bob Briggs.

Rod Romesburg is a lecturer and the first-year writing coordinator at Rollins College in Winter Park, Florida. He has published essays on Ernest Hemingway, Gary Snyder, Ed Abbey, and *Buffy the Vampire Slayer*.

Rosie White is a senior lecturer in English at Northumbria University, UK. She teaches and researches in a variety of fields including popular culture, feminist theory, film noir and active female protagonists in film, fiction and television narratives. She wrote *Violent Femmes: Women as Spies in Popular Culture* (Routledge, 2008).

Meghan K. Winchell is an associate professor of history at Nebraska Wesleyan University in Lincoln, where she teaches courses on twentieth-century U.S. history and women's and African American history. She has taught a full-length *Buffy* course as part of NWU's Liberal Arts Seminar program for the past five years. She is the author of *Good Girls, Good Food, Good Fun: The Story of USO Hostesses During World War Two* (North Carolina, 2008).

Jason Lawton Winslade is an adjunct professor at DePaul University, where he teaches writing, the performance of literature, and interdisciplinary courses on occultism and culture, Irish myth and politics, comics, and *Buffy the Vampire Slayer*. He has published work on occultism, media, and culture in various journals and anthologies.

Kristopher Karl Woofter teaches in the English Department at Dawson College in Montréal, and is a Ph.D. student in film and moving image studies at Concordia University's Mel Hoppenheim School of Cinema. Woofter also serves as a co-chair for the Horror Area of the Popular/American Culture Association.

Index